PERFORMANCE INDICATORS
IN SOCIAL CARE FOR OLDER PEOPLE

Related Titles
in Association with PSSRU

Series Editors:
Professor David Challis, University of Manchester
Professor Martin Knapp, LSE
Professor Ann Netten, University of Kent

Long-Term Care: Matching Resources and Needs
Edited by Martin Knapp, David Challis, José-Luis Fernández and Ann Netten
ISBN 0 7546 4341 7

Towards Quality Care
Outcomes for Older People in Care Homes
Caroline Mozley, Caroline Sutcliffe, Heather Bagley,
Lis Cordingley, David Challis, Peter Huxley and Alistair Burns
ISBN 0 7546 3172 9

Care Management in Social and Primary Health Care
The Gateshead Community Care Scheme
David Challis, John Chesterman, Rosemary Luckett, Karen Stewart
and Rosemary Chessum
ISBN 1 85742 206 6

Equity and Efficiency Policy in Community Care
Needs, Service Productivities, Efficiencies and Their Implications
Bleddyn Davies and José-Luis Fernández
ISBN 0 7546 1281 3

Caring for Older People
An Assessment of Community Care in the 1990s
Linda Bauld, John Chesterman, Bleddyn Davies,
Ken Judge and Roshni Mangalore
ISBN 0 7546 1280 5

The Personal Social Services Research Unit is based at three branches, at the University of Kent, the London School of Economics and the University of Manchester. The Unit undertakes social and health care research, supported mainly by the Department of Health, and focusing particularly on policy research and analysis of equity and efficiency in community care, long-term care and related areas – including services for elderly people, people with mental health problems and children in care.

The PSSRU website is at www.pssru.ac.uk.

Performance Indicators in Social Care For Older People

DAVID CHALLIS
PSSRU, University of Manchester, UK

PAUL CLARKSON
PSSRU, University of Manchester, UK

RAYMOND WARBURTON
Department of Health, UK,
formerly PSSRU, University of Kent, UK

at the University of Kent,
the London School of Economics
and the University of Manchester

ASHGATE

This work was undertaken by the PSSRU, which receives support from the Department of Health; the views expressed in this publications are those of the authors and not necessarily those of the Department of Health.

Published by
Ashgate Publishing Limited
Gower House
Croft Road
Aldershot
Hampshire GU11 3HR
England

Ashgate Publishing Company
Suite 420
101 Cherry Street
Burlington, VT 05401-4405
USA

Ashgate website: http://www.ashgate.com

British Library Cataloguing in Publication Data
Challis, David, 1948-
    Performance indicators in social care for older people
    1.Older people - Services for - Evaluation
    I.Title II. Clarkson, Paul III.Warburton, Raymond
    IV.University of Kent at Canterbury. Personal Social
    Services Research Unit
    362.6

Library of Congress Control Number: 2006928104

ISBN-10: 0 7546 4744 7
ISBN-13: 978 0 7546 4744 7

Typeset by Nick Brawn at the PSSRU, University of Kent
Printed and bound in Great Britain by MPG Books Ltd, Bodmin, Cornwall

Contents

List of Boxes, Figures and Tables

Tables

Preface

Performance indicators are a relatively new development in social care services but their development and use has been of long duration in other areas of private finance and in the public sector more generally. The use of these indicators is not without its problems and it is the purpose of this study to examine their development and use in the area of social care for older people. This has been done though the commissioning of work by a local authority Social Services Department on the use of performance indicators to measure their community care services.

During the 1990s Cheshire Social Services Department (SSD) commissioned the Personal Social Services Research Unit (PSSRU) to recommend, develop and then help to implement and monitor a set of performance indicators for services to older people. The result was an integrated suite of local performance measures set within an organising framework, the *Performance Indicator Analytic Framework* (PIAF) contained within this book.

This book is directed at a social care audience, particularly those policy makers, researchers, managers and practitioners interested in methods of appraisal, which permit their work to be planned and evaluated on a department-wide basis. It has many links and resonances with recent national concerns about how well social services are performing in their functions. In this respect we believe it to be both timely and relevant to the needs of social services personnel at a critical time in the history of social care.

A number of present and former Cheshire County Council staff members have contributed to this study through their work as colleagues in developing this work, interviews with them and in the provision of information concerning services for older people in Cheshire. We thank in particular; Colin Berg, Helen Black, Sue Crompton, Jonathan Cope, Kevin Miller, Judy

Scott, John Webb and David Whyte. They were a very stimulating group of colleagues with whom to work. The analysis in Chapter 7 owes much to David Whyte, Business Manager for his progress reports describing the way performance indicators had been used in Cheshire. We are grateful also to both the Directors of Social Services who were involved during this work, Neil Singleton and Jo Williams, for their support.

Finally at PSSRU, this book has been a genuine tripartite effort of authorship. Raymond Warburton, prior to his work at the Department of Health, was a key driver in the thinking, planning and development of the performance indicators in collaboration with Cheshire colleagues. Paul Clarkson has been central in the crafting of the work into this book reflecting the background, analytic framework, performance measures and their implementation. The manuscript was prepared for publication by Nick Brawn with his customary skill.

David Challis
Professor of Community Care Research,
Personal Social Services Research Unit, University of Manchester

Chapter 1

The Emergence of Performance Review

The Government are very keen on amassing statistics – they collect them, add them, raise them to the nth power, take the cube root and prepare wonderful diagrams. But what you must never forget is that every one of those figures comes in the first instance from the village watchman, who just puts down what he damn pleases.

(Stamp, 1929, pp. 258–259)

Measuring the performance of whole health and long term care systems is set to become a defining issue in the 21st century (Mulligan et al., 2000; United Nations, 2002; World Health Organisation, 2000). In the UK, a number of documents testify to the greater measurement and regulation of both health and social care activity at a national level. Recent initiatives for the organisation and management of community and long-term care are being shaped by the use of performance information in a way inconceivable even ten years ago. Community care services, particularly those for frail older people, which represent the bulk of social care expenditure, lend themselves to the use of such monitoring systems. Problems remain, however, in translating the need for such data into adequate systems for monitoring the quality of services, particularly at the local level. This book brings together a framework for integrated local performance evaluation with a series of exemplar indicators which may be employed as part of this framework grounded in the lessons of early development in one locality. It is designed to contribute to more comprehensive and effective performance measurement processes in social care.

To date performance measurement has assumed importance at the central government level whereby extensive data are being used increasingly to ensure the regular and effective monitoring of health and social services performance. The White Paper *Modernising Social Services* (Cm 4169, 1998) made such measurements of performance a mandatory requirement. This and other guidance (Department of Health, 1999a,b), provided a framework and measures by which the performance of social services authorities could be judged nationally. This has been accompanied by some tough-sounding announcements concerning the consequences if departments do not show improved performance, including powers to take responsibilities away from failing authorities and hand them over to neighbouring councils (Huber, 1999). Despite these warnings, authorities confront real problems in collecting the relevant information and in analysing performance information. Some of these problems are at the conceptual level, concerning which aspects of performance need to be monitored; some are concerned with measurement issues, such as how to devise relevant data and analyse it effectively; and others are at a technical level, such as how to disseminate information effectively within authorities. However, while solutions to these problems are sought, problems remain with the accuracy of such data, as the quotation from Josiah Stamp so effectively illustrates.

The problems of eliciting reliable and useful information from which to monitor care services are not of recent origin. Routine evaluation of the activities of community care has been plagued with difficulties throughout its development. In the original PSSRU case management experiments prior to the UK reforms of the 1990s, some of the barriers to pursuing effective and efficient management practices in support of long-term care for older people have already been described (Challis and Davies, 1986). These included the structure of social work itself which has, until only recently, relied on routine monitoring on a case-by-case basis as a way of establishing its effectiveness. Management practice has also failed to base its operations on more precise generalisations about the deployment of services. From the original Kent study, an early initiative was developed that enabled information to be used by front line staff in improving the performance of their work with frail elderly people (Challis and Chesterman, 1985; 1986). Information from individual client records was fed into a system that made data concerning needs, care processes and resources available to staff. This, at a more aggregated level, could provide management with the information they needed for longer-term planning. The use of information systems in this way is valuable in improving our ability to predict the likely consequences of certain actions in service delivery. However, in contrast to such action research evaluations, the facility to routinely use information has only recently become available, both nationally and, to a lesser extent, within departments themselves. Comparable information is now available to make possible a wider appraisal of performance: to pursue aspects such as efficiency and effectiveness; to invite comparison between teams or districts; and to compare work with other authorities nationally. The fact that a more sophisticated approach to monitoring has now developed across the government's current modernisation programme serves to underline how influential such developments have been and how far we have come. One task of this book is to help managers and senior practitioners in social services departments confront the further challenges ahead in managing the performance of their services.

The work contained in this book considers a scheme for measuring the performance of social care for older people that relies on the introduction and use of a set of performance indicators (PIs). Its intentions are to review the current state of knowledge concerning the use of indicators in this context. Being a relatively new development for social care services, the use of PIs for local and national concerns inevitably covers a number of themes. Quite apart from the current regulatory concerns, there are the pressures (which have always existed in local government planning) for the continued development of financial and monitoring systems. There are themes drawn from academic research in business, public sector management and policy analysis, which have contributed to a conceptual debate concerning the use of indicators. There were also a number of central government initiatives in the 1980s, which forged a climate of opinion around the idea of efficiency in managing public resources, giving impetus to the use of performance indicators in the public sector. Lastly, there have been specific directives, from the Department of the Environment, the Department of Health, and the Audit Commission, which have had particular relevance for the development of these measures within a social care context.

Many of these initiatives have been attempts from the centre to monitor and regulate public services at a national level. The challenge for social care, however, is to devise measurement systems for use in a local context, so that the performance of key aspects of a department's work can be evaluated, monitored and appraised. Indicators can then be used by managers to assess the work of a department against policy priorities, local circumstances and national guidance. They can be used to motivate staff and explore the extent to which services conform to their expected uses. They can also assist in bringing to light concerns about quality and user choice in service provision, both of which are common currencies in the operation of a modern social services department. It is hoped that this book will provide valuable information to help in accomplishing these aims.

Performance indicators in social care for older people are set in context through work undertaken in Cheshire Social Services Department, described later. The was an authority with a particular commitment to the use of computerised information systems in pursuing its objectives more effectively. The work was designed initially to assist in devising a set of performance indicators that could be used within an existing client-based information system. The technical and conceptual work emerging from this collaboration has led to some major refinements to the knowledge base for measuring performance at the local level. The information presented could usefully be extended to other client groups in receipt of long-term care. It could also, we believe, assist departments in setting out a general approach to measurement. This would aid them in complying with some of the recent initiatives. In the remaining sections of this chapter, the scene is set by reviewing some of the arguments concerning performance indicators; why they were originally devised, what they are, and the procedures necessary to implement them.

Social care performance: why and how

The recent trend towards performance measurement within social care has its precedents in an earlier period of social services history. The difficulties in co-ordination, service delivery and flexibility that characterised social care in the past have gradually given rise to an increased emphasis on monitoring performance. At the time of the Seebohm reorganisation (Cmnd 3703, 1968), the focus was on the problems of co-ordination, inadequacies in the amount and range of provision and the quality of such provision throughout the country. Proposals for a unified service were seen as a way of ensuring a more efficient and comprehensive response to meet need (Cmnd 3703, 1968, paras 152, 153). Throughout the early 1980s, debate centred on a more or less constant reappraisal of these changes. So, there occurred an assessment of the problems encountered in a universal, generic service (Challis and Ferlie, 1986; 1987; 1988), such as the relative neglect of work with elderly people, the lack of specificity in service response, and the difficulties in co-ordination brought about by fragmentation of the system (Challis and Davies, 1986). These more general debates about the performance of social care were increasingly replaced by more specific concerns. The major legislative changes of the late 1980s, of which the White Paper on community care, *Caring for People* (Cm 849, 1989) was central, raised a number of issues about the care for older people. These included concerns about poor assessment and targeting of services, the inappropriate placement of many elderly people in residential care and the rising costs of institutional care (Audit Commission, 1986a; Parker, 1990). During the early part of the 1990s the focus was largely on monitoring the impact of the community care changes. Important early work (Wistow et al., 1994) sought to measure the workings of the new system for social services departments. From central government, there was an increased concern with monitoring social services performance from the viewpoint of the consumer (Black, 1994) and the quality dimension emerged as important (Coote, 1994). The emphasis changed in the later part of the 1990s with the incoming Labour government's stress on a consistent national approach to defining social care performance throughout the country (Department of Health, 1999a).

As opposed to previous periods, in which care provision was observed and recorded mostly within the context of individual cases, the recent reforms bear witness to a sea-change in the way overall care is monitored and appraised. In care for older people, many social services departments are now attempting to monitor the work they do in a way that assists managers and practitioners to think on a more global level. Much of this has been bound up with the emergence of a more market-oriented philosophy in social care, stemming from the community care reforms of the early 1990s (Cm 849, 1989). The reforms required the establishment of quality assurance mechanisms within social services departments (Coote, 1994). This engendered a more competitive environment, with many different players operating in the long-term care field. It is therefore now essential for staff to have some grasp of how their activities fit into the overall provision of care. Related to this, there has been a shorter-term history of budgetary constraints, with the needs of older people often outstripping the supply of well-organised and efficient care. Knowing how services perform and whether they are achieving their objectives has thus become one way of responding to these competing pressures.

At the macro level, central government has responded to these demands by setting standards for the way individual local authorities manage the care they provide. However, this has not been a simple linear development. There have been changes in approach, consequent on the overall economic environment. Often standards have been set down in the style of requirements, where financial and other control mechanisms are imposed if departments do not come up to the mark. At other times, performance standards have been more implicit. Central government, through the Department of Health and Social Services Inspectorate, monitored local authorities by inspection and guidance rather than by imposing mandatory standards. Performance has been measured at the local level with departments devising their own monitoring mechanisms. Recent developments, which may be grouped under the banner of the government's modernisation agenda, now seem to be bringing us full circle. The Social Services White Paper (Cm 4169, 1998) and other initiatives stemming from it (Department of Health, 2000), put considerable stress on a central government role of regulator for care standards at a national level. The *consistency* of services across the country is one theme that has emerged as important and relevant. The local nature of social services has still often been emphasised, as authorities must respond to local need as they determine it. However, a reliance solely on local standards of service has led to inconsistencies in response throughout different areas of the country. A framework of national standards by which to view performance is seen as one way to tackle this. There is a tension, therefore, between central and local government requirements in the development of performance indicators, which is an underlying theme for social care. In other words, a tension emerges between the need for workable systems of local performance against those that are relevant to national policy concerns.

The influence of all these factors calls for coherent methods of measuring performance in a way that reflects the actual operation of social care. This necessitates a full description of the care system in order that measures are designed with reference to the environment in which they are to operate. At the design stage and in subsequent analysis, measures must, on the one hand, be simple and understandable to use while, on the other hand, be generalisable to the wider context. Performance measures must act to support enquiries into the way services operate and help raise questions concerning different aspects of the service system. Indicators often do this indirectly by drawing to attention aspects that deviate from what is expected or by reference to important policy concerns. Once analysed and interpreted, these measures have a range of uses, from commenting on efficiency and effectiveness to judging services according to user-defined criteria of choice and acceptability. Throughout this book several of these issues around the use of PIs are discussed and translated into a context for social care.

Performance review and measurement

Performance indicators are part of a structure of activities required to monitor the different aspects of performance in any organisation. Much of this structure was drawn originally from the private business sector. The technical arguments concerned with such a structure have been summarised for some time. Performance measurement, and the use of associated indicators, draws largely on the theory and techniques of management accounting, which uses information summarising the sum total of an organisation's actions in quantitative terms (Emmanuel et al., 1990). From this point, it is argued that control can be brought to bear by the use of techniques which enable output to be measured against the objectives of the organisation. Corrective action can then be taken if there is deviation from these objectives, with possible causes of error being sought by the use of predictive models based on routinely generated data. Correcting errors in the system produces further information which can be used to inform subsequent actions. Such techniques are now well developed in the private business world. For example, Helfert (1965) in his *Techniques of Financial Analysis* outlined a number of measures that could examine the performance of any business unit. These tools were developed to appraise the performance of business organisations according to the relevant concerns of financial prudence, efficiency and profitability. They were designed to ask specific questions of the running of a business unit, such as its productivity and the meeting of objectives. Performance indicators are expressed in the form of ratio measures, which relate units of information to each other. The resulting measures are intended to express important aspects of a company's overall performance. So for example, indices such as the *current ratio* (current assets/current liabilities) and *profitability ratio* (net profit/total assets) are used to assess different aspects of a business's operation (see, for example, Helfert, 1965, pp. 54–68). A fuller picture of performance can only be gained by examining the relationships between these ratios. These relationships, if interpreted in a meaningful way, can comment on the overall workings of an organisation; they can confirm hypothesis and lead to tentative conclusions concerning important aspects of performance.

It is clear from the work contained in this book that ratios are not available in such a ready form for use within social care. Unlike private business, there is no indicator of profit or share price, the famous 'bottom line', which can act as a summary measure of performance. Nor is it possible, as some business analysts have done, to relate indicators together in a precise arithmetical way (see, for example, Kline and Hessler, 1960, p. 799). In social and health care, performance itself becomes more difficult to measure. What is to be measured is often contested and there are no broad, overall measures that can serve as indicators of performance as a whole. Measures must, instead, focus on the particular workings of specific services. In social services, and other public services, there are several outputs reflecting multiple objectives and a variety of measures are needed (Anthony and Herzlinger, 1980; Jackson, 1988). These must help to define and comment on the objectives of services, their efficient operation and their conformity with specific policy targets. Therefore, a challenge has to be faced in devising appropriate indicators that can serve to emphasise major aspects of current service operations. For social care, these measures can help to answer significant questions concerning the purposes and success, or otherwise, of the care provided to vulnerable people.

Various components of performance review have been identified within the wider public sector (Butt and Palmer, 1985). These include, first, setting clear strategies and objectives for the service. Without these, it is difficult to determine whether policy aims have been achieved. Budgetary processes follow on from this as a means of ensuring the accurate consideration of competing priorities. An effective monitoring mechanism needs then to be in place so that performance of key tasks can be reviewed against targets or standards. PIs are measures designed to reflect aspects of the system to enable this to take place. Indicators have commonly been expressed as ratios between the input and output of a service (Beeton, 1988). For social care, these might include measures such as the cost per home help hour or the number of home help cases per organiser. In order to identify wider-ranging dimensions of performance, these may need to be extended to investigate more subtle processes, such as the adequacy of complementary and substitute services in a particular area (for example, district nurse contact rate/elderly population 65 plus). These can be later combined with other indicators to judge the operation of services on a wider level. More often than not, indicators have been used to compare authorities or districts nationally, so that their place in the whole picture can be seen and appraised. However, they can also be used within an individual authority, so that individual districts or service units can be compared. They are intended to identify the potential cause of a problem so that it can be addressed by modifications to services.

In public service management, there are a number of examples of these indicators working in practice. A structure for strategic management is seen as offering benefits, in terms of improved technical and managerial practice. Many social services authorities are now implementing such a structure as part of a systematic approach to planning and to the measurement of performance. As well as focusing attention on aspects of service delivery, this can also encourage learning and problem solving on the part of practitioners. Such a strategic framework has been described by Jackson (1993) and is represented in Figure 1. Included within this are elements with particular relevance for social care.

Such a framework has enabled managers to move beyond operational management functions, such as monitoring costs and activity, towards a strategic focus, commenting on the organisation's longer-term objectives. These objectives can be set in terms of PIs, which can then be used to compare performance, both internally and against other authorities in terms of national data. The advantage of the framework is that staff are made aware of the consequences of certain actions. What is to be achieved becomes clearer and the effects of changes in policy and practice are easier to assimilate. Such an approach was employed in our fieldwork within Cheshire, described in Chapter 4.

In reviewing existing information for this study, we became aware of a lack of development work on performance indicators designed specifically for a social care audience. Only a small number of commentators have sought to describe the information available routinely and its use in monitoring services (Miller, 1986; Warburton, 1993). To a large extent, existing performance measurement work, drawn from business, local authority accounting and operational research, fails to express the particular arrangements and policies characteristic of social care. Many of the terms used in this literature appear of limited relevance to the concerns of social services managers and interested practitioners. Therefore, a range of academic and management argument is drawn upon in framing the present work. Information on PIs and a context is presented by which managers can consider their own performance systems. By not limiting ourselves solely to past work within social care, it is hoped that fresh insights may be offered from which to inform the current picture.

Central government initiatives

Many of the early and most recent initiatives for performance measurement in social care have taken place at the central government level. Throughout the 1980s, there was a continued drive for 'value for money' within central and local departments of government, which was a spur to the development of PIs. The justification for this stemmed from changes in the overall UK

Figure 1.1
A strategic framework for performance measurement

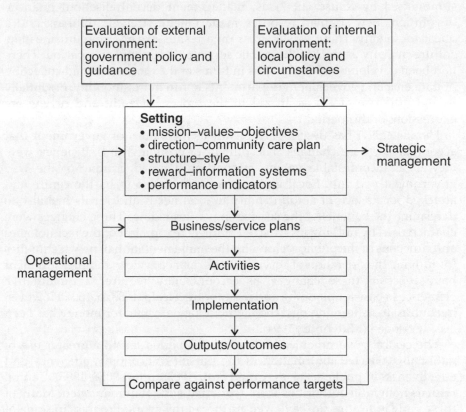

Source: Adapted from Jackson (1993)

economic climate. A constrained economic environment meant that more prudence was seen to be required in the management of the UK economy. No longer was growth in public expenditure to be expected. Reflecting this, there was a change in the way public finances were planned and monitored, from 'volume' to 'cash' planning, with its consequent stress on limits. Some of the arguments concerned with these changes have been neatly summarised by Heald (1983). These include greater calls for accountability with demands for public services to justify and explain their actions and to better demonstrate their use of resources. Political changes too, in particular those stemming from the post-1979 Conservative governments, fostered a climate in which greater accountability, economy and efficiency in all government departments were instigated. The rise of the 'new managerialism', both within social services (Davies, 1987) and health (Vinten, 1993), set considerable store by the use of

PIs as an aid to efficiency in service arrangements of this period. The principles inherent in this reform of public management have already been summarised by Rouse (1997) as: management decentralisation, financial devolution, 'new' human resource management, strategic thinking and a quest for quality. There was a stress on a results-driven, more businesslike culture in many aspects of the public services throughout this period. There had been developments before this in terms of the more sustained collection of data enabling government departments to run more smoothly. Essentially though, the rise of PIs as an aid to the process of audit and review are expressions of this period.

Henkel (1991) has described the shift in the values of government that accompanied these changes. The pursuit of economy and efficiency were viewed as incontestable values, supporting a broad critique of the way government was run. Local government was hauled in by the centre and attacked for its lack of accountability to local needs and for its inability to determine the benefits of the services it was providing. These changes were characterised by nothing less than a complete reappraisal of the technologies and functions of the public sector with the implementation of new techniques for judging the operation of services. Performance review and measurement have reflected these changes, as accountability requires a quantitative element as a base for planning and monitoring (Heald, 1983, p. 160). However, in contrast to its terminology, the methodology of value for money has been less developed (Midwinter, 1994).

The central government initiatives of this period led to a greater use of nationally collected information in the pursuit of economy, efficiency and effectiveness in public services (Cmnd 8616, 1982; Cmnd 9058, 1983). Central returns from local authorities were requested and often mandated. Many of these early indicators are reviewed further in this work. Progress in some of these has already been summarised (Lewis, 1986). The main point to emerge has been that these indicators have stressed certain aspects of performance to the exclusion of others. There has therefore been an emerging debate and criticism of these indicators from a variety of perspectives.

Conceptual arguments

Despite the growth in the use of PIs in local authorities and other public bodies, there has been a tendency to ignore the many conceptual and measurement problems associated with their use. A review of this aspect of performance indicators can never be straightforward. There are a number of linked issues which need to be clarified in order for indicators to be placed in their proper context.

For a social services manager or practitioner reviewing the scene, the world of performance measurement can seem a confusing one. There has been a proliferation of terms and concepts drawn largely from the business sector and the extent to which these can be applied to social care is open to considerable debate. Despite social care being shaped by a greater awareness of economic considerations, some of the definitions associated with this work still sit uneasily with the aspirations of managers and practitioners who wish to develop their own methods of appraisal. A number of related concepts, often used interchangeably, have emerged throughout the evolution of performance measurement. A review of these brings to light the contested nature of performance measurement in the public sector (Yeung, 1989).

Performance statistics, for example, are often collected providing simple information regarding the quantity of services received. Performance indicators, on the other hand, are more sophisticated measures, which look at performance against chosen criteria. Many look to comparisons, across areas and over time. They offer no precise interpretation of the data (Jackson, 1988) but are intended to illuminate specific areas of practice. Human judgement is required to translate an indicator into questions to assist in service review and into proposals for action. Performance indicators are thus but one aspect in the process of measuring performance. Other aspects might include surveys, internal and external inspections and consumer research. Indicators are statistical tools, which permit the performance of an organisation to be measured in a coherent way. This measurement often refers to certain dimensions or reference points such as economy, efficiency, effectiveness and equity, which will be more precisely defined throughout the course of this book. Indicators need to be located within the wider drive for performance review in the public sector which has developed over recent years. This is a generic term for a management system which allows for the use of performance measurement in a review of current and past service development.

Thus, there are many different ways to define performance and there is uncertainty as to how it can most effectively be measured. Terms are used differently by different authors and it is important to define them clearly. However, it is also important to grasp the distinction between the different terms and concepts in order to understand more fully the process of performance measurement. First, the evaluation of performance is impossible without some statement as to the objectives of the organisation. Objectives can be reflective of various dimensions, such as those of efficiency, effectiveness, service quality, equity of provision, and choice. All these terms have been used as yardsticks for performance in social care. It is important to define these dimensions clearly as there may be different methods for evaluating each of them. Indicators can then be devised so as to assess the extent to which the objectives have been achieved. Any shortfalls or discrepancies in achieving them can then be fed into the system of service review. Recommendations can then be put forward which may improve future performance.

Alongside uncertainties around definition, performance measurement is also in need of a framework that can structure the design, collection and interpretation of indicators and assist in their implementation. There are performance models developed from local authority management but these have tended to be rather static in their attempts to comment on the processes at work, particularly for social care. In this book, an analytical framework is put forward, which may comment more faithfully on the performance of social care in delivering its objectives. This framework has been used to structure our work within the social services authority in assisting them in the process of devising and implementing a performance measurement system.

Ideological arguments

In contrast to approaches in business and the wider public sector, there has been a lack of progress in developing performance indicators for social care. Among the many reasons why this might be so, one has been the perceived threat amongst practitioners that indicators will concentrate predominantly on financial aspects to the exclusion of other important areas. So, it is assumed that PIs are solely implemented on the basis of a strategy to contain costs and that other aspects of care, such as whether it meets defined needs, or whether it is provided in an appropriate or timely way, will be neglected in measuring success. This goes hand in hand with a still dominant concern within social services departments that business ethics and principles are being used to control practitioners, leading them away from a concern with the needs of clients.

Such concerns are based on a set of values that contrast the quantitative approach to measuring performance with more qualitative methods and tend to defer to the latter approach over the former. Immediately apparent is the fact that there is an ideological dispute over the use of PIs in this setting and that arguments against using indicators in this context are not always, themselves, value-free. A review of contemporary business approaches to performance measurement makes it clear that these issues are far from simple. While it is true that firms have success in profit maximisation as their final defining standard, there are many non-financial measures of performance available in the private sector. If one were to consult any definitive reference work on business performance, such as that of Holloway et al. (1995) or a guiding article, such as Robert Eccles' *The performance measurement manifesto* (1991), one would see that financial indicators alone are considered too simplistic a measure of performance. Kaplan and Norton (1992) also promoted a 'balanced scorecard' that translated a company's mission statement into a comprehensive set of performance measures, reviewing business activity on a broad front at different levels of the organisation.

It is now generally recognised that a wide range of indicators are important in defining and measuring performance in any organisation. Fundamentally, these measures must relate to performance as a whole, both in relation to organisations of a similar type and as against standards set by the organisation itself and by national guidance. More centrally, the process of measurement and the indicators chosen must reflect the nature of the business in which the organisation is engaged.

Despite this clarification, the value-laden nature of performance indicators cannot be neglected. Many have commented on the debate that surrounds any attempt to assess an organisation's performance. This centres on how the objectives of the organisation are defined, on the criteria to be used in measuring performance and on the interpretation of information (Klein 1982a, p. 385). It will be seen throughout this book that the design and use of these measures is subject to a number of constraints and is the focus of a degree of controversy. This controversy is largely because performance itself is a political issue (Pollitt, 1986, p. 168).

Fundamentally though, the issue is one of how PIs are used by different players in order to justify their own positions. For instance, information support for a top-down management system is not the only way in which PIs can be used. Indicators can also assist, for example, in the more effective pursuit of service provision at the practitioner level (Goldberg and Warburton, 1979). There is therefore a debate centring on which perspective and for whom indicators are devised.

Mechanisms for ensuring accountability

Most debates on the development of and need for PIs centre on their use in upholding accountability, with greater accountability one of the main justifications for the increased stress on public service performance. Within social care, problems of accountability in the early 1980s have been more than adequately discussed elsewhere (Challis and Davies, 1986; Davies and Challis, 1986; Audit Commission, 1986). Clarity about the objectives of social care services and mechanisms for routinely monitoring the success or failure of these was seriously lacking at that time. Coupled with this was an absence of 'technological determinacy' whereby fieldwork staff could appraise the likely consequences of their decisions (Davies and Challis, 1986). The activities of staff could not easily be predicted and so accountability in a professional sense was unclear (Heald, 1983, p. 159). The rise of performance review has permitted the activities of professionals and the processes of departments to become more visible. In this way, they become answerable, to elected representatives, users and the public at large.

There are many strands to accountability including vertical accountability, upwards to elected officials and downwards to service users, and horizontal accountability, outwards to colleagues and managers (Elcock, 1983). Each of these elements has included its own measurement issues. Vertically, accountability requires that those with delegated authority, such as social services managers, are answerable for their actions (Day and Klein, 1987). This requires clear information by which they can be judged, according to clearly labelled criteria of performance, by both political representatives and service users. Horizontally, accountability requires that professionals adopt a clear monitoring process for their work, so that decisions can be communicated reliably to peer-group members. Accountability is, according to Day and Klein (1987), a chameleon-type word representing a host of different functions and practices. These, in turn, reflect the fact that there are multiple audiences for the receipt of information by which to judge performance. A number of different approaches can be outlined that require different sources of information so as to demonstrate accountability. These include budgetary, managerial, political and professional interpretations (Rouse, 1997).

Budgetary accountability requires an authority to adhere to annual budget as a way of demonstrating successful performance. It has been a dominant concern in the policies of local authorities but is an insensitive way of monitoring the quality of services. There have been incentives for managers to ensure spending is completed before the end of the financial year with scant regard to whether services are delivered in an efficient or effective way. Traditional accounting practices associated with this are concerned with costing inputs rather than the outcomes of expenditure, such as services delivered. Indicators of financial activity are therefore required to demonstrate accuracy in accounting practices. However, the budget has often not been scrutinised according to wider concerns, such as whether objectives have been achieved and the value accrued from certain services. For these reasons, adherence to the budget is not necessarily a measure of competence (Flynn, 1993). More recently, in much of the public sector, attempts have been made to set monitoring of resources more in relation to overall priorities and objectives (Cmnd 9058, 1994; Cm 4014, 1998). In order to do this, objectives must be defined and outputs measured in a clearer way. This has called for a review of the indicators used to monitor performance at a local level.

Managerial accountability has been defined as 'making those with delegated authority answerable for carrying out agreed tasks according to agreed criteria of performance' (Day and Klein, 1987, p. 27). This process concerns the construction of an agreed language or currency of discourse by which to assess conduct and the use of technical methods by which performance can be measured (Day and Klein, 1987). This form of accountability was predominant in the early development of indicators during the 1980s, associated with the wider political changes referred to above. It is also present in a range of performance related tasks in which management is engaged, which promote the use of indicators in particular ways.

Political accountability concerns the wider justification of decisions in the interests of the citizen. It includes all the elements referred to above and in addition, it reflects the values of public service, such as equity, fairness, justice and citizenship (Rouse, 1997). It is in this form of accountability that notions of acceptability to, and participation by, the consumer become important drivers for measuring performance. The early 1990s were a period characterised by this type of performance information with the growth in initiatives like the Citizen's Charter (Cm 1599, 1991; Black, 1994). It is difficult to define this type of accountability within a precise set of indicators. However, consumer-related information has become important in the context of recent central government initiatives (Social Services Inspectorate, 2002).

Professional accountability requires that performance be defined by the satisfactory achievement of certain tasks ascribed to the profession. It is in this sense that routine information has been used at the practitioner level to ensure accountability. The main British development of this was the case-review system described by Goldberg and Warburton (1979). In this, a record system was established enabling problems to be identified, the means to tackle them to be stated clearly, and the objectives of intervention to be made explicit. Information concerning social work activity was thus made available for use by individual workers. However, the arguments in favour of such a system are not new. Robert Spano and colleagues in the US described the operation of an accountability system in hospital social work as early as 1977 (Spano et al., 1977; Spano and Lund, 1986). As part of this, standardised client records were fed into a management system to enable a clearer statement of goals and greater feedback to staff concerning the consequences of their activity.

Improvements in accountability require clear statements as to the objectives of services and clear lines of responsibility for the pursuit of them. They also require a credible information system by which client details can be combined with resource data to provide a system for planning and monitoring (Goldberg and Warburton, 1979). PIs provide the measurement basis for such a system. Used properly, they can lead to more explicit decisions concerning resource allocation. The extent to which greater accountability is ensured by the use of such systems remains a crucial question. There has certainly been a more widespread use of computerised systems in social services departments and the sophistication by which modern systems can hold and aggregate information concerning all elements of service opens up much promise, although there is marked variation in the extent to which social services departments can access and use such information. It therefore remains to be seen how far such technology can be utilised in ensuring transparency in the conduct of practice.

Although social care has been touched by many of the national pressures outlined above, devising clear and useable indicators to assist in ensuring the accountability of services has posed some problems. National data sets based on routine returns to organisations such as CIPFA, the Audit Commission and the Department of Health have failed to reflect the changes throughout the late 1980s and early 1990s, particularly the community care reforms and care management. In contrast to the health sector, there have been few publicised accounts of the use of PIs by departments as part of their locally-based information systems. What little is in the public domain remains confined to small-scale research and individual accounts (James, 1987; Fletcher, 1990; Warburton, 1993). In order to improve upon existing work, it is therefore essential that, as well as being clear about the procedures involved in improving accountability and performance, both conceptual and measurement issues are addressed more fully.

From Value for Money to Best Value

In contrast to the 1980s, when value for money initiatives dictated the use of PIs, the end of the 1990s and the beginning of the new century has been characterised by a search for Best Value in public services. Prior to the 1980s, the district auditor was merely required to examine the legality of local authority accounts. This was performance assessment derived from a central government concern to ensure local authorities were acting within their constitutional powers (Jowett and Rothwell, 1988, p. 21). This involved a minimum of central control. However, with the establishment of the Audit Commission in 1982, a philosophy of greater control and regulation by central government was instigated. This moved to a consideration of the three components of value for money – economy, efficiency and effectiveness – by which to measure performance. However, recent inspection and monitoring by such bodies as the Department of Health and Audit Commission has been based on wider responsibilities and functions (SSI/Audit Commission, 1998a). These include the dissemination of information to promote greater clarity concerning aims, the intended purposes of services and the relationship between expenditure and service effects.

In local authorities, accountability to the public now requires the achievement of objectives to be set within a framework fixed by the Best Value regime. This is outlined in the White Paper for local government (Cm 4014, 1998) implemented in April 2000. Best Value is a duty to deliver services to clear standards, covering their cost and quality by the most effective, economic and efficient means available. The performance framework underpinning Best Value requires local social services authorities to establish their own objectives and performance measures. They need to have in place a system of performance reviews and local plans, which set out the performance targets that the authority is to pursue. These local requirements are to be set against a national set of performance indicators, so that authorities can compare their performance.

An outline of the work

As the foregoing commentary makes clear, the study of PIs opens up linked debates concerning the justification for performance and the procedures necessary to measure it. Although these wider organisational concerns of performance evaluation will be alluded to throughout this book, they are not its central concern. This book has a clearly defined purpose in defining and demonstrating the use of measures that assist in making performance review at the local level possible. It is an attempt to provide an interpretation of these measures for use in social care, using services for older people as an example.

This is done by describing the work commissioned by one social services department, who asked PSSRU to develop a set of performance indicators to assist them in their work within older people's services. This book describes the development of PIs within the authority and outlines their use in the monitoring of social care for older people. It does this firstly by placing them in the context of national developments, both historical and conceptual, and within the sphere of social care in general. We then go on to describe our work with Cheshire Social Services in devising and monitoring a set of PIs for use locally, building on many of the arguments set out in earlier chapters. This work is set within a distinctive analytical framework, which we have termed the Performance Indicator Analytical Framework (PIAF) that attempts to overcome many of the difficulties found in earlier PI systems. It attempts to systematically relate indicators of need, supply, process and outcome to one another. In particular, the framework is our attempt to place performance indicators within a proper context for social care so that they can be used more fruitfully (Clarkson and Challis, 2002). Building on this, we describe the use to which indicators were put within Cheshire so that conclusions can be drawn for the future.

Plan of the book

In starting out it was felt that much could be learnt from a review and appraisal of how national and local attempts to create and use performance indicators had fared in the past and what the future held. Chapter 2 therefore serves as a general introduction, setting the scene to the world of performance measurement – its management and regulatory functions – throughout the public sector. We set the agenda for the use of performance indicators with a review of their development in the measurement of social care services in Chapter 3. Chapter 4 deals with the review within Cheshire SSD in setting up a performance indicator scheme for the monitoring of its older people's services. PSSRU felt that they should talk directly to social services staff in Cheshire to understand the experiences of collecting and using information to date and to gain an appreciation of their future needs and aspirations. The chapter therefore covers the interviews that were held with Cheshire staff along with contextual information concerning the aims and practices of the department. Chapter 5 describes a distinctive analytical framework – PIAF – developed by PSSRU, which enables performance indicators to be fitted into the context of service provision. Chapter 6 discusses the indicators and contextual information that were produced. Finally, Chapter 7 goes over some of the processes and systems that need to be in place for the indicators to be collected, analysed and acted upon. It includes some tentative examples of the way these indicators can work in practice. In Chapter 8 we conclude by offering a summary of the main findings from the work and look at some ways forward for performance measurement in social care.

Chapter 2

Indicators: Performance and Regulation

The ... point which needs investigation is the extent to which, working with the local authorities, useful yardsticks of cost or standards of design can be produced by which ... local authorities can measure their own efforts. The central government has the advantage that it can look at the whole of the country, it can obtain information from all the local authorities, and it can, and should, be used as a means of obtaining information for the benefit of local authorities generally rather than to use against them.

(Banwell, 1959, p. 211).

This chapter describes the development of performance indicators nationally in the UK. It begins with an outline of the historical development of PIs, from the early days of monitoring in health and social care to the emergence of more well-defined indicators during the 1980s. This history is predominantly one of regulation, with indicators being used as mechanisms of control of local authorities by central government. The content of these indicator systems is described as a prelude to later chapters where the development of PIs for local social care practice is discussed. Some criticisms of these indicators are also outlined. The discussion then moves on to the use of PIs in terms of other stakeholders: local authorities and the consumer. The historical review concludes with an outline of the use of PIs during the 1990s: in central government; as part of the community care reforms; and as an aid to service review by the public. Finally, the rationale and use of indicators as part of the government's recent modernisation agenda for health and social care is described. In order to consolidate these historical issues, the discussion then moves on to look at conceptual work on PIs with a review of definitions, models and descriptions. The chapter closes with a discussion of the actual use of PIs, focusing on techniques of analysis and some conventions commonly used.

History and context

In the context of the present work, performance indicators have been in vogue in the UK public sector since the early 1980s. However, there were a number of developments before this time and the task of this chapter is to describe these in a general context so that their relevance for social care can be examined later. This is done by concentrating initially on the relationship between central and local government in the design and implementation of performance indicators. A number of questions have been asked: To what extent can central government influence or control local authorities in the pursuit of their activities and in setting standards or benchmarks for them? What are the measurement problems in attempting to devise performance indicators? By what criteria and in what way is performance measured? What are the consequences, at the local level, of this influence on measurement? As witnessed by the quotation from a lecture by Sir Harold Banwell, then secretary to the Association of Municipal Corporations, these questions have assumed importance for a considerable length of time. The control and monitoring of local authorities' performance by central government, while a present-day concern, has, in fact, existed for a good deal of the post-war period (Banwell, 1959). In this work, while the focus is upon the development and design of the measures themselves, these arguments are important. They provide a context for recent debates, as well as an indication of the likely use of performance indicators in the future.

Recently there have been numerous examples of performance indicators in use in many aspects of public life. For example there have been educational performance indicators centring on schools' rates of success in helping their pupils pass exams. There have been health service indicators in the NHS covering a range of process and treatment aspects, some of which have been published so that professionals and the public alike can compare the performance of different hospitals and Primary Care Trusts. There have been Key Indicators of local authority social services, originally developed by the Social Services Inspectorate (SSI) and recently routinised and developed by the Department of Health and there is the work of the Audit Commission across the public sector. These indicators have been put to a number of uses. Many of these indicators have been developed in order to measure the performance of public services in delivering greater productivity and in the more efficient use of resources. Some have sought to measure other aspects such as customer satisfaction, quality and responsiveness. However, many of these terms are difficult to define precisely and, in this context, there has been considerable debate around the use of performance indicators in measuring the success or otherwise of various public agencies.

In the rest of this chapter, PI development for a range of public sector activity is reviewed but the main focus is upon health and social care. These two components are not only the most relevant to the work discussed here, but they have also tended to raise some of the most interesting issues in relation to public sector performance measurement. The review begins by offering a critical review of central government initiatives, which have promoted a range of PIs for management purposes.

The early days

Although not using the term 'performance indicators', there have been a range of statistical measures employed in analysing public sector performance for a number of years. In some quarters, it has been argued that this routine information does not fulfil the criteria for performance indicators, although it does share some attributes commonly associated with them (see, for example, St Leger et al., 1992). In this sense, performance indicators have a long history. In the US, output and performance measurement goes back to the 1960s: Planning Programming and Budgeting Systems (PPBS) and Management by Objectives (MBO) are terms which have been used for initiatives by which US government agencies set clearer objectives for their activities (Brady, 1973; Bovaird, 1981; Carter et al., 1992). Within these mechanisms, the overall costs of a public service were subsumed under the general rubric of objectives rather than measured according to traditional inputs such as wages, capital, equipment and materials (Culyer, 1980). The advantage of budgeting in this manner was that the relationship between expenditure and the actual value of public programmes became more transparent.

There were attempts to transfer these systems from private business practice into the public sector throughout the 1960s and 70s. This proved difficult. The systems required considerable investment and the definition of performance measures often remained elusive (Klein, 1972). In 1970, the then Department of Education and Science, for instance, published a study enquiring into the possibilities of using these techniques to ensure greater clarity in the setting of objectives for social programmes (DES, 1970). Many difficulties were identified, including the very real one of judging the impact of a programme on the local environment. The actual nature of objectives in the public realm was often contested, depending on whose interests were being served by the implementation of a particular programme. There was also a time-lag between the activities of a programme and its impact. Where this was great, as in education for example, it became difficult to pinpoint the link between a programme and its intended consequences. These were arguments that were to resurface later when the technical problems and limitations in PIs were to be debated throughout the public services.

There were other developments, which could be seen, in retrospect, as precursors to the development of performance measurement in the public domain. In Britain, while much of the post war period was directed towards judging the effects of public sector services against 'social' criteria, there were attempts at introducing more commercial measures, evident first in departments of central government. As early as 1968, the Fulton Committee called for managers in the civil service to be held responsible for performance, measured in an objective way. There was a concern that the procedures and practices of government were lacking in efficiency and transparency. If the outputs of government activity could be measured in some way, the Committee argued, this would enable individuals and units to be held accountable for their performance. This would involve developing measures whereby output could be judged against criteria such as costs (Cmnd 3638, 1968). The term 'performance indicator' was first used in this context in 1978 in relation to the nationalised industries (Cmnd 7131, 1978; Rutherford, 1983). This was an early attempt at devising a system of indicators which would help to ensure the closer monitoring of public industry. Non-financial indicators were developed which would inform the public as to an industry's success in controlling its costs and increasing efficiency. The response of the industries to this initiative was, however, mixed; a lack of clear standards being cited as one reason why the response by industries was limited (Jowett and Rothwell, 1988, p. 88).

In health care, the collection of routine statistical information has a longer history still. Goldacre and Griffen (1983) provide a critical review, which traces the development of performance assessment back to the collection of hospital information by Dr Clifton in 1732. From this, there has been a gradual development of crude performance measurement in the NHS, from earlier costing reports (such as SH3 returns from 1948 and a national costing system in 1950) to the 1956 Guillebaud Committee (Cmnd 9663, 1956), which was established to review NHS efficiency. Here, with reference to the use of hospital statistical returns to measure efficiency, it was argued that more precise measures were needed in order to make more meaningful comparisons. In 1972 the Grey Book discussed monitoring NHS performance against health authority plans, which could act as a yardstick by which performance could be adjudged (DHSS, 1972a). In 1977 the House of Commons Social Services Committee recommended the development of performance indicators to the DHSS. They argued that a start should be made in finding ways of relating health expenditure to performance (Goldacre and Griffen, 1983). A Royal Commission on the NHS in 1979 (Cmnd 7615, 1979) discussed some of the inherent difficulties in defining the performance of such a complex organisation. These included the problems in defining the end objectives of the service in improving health. The Commission concluded that, at the time, existing measures of NHS performance were crude and that they did not seek to link measures together in an overall evaluation of the efficiency or 'productivity' of the whole service. These earlier criticisms all pointed to the fact that there was insufficient monitoring and a lack of systems of accountability in the health care sector at that time. The information that was available was often crude and not collected at a national level.

In local government, the *Bains Report* (Department of the Environment, 1972) encouraged local authority departments to set clear objectives for their services and pay more attention to assessing the effectiveness of activities. The

Public Expenditure Committee (House of Commons, 1972) called for a system of information which could guide decisions regarding the allocation of resources to public services. At the time, decisions were not taken on the basis of a framework by which the rationale for allocation of resources to each service could be examined. Expenditure on services was not related to their outputs in non-financial terms. There was also no way to assess the key relationships between all factors in a public programme and relate this to expenditure (House of Commons, 1972, para. 17). The Layfield Committee carried out a review of local government finance in 1976 (Cmnd 6453, 1976). It cited a lack of accountability for local government spending resulting from unclear lines of responsibility between central and local government. There was no generally agreed view as to the aims, objectives and policies of local authorities and contradictory guidance from central government in planning services (Cmnd 6453, 1976, p. 10). An absence of clear information on which to base spending decisions was seen as one reason for the lack of judgement regarding the use of local authority resources (Cmnd 6453, 1976, p. 83). The lack of credible measures of the output of local authority services was another problem cited. These developments stressed the pursuit of value for money in local authority services with accompanying financial control mechanisms.

In general terms, a common theme of all these developments was to stress the need for clarity of objectives and some way of judging public services against these. For example, for social care, the then Department of Health and Social Security in evidence presented to the House of Commons Expenditure Committee identified a number of objectives for social care services for older people (DHSS, 1972a). It is interesting to note the contemporary relevance of these objectives for older people's services: to enable them to live in their own homes as long as they wish and are reasonably able to do so; to enable older people so far as they are able and willing to take part in and contribute to the normal range of social life in their community; and to restore patients with illness or disability to as healthy a state as possible (DHSS, 1972a). There were to be further developments that synthesised these approaches more directly. In 1980, the Local Government, Planning and Land Act (section 2) required every local authority to produce an annual report in which certain performance measures were to be made public. In 1981, The Department of the Environment published a code of practice concerning these reports, which highlighted the aims of making local authorities more accountable and integrating management and financial reporting by the use of statistical data (DoE, 1981). This would include, it was suggested, comparisons with other authorities, trends over time and between plans and achievements. The indicators were intended to measure various aspects of performance on a standard basis, including cost, scale and quality of service, demand for service and client satisfaction. The rationale behind the publication of these indicators was to give local ratepayers clear information and enable them to judge the activity of authorities. A series of key service indicators, published to measure performance, which could be compared by authority, was thus initiated. Contained within this wider set of indicators for local government were a small number of measures designed for social services. However, it took some time before a more comprehensive approach to social services performance measurement was developed.

Regulatory mechanisms: the emergence of the 'new managerialism'

It is not enough to say that earlier indicators were merely measuring aspects of the operation of public services. Already, by the end of the 1970s, these indicators were beginning to focus on issues at a higher level of generality, such as those of efficiency and effectiveness. These issues were also being linked to wider political debates on the state of the UK economy and of the way public services were managed. Probably the greatest spur to the development of performance indicators took place during a period of great change in the political and economic landscape of the UK. This was a period in which the assumptions and activities of all branches of government were being seriously questioned, and some of the early developments in performance measurement were being re-shaped and revived. Many commentators believe that the increasing use of performance indicators was associated with the approach to the public sector taken by successive governments from 1979 onwards (Flynn, 1986; Conner and Black, 1994). This approach was typified by emphases on informed management, value for money, accountability and audit. It was first made concrete by the government's Financial Management Initiative (FMI) of May 1982, whereby public bodies were required to identify efficiency savings and manage their finances more tightly than before. In 1982, a White Paper, *Efficiency and Effectiveness in the Civil Service* (Cmnd 8616, 1982) called on departments in central government to develop plans to implement the FMI whereby performance indicators and output measures could be developed to assess success in achieving objectives. Managers of government departments should have, 'a clear view of their objectives; and assess, and wherever possible measure, outputs or performance in relation to these objectives' (Cmnd 9058, 1983, p. 1).

The initiative thus called for measures of achievement that could translate improved management objectives into targets, which could then be used to hold public managers accountable for their performance (Cmnd 9297, 1984, p. 3). This initiative affected all government departments with reports of performance being made available to Ministers. It was mandated too that the annual Public Expenditure White Paper contain statements of intentions as well as objectives and targets to be achieved. These targets were to be operationalised as measures. The development of these measures continued after the initiative and their progress has been reviewed in a Treasury working paper by Lewis (1986).

Carter and colleagues (1992) have charted the development of these ideas concerning public accountability and effectiveness measurement in government, from a more critical perspective. The 1982 initiative can be seen as a symbolic gesture, largely the result of developments in policy in the US and UK, made concrete by the changing economic fortunes of the late 1970s following the oil crisis. In particular, the FMI was an attempt at devising mechanisms to control the rate of growth in public expenditure, which was then deemed politically unacceptable. It was implemented in the context of calls for economy in public sector services rather than the pursuit of wider efficiency or effectiveness considerations in their own right. This was part of a wider political striving to bring public bodies to account for their activities. It has been argued that this brought about a new concept of public management (Metcalfe and Richards, 1987). An example of this was the efficiency unit headed by Sir Derek Rayner, set up in 1979 to promote value for money throughout government. It carried out a series of small-scale scrutinies of expenditure on government departments (Sheldon, 1986; Bray, 1988).

The developments of this period brought about a host of indicators used in different ways within different public services. Performance indicators certainly increased in number following the 1982 initiative. The 1985 Public Expenditure White Paper contained 500 output and performance measures in all. In the two years after this, the numbers increased to 1200 and 1800 respectively and in 1989 rose to 2,302 (Carter, 1988). A range of public organisations were represented in the growth of PIs, which took place throughout the later half of the 1980s. These included the NHS and social services, social security, the police, education and the former publicly-owned industries that included rail, air and water authorities. However, the rise in the quantity of these indicators was not matched, in all services, by an increase in their scope and quality of design. Many of the indicators being developed, particularly in services such as health, made use of existing statistical data, such as activity or costing information, not specifically designed to measure the success of objectives. Where objectives were more clearly defined, such as in the administration of social security benefits, performance measurement was more straightforward. In other services, performance was more open to debate and technical methods more prone to complexity and misinterpretation. We return to these arguments later. All these developments, however, pointed to the need to develop measures of performance against which the objectives and targets of public services could be assessed. Thus it can be seen that growing political, administrative and accountability pressures combined to focus attention on measures which would allow the activities of government to be scrutinised more thoroughly.

Early organisational responses to performance measurement

Following these developments a number of key public bodies began to formally develop a range of indicators nationally. These developments are discussed below.

CIPFA

The Chartered Institute of Public Finance and Accountancy (CIPFA) had originally published a draft document *Local Authority Accounting – Finance in Management* in 1975, which called for information on the progress towards stated objectives and statistics that would inform the development and effectiveness of services (Woodham, 1980). CIPFA had produced booklets covering different aspects of local authority services on an annual basis for some years. These booklets, which continue to be produced, present activity, cost and unit cost data for all local authorities so that comparisons between them can be made. The information is obtained directly from local authorities and collected and published by CIPFA in estimated and actual form each year. Each booklet contains information about how the indicators have been calculated and, caveats about the use of some, where these are warranted. They have been universally used by local authorities and are seen as an authoritative source to be quoted if bids for additional resources are being made or debates about service rationalisation are being held. There have been criticisms of these data, that they are too prone to error and overly concerned with financial information and elements that can be easily costed. However, until recently, the CIPFA booklets have been the only detailed resources to which social services, in particular, have had access.

The Audit Commission

Real momentum was achieved in 1982 when, under the Local Government Finance Act, the Audit Commission was formed, incorporating within it the old District Audit Service. The brief of the Commission and local District Auditors was to assess public bodies against the criteria of economy, efficiency and effectiveness and to encourage good management (Audit Commission, 1983). This was to be done by a refinement of existing local government performance measures. The Audit Commission embarked on a series of special studies from which audit guides were created for routine use (Audit Commission, 1986b, 1986c). The themes of these studies were the need to emphasise the output of services and relate these to inputs; to make the best use of available services; and for performance review to be an integral part of the management process. These guides comprised lists of performance indicators which auditors and local managers could use in their work.

The Audit Commission (Audit Commission, 1986b) constructed performance indicators to demonstrate the achievement of value for money in public services. Value for money (or the lack of it) was demonstrated through the use of three broad types of indicator covering:

- Economy – that is, how service inputs are acquired, usually by reference to cost.
- Efficiency – that is, the way in which service inputs and service processes, in a context of service quality and service equality, are used or combined to create service outputs.
- Effectiveness – meaning, the way in which service outputs and service processes, in a context of service quality and service equality, bring about service outcomes.

These components of performance measurement have been referred to as the 'three Es'. They figure highly in the Audit Commission's publications and in those of other government departments. The Commission's approach has been to proceed with performance measurement despite its supposed limitations. By making existing performance techniques available to a wide audience it has sought to outline what local councils can do to improve their reviews of performance (Henderson-Stewart, 1990). The Commission's broad values have been to disseminate good practice, taking into account the particular activities of each local authority they are auditing.

The Audit Commission has also been concerned with special studies which, under the provisions of section 27 of the Local Government Finance Act, are intended to illuminate aspects of best practice. It has investigated a range of issues in long-term care, such as the efficient operation of care for older people and the development of community care (Audit Commission, 1985; 1986a). In these studies, a range of indicators have been presented, many derived from existing data sources such as those of CIPFA, in judging the operation of national policies.

More recently, the Commission has also produced Local Authority Profiles, based upon CIPFA data, in which performance indicators for a range of local authority services are presented and comparisons made between the authority in question and similar authorities, grouped within 'families' according to census data. These mainly concentrate on service and expenditure data. These profiles serve to highlight where one authority's performance or activities differed markedly from the average for its group (see for example, Audit Commission, 1996a). Their intention is to inform members of the public about the running of local services and also for local authorities themselves to use as comparative information. They have been published as part of the requirements of the Citizen's Charter. More detail of these is provided later.

The Department of Health

The Department of Health began to take a strong interest in performance indicators in the early 1980s. Earlier, effective comparison of local authorities had been made easier by the creation of clusters of like authorities (Imber, 1977). In particular, there were enquiries as to which indicators could be used at a district level in order to assess performance, with particular emphasis on the efficient use of resources (House of Commons Social Services Committee, 1982a, para. 77). A first package of performance indicators, by the then DHSS, was published in September 1983 and updated annually (DHSS, 1983a). The package consisted of about 70 indicators grouped under a number of headings: clinical activity; finance; manpower; support services and estate management. They covered data on finance, activity and manpower for various groups such as the elderly, the mentally ill and support services. They enabled comparisons to be made between the performance of different hospitals and health authorities with reference to such things as staffing levels, cost per in-patient day, waiting times and the availability of different services. The objective of this package was to assist individual regions and districts in assessing the efficiency of their services. It was intended that the indicators would enable the department and regions to monitor NHS performance on a national basis. Ferguson and McGuire (1984) have produced a review and analysis of this initial package.

A joint group on performance indicators produced an expanded number of indicators in 1985, using 1983/84 and 1984/85 data. This package contained eight groups of indicators covering acute services, services for children, estate management and manpower. The groups were arranged in a hierarchical structure with the most important aspects of performance designated as 'first line'. The 'second' and 'third line' PIs were to be used to illuminate causes for concern identified from the top of the hierarchy. These indicators were presented graphically and ranked by district so that values could be compared to other districts, a regional average and a national average. Indicators included: the consumption of resources (by cost and volume); throughput; unit costs; admission rates; and length of stay in hospital. Indicators of access to services were also included, such as waiting lists and clearance times.

These indicators were a development of existing statistics configured to represent an emerging need for administrative accountability (Klein, 1995). They were heavily biased towards monitoring resources (such as manpower) and activity data, such as the numbers of patients treated, and did not include measures of the impact of health activities on the patient. The health indicators had generally been developed as regulatory mechanisms in order to exert some control over health authorities' performance from the centre. There was therefore no new system of data collection in order to make the indicators work. However, the number of indicators as well as their presentation in a uniform way across all health authorities and the directive that all authorities should address them was a new development (Pollitt 1985). A number of limitations and problems have been highlighted. There was little in the way of interpretation of the data and many of the indicators were incompatible with each other. There was also resistance in some quarters due to the perception that these indicators were intended more to enquire into the efficient use of money and less into the quality of patient care.

The NHS Griffiths enquiry (Griffiths, 1983), in its review of management systems, did not place much emphasis on the PIs on offer at that time. It did mention that indicators should be derived from patients' views and performance monitored against them. There was also the general observation that the NHS lacked a system of continuous performance evaluation against agreed standards. This, it argued, was necessary in order to improve the efficiency of the health service at the local level.

A limited set of complementary health performance indicators was later developed by the Inter-Authority Comparisons and Consultancy Group (IACC), led by John Yates (Yates, 1983; Yates and Davidge, 1984; Yates, 1988), at the University of Birmingham in 1985. This was an attempt to produce PIs that would be acceptable and useful instead of being perceived simply as a tool of managerial control (Carter et al., 1992). One element in this was a faster turnaround of the data, so that the delay between collection and production of the data was around nine months, rather than years as in the Department of Health package. The group selected around 32 indicators covering beds per population; length of stay; patient/staff ratios; and other aspects. They identified some technical and conceptual reservations relating to some of these indicators to help users to interpret the values obtained. For example, a high patient/staff ratio may not necessarily be an indication of good quality care but a low ratio may make it difficult to maintain a high care standard and so should be explored further.

The Korner 'minimum data set'

Later in the 1980s a working party chaired by Edith Korner (The NHS/DHSS Health Services Information Steering Group), charged with examining the entire data system of the NHS, produced its recommendations. This group, in looking at the experience of using performance indicators, found inefficient information systems in use within the NHS at that time. Information was often not analysed in terms of the purposes for which it was collected. The group also referred to the way in which financial and administrative mechanisms in the NHS meant that output of the service was often measured in terms of activity. They argued that information systems directed towards the measurement of those activities that most faithfully reflected the objectives of the service were the least developed (for a review of the group's activities see Mason and Morrison, 1985 and Knox, 1987).

The Group proposed the collection by all district health authorities of a 'minimum data set' for each area of activity or speciality. These data could then be used to decide upon the level of resources to be allocated to each part of the service, dependent on priorities, the delivery of care and the benefits derived from it. The data would be used to match performance against objectives and comparable information in other districts. It was argued that most districts would require additional data to provide them with information for local use. The group operated a pragmatic approach to the revising of health service information systems. They used no theoretical model that could help to define the range of tasks in the NHS, which would provide a coherent framework to logically relate items of information one to another. Instead, they based their approach on the experience of existing methods of data collection in order to produce their recommendations quickly. The group produced its reports for the Secretary of State between 1982 and 1984 (DHSS, 1982a, 1st–6th reports) concentrating on the information needs of different specialist activities such as hospital facilities, transport, manpower, paramedical and community services, and finance.

The characteristics of the Korner minimum data set have largely dictated the type of indicator used in health care up to the present day. For example, the 'finished consultant episode' (the length of time a patient spends in the care of one consultant) was one of the indicators recommended in the group's main report. This type of indicator, together with personal details and details of admissions and discharges, was collected as part of a patient information system designed to track hospital activity over time.

Stemming from the Korner recommendations, a data set of indicators was produced for health authority management purposes from April 1987. This replaced the former Hospital Activity Analysis (HAA) information system, which had been in operation since 1969. It expanded the number of performance indicators and improved methods of feedback (Department of Health, 1988a). As well as developing indicators, the Department published guidance on what indicators were available and how to use them, including warnings on their limitations (Department of Health, 1988b). These indicators were used to indicate variations in performance across districts and trends over time and were aimed at disseminating indicators to a wider audience.

A new set of Health Service Indicators (HSIs), based on the Korner data set, was published in 1989 (Department of Health, 1989). HSIs replaced the PIs published by the Department between 1983/84 and 1986/87 and those of the IACC group. These comprised 42 'family groups' for such activities as accident and emergency and hospital beds, each containing five subject areas relating to: costs of services; costs of staff; manpower related to service; manpower in general; and other data. They included data on waiting lists and destination on discharge, and limited mortality data (for example, WL47 – patients awaiting elective admissions/resident population 75 plus; HA66 – geriatrics discharge rate; and standardised mortality rates for specific conditions). They were intended to comprise a more accessible package of indicators available through computers in every health district. The number of these indicators has been cut back since the original package, largely due to reports of difficulties in their use by managers (Crail, 1994).

The health service indicators concentrated mainly on hospital activity, with information collected at the beginning of a patient's stay in hospital and activity tracked after that point. Information needs for community-based services were not as clearly identified. Indicators for these related mainly to staffing levels (for example, HV23 – health visitors/resident population; CR55 – total chiropody staff/contacts) and expenditure (OT01 – net cost of occupational therapists/resident population). Guidance as to their use as well as some examples of practice has been provided by Day (1989).

Key Indicators for social services

The Department of Health became interested in performance indicators for social services primarily as a result of the transformation of the Social Work Service into the Social Services Inspectorate in 1985. The Social Work Service had focused on policy and practice issues. The Social Services Inspectorate was to retain these roles but add an inspection function and assist local authorities to obtain value for money through the efficient and economic use of resources. Previously, the House of Commons Social Services Committee (1980) had suggested that there were failings in the system of collecting information concerning expenditure levels and service provision. The Social Services Inspectorate worked alongside colleagues in the Statistics Division to merge activity data routinely collected by the Department of Health with social services financial data collected by the Department of Environment and social services cost and activity data collected by CIPFA. Key Indicators (KIs) for personal social services were first produced in December 1988, using data covering the period 1984-85. The principles behind the development of the Key Indicators were exactly the same as those underpinning the development of the health service indicators. They endeavoured to provide a quantitative account of resources, to be used as comparative data, in order to assist the Department of Health and local authority social services departments to monitor service provision over time and to evaluate provision in the context of like local authorities. These indicators were available annually and concentrated on expenditure data for older people's and children's services and also indicators such as: service to client ratios; staffing; needs and service outputs. We discuss individual Key Indicators for social services in more detail in Chapter 3.

Those developing the health service indicators and the Key Indicators for social services stressed that the indicators depended on routine national collections and were only as good or as comprehensive as those collections. They insisted that the indicators were intended to raise questions and to highlight issues for further discussion and investigation in the light of local knowledge. It was stated that the indicators were not precise measures, nor did they cover all aspects of the authorities' health or social care work. They stressed that no single indicator, or even group of indicators, could tell the whole story about an authority's activities (Department of Health and Social Security, 1982b; Department of Health, 1988b; Warburton, 1988). The indicators initially developed were meant to be used to show how each district or authority compared with others and so help to signal potential problems and suggest possible remedies.

Criticisms of early indicators

Despite the care and caveats with which CIPFA, the Audit Commission and the Department of Health covered the indicators they had constructed, they were criticised by many managers and professionals working in health and local authorities as well as by independent commentators. The major criticisms were that:

- Indicators tended to focus on what could be easily quantified and less easily measured aspects relating to quality and standards were overlooked.
- Usually performance indicators focused on service inputs and outputs but rarely looked at outcomes; that is, the impact of services on those using them (McCarthy, 1983).
- Indicators often did not bear any relationship to the wider objectives of the service (Scrivens and Charlton, 1983).
- There were no national standards of care laid down, particularly in relation to the NHS, by which plans could be judged (Downey, 1983).
- Many of the NHS indicators were ambiguous and did not measure performance directly. It was unclear whether they were measuring only the process of care or how the NHS might deliver at some future date. The patient was often left out of the measurement process (Pollitt, 1984).
- Indicators were either too crude or too financially biased to be of use in developing policies and practice (Klein, 1982b; Warburton, 1988).

The NHS indicators have been much criticised for the misleading picture of performance they can apparently give depending on who is reporting on the data. For instance the 'finished consultant episode' indicator has been used to justify claims that more patients have been treated. However, the indicator merely counts episodes of care not the numbers of patients treated. Indeed, the national data returns have concentrated on a number of indicators which have been deemed problematic according to the claims made for them (Radical Statistics Health Group, 1995).

Pollitt (1985) reviewed the initial indicators developed by the Department of Health by corresponding with over 100 health authorities and conducting interviews with the staff involved. He found the NHS PI system to be rather inward looking, failing to set out measures that could inform services from the perspective of the patient. For example, there were no measures of access to services so that the chances of particular patients receiving services in different parts of the country could be assessed. A lack of quality measurement meant that improvements could not be monitored. The scope of indicators was also limited to hospital care with little consideration of the wider aspects of the service. Furthermore, there were a number of technical problems affecting the initial data set. The material was often difficult to digest, containing table after table of figures without any organising structure.

There were other substantial criticisms confirmed by a special study conducted by the SSI in several social services departments as part of a programme to develop key indicators (Duncan and Warburton, 1987):

• Not all indicators had obvious links to key policy goals or topical issues and hence did not relate to matters of local importance;
• There was a lack of validity and reliability for some indicators because of different local understandings of what the indicator was about and how it should be measured;
• The values of printed indicators were often wrong;
• Indicators were too often used to cut rather than develop services;
• Indicator values were sometimes too readily and erroneously equated with good or bad practice. For example, should it automatically be assumed that low unit costs are for the good of users and the service? Should it be automatically assumed that low occupancy rates in homes are bad?
• Linked to the previous point, average values of indicators were often perceived as a norm to which all authorities should aspire without questions being asked about the reasons behind variations from the norm;
• Comparisons between authorities could be facile and misleading if like was not being compared with like and local contexts not understood;
• By themselves, performance indicators often raise more questions than they provide answers but in practice interpretations were often made without reference to a broader review and evaluation process aimed at providing a more complete picture;
• Last, but certainly not least, indicators produced by national bodies using local data were often published years after the period to which they referred, rendering them of little other than historical use.

This review of central initiatives throws light on a number of interlocking issues concerned with indicators in the public sector. There are several recurring themes in the literature. First is the difficulty in finding measures that might be useable in an analysis of performance. Second, linked to this, is the caution which must be adopted in any comparison of the differences between authorities. Third, of central importance, is the difficulty in measuring achievement or the end objectives of a service. Owing to the way indicators were initially developed, from existing information rather than new data collections, they had a tendency to measure activity or process aspects rather than the benefits which might accrue to the service user or patient.

Locally-based indicators

National developments in performance indicators were centralised approaches designed to implement schemes that enabled major public activities to be reviewed. Pollitt (1986, p. 167) terms this 'efficiency from above' and there is an extent to which these developments were intended to exert pressure in the pursuit of political priorities. They were used as part of a control system over central and local departments of government. These indicators were therefore more a part of the managerial process and were not intended to provide review information for the user or the public (Smith, 1993).

In contrast to these central pressures, a number of local authorities made use of indicators and drew on the experience of consultants in order to internally review their performance. Butt and Palmer (1985) provided a performance guide for local authorities in which they described a system commonly used by local authorities for measuring their own performance. These included the councils of Dudley, Birmingham and Bexley who developed an array of performance indicators for a wide range of services in order that comparisons could be made with other local authorities (see Bexley, 1984). Consultancy services such as these have generally helped to clarify the nature of performance measurement for public services. Issues such as the setting of objectives and standards, assessing 'productivity' and defining what impact services are to have on the community, all need clarification before measurement can take place. Yeung (1989) extensively reviewed these systems of performance measurement in a sample of English Local Authorities and related them to the wider UK policy context. This included the directives from the Department of the Environment and the Audit Commission for authorities to produce comparative performance data. Some examples of practice and the use of particular indicators were given in line with these directives.

Burningham (1990, 1992) provided an overview of the use of PIs in local government. There are a range of functions that locally-produced indicators have fulfilled: they have acted to make local authorities accountable for their actions; they have been used as warning signs so that management can take corrective action; and they have enabled development work to be undertaken, where indicators are used for the purposes of learning. The majority of indicators have been used to support the accountability function, rather than to inform the internal management functions of an authority.

For social services, the interpretation of data, such as that provided by national collections, for local use is a key issue. Many authorities have in place mechanisms for collecting data for annual returns to organisations like CIPFA and the Department of Health. Alongside this, however, a structure needs to be in place that supports the internal monitoring of service performance. For example, the Key Indicator package permits the comparison of any one authority with similar authorities. The work described in Chapters 6 and 7 details the establishment of exactly such a structure in a local context.

Consumer indicators

Value for money has not been the only standard by which the performance of public services has been judged. Consumer groups have also used PIs for the wider evaluation of the services provided to the public. Although, initially, the consumer was omitted from performance measurement (Pollitt, 1988), recent periods have witnessed a growth in the use of indicators in this way. A spur to development came in May 1986 when the National Consumer Council (NCC) published its consumer indicators to assess the standards of local government services (National Consumer Council, 1986). These, it hoped, would enable consumers to raise questions concerning the performance of their local authorities in order to ensure accountability. The framework adopted by the NCC widened the criteria by which performance at the local level was to be evaluated. These included economy and efficiency but also judgements about the adequacy of information, representation, quality and choice. Indicators which the NCC considered important from the consumer point of view were those relating to quantity and quality of services, their costs and effectiveness. Indicators of local needs were also included that relied on indicators measuring social conditions such as, for pre-school education services, the number of children on the 'at risk' register. The NCC also offered ten principles of performance measurement, which have wider connotations in evaluating local services. These are listed in Box 2.1.

Stemming from these principles and within a framework of consumer preferences, the NCC developed both quantitative and qualitative measures. They concentrated on specific services such as housing, libraries, day care and

---

Box 2.1
The NCC's 10 principles of performance measurement

- Performance measurement must be set within the political context of policies and objectives.
- It should attempt to relate service provision and quality to consumer needs.
- One must start by asking which aspects of services matter to consumers.
- Consumer performance may be evaluated by: performance indicators, surveys, complaints, 'soft' information, professional self-evaluation.
- Performance indicators mean little on their own: they should be used to demonstrate relationships; to show trends; or to make comparisons.
- Surveys may be needed to assess aspects not easily quantified.
- Number and nature of complaints can be used to assess satisfaction with services. This information needs to be fed back into the process of performance planning and review.
- Performance measurement should be firmly established as part of an authority's review system.
- Attention must be given to the public reporting of performance information.
- Authorities should adopt a more marketing approach to the provision of services.

---

education services. Wide gaps between local authorities' statements concerning their services and actual achievements in practice were identified. A modified version of their framework, listing some of the wider consumer criteria for performance measurement, is outlined in Table 2.1. Against the criteria identified, a number of aspects were distinguished and these were related to the questions that might be asked by the consumer.

The main findings of the NCC in relation to the local services studied were that indicators were more easily devised where the service could clearly express its objectives in terms of relevant criteria. Services where there was a straightforward technical relationship between functions and consumer needs, such as in housing maintenance, could easily express these relationships statistically. Services involving complex relationships between functions, such as education and social services, provided greater difficulty in measurement. In all the services studied, some types of indicator information were more easily available than others. Quantity of services and costs were routinely available, whereas indicators relating to more qualitative dimensions, such as timeliness and customer satisfaction, were harder to collect. This was dependent on the particular services chosen so that, for example, the quality of housing repairs – judged by the time taken to complete work or satisfaction with standards of repair – was more clearly defined than the quality of children's services, which had to rely on proxy indicators such as child/staff ratios. The latter indicators contain problematic assumptions, such

Table 2.1
Consumer-based criteria for performance assessment (NCC 1986)
Effectiveness – does the service do what it is supposed to do?

Criteria	Aspects	Consumer questions
Redress Side-effects	Channels to pursue complaints Environmental impact Safety	Does the service do what it is not supposed to do?
Access Choice Quality Benefits	Availability Equity Provision of consumer choice Comprehensiveness Reliability Speed To users To community	Does the service do what it is supposed to do?
Information Ease and pleasantness Representation	Awareness and use Comfort and convenience Staff/public contact Channels to communicate users' views	What is the service like to use?
Economy and efficiency	The user The ratepayer and taxpayer	What does the service cost?

as whether a high staff/child ratio is necessarily a good thing.

The NCC's framework was important for the insights it gave for the further development of indicators. It also attempted to operationalise some of the performance criteria chosen in terms of the activity aspects of local authority services, thereby linking performance measures to the actual work done in authorities. The framework contained developments such as the importance of need indicators that can be readily translated into a social services context. It also provided a context for the recent period where consumer-related indicators have been widely disseminated, particularly through the Citizen's Charter initiative.

Performance indicators in the 1990s

The review so far in this chapter has covered some of the initial developments in performance indicators concerning the scrutiny of the activities of major areas of central and local government. The development of performance measurement, continued apace during the 1990s. There were developments such as the 'Next Steps' initiative in central government; the 'Citizen's

Charter' and Charter marks and the setting of national standards for public services; the community care reforms and enhancements in NHS performance; and the new system of performance measurement for social care beginning to be established. Associated with this has been the raft of initiatives which may be summarised under the banner of the government's modernisation agenda. Each of these is reviewed briefly below.

The 'Next Steps' initiative

The 'Next Steps' initiative (Treasury and Civil Service Committee, 1990: V) took over from the FMI as a reforming spirit in central government. This set up a number of agencies, most notably in the area of social security, decentralised in their activities. A number of performance targets were set in order to evaluate objectives through business plans. This initiative appeared in the wake of a substantial amount of criticism from various government departments regarding the implementation of performance measures. Most notable of these was the lack of availability of reliable data and the difficulties in integrating current PI systems into management practices (Carter and Greer, 1993). However, again, there appear to have been considerable difficulties in relating these performance indicators to the aims and objectives of the agencies concerned.

In contrast to the FMI, which encouraged the wider development of PIs in the public sector but tended to use them only cosmetically, the Next Steps offered a more robust conception of PIs (Greer and Carter, 1995). The initiative also attempted to use clearer measurement techniques such as target setting in order to seek control over decentralised agencies. Greer and Carter (1995) offered a case study of the early experiences of implementing the initiative in the Department of Social Security. While the use of performance information was linked more clearly to managerial incentives, there were still some objectives for which no indicators existed at all and a predominance of process related measures to the exclusion of outcome based measures. However, there were clear improvements both in the design of PIs and in the quality and reliability of the information systems which supported them.

The Citizen's Charter and Charter marks

In terms of PIs being used for the judgement of the consumer, the introduction of the 'Citizen's Charter' initiative (Cm 1599, 1991) grew in tandem with these developments. This required organisations to publicly display details of performance against targets and 'league tables', which informed users what to expect if they came for help. The Charter applied to a wide range of public sector activity. Originally, the initiative was intended to stand for quality, choice, the setting of standards and value for money (Black,

1994). In the health service there was the Patient's Charter (Department of Health, 1991a). For local government the Audit Commission, at the request of the government, produced a framework for performance measures (Audit Commission, 1992). This contained 77 separate indicators covering expenditure and targets for a variety of local services, from speed of response to queries and service accessibility. Only a limited number of these indicators were intended to compare performance against a designated standard.

From 1993, all local authorities were required to publish annually details of their performance against the Audit Commission's indicators. These are collated nationally by the Audit Commission, through the requirements of the Local Government Act 1992, which requires that the Commission define appropriate indicators, publish comparative information and provide support and guidance to local authorities. Annually also, the Commission publishes a national set of indicators for a range of local authority services, covering various dimensions. These include such general factors as the way an authority deals with the public or provides universal services such as refuse collection and leisure services. The indicators also assess the way authorities comply with specific legislative responsibilities such as provision of housing and social services to vulnerable groups. A description of more detailed definitions and methods for measuring performance is contained within the *Publication of Information Directions* published each year (see, for example, Audit Commission, 1998a).

In a consultation document on performance indicators (Audit Commission, 1998b), the Commission also proposed to introduce a set of 'general health' indicators for local authorities. These would be council-wide indicators intended to express the wider capacity of councils to act as democratic institutions and measure their extent of financial accountability. They suggested 13 indicators in the areas of: financial health; people management; democratic vitality; and quality of service management. A pilot exercise was run through 1999/2000 in order to examine the potential of these indicators in producing useful data.

The idea of the Charter was for citizens to compare indicators over time and across the country to help ensure the accountability of local councils. These developments represent how PIs can be used for the external appraisal of services by consumers and the public rather than for internal departmental review. They thus represent a populist revision of the indicators first introduced in the early 1980s (Klein, 1995). They have a curious place in the history of regulation in the UK public sector; standards are set for the performance of public services but without any legislative rights or entitlements for the consumer. Instead, rights are 'procedural' according to what the citizen can expect from the emerging markets operating in social and health care (Black, 1994).

There have been dissenting voices raised against the initiative. A number of conceptual criticisms were levelled at the initial Charter publications, such as the Patient's Charter (Pollitt, 1994). Priority was given to standards of timeliness or responsiveness of services to the exclusion of other performance criteria. A new Patient's Charter has been developed (Department of Health, 1998a), designed to stress other criteria, such as openness, accountability, equity, service access, quality and responsibility (Whitfield, 1998). Although the Charter was initially a central initiative, designed to protect the consumer by promoting standards, the new Patient's Charter recommends local charters backed up by national standards. The extent to which the Audit Commission should become involved in such an enterprise has also been questioned (Bowerman, 1995). The way in which indicators are used within the Citizen's Charter may cause the apparent neutrality of the Commission to be compromised by its involvement in the monitoring of local government performance. If linked to financial control mechanisms, this could cause further concern to local authorities who wish to maintain their local independence. Hence, the monitoring of performance nationally remains a political as well as a technical issue.

It is interesting that, in the public mind at least, the Charter represents the most visible way in which PIs have been used in recent times. This is despite the fact that there are numerous difficulties associated with the use of league tables in judging comparative performance (Goldstein and Spiegelhalter, 1996). In line with these developments has been a drive to develop wider-ranging measures such as those of customer satisfaction, the handling of complaints, timeliness, responsiveness (such as targets for planning applications) and reliability (such as missed refuse collections). There has also been an attempt to link indicators to more procedural concerns such as the adherence to codes of practice for housing lettings and equal opportunities legislation. Finally, attempts have been made to set clearer standards for activities, either those set down nationally or those adopted by an individual authority (Audit Commission, 1998).

The community care reforms

The comprehensive changes brought about by the *Working for Patients* (Cm 555, 1989) and *Caring for People* (Cm 849, 1989) reforms also set in train a greater use of indicators in order to better inform purchasing and contractual arrangements in health and social care. The market reforms in both the NHS and social care brought about a greater need for information to enable management to judge the operation of the market locally. In the NHS, there had already been pressure for greater clarity in defining standards of service in relation to contracts and ways of providing measurement for these. In social services, the development of community care plans brought into focus the need for a variety of information to be used in planning and appraisal and in the effective dissemination of the work of a department to the public (Cm 849, 1989, para. 5.6). Performance information will also be increasingly relevant to a range of stakeholders. In terms of contractual arrangements for care, agencies will need to continue to provide information as to their achievements and the types of services they offer in order to demonstrate their place in the market. Agencies which use quantitative information in assessing the achievements of their services will have a distinct advantage in negotiating contracts with local authorities (Hunter, 1989).

At a practitioner level, a greater range of reliable information is needed to permit care management activities to be more faithfully monitored. Clearer specification of eligibility for service, need and resource costs will need to be available so that care alternatives can be weighed up. Measurable indicators could, in the future, be attached to individual packages of care, permitting care managers to monitor progress in meeting client need. This information could be fed back into service review, increasing the opportunities for measuring equity, efficiency, effectiveness and levels of service.

The reforms can be seen as potentially one of the greatest spurs to the development of reliable information at successive levels of the care environment. They enabled information to be devised to take account of a range of performance dimensions. However, local data sets still require refinement with such factors as targeting and eligibility for service also needing to be monitored by managers. This will require very marked improvements in the design and collection of information available at the local level.

The modernisation agenda of the late 1990s and beyond

A number of major developments, articulated by central government, have brought the concerns of performance measurement to centre stage, especially for health and social care. There is considerable activity at the central government level in the present period. Much of this reflects general public and professional criticisms of the way public services have operated. Regulation has taken the form of national standards, laid down as requirements for local authorities to meet, in tandem with their own particular local assessment systems. The scope of performance measurement has widened and a variety of indicators have been promoted, often reflecting quality and outcome dimensions in addition to the traditional measures of output. Here, some of the more important initiatives are reviewed, keeping in mind the differing performance elements that have been discussed so far.

National priorities guidance

The guidance, *Modernising Health and Social Services: National Priorities 1999/00–2001/02* (Department of Health, 1998b) and its successors set out a joint programme to modernise health and social care services into the new century. Performance was a central theme. There was a focus on targets and standards and on accountability for these. A main topic was how to regulate local services so that they can be judged against national objectives and standards. The government's plans were set out in a series of initiatives reaching across health and social care.

Performance was a particular concern of the NHS White Paper (Cm 3807, 1997). This envisaged the establishment of a national performance framework with a broad set of performance indicators, intended to be set against a national schedule of 'reference costs'. NHS trusts are now required to publish and benchmark these on the same basis. These new broader measures include health improvement, access to services, quality, and outcomes. There is also a new Information Technology Strategy to support these developments, whereby financial and performance information can be accessed quickly. The White Paper makes reference to the ways in which past indicators mostly made reference to activity data and did not capture the ways in which services were provided for patients, which tended to create perverse incentives. The new framework is expected to demonstrate progress according to the wider goals of the NHS. A consultation document (Department of Health, 1998c) was published in January 1998 and the new framework was introduced in 1999. The new performance framework sets out six areas where indicators are to be used. These are listed in Table 2.2, which also gives examples, quoted in the consultation document, of performance indicators for care of the elderly.

A major step forward in the new drive for performance indicators in the NHS is the stress on health outcomes. Publication of data relating to mortality and other outcomes has been proposed in new league tables of outcomes (McKee, 1997). As opposed to judging the performance of management and resources, through indicators such as waiting times, this new emphasis is meant to enable the consumer to evaluate the effectiveness of care available in their locality. The major difficulties in the interpretation and analysis of outcome data, discussed earlier, apply equally to this recent initiative.

Modernising Social Services

The social services White Paper (Cm 4169, 1998) similarly stressed performance as a defining attribute of good public services. It sought to set out a new regulatory framework for social care services implemented by the Care Standards Commission. New standards of performance were set out and detailed in annual reports of each council's performance. Amongst the many

Table 2.2
The NHS framework for assessing performance in relation to older people

Areas	Aspects of performance	Examples of indicators for healthcare for older people
Health Improvement	Overall health of populations	Standardised mortality ratio (65–74)
Fair access	Fairness of service provision in relation to need	No. of district nurse contacts for over 75s per 1000 population
Effective delivery of appropriate healthcare	Extent to which services are: – clinically effective – appropriate to need – timely – in line with agreed standards – provided according to best practice – delivered by appropriately trained staff	Age standardised rate for hip replacement for over 65s
Efficiency	Cost per unit of care Productivity of capital estate Labour productivity	Rate of discharge home within 56 days of admission with fractured neck of femur
Patient/carer experience	Experiences of response to needs, skill and continuity of car, information and choice, accessibility	No. of delayed discharges for over 75s
Health outcomes of NHS care	Reduction in levels of disease/impairment Quality of life Reduction in premature death	Emergency admissions to hospital for over 75s per 1000 population

Source: Department of Health 1998c.

themes in the White Paper was the inflexible and unclear way in which social services had operated in the past. Performance measurement is linked to this with the advocating of clearer objectives and standards for social care. There is a focus on consistency and equity through initiatives such as Fair Access to Care (Department of Health, 2002a), which imply the reduction of spurious variation through the establishment of a national eligibility framework. These all require the comparison and measurement of both process and outcome in ways more systematic than ever before. The next chapter deals with these specific proposals in more detail.

Joint reviews

In the late 1990s, the SSI together with the Audit Commission set out a combined approach to evaluating the overall performance of each social services authority (SSI/Audit Commission, 1998a). A rolling programme of reviews was instigated, established through the Audit (Miscellaneous Provisions) Act 1996. A framework has been published which is based on four key aspects, judged to be important in measuring performance: to assess whether services focus on the meeting of needs; whether an authority can shape its services for the future; whether overall performance is effectively managed; and whether resources are managed to secure value for money and quality. The evidence collected during reviews has a particular focus on users' views and includes trends drawn from published data, interviews with staff and questionnaires for users and carers. The joint review team attempts to relate its evidence to the standards and policies of the authority under review. The published data to be analysed are drawn from the Department of Health's Key Indicators, the CIPFA Social Services Statistics, and the Audit Commission's Performance Indicators, Financial Profiles and Key Comparisons. The data are analysed and comparisons are made with those of like authorities and with a particular authority's performance over time. Relationships between these indicators are also examined and classified under the four key areas of the review framework. Readers interested in pursuing some of these lines of enquiry are referred to the Commission's publication *Getting the Best from Social Services* (SSI/Audit Commission, 1998b), which outlines a number of professional and consumer questions that can be examined by the use of indicators and comparable data.

Improving local government – 'Best Value'

The government White Paper *Modern Local Government: In Touch with the People* (Cm 4014, 1998) discusses the Best Value approach to measuring performance in local authorities. The principles of Best Value dictate that performance should be set against standards derived not just from comparison with other local authorities, but with those of other agencies, whether in the public or private sector. It involves the delivery of services based on clarity of standards, covering quality and cost and their delivery in a way that ensures economy, efficiency and effectiveness. Best Value articulates a new emphasis on outcome as essential in judging how public services are performing. The end product and objectives that need to be achieved are to be more important than who provides the service or the source of the resources used. The Department of Health has linked performance management in social services to local Best Value arrangements. The Best Value proposals bring the discussion of performance measurement and accountability full circle. In the setting of their own targets for improving performance, local authorities will demonstrate their accountability to local interests. This, however, is to be done against a background of national standards laid down by central government. For social services, the Social Services Inspectorate and the Audit Commission have jointly externally assessed the performance of each authority in delivering the standards of Best Value.

Best Value constitutes a duty, not merely guidance. Authorities have to work within a legislative framework for performance measurement. The government has the power not only to monitor, but also to regulate authorities against standards when they are shown to be deficient in important respects. The performance framework which articulates the mechanisms for Best Value is set out in Figure 2.1. This indicates, in particular, the distinctions and links between national and local foci in the management of performance.

The Best Value regime sets forth a more explicit structure for local performance management. For social services, it is necessary to set clear corporate objectives against national requirements. From these, the principles necessary to pursue performance measurement can be clearly articulated. These include: the establishment of mechanisms to identify the extent of need in the local community; the relating of components of services to each other; surveys to seek the opinions of users and carers concerning services; and identifying information from other authorities and the private and voluntary sector for examples of best practice.

Drawing on the principles of Best Value, a new set of national performance indicators was developed with the assistance of the Audit Commission and local government associations (Cm 4014, 1998, pp. 67-76). These include a limited number of 'general health' indicators, to operate council-wide. Key indicators were to be developed for each particular local authority service. Rather than their use as comparative information, these indicators are expected to support local performance plans on an annual basis whereby local targets are set by which to measure the performance of individual authorities.

The local authority White Paper (Cm 4014, 1998) stresses that these indicators are designed to reflect outcomes – what services have been delivered – rather than merely the resource inputs devoted to each service. These are assessed in relation to a range of indicators, so that performance can be compared between authorities and tracked on a consistent basis over time. The basic aspects of performance to be measured are listed in Box 2.2.

It is intended that local targets be set for each of these performance aspects on at least a five year basis as part of authority-wide performance reviews. These reviews report on current performance using comparative information from other authorities as well as identifying future targets to be achieved. It was also intended that there would be external audit, by such organisations as the Audit Commission, to ensure that these plans comply with the

Figure 2.1
The Best Value performance framework

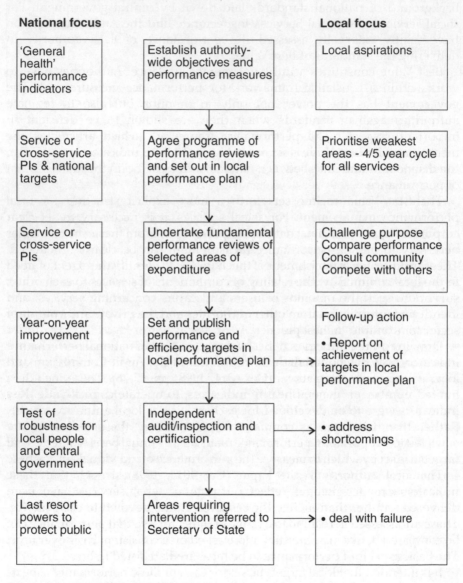

National focus		Local focus
'General health' performance indicators	Establish authority-wide objectives and performance measures	Local aspirations
Service or cross-service PIs & national targets	Agree programme of performance reviews and set out in local performance plan	Prioritise weakest areas - 4/5 year cycle for all services
Service or cross-service PIs	Undertake fundamental performance reviews of selected areas of expenditure	Challenge purpose Compare performance Consult community Compete with others
Year-on-year improvement	Set and publish performance and efficiency targets in local performance plan	Follow-up action • Report on achievement of targets in local performance plan
Test of robustness for local people and central government	Independent audit/inspection and certification	• address shortcomings
Last resort powers to protect public	Areas requiring intervention referred to Secretary of State	• deal with failure

Source: Cm 4014, (1998); Cm 4169, (1998).

requirements for Best Value. The targets to be set comply significantly with a best practice model of performance. As a minimum, local authorities are required to set targets for quality, cost and efficiency that are consistent with

---

Box 2.2
Aspects of performance measured in the Best Value initiative (Cm 4014, 1998)

- Strategic objectives
- Cost and efficiency
- Effectiveness
- Quality
- Fair access

---

the performance of the top 25 per cent of authorities. The performance reviews attempt to highlight areas of weakness in practice, judged against national performance indicators. Where authorities are consistently failing to come up to standard, they will be expected to review service delivery quickly.

The reviews assess services against the '4Cs' – to challenge purpose, compare performance, consult the community, and compete with others. Challenging purpose is a way in which each authority can seek justification for the services it provides. Current services may not meet changing needs or there may be a case for substituting some services for others in order to deliver the desired effects. Comparing performance is derived from a best practice methodology which attempts to compare performance with the best, using the national performance indicators as a guide. Best practice comparisons aim to move beyond the local authority context to embrace the best practices of other agencies and the private sector. Consulting communities is done under statutory requirements in some areas of service. It is a means of seeking information by which to inform the performance reviews. Competing with others is a way of seeking continuous improvements in services.

Two of the major themes in the government's recent initiatives are a stress on measuring outcomes rather than activity and devising mechanisms for financial funding dependent on the meeting of targets. The guidance gives a new scope for performance indicators to be used in order to underpin accountability mechanisms, evaluate the success of targets and inform service agreements. Also present is a restatement of the use of PIs to inform the public and assist them in judging the benefits of local services. It is stated that PIs are to be used as *diagnostic tools*, helping to improve performance at a local level by benchmarking and sharing best practice (Department of Health, 1998b). The proposals highlight the need for better joint working between health and social services in developing national objectives (Department of Health, 1999a).

Conceptual issues: defining and using indicators

In the context of applying indicators to measure performance in public services, a number of definitions and conceptual tools have been considered alongside the growth of indicators. A number of indicator systems have used existing data without placing it within an analytical framework. In doing so, they may function to simply describe the system, not measure its success in pursuing such dimensions as efficiency or effectiveness relating to the system's objectives. Several of the conceptual issues regarding the development of indicators have been extensively reviewed (see Carter, 1991; Carter et al., 1992; Cave et al., 1990; Pollitt, 1986). These debates offer some clarification in the use of indicators that have so far been developed and open up areas of complexity required to place the subsequent discussion in context. In particular, these debates inform the approach to the initiative discussed in succeeding chapters.

What is performance?

'Performance' itself is an attractive label, with its connotations of purposeful movement and action (Pollitt, 1986). It seems a neutral and obvious objective to pursue. However, it is an umbrella term, as usually within it there are a number of components that can be identified. These include the 'three Es' (economy, efficiency, effectiveness – see p. 27), along with availability, awareness, extensiveness and acceptability (Clarke, 1984). Added to this, we can assess performance with reference to the concerns of quality, fairness, equity, predictability and democratic control (Pollitt, 1986). Equity has often been termed the 'fourth E' (Bovaird et al., 1988) and refers to the fairness by which resources or services are allocated. Arvidsson (1986) distinguished the major dimensions of performance operating in the public sector as: economic (cost per product); democratic (fair treatment); legal (complaints and appeals); and professional (professional standards and ethics). Performance is therefore multidimensional and its definition is fundamentally related to which aspects are presently being identified. Some have argued that there are two basic ways in which performance may be assessed. One is by the behaviours of the people involved in any activity or service and the other is by the outcomes of that activity on its recipients, whether these are customers or service users. Both these senses of performance seem necessary if we are to judge the operation of a service as a whole; both *how* things are done as well as *what* is done (Hartle, 1995).

Performance may be defined as, 'the amount made or done in relation to the resources used to make or produce or do it' (Harper, 1986, p. 26) or, in the terms discussed here, as 'the way the organisation carries its objectives into effect' (Flapper et al., 1996, p. 27). Performance is therefore an expression of the relationship between input and output. An indicator should point out or signify this relationship and be a sign, token or explanation of how the system performs. Performance indicators are most effective when they express this relationship in the form of ratios between input and output and when differing outputs are related to each other in an integrated system which expresses the overall objective of the service (Harper, 1986). An integrated system moves us beyond the mere presentation of a list of indicators. It effectively pulls them together as a basis for evaluating wider organisational goals. Some indicators may comment directly on these, while others may do so indirectly or in combination with other indicators and other background information. By defining an indicator set – a set of related measures within an integrated system – it is possible to more easily identify the 'right' measures for any particular purpose.

If one were to look back over the PIs which were developed following the 1982 initiative, this complexity in the measurement of performance becomes clearer. It involves a question of priorities as to which components are to be identified. Some commentators have gone so far as to attempt to place some of these PI developments within a framework set by the differing dimensions of performance (most notably Pollitt, 1986, p. 162). Table 2.3 outlines the results of such an enterprise, building on Pollitt's work, framing three important PI schemes for health and social care during the 1980s, according to some of the components of performance that can be identified.

What is striking from this descriptive analysis is first of all the difficulty in classifying the indicators within such a framework. Much of the data has not been aggregated in a way that reflects these differing dimensions. Second, there is the relative imbalance between the different components of performance that are identified. Judging by the primacy of measures reflecting economy and efficiency, the focus of the reforms throughout the 1980s becomes clearer. At the time, there was little in the way of measures which reflected quality or customer satisfaction other than, for instance in the Audit Commission scheme, reviews of complaints that were non-quantified.

Effectiveness measures were rarely identified, relying as they do on notions concerning the impact of a service on its clientele. This element (the final outcome of a service) has been difficult to identify and measure, which is another recurrent theme in the literature. The Treasury, in its 1986 review of performance measurement in central government (Lewis, 1986, p. 6), also emphasised this point. The difficulties in measuring the outcome of programmes were related to the broad nature of aims in the public services, their multiple objectives, the interpretation of conflicting policies and discrimination of the effect of a programme from other competing factors.

Other dimensions of performance have been measured as part of the central government initiatives described earlier. There was progress in some departments rather than others (for an analysis of these developments, see

Table 2.3
Components of performance identified by national PI schemes[a]

Component	CIPFA social services actuals – general (1986/87)	Audit Commission social services PIs – general (1986b)	NHS PIs (July 1985)
Efficiency (input to output)	–	20%	43%
Economy (input-based measures)	58%	30%	11%
Effectiveness (outcome-based measures)	–	–	5%
Service quality	–	5%	1%
Customer satisfaction	–	5%	–
Other[b]	42%	40%	40%
Number of measures included	26	20	135

Notes
a Figures are percentages of total measures identified in each scheme.
b 'Other' refers to levels of activity/lists of services provided or general (unquantified)
  definitions of policy.

Lewis, 1986, Annex A). Some departments devised wider measures for use but efficiency or value for money were still stressed in the major reports for external appraisal (Cmnd 6453, 1976; Cmnd 8616, 1982). Some of the alternative measures that were used are listed in Box 2.3.

The Treasury offered a definition of the value for money framework as consisting of an 'optimal' combination of economy, efficiency and effectiveness (Lewis, 1986). We may conclude from a review of the available information in major publications, that the notion of value for money throughout the 1980s rested on crude notions of efficiency and did not include wider ranging dimensions of performance. Notions of efficiency need to be explored further, especially within social care, in order to come to a clearer view regarding its relationship to performance.

Performance then, can only be fully explored by taking into account a range of different aspects. It is a dynamic concept (Jackson, 1990) and measurement requires a host of indicators designed to comment on or express these aspects. These will differ according to the nature of the organisation or programme under review. It is most important to recognise the multidimensional nature of performance and that there may be trade-offs occurring between different performance elements. Efficiency may be at the expense of longer-term effectiveness, for example, or a unit may handle an increased number of cases but this may not necessarily indicate a better service for the user. The identification of performance solely with one aspect, such as efficiency, neglects this fact. The fact that, at different times, some of these aspects have been stressed at the expense of others should also be noted.

Box 2.3
Alternative performance measures in central government (after Lewis, 1986)

- Staff utilisation — actual number of staff available compared with number required.
- Unit cost — total cost / total output.
- Productivity — average output per person.
- Throughput — number of cases dealt with.
- Timeliness — response time, backlog or number of deadlines missed.
- Accuracy — proportion of errors in work (e.g. social security payments).
- Customer satisfaction — number of complaints.

Performance can best be measured on a number of different levels. These describe our aspirations to achieve particular standards of performance. The evidence, collected by using PIs, of how an organisation is working towards fulfilling its objectives can thus be framed. A hierarchy of performance has been suggested by Maxwell (1992), outlined in Box 2.4. This describes a series of steps, from the current performance of the organisation to a theoretical optimum. Looking at performance in this way helps us to signal where improvements can be made according to where the organisation is now, what it can hope to achieve and by reference to a 'gold standard', derived perhaps from current research evidence or what is thought to be theoretically possible at a given time. This hierarchy also draws attention to what successive targets might look like in framing the use of statistical information.

Box 2.4
Levels of performance (from Maxwell, 1992)

- Theoretical optimum — within current technologies.
- Known attainable level — achieved somewhere, under realistic operating conditions.
- Current target level — one realistically attainable on current plans.
- Present performance level — by analysis of variations.

Models of performance measurement

It is clear that there are a variety of perspectives or criteria from which it is possible to define performance. So far, these have been stated more or less implicitly. A number of aspects that distinguish performance have been identified more clearly within differing models or typologies. Much of this is derived from performance measurement work in local government. The terms differ by commentator but a common process can be identified. Box 2.5 describes some of the models of performance measurement, reviewing the terms used by different authors. Some of the developments referred to later, including the PSSRU's own work, describe how these might be translated into a context for social care. For now, some of the terms used to determine the process of performance measurement in general are included.

Box 2.5
Models of performance measurement

Bovaird (1981):	Input – Level of Activities – Final Outputs
Audit Commission (1986a):	Input – Output – Impact
Flynn (1986):	Input – Intermediate Output – Output – Outcome
Levitt and Joyce (1987):	Input – Activity – Throughput – Consequences
Klein and Carter (1988):	Input – Processes – Output – Outcomes

---

In the public services in particular, these models underpin (often implicitly) much of the analysis of data collected in order to review performance. We can describe these models more explicitly by referring to the process by which public services are produced.

The *inputs* into public service production are such things as the staffing of hospitals or residential units and the capital and materials that go into them. *Process* refers to the activities of staff, or what they do. *Intermediate outputs* relate to what staff actually produce in their work such as the treatment of patients, the amount of home care delivered or the number of assessments completed. The *final outputs or outcomes* are the end consequences of the service process and include such things as improved health or functioning or better quality of life. These final outputs are often more difficult to define and measure, particularly from the perspective of routinely collected indicator data. Indicators so far devised, therefore, either concentrate on proxies for final outputs, such as mortality rates, or on intermediate outputs, such as the number of meals provided for an older person. Although these elements can be measured in stand-alone form, it is the ratios between them that provide some of the criteria used in performance measurement. For instance, the relationship between inputs and intermediate output measures indicates efficiency and that between intermediate outputs and final outputs indicates effectiveness. There is confusion, however, not only in terminology but also in the way these measures have been utilised. Some commentators have linked efficiency, for example, purely with the volume of service achieved at the lowest input (for example, Audit Commission, 1986a, p. 8). It can also be looked at by emphasis on the maximum output from a given input. Effectiveness is also a concept ripe for differential interpretation. It can mean merely achieving what was narrowly intended or, more widely, as an assessment of overall policy.

These models do not give sufficient scope to the quality dimension, although underlying them is an assumption that ratios are built on a notion of constant quality (Carter et al., 1992). From a different perspective, Donabedian (1980; 1982) developed a useful framework for analysing quality in health care, which is based upon the extent to which the process of care contributes to valued outcomes. He wrote about the need to examine quality with reference to three domains – structure, processes and outcome. *Structure* refers to the resources used in the provision of care, which largely set out the context for the way the service operates; *process* refers to the varied forms and types of activities that constitute care – how services are organised and accomplished; and *outcome* refers to the consequences of the resources and care processes, the benefit received by the user from contact with the service. It is difficult to provide quantifiable measures of quality. This is usually done with reference to criteria of process – such as speed and accuracy of service. Notions of quality are, however, very much dependent on a particular organisation's principles, functions and structure. There are advantages and disadvantages to measuring quality in terms of all three aspects and consequently these should be measured simultaneously.

The emergence of models of public sector performance is not only a recent development. In the US, Ridley and Simon (1938) presented a classification of measures of local government activity. These included: costs; efforts – physical units such as 'man hours'; performances; results; and service needs. These measurements could be used to answer questions concerning the adequacy and efficiency of a service. They saw their performance indicators as the effect of physical units, such as the number of pupils taught or the numbers of meals-on-wheels served (see also Davies, 1968, p. 41). Whether or not these inputs contributed to meeting the desired objectives of a service, they termed 'results indices'. The evolution of these models and the terms used are intended to express similar processes.

Without a clear model by which to follow the production process, it is difficult to come to a view regarding the overall performance of a service. Rouse (1997) sees these models as reflecting the value-adding process of performance; ways of measuring the increased productivity in the relationship between inputs, delivered outputs and outcomes achieved. It is striking in reviewing the national developments in PIs how little account has been taken of these models in the analysis of what performance means and how the data might fit into such a scheme. Some commentators (for example, Allen et al., 1987) have even criticised national PI schemes for not measuring performance at all but only aspects of it. Many PIs in use are indications of inputs, such as numbers of staff employed, or intermediate outputs, such as numbers of people receiving home helps. The measurement of outcome often poses special problems as relevant indicators are often unavailable. Taking account of this, many centralised indicator sets use process indicators – the different activities undertaken – in assessing performance. These indicators may be less stable and more prone to manipulation but have the advantage of being easier to collect. However, performance as a whole is only really fully evaluated by taking into account all of the elements of the production process. Indicators can be devised for each of these aspects in turn, which can then be used in examining performance against particular criteria.

Models of performance help to place indicators in their proper context and assist in judging their use. Any performance measurement scheme should ideally attempt to build upon this conceptual work in order that performance is defined more satisfactorily. In certain services, such as in social care, these models may need to be extended to include such factors as: the differing goals of the agency, both in terms of the production of relevant services and wider organisational goals; differing resources, in terms of finances, material and non-material factors; the variety of staff activity; and quality dimensions, such as public accountability, due process, professional and policy standards (Arvidsson, 1986). An expanded performance model for social care is pre-sented in Chapter 5.

Defining performance indicators

During the 1980s there were linked debates about the definition of performance indicators. Some commentators tried to distinguish between performance indicators and performance measurement (Jackson, 1988; Jackson and Palmer, 1989; Roberts, 1990). Performance indicators were said to be less accurate and more suggestive than performance measures, which were definitive measures of aspects such as productivity or efficiency. The Department of Health in a number of publications attempted to emphasise that performance indicators were crude proxies for accurate performance measures and that performance indicators were starting points rather than end points in service investigations. In many ways, this debate is not a particularly fruitful one. While definitions are important, these must not obscure the very real technical issues in devising indicators that are useable and which inform managers of the degree of success in pursuing objectives. The overall conclusion that can be drawn is that performance indicators, if they are to be produced speedily and often, must be broad-brush. They can be based on information of variable quality and subject to varying interpretation and hence, must be analysed over time in the context of more reliable information and more informed debate.

Bearing in mind the inconsistent development of PIs in the public sphere, it is perhaps not surprising that there has been much comment concerning the ways in which they are to be used in any organisation. Various commentators have mentioned that performance indicators may be used:

- To monitor the overall operational performance of an organisation. This may be done individually against certain standards or guidance, against the performance of previous periods, or as against other organisations of a similar type or function (Jackson, 1988).
- As an instrument of 'hands-off' control over the organisation's lower levels (Carter, 1989).
- As a tool for the day to day management of an organisation by managers or practitioners.
- As part of a process of individual appraisal.
- To inform users or the public of certain aspects of the organisation.

Designing PIs for use requires an acknowledgement of this multiplicity of functions (Audit Commission, 2000). Different kinds of measures may be advocated and used by different stakeholders within an organisation. Before any type of indicator is designed, it may be fruitful to ask the following question of any organisation: *who wants PIs, who uses them, and why*? (Carter et al., 1992 p. 42).

Various commentators have further suggested a number of attributes that a PI system should satisfy (Jackson, 1988; Cave et al., 1990; Carter, 1991; Audit Commission, 2000). In essence, these include the requirements that:

- Definitions must be clear and consistent.
- A PI should measure performance that is 'owned' by the organisation and not dependent on external factors.
- PIs should be relevant to the needs and objectives of the organisation.
- PIs should be comprehensive but also 'bounded' (concentrating on a limited number of PIs). A large number of PIs may be unwieldy in a public sector organisation. These two criteria may be in tension with each other.
- PIs should be verifiable by senior managers, auditors and inspectors. This reduces the risk of manipulation by the person or unit to be assessed.
- PIs must be built on credible information systems. An investment in information technology is critical in enabling PIs to be used in a sophisticated way in the organisation. In many senses, the quality of the data that are available dictates the choice of performance indicator.
- PIs must be statistically valid in order to draw valid conclusions from them.
- PIs must be cost effective to collect so that the benefits of using them outweigh the costs involved in collection.
- PIs must be timely. In order to have relevance for current practice it is essential that PIs are produced quickly enough to reflect how resources are presently being deployed in an organisation so that an appropriate response can be made.

• PIs must be acceptable to members of the organisation. It is important that practitioners see the benefits of introducing a system of PIs or this may be interpreted as an instrument of cost-cutting or redundancies.

Carter (1989) has provided a classification to assess the use of PIs in any organisation, which involves their use as 'dials' or 'tin-openers'. Using PIs as 'dials' means that an indicator provides a precise measure of outputs and a clear understanding of when progress towards objectives is being achieved. Most public sector services cannot claim to have, as yet, sophisticated enough systems that would enable this prescriptive use of PIs to take place. Most of the indicators developed so far act rather like 'tin-openers'; they do not provide complete answers but open up a 'can of worms' by directing attention to inconsistencies and problems which may or may not be amenable to solution. Many of the indicators currently in circulation are measures of process or throughput that enable this to take place. The measurement of the success of overall objectives is proceeding although at a slower pace.

Classifying performance indicators

Classification is essentially about ordering information so that it can be used in a more logical way. In contrast to models for the analysis of performance, classifying indicators can be important in initially selecting the 'right tools for the job'. There are currently a number of classifications in existence. Some of these have been drawn from the business and management literature but have relevance to wider concerns in the public sector. They include classifying PIs according to whether they are: financial or non-financial (McNair et al., 1990); global or local (Fry and Cox, 1989); internal or external (Fortuin, 1988); and according to which part of the organisation they belong (Kaydos, 1991). Kaplan and Norton's (1992) 'balanced scorecard' promoted business performance measures across financial, customer and internal business processes and learning and growth perspectives. These classifications are useful but can be limited. They offer a source of information concerning what may be measured but often do not help in establishing the ways in which indicators can be used for monitoring organisational performance.

Flapper and colleagues (1996) offer an overview that takes into account many of these approaches. They offer a classification that seeks to widen the scope of indicators. This particular classification is based on three elements that are part of each indicator, namely: the type of decision supported by the PI; the level of aggregation; and the measurement unit by which the PI is expressed. The classification scheme is outlined in Table 2.4. A scheme such as this enables managers and those devising indicator sets to establish performance measures that are consistent and reflect many different attributes of the organisation. It also enables indicators to capture aspects of work at different levels of the

Table 2.4
A scheme for classifying performance indicators (from Flapper et al., 1996)

Indicator dimensions	Element	Examples
Decision type	Strategic	Long-term policy objectives
	Tactical	Short-term activities – weeks/months
	Operational	Daily activities
Level of aggregation	Overall	Whole system – overall performance
	Partial	Particular details – tracing instances of performance
Measurement unit	Monetary	Financial – costs and expenditure
	Physical	Number of products or customers/ unit of time
	Dimensionless	Abstract – service levels

organisation. It is by no means exhaustive. There may be certain types of information that do not sit easily within a scheme such as this. However, classifying indicators in this way at least enables staff in an organisation to analyse critically the basis on which they are chosen. We must move beyond classification if we are to use indicators to comment on, rather than merely describe, the operation of services.

Using indicators as evidence

The use of indicators in practice is dependent upon their capacity to provide clear statements as to how well an organisation is performing its tasks. In line with the use of indicators as diagnostic tools, a number of observers have outlined the steps that must be completed in order that PIs can act as sources of evidence. Some pointers have come from the wider literature on programme evaluation, much of it from the US. A recent example is the text by Owen and Rodgers (1999). Other sources that may illuminate aspects of good practice are drawn from texts on management and planning in both health and social services (for example, Tyrrell, 1975; Falk and Lee, 1978). Jackson and Palmer (1989) also offer a management guide to using indicators in the wider public sector. These and other commentaries highlight some explicit methods for using PIs at a more local level. Such processes can offer greater consistency in the techniques available for gaining evidence of performance.

The process of formulating and using indicators is best thought of as a series of steps. Firstly, it is important to define PIs and to select relevant means of measurement. Secondly, the relationships between PIs can be stated or assumed – this involves the use of models or hierarchies. Lastly, a range of target values can be set that involve standards or values to meet, indicative of certain levels of performance. Indicators are then presented and analysed and questions asked concerning organisational variance from established yardsticks. Arvidsson (1986) has outlined these steps as first *performance description*, where the benefits and limitations of a particular activity are expressed in quantitative terms. For each performance dimension identified, valid and reliable measures are found that describe service operations. Second, *performance analysis* is then undertaken, which attempts to relate the data to each other, to performance standards and to the objectives of the activities. Third, *performance monitoring or follow-up* then compares actual performance data to criteria set by budgets or other standards. This is then used to draw conclusions which can inform management decisions. These decisions are set within a framework of evaluation whereby data are related to the overall goals of the organisation.

At the present stage of development, attempts should be made to make indicators as unambiguous as possible. Investigating the operation of PIs in an evidential way imposes clarity about the steps needed to translate them into a useable form. For health and social services, it is now possible to state these steps with some clarity.

Thus, indicators need to be defined with reference to overall objectives. After setting objectives, the organisation may then be in a position to critically assess the performance measures that present themselves as most useful in supplying the means to assess these objectives. These objectives may be broad statements (for example to save or extend life or maintain an acceptable level of functioning) and so will need to be broken down into specific dimensions, such as efficiency, effectiveness or equity. These lower-order objectives will reflect the operation of different aspects of the service. A list of key questions may then be asked relating to how these parameters are defined. So, for example, for effectiveness it could be considered whether the right amount of service is being supplied, or whether services are having the desired results. Indicators can then be devised that may help to answer these questions. However, because available data will only indirectly point to the answers to these questions, it is better to examine indicators that relate to aspects thought likely to lead to these answers, or at least lead to further questions requiring more detailed examination. For example, in order to point to effectiveness it is necessary to consider the impact of services. Since it is difficult to assess this directly, this dimension might be more reasonably examined by investigating the level and quality of provision, its range and whether it reaches those for whom it is intended (Falk and Lee, 1978). These data can then be used to test initial hypotheses concerning the likely impact of the service on a local area.

Once useable data are defined and presented they can then be analysed, reflecting the initial questions that were of concern. It is helpful in this process if relevant norms are in place against which to judge the appropriate operation of services. Norms relate a policy to specific decisions that need to be made under local conditions (Tyrrell, 1975). These are most properly set in relation to local policy or what is felt to be a desirable level of service. However, they are more often set as the average for a particular unit or organisation or that pertaining nationally. Norms provide a basis for directing appropriate questions at the way services are currently distributed. So, for example, the staffing levels or numbers of day places nationally can be compared with those of a particular health or social services authority. Further questions can then be asked dependent on the results of this comparison.

Owen and Rodgers (1999) cite a number of questions to ask of each indicator. These consider first, relevant issues around the use of the indicators. These include: *validity* – does what is measured relate to the work of the organisation in a credible way? *Accuracy (reliability)* – does it truly measure the variable of interest? *Availability* – are the right data available? In addition, are they available at the right time? *Practicability* – can the information be collected and processed without undue strain on the organisation? Second, they offer a check on each indicator against the following criteria: *significance* – are the data worth collecting? Do they point to issues of particular significance for the organisation concerned? *Uniqueness* – does each indicator measure an element that is important and distinguishable from other indicators? *Comprehensiveness* – will the indicators in combination cover all aspects of interest to the working of the organisation? *Interpretability* – is the information from the indicator easily digestible and understood?

Due to the multiplicity of objectives in areas like social care, it may prove difficult to provide measures of the ultimate objectives of a policy or programme. Therefore, PIs can act as indirect pointers to these objectives through the use of intermediate measures. An important point is that a particular indicator should offer a statement as to the direction judged important in any subsequent analysis; for example, whether a high value is indicative of a positive direction and a low value a negative one. In any set of PIs, a number of complementary measures are often used which, in combination, offer a broader scope for evaluation (Jackson and Palmer, 1989). These measures are set at differing degrees of aggregation suitable to the degree of detail required by the manager or practitioner concerned.

The foregoing has outlined a strategic and planned approach to the use of indicators. Although much can be gained by an initial review of the distribution of indicator values for a particular function, these can be misleading. It is important to first of all have a number of questions in mind that relate to the key issues of performance to be considered. These questions will dictate how information supporting these issues is to be operationalised as indicators.

Using indicators: analysis and comparison

Alongside the design and development of PIs there has been considerable academic debate as to how they can best be used in measuring performance. Much of this work has been at the conceptual level in attempting to define more clearly the measures to be used and how these might relate to the wider objectives of the organisation under review. There has thus been an attempt to overcome some of the criticisms identified in the foregoing discussion.

Technical methods by which performance can be made explicit through the analysis of routinely collected data have also been discussed. Some of the arguments are complex and a number of these are outlined and discussed in Levitt and Joyce (1987). A description of more sophisticated methods of performance measurement, along with relevant guidance and a consideration of mathematical techniques, is contained in a Treasury publication by Jones et al. (1988). It must be remembered that not all of the measurement problems have been overcome and there is still considerable room for further enquiry. Some methods for using indicators that have been examined are discussed below.

Statistical analysis

Most indicator systems available at present use techniques commonly encountered in research evaluations, with particular applications depending on the problem being addressed. Judgement is required in their use and it is important to make explicit the questions to be addressed before consulting them. The relevance of any indicator can only be established if a prior specification is made on this point.

Once indicators have been derived, they provide little evidence unless there are explicit methods for employing them. Most of the national indicator sets already described use data in a comparative way (Audit Commission, 1986a; Flynn, 1986). These comparisons can be made in three basic ways: they can be used to compare geographical areas; to compare in terms of changes over time; or to compare the distribution of an indicator against some relevant criteria. The first of these, comparing geographical areas, is the method most used in formulating performance league tables within various schemas (for example, Audit Commission, 1996a). The second type of analysis, data measured over time, often avoids the compatibility problems when comparisons are made with other authorities or districts. This is a useful method in analysing performance in relation to targets. Alternatively, the third type of analysis, looking at the distribution of values for an indicator against an external standard, is often used to signal exceptions to established practice or to raise questions for further investigation.

Statistical methods may be employed to support each of these uses of indicator information and different yardsticks may be required for each of them. The setting of norms or standards enables values to be plotted and the deviation from the standard to be clearly seen. However, interpretation is required in order to judge the importance of any deviation from that which is expected. In comparison across areas, for example, deviation might be dependent on a particular area's characteristics, the population served, or unexpected local conditions. In comparing trends over time, the data are dependent upon the assumptions made about the likely effects of such things as population or staff changes on the variable of interest. There is also no reason to believe that a current trend is either appropriate or desirable in the longer-term. Of course, in comparing the distribution of an indicator against an external criterion, the analysis is dependent upon the validity of that criterion itself. Such analyses of indicators are intended to form a basis for subsequent questions to explain organisational performance further. So, the significance of any particular deviation might not be analysed using formal statistical methods but may, in the first instance, be the product of simple judgement.

Most indicator systems enable routine descriptive statistics to be analysed in this way. Day (1989), for example, explored the usefulness of the health service indicators and provided a practical guide with examples of their use by a number of authorities. Common features of the health indicators, as well as those from other packages, are: the provision of information in graphical form where values are compared across all districts or units; ratios of a district or unit value to the national average; scattergrams to highlight extreme values and test initial hypotheses; and time series descriptions to illustrate changes in PI values over time. All these methods can be interpreted numerically with the usual warnings for care in the analysis of data and comparison of like with like.

Once data are collected concerning key areas of an organisation's work, they must then be analysed in a way that enables some of the important issues of performance to be clarified. A number of statistical tools have been used to judge the relative performance of different authorities or agencies. However, before the analysis of data can proceed, clarity as to the nature of the comparison is first of all required. For example, this could be whether it is desired to compare performance relative to the average, or to some standard or yardstick set by national or local guidance, to past performance, or to some 'best practice' unit or authority. Different methods are available in order to judge performance by these differing criteria. Analytical tools have been derived from various disciplines including financial accounting, operational management and economics.

Comparative approaches

Many of the nationally collected indicator sets have as their objective a comparison of those units – authorities, hospitals or departments – which deviate significantly from the norm for that area. Often these comparisons are presented as histograms or box plots, showing the position of a district or authority on a particular indicator in relation to others (often expressed on a percentile basis). These comparisons tend to look at data descriptively around the average so as to identify statistical 'outliers'. However, there are limitations in doing this as a number of factors peculiar to the unit in question may be responsible for the differences that are found. In comparing whole authorities some examples of these might be: population density; social deprivation; age trends; housing; and historical area differences (Audit Commission, 1996a, pp. 6–8). Attempts at standardisation can take account of these. Often such standardisation permits comparison of actual with expected values (generated statistically). In the health service indicators, length of stay is one indicator which uses this method. However, the use of more detailed adjustments to data can often make the information more difficult to interpret. Comparative data has been viewed as a simplistic method with unsatisfactory results in terms of its likely interpretation and use (Yeung, 1989, p. 126).

Measurement of comparative data against the average also has many disadvantages from the conceptual point of view. An average is not an optimum (Ehreth, 1994, p. 569) and comparisons against the average cannot really assess overall performance against standards or targets. Comparative data are useful to identify questions for further examination but are inadequate to measure an organisation against criteria such as efficiency. For this, some form of multivariate procedure is necessary.

Correlation analysis

One useful way of analysing indicators is to examine the relationships that exist between them. This not only throws up useful information regarding trends but it may also point to the further properties of the indicators themselves. Ferguson and McGuire (1984), for instance, examined the statistical relationships that existed between specific sets of the initial NHS indicators. This was done in order to identify 'compound indicators'; pooled data which may reflect a single measure of performance. Correlation analysis was used to reflect any associations existing between ranked variables. From this, they found that the indicator of 'throughput' could be useful in acting as a proxy indicator to judge overall hospital performance. In examining measures of association, care must be taken to compare like with like. For example, in the initial NHS package of PIs, clinical activity data and financial data were aggregated on a different basis, the former by specialty and the latter by hospital; the two sets of measures are therefore not open to any meaningful comparisons.

Benchmarking (standard setting)

This is a methodology that can be applied to performance indicators in which performance is evaluated with reference to the 'best practice' of comparable organisations. It contrasts with the process by which an organisation internally measures itself in relation to yardsticks set by past performance or by comparison with other units. Its origins lie in the business sector in the US in the 1980s, and it has been used by companies to gain competitive advantage by identifying performance gaps and in improving performance to meet the standards of the best in the business (Balm, 1992; Dence, 1995). As a method, it can be traced to the original work of Camp (1989), who articulated the process of sharing industry information in the search for best practice. He defined benchmarking as 'an ongoing investigation and learning experience that ensures that best industry practices are uncovered, analyzed, adopted and implemented' (Camp, 1989, p. 12).

From a business perspective, benchmarking as a technique has been explained clearly by Syrett (1993). It is important first to focus on which aspects of practice to benchmark and why. Many of the performance criteria already identified can be benchmarked. Some useful elements include: speed of service, communications, training aspects, management functions and financial management. The more effective businesses limit their benchmarking operations to a few key areas, usually ones directly linked to their overall objectives. These aspects are then broken down into quantifiable measures. Bullivant (1997) describes the process of benchmarking according to five phases: first, a clear definition of the process to be studied is set out; second, a database describing the process is developed; third, those organisations performing in a superior way are identified; fourth, the factors that account for this superior performance are described; and lastly, these critical factors are adapted by the organisation in a way that suits its particular processes.

Many of the approaches chosen in the business sector are equally applicable and relevant to work in health and social care. Gunther and Hawkins (1996) describe the three most relevant processes that can be benchmarked within the social and health care sector: the business function; the clinical (or professional) function; and the support function. The business function is the easiest to benchmark. Most of the business processes in social services and health authorities are now broadly comparable to those in business organisations. Aspects such as resource costs and staff administration can be readily compared across settings. The clinical or professional function is more difficult to benchmark. The functions of different professionals are particular to their discipline and sometimes to their area of work. For example, professional functions in relation to older people are different to those in adult mental health, even within the same discipline such as social work. Care must therefore be taken in comparing between organisations, unless these functions are clearly described. For support functions, such as the maintenance of equipment and the purchase of supplies, the situation is more complex. For health care, there is a specific relationship between particular clinical functions and their support services. In social care this is less of an issue, and the various support functions may be more easily compared to others outside those of a particular department.

Benchmarking these functions in social and health care is of real importance. If done properly, it can bring about increased knowledge concerning which processes lead to which outcomes for comparable organisations. It becomes a way of searching out critical variables thought to be necessary in achieving the effective or efficient delivery of services. When this knowledge is translated into practice within the organisation, it offers scope for improving processes based on those that have been found useful and relevant for others in similar circumstances. However, the validity of a chosen benchmark should be considered carefully in any analysis (Yeung, 1989). Analysis of performance against a previously failing organisation will lead to distorted interpretation of the data. Many indicators will show improvement against a poor baseline. The converse is also the case; many organisations exhibiting excellence will show little scope for future improvement. Interpreting the results of any indicator against a model of best practice needs to be done with great care. Manipulation of data is a constant threat and should be guarded against.

The source of measurement is crucial and need not be limited to one focus. Information on the good practices of other organisations can be gathered from publications, electronic databases, relevant personnel, and consultants. Benchmarking should also be a continuous activity as the standards by which good practice is compared today can become merely commonplace or deficient tomorrow. In the public sector these standards are often set by national or local policy, building on identified best practice. Benchmarking is currently in vogue, particularly in local authority performance systems and in central initiatives to modernise health and social care, some of which are discussed in the next chapter. However, its use in social services may be constrained by the difficulties in maintaining reliable partnerships between authorities (Bullivant, 1997; Cmnd 3588, 1997).

Benchmarking as a technical method is not to be confused with the setting of standards in general. This has often been the case within social care as it is difficult to identify best practices from other authorities. Standards can be any points of reference by which to judge the performance of an organisation. They are relatively precise statements that require measurement to support them. Benchmarks, on the other hand, include the practices necessary to uncover the standard and the mechanisms for achieving it (Camp, 1989). They are standards of an 'exemplary' type, used in order to guide practice. On the whole, standards can be set for the judgement of various players in the organisation. They can be of an ideal or normative type or may be 'ratchet' standards, judged by current performance, or minimum standards, whereby a threshold is identified, under which performance is not allowed to fall (Ritche, 1992, p. 69). Bovaird (1981) has described a general hierarchical approach to the setting of standards. Standards can be set at each stage of the hierarchy, for instance for inputs, outputs or outcomes, in order to make clear their relationships to the overall achievement of desired objectives. Performance indicators can then be used to measure various aspects of an organisation's work, against these differing standards. Caution is warranted in judging performance against standards which are too ideal in character.

Many elements from the benchmarking literature pose problems for public care agencies. Before the practice of other organisations is examined, it is necessary to first of all develop a culture of continuous improvement and learning by evidence. Without this it will be unclear which aspects of activity to benchmark. There is also the danger of choosing an incompatible organisation with which to compare practice. Careful thought needs to be given to which processes can benefit from comparison; these must be ones that have similar purposes for each organisation. Particularly in social care, where many performance standards are set by government policy, taking account of comparable circumstances is crucial for comparisons to have real meaning. Indicators can then be used to comment on the achievements of policy, reflecting their use in the real world rather than under ideal conditions (Ferguson and McGuire, 1984). Overall, standards should be clear, owned and understood by members of the organisation under review; and they should be periodically reviewed to ensure compliance.

Multivariate analysis

In contrast to descriptive methods, which compare organisations against average or static standards, inferential methods which generalise from a sample to a population, are a valuable way in which control of the system can become more effective in the future. Multivariate statistical techniques enable conclusions to be drawn concerning the system and its performance at a more general level. Rather than computing ratios of comparative performance, used singularly in a descriptive fashion, multivariate procedures model the processes at work to arrive at estimates of the relative impact of particular variables on others. This can be particularly useful if one wishes to move beyond description to offer explanations of the factors at work.

Multiple regression analysis, for example, permits us to estimate the extent to which differences in one particular measure may be explained by the variation in a number of other factors. For instance, differences in service costs between authorities could be explained by the characteristics of clients or staff, the nature of services and local variations in other factors such as the characteristics of the population. A so-called 'cost function', used in health economics, uses this method to help explain the variation in costs dependent on a number of other factors (Knapp, 1998). Regression takes all these factors into account, measuring their combined influence on the variable of interest. It thus helps to control for the influence of potentially confounding factors when making comparisons. Levitt and Joyce (1987, pp. 96–103) discuss some of the uses and also problems encountered with this approach. Some points to note are factors such as socio-economic variations between authorities and how these may influence some of the differences in the values of chosen indicators. There is also the question of existing associations between the variables chosen (multicollinearity), which may inadvertently distort the variable of interest. Regression analysis is mostly used as a prediction tool to estimate average expected performance. For example, in examining the efficiency of home care, one could use the method to consider whether a particular authority is spending more or less than one would expect, given the conditions under which it operates. These conditions could include: the dependency of its population; the size of the authority; its population density; the extent of rurality and other needs-related factors such as the extent of deprivation. The method thus provides a summary measure of performance, based on an analysis of how one set of data varies in relation to, or statistically 'explains', another set of data.

Data envelope analysis (DEA)

In contrast to using comparative data to evaluate performance against the average, indicators can also be assessed against a model of 'best practice' or criteria reflecting some notion of optimum performance. This is, as yet, relatively unexplored territory in performance measurement, especially in areas such as social care. Here the comparator is derived from a more theoretical basis, from which an optimal yardstick of performance may be identified. This involves a more complex analysis of the data and may be outside the present scope of many authorities. However, this method is described here as a way of identifying future possibilities.

Data envelope analysis (DEA) is a procedure derived from the economic literature on production efficiency (Farrell, 1957; Charnes et al., 1978). It is a useful method to assess public sector performance since it is intended to deal with organisations where there are a range of inputs and multiple outputs. It analyses the way in which the inputs of units are combined to produce differing outputs so that units that produce the best output in relation to their inputs can be identified. The relative performance of different management units are then assessed against these best performing units. A 'unit' could be a private firm or a public agency such as a health authority, local authority social services department or even a residential home or hospital. This type of analysis, instead of initially specifying a model to explain the variation of one set of data in relation to another, attempts to measure relative performance (in terms of technical efficiency) from the actual observation of units against best practice in the sample. From this, efficiency scores are calculated for each unit enabling comparison of their relative mix of inputs and outputs compared to the most efficient units in the sample of analysis. Efficiency scores are calculated in terms of either output efficiency (actual output as a percentage of maximum feasible output, given inputs) or input efficiency (minimum possible inputs as a percentage of actual inputs, given outputs). The different mixes of inputs and outputs for each unit are weighted to produce a single summary measure for each unit; scores of 100 per cent indicating maximum possible efficiency and scores approaching zero indicating greater degrees of inefficiency.

DEA is a 'best practice' method of analysing performance in that it relates efficiency scores for a number of units to the best performing units operating under current constraints. There are certain assumptions made in the approach which need to be articulated clearly and a number of issues remain to be resolved. For example, different specifications are needed in the method depending on whether assumptions are made concerning constant or diminishing returns to scale. Problems can also occur in that a unit is assessed as technically efficient if it has the best ratio of any chosen output to any input. Therefore, great care needs to be taken in choosing which inputs and outputs to include. Problems also exist in that efficiency scores are calculated relative to the best performing units. This can result in measurement error and extreme values being reported. A summary and application of the approach can be found in Levitt and Joyce (1987, pp. 103–106 and 169–178) and Thanassoulis (2001). DEA has also been used in many studies of efficiency across general hospital settings (Ozcan et al., 1992; Ehreth, 1994) and there are a limited number of examples in the social care field, which will be examined in more detail later.

Overview of analytic and comparative approaches

Many of the methods described above concentrate on the comparative analysis of performance between like units or authorities. Performance can also be measured internally against standards or guidelines. In social care, many of these will be set by local and national policy or by legislation. There is much progress still to be made in the quantitative analysis of performance in public services. Many of the analytic methods described above offer more complex alternatives than those currently in use within the national indicator sets. Some, such as multiple regression and DEA, are information-hungry tools and current routine data sets frequently lack sufficient sophistication to enable these methods to be used more widely. Progress is therefore required in devising clearer and more thorough measures, particularly of costs and outputs. Thus, although a particular approach may represent the best way to analyse performance, the required measures may not be available. Furthermore, measurement development needs to be part of a system which encourages planning and management implementation of some of the tools listed above. The further development of all these aspects is needed before wider ranging performance measurement is possible.

Constructive use of indicators

In many past indicator systems table after table of information was provided in the absence of an organising structure, which consequently served to baffle the reader or user. Day (1989), in describing the use of health service indicators, gives some useful pointers as to how they can be used more constructively. These include: the careful analysis of the issue under investigation; the selection of relevant information in a rational and systematic way; and its presentation and interpretation in a manner likely to have interest and immediacy. Coupled with this is the imperative that things must be made to happen as a result of the analysis of indicators (Day, 1989, p. 113). There are a small number of techniques that can assist in the better interpretation of indicators. These can be described in relation to both health and social care.

Ratio measurement

It was noted earlier that measurement provided in ratio form is a defining attribute of performance indicators. There is much information that can be provided in non-ratio form and a substantial part of this will be to provide contextual information. Ratio measurement, however, permits all data to be expressed according to a common baseline so that meaningful comparisons can be made. Indicator ratios therefore have both numerators and denominators. *Numerators* express the point of interest, such as numbers of fieldwork staff or numbers of admissions to local authority homes. Common *denominators* are numbers of beds, populations (often per 1000) and members of staff (such as discharges per consultant or numbers of whole time equivalents). Unit costs express a measurement of expenditure in relation to the number of units of output; for example, gross expenditure on meals/per meal served. This is a useful measure in judging comparative efficiency. Other ratios can, however, be expressions of more complex concepts such as whether older people are diverted from institutional care or whether access to services is fair and equal based upon levels of need or personal characteristics.

Although the baseline in these measures appears easy to calculate, there can be problems in the estimation of the figures. Tyrrell (1975) mentions problems in the use of national population figures (such as those of the Registrar General), which may underestimate local migration of certain age groups. This may alter judgement if age-related figures are used in local planning. Locally calculated estimates can therefore sometimes serve as more reliable figures. Also care must be taken if the baseline is of a time component, such as per week or per year. Should a week be five days or seven? Is a month a designated number of days or a calendar month? These are serious questions if the service is an emergency one, operating out of hours, or if it serves a particular function such as a day hospital or ward. Careful judgement is required in estimating the baseline figure for the purposes of any particular analysis.

Variance analysis

The problems in coming to a clearer view of performance in local authority services has meant that this is often measured by comparing actual with budgeted performance. This technique involves looking at the difference (variance) between planned performance, described in relation to the budget for a particular programme, and actual performance. There is no need to conduct specific statistical techniques here as these differences can often be seen in tabular or graphical form. Anthony and Herzlinger (1980) discuss the need to consider variances in volume, price, efficiency and effectiveness separately. They have outlined various calculations for these comparisons. The authors of a technical guide to performance measurement in central government departments (Jones et al., 1988) have also included more detailed calculations based on judging the efficiency of a programme against the plan. It must be remembered that this sort of analysis is only worthwhile if planned performance is a reasonably satisfactory measure of an organisation's achievements. In other words, it assumes that the original plan has some validity. If the nature of an organisation's activity means that the plan needs to be changed, then further higher-level analysis would need to be undertaken.

The analysis of variance from planned budgets is a technique common in public accountancy and project control. It attempts to assist managers in assessing the reasons why work may be going off-plan and to attempt to implement corrective action within their sphere of responsibility (Jones et al., 1988). It is a simple input-output method for the use of indicators. As such, it may represent a useful initial analysis of certain data but, as part of the analysis of more complex service-delivery systems, it may be inappropriate.

Indicator inversions

An easier way to understand the relevance of some indicators within a particular domain is to invert them. For example, 0.25 district nurses per 100 first visits becomes 400 first visits per district nurse (Day, 1989, p. 113). This is more easily digested and permits quick interpretation of the data to enable key issues to be identified. The technique is applicable to data produced in ratio form once the indicator has been devised. The nature of the indicator will usually offer a clue as to whether data obtained from it need to be put into a different form.

Problems in application

There has been much comment made about the practical difficulties in using the national indicator sets, such as those of the NHS (Goldacre and Griffen, 1983, pp. 82-89). Some of these arguments have already been mentioned. Problems include the difficulty in establishing objectives – for instance, which PI or set of PIs are to be used in measuring which objectives. There is a need to define individual PIs as precisely as possible and to agree what is meant by them and which aspect of performance they are intended to measure. Other problems which have been identified, are the lack of incentives and time for staff to use routine data. Some data exist but have not been fully explored in PI packages and other data are not routinely available. Running through the literature is the central theme of the need to find credible ways of linking existing data, conceptual work, and the technology and techniques for using the data in a system which is useable in examining comparative performance.

'Gaming'

A further problem in the use of indicators has been the opportunities afforded for the manipulation and misrepresentation of the data – the so-called 'gaming' problem. This is often discussed in response to the perceived failings of the performance measurement approach. It is also pursued for wider political ends by the organisations concerned. It is therefore presented as a particular problem to do with how people deal with the data. This is evident, perhaps nowhere more so, in the use of PIs by the previously publicly owned industries, such as the reformed rail companies. There are many examples of PIs being set to measure some attributes of a service at the expense of others. Good performance is often highlighted when, in fact, an overall view would lead to conclusions of serious shortcomings in the service. A recent report by the Consumer Association (Which?, 1999), has highlighted the problem of PIs being put to many different uses, not all necessarily reflecting a value-free idea of performance in the service of the consumer. They examined the rail companies' use of performance data. Although the companies are obliged to regularly monitor customer satisfaction (as a notion of outcome), the questions asked in surveys often do not concur with passengers' priorities. So, for example, companies ask about the appearance of their staff and on-train catering but questions concerning punctuality and overcrowding, rated highly by customers, are not given the same priority. The companies' benchmarks are also not standardised across the country and so there is no way of easily comparing their performance. Train companies' punctuality and reliability levels are also measured against benchmarks based on pre-privatisation levels and so can rise and fall regularly but not show up in official figures. The benchmarks themselves are also not very demanding, set as they are at a low initial baseline.

These issues are to do with the behaviour of those using the indicators and such problems can also occur at the level of individual staff or teams. For example, a certain performance management strategy might unintentionally give staff an incentive to accept certain types of cases and not others. This could lead to a distortion in targeting as an unintended consequence of performance management. It is an emphasis on the short term in many systems that can create these perverse incentives to manipulate the data for specific ends. For this reason performance systems need to be linked to more long-term strategic concerns, such as the achievement of agreed objectives. There are many examples, both in the private and public sectors, of performance measures becoming 'ends in themselves' (Jackson and Palmer, 1989). In order to counter this trend, the purpose of measurement must always be borne in mind and communicated regularly to staff.

These examples, and others that have come to attention in recent years, signal the problems which can arise in the use of PIs. As performance measurement, from its very beginnings, has been part of the political environment, it is not surprising if the data become ripe for manipulation to suit other, more covert, objectives. This can also be viewed as a conceptual problem. The rejection of measurement and its use in ways that were not intended stems from a way of thinking about information which is both uninformed and misguided. Tyrrell (1975) refers to the importance of following the 'rules of the game' when using indicators. Statistical information is built on assumptions and conventions that relate to how information is used and what it is intended to express in the real world. Becoming aware of these assumptions and being critical in the ways we appraise data will go some way to making data such as these more interpretable. In order to avoid the problems of misuse, there is a need for clearer definitions of indicators, well-established comparators and more precise baseline estimates. There is a need also to fully brief staff and consumers in the assumptions that lie behind the uses of data.

Indicators in practice

Studies have been undertaken using indicators to measure performance in various ways. The health-care field, in particular, has provided opportunities for analysing routinely generated data in a way that helps to clarify some of the issues already discussed. Some of these studies have employed specifically funded academic research, while others have analysed the data available nationally. Still others have sought to comment more generally on the uses and abuses of indicator data. Goldacre and Griffen (1983) have reviewed many of the health studies available, which examine indicators such as admission rates, manpower, length of stay, throughput, waiting lists and outcome and identified many of the problems associated with their routine use. Some smaller-scale studies using indicators for social care are outlined in Chapter 3. For now, some of the types of indicators used in measuring the various performance dimensions identified are considered. Below, evidence of sources is provided as well as discussion of limitations in the data used.

General aspects

General studies of hospital efficiency over time were undertaken by Barr (1968) and by the DHSS (1983b). These used a range of indicators to compare rates of expenditure to numbers of patients treated or to episodes of care, which may not be the same thing. Geographical comparisons of health indicators were reported in a comprehensive study in Liverpool by Logan and colleagues (1972). These included: indicators of resource inputs, such as numbers of beds per 1000 population; those of activity (or process), such as average length of stay and discharges per bed; and proxy outcome indicators, such as standardised mortality rates. They also included some indication of the local policies of the health regions studied, such as the time from operation to discharge. These indicators were used to compare the health care of a number of regions in the UK according to a range of criteria. Information was analysed from various national sources at the time including SH3 returns and Hospital Inpatient Enquiry Reports (HIPE). They also analysed indicators of need, drawn from census data, and related these to the use of resources.

A number of studies have reviewed the uses of routinely available data from the health services. Ashley (1972) argued that although, at the time, a wealth of data existed, this was often not put to good use. The national data sets, described above, did describe trends across health authorities such as morbidity for certain illnesses and reasons for hospital admissions. However, in order for the information to assist in the planning and distribution of resources, more rapid feedback from returns was required as well as greater accuracy in data collection. One of the main measures of hospital performance at the time – length of stay – was often compared in terms of average values across districts, ignoring the differences in distribution patterns across areas and specialties. In conclusion, Ashley reported that the existing data sets needed to be extended to include additional social indicators within a fully integrated information system.

Barber and Johnson (1973) examined the variety of performance measures used within hospital in-patient services. These included bed occupancy, admission rates, length of stay and patient turnover. They outlined a graphical method for the linking and analysis of this information. This method was used to estimate the effects on some indicators of changes in the values of others. A model of efficiency was provided by considering the greatest change in productivity (discharges per available bed) likely from the minimum change in length of stay and turnover interval. A range of values were investigated that could act as a signal for efficiency reviews of the way hospital services were operating.

Tyrrell (1975) described the use of data to assist health service managers in their work. In a relatively simple exposition, he outlined the usefulness of a range of numerical information used in measuring various aspects of the manager's task. The advantages of using indicators to support management decisions were described. These included the ability of data to compare situations, so that the effects of different policies and local conditions could be appraised, their use in comparing present performance with a previously agreed standard, and in helping to decide whether reported difficulties merit further action. The limitations and problems inherent in the use of routine data were also outlined. These included error and inconsistency in the data itself and a lack of clarity concerning both the assumptions on which the data rested and the eventual use of the data once it had been analysed. This work also gives a useful overview not only of ways to present data more coherently but also of the data available nationally at the time. Yates and colleagues (Yates, 1981; Yates and Vickerstaff, 1982) also provided access to indicators generated by local health authorities, designed to complement those nationally available.

One of the conclusions to be drawn from analyses such as these is the need to standardise indicators according to various factors such as age and diagnostic (or service-related) groups. Without this, indicators may express a wide range of summary statistics without really pointing to the significance of any differences between them. For instance, it is known that hospital admission rates vary with age. To compare admission rates over districts therefore requires age-related indicators to be included in order to draw valid conclusions from any comparisons. These considerations need to be borne in mind in the use of any indicators, whether these are of activity, costs, process or output.

Financial indicators

A number of themes have been discussed in relation to attempts at devising financial indicators of performance. There are difficulties in accurately costing particular activities and in relating costs to their outcomes. The limitations of costing systems within the NHS have long been recognised. For health care, there are enormous problems in devising PI systems for whole districts which can link financial data to the outcomes of care. It is more likely that this will be done for specific diseases or functions (Goldacre and Griffen, 1983). Research has been undertaken, using routinely available data, which attempts to link costs to other factors. Statistical techniques, such as multiple regression analysis, have been used to account for variations in total hospital costs, taking into account a range of other variables (Ashford et al., 1981). Interpretation of these studies is made difficult by the many problems encountered in analysing cost information. Such factors as the organisational structure of a hospital, the efficiency with which it operates and inclusion of overhead charges, such as those for investigations and support services, all have a bearing on the way costs are calculated (Ferguson and McGuire, 1984, pp. 17-22). In national collections, such as those using comparative figures for local authorities, there are also problems in interpretation. The different accounting practices in local authorities tend to make financial comparisons difficult and unreliable. Low expenditure of itself, for example, should not necessarily be considered as a sign that one authority is more efficient than another.

In social care, Knapp (1987a) provided a brief critique of some of the cost information available to social services departments in guiding policy decisions. Much of this, for example the routine returns made to CIPFA and the Department of Health, was incomplete and ignored cost variations between authorities. The data often related to the direct costs of care borne by social services, such as expenditure on residential homes. It did not take account of indirect costs, such as those borne by other agencies associated with the support of clients. If cost information is incomplete, this can lead to erroneous conclusions being drawn about the consequences of changing policies.

Netten (1997) has presented arguments concerning the derivation and use of cost information in both health and social care settings. The wider use of financial indicators has meant that there is a need to consider more comprehensive methods for the calculation and presentation of cost information. Many previous problems associated with financial indicators were due to the difficulties in linking service activity to expenditure. For example, the costs of services reflected in annual returns to bodies like CIPFA may not reflect changes in resource use as the nature of staff activities change. There is also confusion in national data owing to the variety of independent organisations now operating in the social care market. Owing to contractual arrangements, data on these services at a national level may be reflecting *prices* rather than costs. Care is therefore warranted in using these indicator sets to express the overall efficiency of services.

Need indicators

Early indicator systems said little about need, even though in health and social care this is an important element to consider as it helps us to discover how demand for services is linked to illness and disability characteristics. Need is notoriously difficult to define and so operationalise clearly. There is a distinction between need for a service, which may be latent and unarticulated, and wants or preferences, which are more akin to wishes and demands for services. Needs can exist without corresponding services, or before they are provided. Demand, however, mediates between need and the actual use of services. Need is therefore a first step in considering the performance of a whole service or authority. Without some indication of need, it is difficult to link together resource inputs, service activity and effects in a complete system by which overall performance can be gauged.

Need is difficult to establish empirically. Its use in planning has been subject to much debate and academic work. Surveys of a wide range of need, which might translate into demand for services, can often be expensive and time consuming. An alternative to this method is the use of proxy indicators, which measure social conditions. The former technique attempts to discover from service users themselves what kinds of services they require. The latter method is intended to investigate the factors which are likely, either intuitively or empirically, to give rise to needs in the first place.

The survey approach was used by the National Consumer Council (NCC, 1986), in conjunction with local authorities, in their study of consumer indicators. Questionnaires intended to elicit needs from users of a variety of services, including housing maintenance, libraries, and pre-school education, were administered to gather absolute figures on types of need. A large difficulty with this approach is its piecemeal nature; needs are constantly changing and so measures are required that can track needs across time. Surveys such as these take up resources which may be better employed in initiating a routine measurement system likely to predict future resource use and service deployment.

The indicator approach uses routinely available data to establish the likely prevalence of need in certain defined groups of people. This can then be used to judge whether existing services and resources are directed towards those likely to require them. The NCC, in their appraisal of local authority services for the under-fives for example, used indices of social conditions available from national sources such as the Census or local education authority bulletins, likely to predict needs for the service in question (NCC, 1986). Logan and colleagues (1972), in their study of hospital resources, based their need indicators on Census data, investigating factors such as age structure, housing amenities, overcrowding and social status. The complexities identified in measuring need included the fact that need is not a static concept and so indicators may fail to reflect the variability in need, both across time and culture. An analysis of early need indicators for judging the allocation of services across local authority areas was provided by Davies (1968). He discussed the necessity for more precise indicators of need to be available than was the case at the time. He analysed indicators of resource use and the extensiveness of service provision as against need indices to investigate justice in the allocation of services.

Due to the broad nature of definitions of need, there are numerous problems involved in devising suitable indicators. Absolute numbers of people in different social categories are often available through national data, such as the Census. If comparable information is needed across authorities, then these should be expressed per 1000 population of the group concerned. This is in order to allow for the mix of size and population differences in individual authorities. Allowance must also be made for the timeliness of the information available routinely. The national Census is carried out only once every ten years and so data can become out of date although estimated updates are provided. Considerable care is therefore needed in devising credible need indicators and ensuring that the information is available in a useable form.

Output indicators

Outputs are broadly those things which a system produces. They are indicators of the amount of services provided. Some commentators equate them with performance per se, but they are, in fact, a reflection of the type and extent of services or products produced (Martin and Kettner, 1996). Output data are generally easy to collect and are often routinely available. Output measures can often be combined with those of inputs (predominantly costs) to express relative efficiency. In models of the production process, highlighted earlier, outputs are contrasted with outcomes, which are the end products of the system – consequences that are valued in their own right. Outputs are, in fact, those services or products consumed in order to produce final outcomes.

In the production of public services, output measures have often taken the form of units of service (Kettner et al., 1999). The volume of services provided for each service category is often used as a measure of output. This can be measured in three ways: an episode or contact unit, a material unit, or a time unit (Kettner et al., 1999). For example, an indicator of contact could be per visit or referral, that of material would be per meal served, or that of time, per home help hour. A time unit of service can be considered more precise than other types of output as it is a standardised measure, reflecting the same increment of time across service units.

Output indicators have commonly been used in the planning of public services in order to judge the allocation of resources. In the development of policy, it has long been recognised at a national level that a comprehensive measurement of outputs is needed by which governments can judge whether broad aims have been achieved (House of Commons, 1972, para. 19). They are not stand alone measures of effectiveness but were used in an earlier period to reflect the operation of services nationally.

Outcome indicators

There has been much debate on the difficulty of measuring the outcome of care from routine data. This is the most problematic area of performance indicator development. In the health field, measures of population-based outcome, such as mortality rates, have been the preferred measures used. These are relatively easy to collect but are subject to so many non-health care influences as to warrant caution in their use. Morbidity measures are also used but are less routinely available. Data on illness are also not routinely linked with other data on follow-up care from hospital. In the social care field, ways of measuring achievement of objectives and identifying domains of welfare have also been debated (House of Commons 1972, para. 23).

Outcomes may be conceptualised in two ways dependent on whose valuation one takes to be important in judging care delivery (Williams and Anderson, 1975). The first is in terms of an 'expert' approach, which is often advocated in academic research or by professionals involved in the care for older people. This approach explores a number of outcome domains by which to judge effective practice, drawing on the psychological and survey literature. Here, outcomes can be conceived of as at a number of different levels. At the most specific level are disease specific measures such as those capturing depression or cognitive impairment (Yesavage et al., 1983; Folstein et al., 1975). At a slightly more general level are health status measures, which aggregate a number of health states into a common scale. Examples include the Index of Activities of Daily Living (Katz et al., 1963) or the Barthel Index (Mahoney and Barthel, 1965) used in many evaluative studies of geriatric care. At an intermediate level are health-related quality of life measures that can examine changes in symptoms or health status as a result of service receipt (Hunt et al., 1986; Deyo et al., 1983). More general, are aspects of user satisfaction, which can be used to monitor the quality of services (Geron, 1998; Applebaum et al., 2000; Bauld et al., 2000). At the most general level are indicators of quality of life that include a number of dimensions such as life satisfaction (Neugarten et al., 1961), psychological well-being (Bradburn,

1969), and morale (Lawton, 1975). There are a number of reviews of assessment scales that focus on dimensions of life quality that may be drawn on to offer more determinacy in routine settings (Challis, 1981; Kane and Kane, 1981, 2000; McDowell and Newell, 1987; Applegate et al., 1990; Royal College of Physicians and British Geriatrics Society, 1992; Philp, 1993; Rubenstein et al., 1995; Bowling 1991, 1995). Some measures have been developed at a higher order of generality to provide a single unit of outcome to judge cost effectiveness. For example, a system-level measurement of general hospital output (or in our terms, outcome), which included patient disability and distress, was described by Rosser and Watts (1972). They introduced an outcome scale for routine use, to measure improvements in patient health as a consequence of episodes of care. It was possible from this, to derive a measure of overall output and compare this with the optimum potential of a hospital in improving health over a one-month period. Similarly, others have attempted to produce single aggregate measures of health status such as Quality Adjusted Life Years (QALYs) (Williams and Kind, 1992), Euroqol (Euroqol Group, 1990), and Healthy Active Life Expectancy (HALE) (Grimley Evans, 1993).

The second way in which to conceptualise outcome relies on a 'bottom up' approach with evidence collected from users and carers as to the domains considered most important to them in judging the conduct of services (Nocon et al., 1997). Such an approach can generate tools to routinely monitor such outcomes. For example, Qureshi and Nicholas (2001) developed an outcomes monitoring tool generated from exploratory research with older service users and carers designed to monitor care management practice at the point of assessment. The framework around which the tool was based gives prominence to three main areas: maintenance of quality of life for the user, such as maintaining acceptable levels of comfort and safety; the achievement of change, such as improving confidence or self care skills; and the impacts of service processes, such as whether the user feels valued or has their preferences respected. In a similar vein, Netten and colleagues (2002) have developed a measure of social care outcome, OPUS (Older People's Utility Scale), which draws its domains from those considered most important by older users. This measure aims to identify changes in the levels of met need arising from social care intervention in the areas of food and nutrition, personal care, safety, social participation or involvement, and control over daily life. Findings from an analysis of the preferences of older people revealed that the domains of personal care and social participation and involvement were rated as the most important for them.

There may be ways of reconciling these two approaches since both older users and social services managers have identified the maintenance of 'quality of life' as a central aim in monitoring outcome (Nocon et al., 1997). Moreover, the standardised scales identified for use in 'expert' evaluations were, in fact, originally developed from large samples of service users. These scales, in directing attention towards assessments of physical and mental functioning, also focus upon issues concerned with the well-being and quality of life of older people. Therefore, there may not, despite the academic debate surrounding the construction of assessment tools, be wide discrepancies in the way outcome is conceptualised by users and by professionals and researchers. If such information, linking user and professionally derived outcomes, could be made available routinely then this could enable linkages to be made between a number of concerns, such as the managerial concern with value for money and service effectiveness as against the user concern with services' impact on lifestyle and choices (Qureshi, 1999).

However, translating these outcome domains into indicators that can be used to judge service effectiveness represents the greatest challenge in routine monitoring. Previous indicator developments have, conceptually speaking, failed to separate ends from means: outcome has been viewed in terms of service activity rather than the consequences of this activity for the welfare of older people (Harding, 1999). However, ways are emerging for monitoring the final outcomes of social care interventions. Gathering routine evidence as to the success of services – the achievement of these ends – could involve the routine collection of data from standardised assessment tools, appropriately aggregated to signal changes in older people's welfare. Here, tools measuring conditions, behaviours, attitudes, feelings and functioning (Martin and Kettner, 1996) often produce a single summary score, which can be useful in measuring the degree of improvement in the domains being identified. These measures could be completed at regular intervals in order to monitor changes in outcome – so-called 'concurrent measurement' (Brill *et al.*, 1995). This can provide comparisons of groups of cases against normative information collected over time. *Numeric counts* – counts of how many users achieve a change in outcome as a result of a particular service (Martin and Kettner, 1996, pp. 62-83) can be translated into indicators reflecting the number of cases demonstrating improvement, or the proportion of those demonstrating improvement as against the total number of clients receiving services. Alternatively, data from the routine administration of user-derived tools could be compared with target standards for maintaining quality of life or achieving change, which may be set by a social services department (Qureshi and Nichols, 2001). Data from these tools could also be used to compare levels of met need across social services areas, those before and after an intervention, or current levels with expected levels (Netten et al., 2002).

However, while reliable tools exist that can monitor these outcome domains, their use in the routine setting has not, as yet, become commonplace. Not only is their use not formally approved in the context of routine practice, but also the range of domains identified as important for judging the impact of social care are not always included as part of assessment documentation (Stewart et al., 1999). A transfer of knowledge from other areas, such as old age psychiatry services, where the routine use of outcomes data is more commonplace (Macdonald, 2002) may help. Such services are in the process of implementing the routine administration of outcomes data, such as the Health of the Nation Outcome Scales (HoNOS 65+) (Burns et al., 1999), and in examining outcome changes over time and between areas and teams. Establishing such practice and linking it to management feedback and resource use would have much to offer community care services and would extend the traditional approach of performance measurement in this area.

There are also methodological difficulties presenting a challenge to the use of outcome measures in practice. As opposed to the health care arena, relating final outcomes to the objectives of care delivery has been problematic in social care. Community-based social care is often concerned with maintaining clients in a steady-state or in minimising risk rather than with achieving an end-state of welfare (Stevenson and Parsloe, 1993). It may therefore be inappropriate to measure outcome as a change in users' welfare before and after an intervention. The appropriate time scale over which to measure outcome is also a problematic area. Service impact may be slow to materialise and there are often no comparative data available on the consequences if no service is received. There is also the difficulty in establishing a causal relationship between care services used and the final outcome for the user. Factors other than the care received may influence outcome to a greater or lesser extent. These difficulties are familiar to researchers and they can be controlled for by the use of multivariate procedures in order to allow for confounding variables. Indicators may be more difficult to interpret, however, unless care is taken to include a range of extraneous factors within indicator sets, which are thought likely to influence outcome (Goldacre and Griffen, 1983, p. 41).

Some commentators have attempted to respond to these difficulties by using indicators of *service completion* as a proxy for final outcome. This relates not to the direct outcome of a service for the user but to the completion of treatment or the full receipt of those services considered necessary in any care programme (Kettner and Martin, 1993). The justification for using such indirect indicators is that there is an expectation of improvement if a user completes a full course of treatment or receives a full complement of services. Service completion may, therefore, indirectly reflect the outcome to the user, which is not directly measurable routinely. This argument raises difficult issues regarding the relationships between receipt of a service and its effects on the individual user. Measurable improvement is more likely to be the case as a result of treatment with, for example, the administration of drugs whereas for social care it is more difficult to provide evidence that service completion can serve as an adequate measure of final outcome. This is especially the case for long-term care. Martin and Kettner (1996) illustrate two methods to describe how service completions can be defined; the standardised approach and the case-plan approach. The standardised approach assumes that a minimum number of service units are necessary for the client to complete an episode of service. A client completing the prescribed number of therapy sessions would be one such measure of service completion. The case-plan approach defines service completion in terms of when a client has completed a designated plan of care. The care plan can be divided into episodes of care necessary for the effective performance of the plan. For long-term care, one such measure would be the point at which an older person is reassessed for care, having received a full complement of services based on needs identified at initial assessment. Indicators can then be devised which express whether a service has been completed. These can be expressed as raw numbers (the numbers of people reassessed as needing residential care) or as proportions of the population served (proportion of clients assessed who enter residential care).

Problems still remain in translating outcome measurement into use as part of routine indicators. The *utility* of using numeric counts or service completion measures as outcome indicators may be high. Their use may have high acceptance and it is reasonably easy to collect data relating to service use as a proxy for final outcome. The *validity* of these indicators may, however, be low. They remain imprecise reflections of final outcome, which can only be faithfully recorded as elements that are valued in their own right (Davies, 1977). These challenges inherent in attempting to measure outcome with routinely generated indicators mean there is considerable room for further enquiry.

Quality indicators

The literature on quality assurance techniques and monitoring has become substantial in recent years. However, indicators designed to express quality are hard to come by. Most of the models reviewed earlier failed to take account of the quality dimension. The studies undertaken often fail to present measurements of quality, tending instead to hide behind a flavour of managerial analysis that can appear vague and confusing. There have been a number of recent exceptions. Martin and Kettner (1996) present a number of generally accepted dimensions of quality from the US literature. These are listed in Table 2.5. Similar dimensions have been articulated by other authors from a health perspective (see Maxwell, 1992). Devising indicators for these dimensions poses further difficulties. There are potential trade-offs between one element and another. A service may be accessible, for example, without necessarily offering competent care once the user has received it. In addition, some dimensions denote positive attributes of a service whereas others express deficiencies. Deciding on which measures faithfully express these different aspects is full of methodological pitfalls.

Quality indicators have usually had a customer or user focus. Gunter and Hawkins (1996) see them as characteristics of service delivery and the way this is perceived by the consumer. This can be contrasted with measures of productivity, which focus on the structure of services and their appraisal by management. One measurement issue in devising indicators of quality has been the extent to which client judgements about a service are founded on the dimensions above. Two elements identified as important by customers are reliability and responsiveness (Zeithaml et al., 1990). Indicator sets that make some reference to quality might consider including measurements for these aspects as a minimum requirement. Thus, to an extent, customer satisfaction can be an indicator of quality so long as this is rated against a number of domains reflecting different aspects of quality. This may be difficult to implement as part of routine indicator sets and often the number of complaints are used as indicators of quality, focussing attention only upon the deficiencies in the service.

In order to operationalise these quality dimensions, they need to be translated into characteristics that reflect the context of the particular services studied (Martin and Kettner, 1996). So, for example, responsiveness might mean something different for a meals-on-wheels service than it does for a surgical procedure. In terms of some of the concepts outlined here, contextualisation is often achieved by attaching quality measures to existing output indicators. In other words, this involves 'weighting' outputs according to some quality dimension (Beeton, 1988). For example, an output indicator of a delivered meal might have a dimension of reliability attached to it (whether the meal is delivered to a certain temperature), or one of responsiveness (whether the meal is delivered on time). In so doing, it is possible to come to some agreement on targets, which can then express a dimension of quality in the service.

Summary

This chapter has outlined many of the developments and arguments associated with the growth in performance indicators over the last two decades. A central theme has been the need for central government to monitor and regulate the affairs of local public services. The mechanisms and measurements needed for this have gradually developed in response to the general economic climate. Political priorities too, have led to the development of particular forms of measurement. These developments have been discussed in the UK context. Similar processes have been at work in the US (Wholey and Hatry, 1992; Martin and Kettner, 1996) and in other countries, such as New Zealand (Irwin, 1996), Sweden (Fortin, 1996), the Netherlands

Table 2.5
Dimensions of quality (from Kettner and Martin, 1996)

Dimension	Definition
Accessibility	Easy to access or acquire.
Assurance	Staff are friendly, polite, considerate.
Communication	Information provided in understandable language.
Competency	Staff possess required knowledge and skills.
Conformity	The service meets established standards.
Courtesy	Staff demonstrate respect towards clients.
Deficiency	The service is missing a characteristic or element.
Durability	The results from the service do not dissipate quickly.
Empathy	Staff provide individual attention and understand need.
Humaneness	Service protects client dignity and self-worth.
Reliability	Service is dependable with minimum variation between clients.
Responsiveness	The service is delivered in a timely way.
Security	The service is in a safe setting free from risk
Tangibles	Appropriate appearance of facilities, personnel and materials.

(Sorber, 1996) and Japan (Tanaka and Ono, 2002). Similar accountability mechanisms and budgetary constraints are in operation in these countries that provide a context for the rise of performance measurement systems. In many cases, these mechanisms have been enshrined in legislation, permitting the wider and more direct use of performance indicators in the regulation of both central and local government. In the US, for example, the Government Performance and Results Act (GPRA) (US Congress, 1993) dictated that, from 1998, departments report on performance measures set to investigate the effectiveness of public services. In both the US and Sweden, for example, governments are now requiring agencies to set out annual performance review plans with which to account for the success of public services. Similar requirements are present in the UK care environment and similar mechanisms and processes have been introduced.

In the social and health care context in the UK, indicators were initially introduced that relied purely on what can be termed 'counting and costing' information. In a sense, these were sound measures but were devoid of any theoretical content. These were replaced by a dramatic growth in indicators throughout the 1980s, based on the political pressure to regulate and monitor aspects of central and local government. These, however, mostly related to activity data such as length of stay in hospital or number of admissions to care homes. They stressed efficiency, crudely translated as 'value for money', as the guiding standard by which performance should be judged. More recently, performance measurement in local government has stressed Best Value as a core framework within which performance is defined. Wider criteria for performance have been added, including fair access to services. There has been increasing pressure to devise indicators of performance which more closely match the objectives of the organisation, albeit with varying degrees of success. There still remain substantial design and conceptual problems in using PIs in the public sector, particularly the difficulties of most performance systems in measuring the final outcomes of the service in question. The growth in some performance indicators, in particular those of the NHS, has been more rapid than in other quarters such as in social care. However, this rise in the number of indicators has not always been in useable measures that permit the nature of the organisation to be measured against its objectives. Some of the difficulties found in successive generations of health indicators need to be borne in mind when examining the development of indicators for social care. These problems include their all-inclusive nature, difficulties in presentation and a reliance on inputs and processes to the exclusion of outcomes.

It is not only technical issues that are important in the development of indicators. Definitions of performance are also dependent on who is interested in the results of measurement (Jowett and Rothwell, 1988). There are thus political implications in the choice and use of particular measures. There is also a sense in which performance measurement is 'context dependent' (Yeung, 1989). In the 1980s, for example, economy and efficiency were the defining criteria of performance. Notions of effectiveness, service quality and customer satisfaction were largely neglected at that time but have recently achieved more prominence.

Performance measurement, and the indicators used to support it, are thus a child of their times, subject to political priorities and dependent on the nature and purposes of the organisation under review. There will therefore be no 'best' measures of performance for any organisation. Indicators will need to be devised which allow for and reflect an organisation's particular circumstances and objectives. The concerns of performance measurement in social care, for example, have been shaped by organisational and legislative factors different from those in the NHS. This has influenced the nature of the indicators chosen. The next chapter therefore examines specifically performance indicators for social care.

Chapter 3

Performance Indicators in Social Care

Much of the discussion in Chapter 2 focused on national developments in performance measurement outlined by central government in the UK. To an extent these approaches have relied on aggregated information not immediately in tune with the needs of managers and practitioners in individual services such as social or health care (Roberts, 1990). For social care, a primary issue is how these central initiatives can be translated into a form fit for local use. This reflects the discussion of the importance of recognising issues concerning the balance of central–local control in the measurement of performance.

In the mid 1980s, on the social care side, other bodies began to take an interest in performance indicators. Part of their motivation was to address the previous criticisms and to relate indicators to practice in a way in which it was generally perceived the CIPFA, the Audit Commission or the Department of Health indicators had not done. This emphasis can be seen to stem from the need to comment on the wider political changes already discussed and their implications for social care.

This chapter reviews performance indicator development for social services, in particular for services for older people. It begins with a review of how central planning mechanisms may have shaped the early development of PIs for social care. It then reviews some of the more recent developments concerning routinely collected data for social services. Academic arguments associated with some of the conceptual problems in devising indicators for social care are also reviewed. One important aspect of this is the long running problem of measuring the achievements of social care services, the definition of outcome. It concludes by reviewing more recent developments in social services performance measurement in more detail in order to bring the discussion up to date.

Social services planning and measurement

Performance in social services is set within the context of planning. In order for publicly funded authorities to provide services that are relevant to a range of needs, decisions have to be made concerning competing priorities. Planning thus attempts to identify current needs and circumstances and how these might change in the future. Planning should lead to a clear direction and flexibility in the way services can respond to a variety of changing needs. It can also lead to the better management of existing resources based on an understanding of the likelihood of these changes (Falk and Lee, 1978). Planning inevitably involves measurement. Targets need to be set in advance and modified in the light of new information.

The history of planning in the social services offers a particular instance of dashed expectations in the ability of the state to measure and evaluate its social welfare activities. As with the general developments mentioned earlier, the planning of particular services and their functions has been based, to a large extent, on the changing relationships between central and local government (Davies, 1968). Measures designed to assist in this planning have varied with these changing circumstances and there has been a tension between national and local demands for information. The type of indicators produced so far in social care can be reviewed in the light of these shifting relationships.

The early history of social services planning

The history of social services planning has inevitably not been an entirely rational process based on clear assumptions about resources (Bamford, 1982). There has been a general limitation in the capacity to plan by evidence. This has occurred because of not only restrictions in resources, but also a lack of expertise in social services departments in their capacity to use measurement as an aid to planning. The long-term planning of an earlier period was replaced by a more incremental approach to planning due to economic pressures and reductions in spending (Webb and Wistow, 1986). The indicators used as an aid to planning have varied as a result, particularly after the end of the 1970s.

At the time of the 1948 National Assistance Act, legislation conferred major powers on central government over the approval and conduct of local services. In plans put forward by local authorities at that time, measures of the extent of services available and estimated future demand (such as bed ratios in old people's homes) were included (see Davies, 1968, pp. 90–96 for a more detailed exposition of these). These were, however, not of great detail and were often vague.

A change of emphasis occurred during the 1960s as central government wished to influence local authority activity more indirectly. They did this by requesting advance guidance or plans of specific activity and expenditure. The first of these ten-year plans was published in a White Paper for Health and Community Care in 1963 (Cmnd 1973, 1963). The Ministry of Health, at that time, used these plans as a basis for following up authorities who showed the lowest standards of provision. Indicators were used as a measurement basis for this and measures were provided such as the ratio of places in residential care relative to the elderly population and the provision of home nurses and home helps. Davies, in his analysis (Davies, 1968, p. 206), cites at least 120 items of statistical information collected from each authority in pursuit of these plans. However, the range of this information was limited to resources (such as numbers of places in homes), numbers of staff and capital expenditures. The routine data available, both to individual local authorities and nationally, were therefore rather limited. The provision of information was also not related in any coherent way to the wider stated objectives of social care.

There are echoes with more recent periods both in the way in which these plans were formulated and in the manner of their execution. An attempt to exert central government control over the extent of local provision, if not its quality, was made while still allowing local authorities to maintain their own responsibility for planning (Cmnd 1973, 1963, para. 4). The measures used to support this can be taken to be an indication of a crude beginning to performance evaluation. There were no large scale statistical evaluations of these measures, which often meant that details were overtaken by a new set of planning returns for the next period (Davies, 1968, p. 98). Although this planning process called for the measurement of social services activity on a comparable basis, it did not, however, call for explicit central government control mechanisms. Local authorities were left to modify their own planning in relation to the activities of other authorities.

From the Seebohm reorganisation in the 1970s there was an increased drive towards forward planning within social services departments. A DHSS circular in August 1972 (DHSS, 1972b, circular 35/72) requested that a further ten-year plan be developed for social services capital and revenue programmes up until 31 March 1983. This would enable, it was argued, local and central government systematically to review the development of services at regular points in time. It would also enable an evaluation to be made of the best use of resources. Data were requested from authorities in order to make this happen; measures such as the amount of capital investment, net revenue expenditure, numbers of premises in use and staffing were requested. Some (such as Webb and Wistow (1986)) have argued that the actual production of this plan took precedence over the development of more accurate methods, which would permit departments to evaluate their activities in relation to objectives.

Although the term 'performance indicator' was not used at this time, the guidelines to the 1972 circular contained indices for such things as numbers of day care places per 1000 population and staffing ratios. The ten-year plan did enable the collection of data concerning manpower, such as numbers of staff in old people's homes, which were hitherto not available. The guidelines did not contain suggestions for the measurement of need or service quality and in some respects they were imprecise (Falk and Lee, 1978). However, this period was the first to generate information to show the level of activities across all local authorities on a comparable basis. At the time, the measurement of output levels was an attempt to provide a basis for planning to determine the allocation of resources to each area of public expenditure (House of Commons, 1972). For older people's services, there was still a lack of precision regarding measurement of the achievement of specific aims. Work was being done at a central level in seeking new measurements of output by which to judge the operation of services and relate these more specifically to need (House of Commons, 1972, para. 23). These guidelines also encouraged an analytical approach to the collection and return of information. However, the data requested were limited to inputs and gave only a partial indication of how objectives were to be achieved with particular resources. A comprehensive system for judging resource accountability did not, at that time, exist.

A further development in 1976 was the introduction of a set of planning priorities for health and social services (DHSS, 1976). This provided a quantitative base for planning. The document mostly concentrated on the NHS, with social services relegated to a subsidiary role in the development of community care. Planning, after this, was requested on a three-year basis by Local Authority Planning Statements (LAPS) (DHSS, 1977). The first year of these returns was used to feed back to authorities details of their performance in relation to other authorities. In the second year, statistical tables in these returns were to be accompanied by an outline from social services departments of the objectives of their planning. In some respects, this initiative called for a national database but useful data were not produced as the completion of these returns was resisted. It was felt that processing the required information committed valuable resources leaving little time for a consideration of more fundamental questions of social services planning (Webb and Wistow, 1986). Already, by the third year, limited growth in public expenditure meant that the requirement for authorities to produce returns was scrapped. The LAPS guidelines were eventually abandoned in 1981.

Bamford (1982) sees the history of social services planning as one of rationalism being replaced by opportunism. Long-term planning was severely curtailed by the early 1980s, to be replaced by a style of planning that merely responded to recent changes, rather than being part of a coherent strategy. In particular, the plans had assumed a rate of economic growth which, by the late 1970s, could not be guaranteed. In this early period, social services performance measurement followed a similar trajectory to that in the rest of the public sector. The changing economic fortunes of the late 1970s and early 1980s brought about a change in emphasis; concerns about efficiency and value for money taking precedence over traditional long-term, rational planning mechanisms. Indicative of this change was the general discussion of the Layfield Committee (Cmnd 6453, 1976), whose remit to enquire into the structure and administration of local authority finance as a whole, was eventually bounded by a general concern with efficiency in local authority spending.

The availability of early indicators to assist in planning

The nature of the data required for planning reflected these pressures. Information was restricted to data on activities, manpower and finance, rather than that reflecting service quality or more focused aspects of service delivery, such as the pursuit of certain service-related objectives. This could be seen as 'informational pragmatism' (employing the data available), combining with immediate pressures. The Rayner scrutinies at the DHSS in the early 1980s also restricted the availability of data relating to such things as social services staffing. Departments often reviewed their own services internally after this time and there are some examples of the use of research information to investigate performance locally, which led to some improvements in the collection of information. However, nationally collected information from departments' returns was severely restricted from the early 1980s onwards. Indeed, there was the accusation from a Social Services Select Committee in 1982 that the DHSS had abandoned any notion of social services planning entirely (House of Commons, 1982b). This restriction led to problems in the availability of useable information on which to base the indicator sets throughout the later part of the 1980s and beyond. Thus, the history of central planning and monitoring of social services may have been responsible, in part, for some early difficulties in the availability of relevant data to monitor social services performance at a national level.

In measurement terms, the data available in this early period at least enabled central government and the local authorities themselves to assess the rates of development of different services. However, as Davies (1968) showed in his analysis of the content of the plans, this capability did not extend to using these measures to permit service changes to be made, dependent on the extent of provision and its relationship to the needs of the local communities concerned. The indicators used in this planning were, 'insufficiently specific, insufficiently numerous and not the ones logically related to decisions about the most appropriate techniques to use' (Davies, 1968, p. 299). In many respects, earlier social services planning was unresponsive to both local financial information and wider social policy. The measures themselves were often crude reflections of what services were available, rather than their being used to inform service delivery based upon more comprehensive concerns of efficiency, fairness and responsiveness. Indicators at that time also did not adequately reflect the provision of complementary services in the voluntary and private sectors – an important consideration more recently in order to monitor the operation of the market for social care. Davies (1968) also pointed out the lack of resources available in this early period that could have been used to process measures and identify shortfalls in service provision.

Nationally collected social services data

Thus, changing priorities, uncertainties about measurement and the pattern of central–local relations in planning have been influential in the types of performance data collected at a national level. In the following section, the social services indicators that have had the most relevance in the pursuit of performance measurement up to the present are reviewed.

Early indicators

In line with the increased use of PIs in the early 1980s, to ensure accountability in public services, the *Local Government, Land and Planning Act* 1980 laid down statutory requirements for local authorities to publish annual reports of their activities. For social services, a brief selection of seven indicators was given in order to account for their work and to provide a comparison with other authorities. The indicators were mainly cost and activity data and are listed in Box 3.1. These indicators were expected to be based on information readily available to authorities and there were thus no new developments in measurement. There were no statements in the Code of Practice (Department of the Environment, 1981) concerning reasons for the choice of particular

---

Box 3.1

Social services indicators under Local Government, Land and Planning Act 1980 (Department of the Environment, 1981)

- Net costs of social services per capita
- Children in care as percentage of under 18s
- Net cost per child/week in childrens homes
- Gross cost per resident week in local authority homes for the elderly
- Per cent of elderly population aged 75 plus supported in residential care
- Home help contact hours per 1000 65 plus
- Fieldwork staff per 1000 population

indicators. There were developments in other nationally collected data for social services after this time, which made more reference to frameworks rather than ad hoc pieces of information.

Taking into account some of the points discussed previously in our review of general developments in PIs, these indicators can be seen as a first attempt at designing measures with particular relevance to social services. They do not fit into any framework but are basically measures reflecting the inputs and resources used. Even at the time of their publication, events were occurring (such as the changes in patterns of funding in residential and nursing home care) which would render at least two of the indicators increasingly redundant.

CIPFA's personal social services statistics

CIPFA's booklets of estimates and actuals for social services have been published annually since 1951. They were originally the *Welfare Services Statistics* and after this, the *Local Health and Social Services Statistics* following the 1970 *Social Services Act*. The information contained in them has been mainly concerned with activity and expenditure. A revised standard classification for the social services statistical returns was published in February 1993 (CIPFA, 1993). This applied to all published statements for periods from 1 April 1993 onwards. From this point, costs were more clearly identified to reflect the community care reforms and the separation of purchaser and provider roles within social services departments. These booklets provide an analysis of expenditure and income for major client groups. For older people, they provide indicators such as average numbers of clients, gross cost and expenditure on nursing homes, residential care, day centres and home care. For home care, more detailed data are given such as numbers of hours of service received (per annum and per week). For meals on wheels the standard charge per meal is given as well as gross cost and expenditure. Unit costs are calculated from this, such as net cost per hour of home care.

These statistics concentrated on local authority social services provision and did not include data on other aspects of care such as that by private and voluntary agencies. However, they did include the numbers of clients financed by the local authority in other sectors of care. There has been much comment (see for example, Hoyes et al., 1992, p. 19) about the inaccuracy of these data, in part reflected by the voluntary nature of the returns from local authorities. Many authorities made no returns at all or only partial data were provided. CIPFA themselves included caveats as to the use of these data in their booklets. In particular, warnings were given concerning using the data for comparative purposes as many local factors were not included in the costing procedures. In terms of measuring performance on a wider basis, the

CIPFA statistics were severely limited. Expenditure and service levels were only presented in broad terms and failed to reflect the variety of service provision. They did not enable an evaluation of whether services were appropriate to the needs of clients served.

The Audit Commission's performance indicators

The Audit Commission published its handbook for performance review in social services in 1986. It was designed to assist auditors and local authorities appraise their services. This described PIs to answer questions which were likely to arise from reviews. These included questions relating to the underlying policies of SSDs, and queries concerning service planning, the organisation of social work and the management of resources. Appropriate benchmarks were listed in an annual statistical supplement from this point. These indicators, it was stated, should not be seen as definitive. They were considered to be a starting point from which to review services and explore differences between one authority and another. Questions designed to assist in review are listed along with appropriate indicators for older people in Table 3.1.

Local authority profiles prepared by the Commission each year also outline service and expenditure data for social services whereby data from authorities in the same 'family' are compared. These have been mentioned in an earlier section dealing with the Citizen's Charter initiative (p. 39). Indicators have been used comparatively across similar authorities and judged against the average for that group. For social services provision, a small number of indicators are provided for the judgement of the public and for local authorities themselves. A number of statements are also provided so as to shape comparative judgements (Audit Commission, 1996a, pp. 6–8). Examples of these indicators provided for social services are listed in Box 3.2. They focus on the type and intensity of service provision rather than providing a basis for wider considerations. In themselves, they offer limited assistance as measures of performance against criteria judged to be important in social care. However, a separate statistical appendix to the profiles (Audit Commission, 1996b) lists further information making it possible to form judgements concerning targeting issues by employing indicators such as the proportion of older people being helped to live at home in comparison with levels of need. This supplement includes expenditure data and indicators of the numbers of people referred for assessment and the outcome of that assessment and therefore provides a limited focus for the analysis of service related issues.

The Commission has also produced value for money studies, such as that examining the care of the elderly (Audit Commission, 1985). These are more sophisticated than the local authority profiles, usually taking into account a particular authority's policies and procedures. The Audit Commission's

Table 3.1
Audit Commission indicators for performance review of older people (Audit Commission, 1986c)

Review questions	Suggested indicators
Scale and nature of provision	
Estimates of need	Elderly population in age groups
Has the council produced a clear policy statement on the scale and nature of services to be provided? Is this based on an analysis of demographic trends and likely numbers needing services?	Percentage needing services Percentage needing residential care Percentage in receipt of day/domiciliary services
Liaison	Waiting lists
What are the arrangements for meeting the housing needs of elderly people?	Placements in sheltered and other dwellings
Service delivery	Dates of initial and review assessments
Are assessments and reviews of dependency and need undertaken by a multidisciplinary team?	
Community services	Net expenditure on domiciliary services as percentage of total
How does council policy provide positive support in enabling older people to live independently?	Net expenditure per 1000 elderly Attendances at day centres Meals taken
Residential accommodation	
Is this graded according to dependency?	—
Management of services	Net expenditure per 1000 elderly Costs per home help organiser Gross cost/hour for home help

---

Box 3.2
Local authority performance indicators for social services (Audit Commission, 1996a)

- Percentage of elderly people over 75 helped to live at home
- Percentage of minor items of equipment to help people live at home, provided within three weeks
- Percentage of adults going into residential care who were offered single rooms
- Percentage of children in local authority care who were in foster homes
- Number of children on the Child Protection Register per thousand children

report, *Making a Reality of Community Care* (Audit Commission, 1986a), also sought to examine the provision of community care nationally and outlined its arguments using a range of comparative indicators. The aim of this study was to help judge whether the financial and organisational arrangements for community care were promoting the 'three Es' of economy, efficiency and effectiveness. A range of data sources was used in an attempt to judge national policy and targets against current provision of services. The indicators used mostly related to staffing and service provision, such as home help numbers and expenditure, and numbers of residents per 1000 population in private and voluntary homes. There were attempts to use these indicators to enquire into the balance of care between residential and community-based services and relate these to targets in previous White Papers. The Audit Commission thus used these measures to comment on the response of authorities to the host of legislative guidance produced throughout the 1980s.

The Social Services Inspectorate's 'Key Indicators'

The SSI, charged with a regular programme of performance review in social services, originally released its 'Key Indicators' as a demonstration package in December 1988 (Warburton, 1988). Some of the criticisms of these data have already been discussed. Many of these relate to the limitations in data provided by authorities in their returns. The package was based on the integration of data from a number of sources: a possible source of bias. The bulk of the information collected related to service activity and manpower. The indicators were oriented to financial issues and did not clearly relate performance to overall policies and objectives. Like the Audit Commission's profiles, the intention of these indicators was to identify norms by which authorities could be judged. Indicators were presented in comparable form across authorities and against national averages.

There have been limitations in using these indicators as measures of performance (Lupton, 1989). Not least, there was a lack of comprehensiveness in that they only sought to identify issues of importance centrally and highlighted only issues of particular concern (Gostick, 1989). Data were unavailable for some authorities and the data were based mostly on older people's and children's services. Some of these limitations were mentioned in the detailed notes to the package. There were many sources of bias that could intrude during the collection and aggregation of the data. Some sources for the data, such as that from CIPFA, did not provide rigorous validation of the data they provided. Local authorities may also have had different interpretations and categorisations of the data, which could lead to further sources of error.

The Social Services Inspectorate produced an analytical framework for its key indicators, which it hoped would ensure their proper and considered use

(Warburton, 1988). This framework identified nine types of indicator: scale, extent, level, cover, intensity, turnover, management, occupancy and unit costs. The framework also highlighted the need to relate the nine types of indicator to national policies, the policy and goals of the local authority and the policies and practices of other agencies, and to user and policy-related outcomes. The Inspectorate also published articles in the professional press in the hope of explaining indicators to a wider audience of managers and practitioners (Warburton, 1989).

During the development of the Key Indicator package, the relevance of some measures to community care activity was questioned. There was a lack of data relating to the activities of other service providers, such as services in the independent sector. There were also problems in the way in which these data were recorded and used by SSDs, with serious shortcomings in the input of data and its interpretation (Miller, 1986; Hardingham, 1986). The nature of some of these data, particularly regarding costs, was also of variable quality and some basic 'rules of thumb' were neglected in examining cost comparisons between authorities (Knapp, 1987a). However, in terms of its conception, the SSI Key Indicator package represented a major development at the time.

The aspects of social services' work detailed in a subsequent version of the package (Department of Health, 1991b), with some examples of indicators, are shown in Table 3.2. The indicators present comparative data for local authority social services according to a number of aspects: financial information, social needs indicators, staffing, overall expenditure, and patterns of expenditure. For older people's services, indicators were included on expenditure patterns and service outputs, services-to-client ratios, unit costs, and the numbers of elderly people in residential and community settings. Notes were provided as to the source and interpretation of some of the information contained in the package.

The Statistics Branch of the Department of Health has recently had responsibility for the generation and publication of these Key Indicators on an annual basis and has sought to improve the information available. An expert system and a graphics package now complements the printed indicators (Department of Health, 2002b) and latterly, these indicators have been available as part of a web-based application (Department of Health, 2005).

Scope of indicators

By the end of the 1980s it was possible to see the beginnings of a consensus emerging about the appropriate use of performance indicators and the necessary conditions for generating and using them, arising from both the developmental work on performance indicators and the experience of their

Table 3.2
Examples of the SSIs 'Key Indicators' for social services

Indicator type	Examples
Financial	Net current expenditure per capita
Social need	Percentage of population in different age groups (0–4 / 5–9 / 10–17 / 18–64 / 65–74 / 75–84 / 85 plus) Total population Projected percentage growth in population Percentage of economically active residents unemployed Percentage of households overcrowded / with one pensioner living alone / lacking bath / WC Standardised mortality ratio Deprivation scores Percentage breakdown of housing tenure
Staffing	Number of senior managers (WTEs) / administration / ancillary staff / fieldwork staff / home help / day care / residential staff: as a percentage of all SSD staff Total numbers of SSD staff
Overall expenditure (also by client group and administration)	SSD total gross current expenditure (£000s) SSD total gross current expenditure per capita Capital expenditure as percentage of gross current and per capita expenditure
Expenditure patterns	Percentage net current expenditure in support of: residential/day care, home help, meals, other Percentage of gross SSD expenditure on residential care accrued through charges
Service outputs	Number of places in LA / private/voluntary residential care per 1000 population 75 plus
Service-to-client ratios	Percentage occupancy in residential care run by LA / private/voluntary sector Number of home help cases per organiser Number of residents per 10 manual staff in LA residential care
Unit costs	Expenditure on residential care/supported resident 65 plus per week Gross weekly cost/place filled for LA homes Weekly gross expenditure on day care/place Net cost/received hour of home help Gross expenditure on meals/per meals served
Client data	Number of people in receipt of home help/1000 population Number of admissions to LA homes/1000 population 75 plus

Source: Department of Health (1991b)

use by managers and practitioners. In terms of the scope and types of indicator that CIPFA, the Audit Commission and the Department of Health produced in the 1980s, they were usually limited to two types:

* *Service inputs* – such as the amount of money allocated to social services by local councils, the quantity and type of people employed by social services departments, and the type of buildings used as social services facilities;
* *Service outputs* – such as the number of delivered meals kitchens produced, the number of home care hours provided, or the number of residential care places available.

All three national bodies recognised that the scope of their indicators was limited and that for social services these needed to be broadened to take in indicators of:

* *Service outcomes* – meaning either the impact of services on users and carers or the comparison of stated policy targets set against target achievement;
* *Service quality* – such as the attention given by staff to customer care, to ensuring user choice, to safeguarding the privacy and independence of users;
* *Service equality (equity)* – meaning the equal and appropriate access and provision of services to all users from all backgrounds;
* *Service processes* – meaning the way in which organisational structures, line management arrangements, and agency procedures and systems are designed and operated.

Recognition of these deficits was one thing; to do something about them was another. Much of the data that were missing, while essential for understanding the impact of services, were difficult to collect at the local level on any consistent or comparable basis. The national bodies relied on locally generated data and could not make unreasonable information demands of local authorities. Hence, the best that the national bodies could do was to note that information on, say, service outcomes, was not available to them, but should be collected locally if and when the opportunity arose (Warburton, 1989).

Other developments

These limitations in centrally collected data echo a main theme in the current work, namely how insights taken from data generated at a national level can be interpreted into a framework for local use. In this context there were two notable developments towards the later part of the 1980s. The first came from the Social Services Research Group (SSRG) and the second from Social Information Systems (SIS).

The SSRG published their ideas for performance measurement in a series of monographs, covering different user groups in turn. The SSRG's first monograph was published in 1988 (Barnes and Miller, 1988). Rather in the style of the Social Services Inspectorate's analytical framework, it included a basic model for the development and interpretation of performance measures for a service unit. The ten elements included in the model are shown in Box 3.3.

Box 3.3
SSRG's model for performance measures

• Measures of need
• Statements of policy and service objectives
• Statements about the service unit's function or tasks
• Measures about the users of the service
• Measures to describe the service unit such as staffing
• Quality of the resource inputs used by the service
• Measures about how and when the service is used
• Outcome measures
• Unit costs and charges
• Presence and impact of substitute or complementary services

---

The model was an attempt to reply to the many criticisms of existing information sources. Among the key elements which had not been included in national statistics were: estimates of likely community needs; statements of a department's policy (without which it was difficult to measure performance in relation to objectives) information on the characteristics of users (in order to interpret routine data) the pattern of service receipt; outcome measures to judge effectiveness; and an outline of other agencies providing a service.

Within this model SSRG produced a range of indicators – some of which it was advised should be routinely collected as part of management information systems, some of which should be part of once-off collections, and others which provided qualitative information to occasionally supplement the routine information. Indicators were drawn up in conjunction with some social services authorities in a review of their management information systems. Each indicator was related to a policy or objective. For older people, these centred on the departments' overall policies to support the most frail, provide support for carers and encourage rehabilitation. As an illustrative approach, the group applied performance indicators to the areas of residential care, day care and home help services. Examples of the group's performance measures for home care services are set out in Table 3.3. In addition, PIs were developed to reflect the measurement of certain objectives relating to policy. These included: assessment, choice, responsiveness, service

Table 3.3
SSRG's performance measures for home care services for older people – policies (Barnes and Miller, 1988)

Policy area	Management information	'One off' collection	Qualitative measures
Maintain independence of most frail	Hours/client: inference from low numbers of high support cases that numbers of very frail are low.	Measures of dependency. Number of admissions to homes for elderly/day care by number of hours of service	'Feel' from home care organisers.
Support and relieve carers	Numbers of clients living alone – if high, inference that those with resident carers insufficiently supported.	percentage of cases with carer support x level. Carer satisfaction interviews.	–
Rehabilitation	–	Hospital discharges who are newly allocated service. Reason for termination of cases – successful achievement of plans?	Working to contracts with clients and carers. Any special rehabilitative schemes.

integration, equality of access, timeliness, resource efficiency and quality of service. These are outlined in Table 3.4.

In some cases data were not available to produce useable measures, but the group's approach represented a step forward in the broader development of PIs for measurement in social services. It was a first step in enabling PIs to be collected at a local level, which could assist local management in judging the performance of specific aspects of their services. The SSRG were keen to point out that their indicators were very much in line with developments like those of the SSI, in that it would be necessary for individual departments to supplement the framework with their own information, particularly with respect to measures of outcome.

It was intended that this model would become a standard reference point in any attempts to review a department's services for specific client groups. Earlier, in 1986, Miller had outlined this model highlighting the way in which management information could be used in social services to measure performance (Miller, 1986). He usefully distinguished between the routine management information collected within social services departments and

Table 3.4
*SSRG's performance measures for home care services for older people –
objectives (Barnes and Miller, 1988)*

Objectives	Management information	'One off' collection	Qualitative measures
Assessment/ review	Percent refused/refusing service. Percentage of reviews achieved.	Reasons for people declining the service (leavers' surveys).	All cases assessed – is there a procedure?
Choice	–	Client satisfaction survey.	Information that clients get. Information available to referrers. Involvement of client/carer in assessment.
Flexibility/ responsive- ness	Range of hours of service delivered. Extent of specialist services – eg. night sitting, clean ups, weekends.	Tasks done. Hours of the day and weekend working. Change of hours over time.	Task explicitly excluded – window cleaning? medication?
Integrated with other services and Carer input	–	Survey of other services received. Carer support x level.	Who participates in assessment/ review. Key worker arrangements. Other services available.
Equality of access	Equity in resource distribution. Impact of charges for service.	Ethnic minority clients and staff. Consistency in service response. Waiting list/under allocation of hours.	Experience of impact of charges on demand. Availability of information.
Timeliness	–	Time between: referral – assessment/ assessment – delivery	Reliability of service delivery as promised.
Efficient use of resources	Travel time as percentage of total hours. Cost of maximum service/cost of Elderly People's Home	Home Help Organiser's time spent on administrative tasks.	Unpaid extra duties.
Quality of service	Sickness and staff turnover.	Staff and client views (surveys)	Complaints procedure.

data collected by research teams, often used to supplement this. Existing
national statistical data collected on social services activity and manpower
were also reviewed. The model the SSRG employed was based on a
recognition of the limitations of existing indicator information. In particular,
Miller made reference to some of the problems inherent in the value for
money guides published by the Audit Commission. Indicators suggested in

the guide for care of the elderly (Audit Commission, 1985), for example, were subjected to scrutiny. Among the problems cited with these data were: the lack of information relating to the private and voluntary sector; a lack of definition and guidance on the use of data relating to intensive alternatives to residential care; misleading treatment of costs; and the difficulty in setting an appropriate level for home help caseloads. In all, there were problems with these previous indicators in that they did not adequately reflect the real world of service provision.

Social Information Systems (SIS) also produced a series of monographs, covering the performance review information for different user groups (Social Information Systems, 1988). SIS saw the need for core information augmented by second order information. The notion of core information approximated to what others have referred to as a minimum data set (Glover et al., 1997; Morris et al., 1990). SIS emphasised in their work that performance indicators are not meant to give insights into every nuance of every case, but rather to indicate areas of concern or interest which can be pursued by more detailed reviews or investigation if necessary. Hence the distinction between core (that is, indicator) and second order (that is, review-based) information.

The experience of the SIS group showed again that it was easiest to collect data from social services departments in order to measure *process* but more difficult to produce *output* and *outcome* data. It is relatively simple for management to use inputs in order to measure the activities of the organisation. However, the changes in organisation brought about by the *Caring for People* reforms meant that the nature of control had shifted to an emphasis on competition between different players in the social care market. In order to measure performance in the future, departments would therefore need to base their data more on output and outcome rather than input (Sumpton, 1995).

Charters and quality standards

In subsequent years, much happened in social and health services to deflect attention away from performance indicators. From 1989 onwards health and social services authorities were rightly pre-occupied with the implementation of the two White Papers *Working for Patients* (Cm 555, 1989) and *Caring for People* (Cm 849, 1989) the principles of the latter being enshrined in the NHS and Community Care Act 1990 and associated policy guidance. However, attention was recently shifted back to how all these changes – some of which were quite radical – can be monitored and interpreted at both local and national levels.

The market reforms and community care changes ushered in by the two White Papers also meant that there were many new or different aspects of policy and practice for local authorities to monitor and evaluate. To some extent, those responsible for collecting data at the national level appeared not to have re-evaluated their data collections to reflect the reforms and changes. For example, nationally there was little or no information on the operation of the market in health and social welfare and no systematic information on all the various stages of care management, nor information on the development of user choice, services and support for carers. All these aspects were key elements in *Caring for People*, yet nationally there was no systematic evidence about them. Indicators were slow to develop to support and monitor these changes at the local level also.

Quality has come to the forefront in recent years, also reinforced by the community care reforms. The Griffiths Report (Griffiths, 1988) and the consequent White Paper (Cm 849, 1989) can be seen to have introduced quality control as a necessary condition to obtaining high quality care (Cm 849, 1989, para. 3.4.9). This can be seen to represent the implementation of a business-like conception of quality for community care (Department of Health, 1992). Departments were required to check that their services were meeting designated standards through the use of regular information and feedback (Cm 849, 1989, para. 5.14-5.15). However, mechanisms by which quality can be measured have been slow to develop. One possible reason for this is the vagueness of the concept. There is also an evangelical flavour in the way it is described by some commentators. Quality is a highly generalised notion (James, 1992, p. 50) and is open to a number of interpretations. It has been variously defined as: the satisfaction of consumer need (for instance, Department of Health, 1992); an absence of faults or failure in the system; conforming to requirements (Crosby, 1979); or 'fitness for purpose'. Quality may also be defined as by Osborne (1992) as a function of the performance of services in relation to their consumers. It is thus another element of performance, albeit one more focused on the receipt of care rather than its wider ramifications, such as that of efficiency.

In business practice, quality can be defined in a more circumscribed way as 'fitness for purpose'. This is because a product must precisely fulfil the purpose for which it was designed, otherwise it will not be fit for use (Osborne, 1992). Here, quality is thus equated with output. However, in social care services quality needs to be more broadly defined. In a general way, quality can be seen in the achievement of outcomes, but these must also be accomplished in an appropriate way. For older people, it is not only the end results of care that matter but also the way in which care processes are carried out – in the context of relationships with staff and the mechanisms by which services are provided. Therefore, in the sense in which it is pursued here, quality concerns not only outcome but also process. It concerns not only services which fit their intended purposes but also ones that are 'excellent in their disposition' (Osborne, 1992). Within the reality of social services provision, the qualities of process are demonstrated predominantly through inspection arrangements.

The emergence of the quality dimension in social care (Kelly and Warr, 1992) calls for more indirect measures of the impact a service has on the consumer. These must be operationally defined in relation to the objectives of care. This means a consideration of wider criteria of performance such as responsiveness, the handling of complaints, consumer satisfaction and choice. Performance indicators have thus to become a part of quality assurance systems, designed to monitor all aspects of service provision including inputs, process and output/outcomes and often the relationships between them. The pursuit of quality thus also requires the setting of more effective standards for services and monitoring progress towards their achievement.

Defining and setting standards

Standards describe the level of service to be achieved (Dunnachie, 1992). Once standards are set, indicators can then be devised which measure the extent to which these standards have been achieved. The setting of standards has been important in a number of ways. First, it ensures that services are judged in a comparable way. The local authority, in its role as purchaser, needs some yardstick by which to compare the different care services on offer. Second, for the user, standards provide some way of judging services, although this yardstick is less developed at present. Third, standards can be used as a reference point, around which the performance of the whole department is organised (Ritchie, 1992).

Differing standards can be set for social care services. Standards can be defined for a range of factors in the production process. Those for inputs are easier for departments to define. Outputs are controllable but standards based on these may not relate well to outcomes, which are not entirely within a department's control (Ritchie, 1992).

Standards for quality

In terms of the application of quality assurance mechanisms, the Social Services Inspectorate have taken a lead through a number of publications about standards and inspection methods for different forms of provision, such as home care (Social Services Inspectorate, 1990) day care (Social Services Inspectorate, 1992) and residential care (Social Services Inspectorate, 1989). For residential care, the Wagner Report (Wagner, 1988) articulated a new emphasis on outcomes, such as the quality of care.

Contracts for community care have been used by many local authorities to revisit the standards of care required in residential care homes and nursing homes, and in many instances to raise them. The majority of local authorities have opted for approved lists or preferred supplier lists of independent providers which require home owners to meet certain standards if they wish their homes to be added to the lists. These contract standards give local authorities the potential to monitor performance with respect to these standards on an aggregated basis across types of home. On occasions, a ranking system such as a 'star rating' has been developed to indicate enhanced quality, analogous to systems for hotels (Peterborough UK, 2004).

The Department of Health has also produced a review of quality assurance initiatives in a small number of SSDs (Department of Health, 1992). In this, it is stated that the pursuit of quality requires ways of measuring performance, giving prompt feedback to staff and including the judgements of service users. The SSI has obtained a wide range of information from departments concerning their performance. Its inspection methods have included formal instruments, such as questionnaires, which are then analysed to produce indicators relating to a particular standard (Mitchell and Tolan, 1994). Gibbs and Sinclair (1992a,b), for example, described a checklist used to inform the inspection process in care homes that attempted to operationalise some of the dimensions within the quality of care literature. This concentrated predominantly on structural elements and their relationship to the process of care within homes. Care was evaluated along a number of dimensions that could be shown to influence overall quality of care. These included the availability of single rooms, staffing, qualification of the heads of home, resident dependency, and building suitability. These dimensions were based on current professional thinking and were intended to act as pointers for the testing of later hypotheses concerning the influences on quality in residential care.

The Department of Health also produced a framework for local community care charters. The idea of this framework was to reinforce the centrality of users and carers to community-based care. The framework set out standards that might be expected of social services departments as they carry out their community care responsibilities (Department of Health, 1994a). For example, standards were suggested for: the times between the completion of the various stages of screening, assessment and service delivery; the speed with which disability equipment is repaired; whether or not day care users have a choice of activities and transport to take them there and back; full and clear information about assessment, services and charges; and so on. Local authorities planning or revising their management information systems were expected to consider how to include Citizen's Charter and Community Care Charter indicators into their management information and performance indicator systems. These developments can be seen as the promotion of adequate information for the consumer in order for the market reforms in social care to work more effectively (Roberts, 1993). It is through the establishment of standards that the service user can make choices between competing services. Charters become a mechanism by which the user is guaranteed a certain level and responsiveness of service.

Measures of quality were difficult to provide in an earlier period of social services history including, as they do, a measure of the 'value-added' attributes of a resource or service. In devising quality indicators, a judgement is required as to what is considered important or what techniques are thought worthy of promotion (Davies, 1968, p. 54). Quality indicators may be used to indicate the fulfilment of policy aims judged important in terms of the wider social objectives of the service. For example, the principles set out in *Homes are for Living In* (Social Services Inspectorate, 1989) sought minimum standards for the residential care of older people through the promotion of core values. These values (privacy, dignity, independence, choice, rights and fulfilment) can be operationalised as measures relating to an acceptable standard of care. For instance, the degree of privacy could be expressed by an indicator relating to the proportion of residents given a choice as to rooms. Choice could be expressed in whether likes and dislikes were addressed in an individual programme. Quality could also be evaluated by the relative prevalence of need-related factors. For example, in US nursing homes employing a standard system of assessment and review of residents (Morris et al, 1990; Challis et al, 1996), a system of quality indicators has been derived from aggregating individual resident information. This provides information, at the level of residents or the facility, on prevalence and incidence of conditions and on both process and outcome of care (Ramsay et al., 1995; Zimmerman et al., 1995; Zimmerman, 2003).

Academic contributions

Throughout the 1970s and 1980s, academic institutions also addressed efficiency arguments in the social services. In particular, they sought to define more precisely the concept of efficiency in the context of social care. A narrow interpretation of efficiency operated within social services at that time (Williams and Anderson, 1975). The value for money judgements, stressed in the performance debate throughout the 1980s, influenced many of the initiatives for large-scale data collection, which have already been reviewed. These were often translated into cost-minimisation policies, which are more correctly a function of economy rather than efficiency (Knapp, 1987b). Jackson (1993) has stated that value for money was able to comment on only one aspect of efficiency, namely technical efficiency; the issue of how inputs are translated into outputs. It said nothing about allocative efficiency, of particular relevance to the production and delivery of social services. Allocative efficiency investigates how the output of a service relates to demand. Is there enough home care, for example, to fulfil the needs of certain groups of clients? Is the range of provision adequate in relation to specific levels of disability? Are services being targeted correctly to those who need them? It is not enough, therefore, for an indicator of output to show increased levels of service in relation to the resources necessary to produce it (the commonly accepted view of economic efficiency). The service also has to be received by clients who truly need it, and it must be targeted correctly to reflect certain objectives, or to comply with certain policies. To permit more advanced work on performance measurement, it is necessary to take more extensive account of some of this academic work in reviewing efficiency.

At its simplest level, efficiency can be thought of as an equation setting out the relationship between inputs and outputs (the 'productivity' of a service). It can mean either maximising the outputs from given inputs or minimising the inputs needed for a given output. So, in these terms, measurements of efficiency would include costs per unit of service (such as the cost per home help hour), and the extent to which this figure was minimised would indicate greater efficiency. However, this simple notion of efficiency ignores ideas concerning the benefits of services, their wider impact or quality. An exclusive reliance on cost has also led to crude assumptions concerning efficiency and left the concept open to attack and misrepresentation. For social care, the idea of allocative efficiency brings us nearer to an expression of efficiency in the context of service provision. It relates costs of services to their benefits. Several efficiency concepts emerge in relation to social care and each has its own particular measurement problems. It is necessary to make these differing concepts clear as they may be measuring different aspects of performance. Unlike the private firm, social care services exhibit complex relationships in their use of resources and in the way in which these are delivered. Hence, there is a complex differentiation of product. This can have consequences for the way performance is defined and measured. A review of academic arguments also enables us to put the elements of performance measurement defined previously into their proper context.

The PSSRU and 'the production of welfare'

While not part of performance indicator development per se, the work of the PSSRU is important. The PSSRU set up a number of projects to explore, through a Production of Welfare model, various aspects of efficiency in the care management and service delivery of community care for older people. This model frames much of the PSSRU's research work and has been described in a number of publications (Challis and Darton, 1990; Challis et al., 1988). A diagrammatic outline of the model is provided in Figure 3.1. This Production of Welfare model has been used to evaluate the relationship between needs, resources and outcomes in community care and to consider issues such as targeting, cost-effectiveness and the marginal productiveness

Figure 3.1
The production of welfare

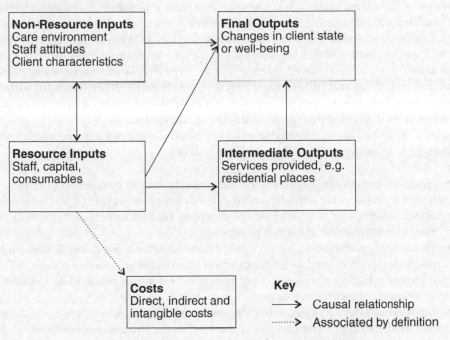

of services (Challis and Davies, 1986; Davies and Challis, 1986; Davies et al., 1990; Challis et al., 1995; Challis et al., 2002). The model is useful for a number of reasons. It enables us to see how improvements in performance can be judged in terms of their influence on aspects of the production process. It also helps to identify some of the criteria mentioned earlier as being important in measuring social services performance. The main elements of the Production of Welfare framework are:

- *Resource inputs* into an organisation or unit of activity, such as staff, capital or volunteers;
- *Costs* of the inputs, usually expressed in financial terms but not always so (for example, the 'non-monetary' costs to other players, such as carers);
- *Non-resource inputs*, such as the wider influence of ideas, 'ethos' and style of work in the care setting, the assumptions and opinions of staff and managers which do not have a monetary value attached to them;
- *Intermediate outputs*, or volumes of services produced in social care by a combination of resource and non-resource inputs;
- *Final outputs*, defined as the changes in the welfare and status of clients produced by the care services; the end result of the process of care.

These elements are in a dynamic relationship to each other and reflect the way in which service elements combine in the production of social care services. If they are considered together, and their relationships examined, it is possible to comment more faithfully on performance in social care.

Examining aspects such as efficiency in service delivery demands that we explore the relationships between these elements. A large part of PSSRU's evaluative work has focused on these issues. In particular, ongoing work, such as that by Davies and colleagues (1990) seeks to examine the relationships that exist between the outcomes for the client and the comparative costs of differences in service provision within local authorities.

The PSSRU has identified five types of efficiency which are useful to outline in this context (Challis and Davies, 1986):

- *Horizontal target efficiency* (HTE) – the extent to which people deemed to be in need of a service actually receive it. Put another way, HTE is therefore about whether or not services are reaching those in need of them and it provides a measure of unmet need;
- *Vertical target efficiency* (VTE) – the extent to which available social care resources are received by those deemed to be in need. More precisely, VTE explores whether those with equal levels and types of need get similar levels and types of services;
- *Input mix efficiency* (IME) – the degree to which the mix of care inputs is adjusted to reflect the costs and constraints in their supply. IME is also about how well different services or inputs are coordinated or used together for the benefit of the user;
- *Output mix efficiency* (OME) – measures the degree to which the balance of service outputs and outcomes sufficiently reflects the valuations placed on them, or in social care, user and carer preferences. OME ensures that the outcomes achieved reflect the aims of intervention;
- *Technical efficiency* (TE) – describes the relationship between inputs and outputs, and how structures, procedures, training programmes and technical aspects of approaching and carrying out care tasks affect the services that users get and how well the services perform.

All these aspects of efficiency have been judged as important in the range of policy documents produced throughout the 1980s, to which reference has already been made. They have also been cited in the Department of Health's guidance for managers (Social Services Inspectorate and Social Work Services Group, 1991). They represent different dimensions to consider in any evaluation as to the efficiency of any unit of organisation. A range of indicators can be used to offer insights into these different measurements of efficiency (Ferlie et al., 1989). Each aspect may be examined in turn to inquire into our present state of knowledge concerning the possibilities for routine indicator information in measuring efficiency:

Horizontal target efficiency refers to the extent to which those for whom a particular service is deemed appropriate receive it. HTE has been difficult to judge without properly conducted studies, but the extent to which needs have remained unmet has been a theme of some reports (Audit Commission, 1985). The measurement of HTE requires indicators of need to be combined with service output data in order to measure the proportion of each target group for particular forms of service who actually receive that service. So, for example, indicators of need could focus on those older people with designated disability such as visual or cognitive impairment, depression or physical frailty. Referral levels or the level of service receipt can then be compared against these groups to assess the extent to which those in need are in touch with services. Appropriate case finding or screening techniques could be used to improve the extent of HTE including attempts at identifying undetected pathology for which an appropriate service response exists (Bowns et al., 1991).

Vertical target efficiency, on the other hand, looks at the distribution of social care services and to what extent it is those in need who actually receive them. It is a measure of the proportion of actual users who are in the target group. Analysis to explore the extent of VTE would therefore concentrate on the distribution of service receipt as against categories of need. Appropriate need indicators can be devised where their relationship to risk or morbidity is known. For example, defined categories of need could be represented by the numbers of those at risk of entering residential care, such as the very old or frail, those living alone, or those having particular conditions such as a diagnosis of dementia. Service receipt data, plotted against these criteria, would indicate the spread of services over defined client populations. If services are spread too thinly over such priority groups, this would indicate poor VTE and the need to target appropriate populations for different forms of intervention. VTE could be improved by the establishment of clear eligibility criteria for services rather than attempting to spread a universal service over a larger number of clients (Bebbington, 1979; Ferlie et al., 1989).

Input mix efficiency concerns the coordination of care. In this respect there is often inefficiency in the provision of care from multiple agencies, concerned with the welfare of an elderly person. The mix of care inputs can be examined by looking at how different agencies combine in meeting the needs of elderly people or by, for example, investigating the allocation of resources between different geographical areas. Indicators representing the supply of different modes of care between hospital, residential care and home care may be used to investigate the cost differentials between them and to judge the optimum mix in desired circumstances. The opportunities for service substitution can then be assessed, such as whether it might be possible to make use of alternative services to achieve the same ends. IME can thus be improved by the development of cost-sensitive care packages and by factors such as more effectively linking formal and informal care.

Output mix efficiency examines the degree to which different components of care are differentially valued. For instance, is the value placed on supporting the carers of elderly people at the expense of providing certain care inputs designed to benefit the elderly people themselves? Should social services concentrate their efforts on providing direct services to elderly people and encourage other agencies to provide support for carers? Are there certain outputs which are more important than others in promoting certain aspects of well-being? Such issues can be examined by the use of indicators which point to the use made of different services and the differential benefits gained from them. Where data on the effects of services (such as improved client well-being) are unavailable, as is usually the case, proxy indicators of process may be devised to comment on these aspects. Thus, indicators examining the content of care packages, such as the proportion of units of different services actually provided to older people compared with the units purchased, can act as an output efficiency index. OME can be enhanced by improving the core tasks of care management: assessment procedures that clearly identify need; care planning focusing on the most appropriate ways to meet need, including the mobilisation of resources from multiple sources; and monitoring that enables links to be made between service provision and improved client outcomes (Ferlie et al., 1989).

Technical efficiency reflects the manner in which services are provided, in other words how care processes operate to define what kinds of service clients receive. Improvements in technical efficiency may not require service configuration to be changed in a dramatic way; many improvements may be sought by a rationalisation of existing resources and the manner in which they are used. An example for routine evaluation might include the procedures by which services like home care or meals take account of travel or delivery costs. Indicators such as the number of hours worked by home helps, when analysed in relation to outputs, represent a measure of technical efficiency. Technical efficiency has been the most thoroughly measured aspect of efficiency using routine data. It could be said to be the type of efficiency most commonly thought of in the way authorities currently measure their performance. One approach to improving technical efficiency might be by developing varied and flexible services that can respond in innovative ways and which are not impeded by established practices.

These different types of efficiency are tools to describe different facets of the provision and distribution of various forms of service and how these might best benefit the user. They are interrelated concepts. They examine how the various inputs into the care process work to meet the needs of older people and whether the services are productive in their operation. Jackson (1993) states that many public services may already be operating close to their efficiency frontiers in the way they are run and so may be operating at close to a technically efficient level. A more significant source of enquiry when examining social care performance is likely to be an appraisal of the extent of allocative efficiency which exists. So, indicators need to be devised that comment more clearly on aspects such as targeting in relation to need or demand and the mix of services available. It may not be possible at present to explore these elements as comprehensively as one would wish, owing to the difficulties in collecting appropriate information locally as well as nationally.

On the output side of the equation, certain improvements in efficiency can translate into improved benefits for the client – an improvement in what is termed the 'marginal productivities' of services. More correctly, marginal productivity can be defined as the greater benefit to the client which is derived from variations in the inputs into care. It is, 'the increment of a final output associated with an increase in a resource or service input by one unit, given the level of output postulated and the need-related circumstances of the client' (Davies et al., 1990, p. 481). The concept asks the basic question; are clients who receive increases in the services offered to them relatively better off, given their existing levels of need, than clients who do not receive a corresponding level of increase? 'Better off', in these terms, is judged according to the final outcome criteria of the service. These criteria include general satisfaction, feelings of vulnerability and welfare shortfalls experienced by the client. Marginal productivity therefore examines the value of additional services delivered to the client, in terms of the variations in outcome judged to be important in maintaining independence. Aspects of the PSSRU's work have analysed marginal productivity as it relates to social care, and a number of techniques have been described (Davies et al., 1990). In essence, these analyses have sought to estimate, using multiple regression, how the use of different service elements, combined with the circumstances of clients, predicts the achievement of certain outcomes. As outcomes reflect the achievement of service objectives, judging the marginal effects of services is of importance in evaluating productivity and performance as a whole and the likely gain from increased investment in one service rather than another.

Davies and colleagues (1990) outlined their data from the first phase of a national evaluation of community care services for older people, across ten local authorities in England and Wales. This was intended to evaluate, *inter alia*, using complex statistical modelling, whether providing greater resources to those persons needing help in remaining at home would reduce the need for residential care. It thus explored, in a research context, the workings of community services prior to the 1993 reforms. In this study, the authors judged the marginal productivities of pre-reform community care services to be low (Davies et al., 1990, p. 290). In other words, the outcomes for the welfare of older people were often quite small in relation to the costs of the care packages implemented. The clients were thus not receiving the full benefits, in terms of factors such as increased functional capacity, morale and relief of disability, of the services provided for them. Final outcomes appeared, in fact, to be small in relation to the increased contribution of resource inputs. To explore the reasons why this might be so, under current service arrangements, necessitates an examination of the performance of the tasks of care management itself. There may be little direct benefit to the client of merely providing additional resources. Better predictions of improvements in outcome may be derived from examining how each care management task relates to the criteria of efficiency, highlighted above. For instance, enhancement of case finding and screening relates particularly to improvements in horizontal and vertical target efficiencies. Improvements in assessment procedures and care planning have direct impact on output and input mix efficiencies. The tasks involved in ongoing contact and monitoring are relevant to attempts at enhancing both input mix and technical efficiencies (Davies and Challis, 1986).

Social services managers can use the insights gained from exploring these different aspects of efficiency to change working practices through improvements in the tasks of care management. This requires information to be generally available within departments concerning the different characteristics of clients in differing categories of need; both the supply of different services and the manner in which they are provided; and the differential benefits that are derived from providing one service and not another. Improvements in the availability of this information and its greater use will tend to lead to better knowledge of how the core tasks of care management are being performed. Greater knowledge of the range of complementary services and the extent of informal care could, for instance, lead to a reduction in the duplication of services. This could enhance the ability of care planning to direct services towards improving welfare for the client, through enhanced input mix efficiency. A greater knowledge of how different procedures affect the kinds of services users receive is likely to lead to better monitoring and readjustment of services in the light of changing needs, thus enhancing technical efficiency. Potentially, better use of indicator information also has the capacity to reduce the necessary crisis responses. It can lead to a more systematic response to changing needs and more accurate feedback to frontline staff to assist in the performance of their tasks.

The real challenge for social services management is to attempt to estimate more complex processes, such as marginal productivities, from indicator information. This is at present difficult with the range and quality of information generally available within social services departments, which also prohibits wider evaluation. In examining outcomes, thought could be given to some of the measures discussed below. These seek to define what are the characteristic end-points for clients of the services provided. Although these analyses could prove technically difficult, it would be a way in which indicators could more truly appropriately measure performance: to identify the added value derived from the use of services matched more appropriately to users' needs and for which the social services department could claim some responsibility.

The production of welfare and performance

The ideas expressed by the Production of Welfare framework have become part of the language of performance. It is a helpful organisational schema by which to review some of the academic outputs in social care with reference to the different stages in the production process outlined by the model. This highlights some of the issues around the feasibility of deriving routine indicators in this setting.

Resource inputs

Resource inputs (such as staff, buildings and consumables) are factors that have received the most attention in past indicator systems. They can be divided into labour and capital inputs. The former comprise the human resources necessary to produce care and the latter the physical plant such as buildings. Indicators of labour inputs usually focus on the numbers of staff (in terms of their 'whole time equivalent' baseline), their hours worked and the nature of the services provided. The first two are traditional inputs and are easily measured. It is when we consider the nature of the services provided that a quality dimension can be added, such as the training, support and adequacy of staff coverage in a particular area.

The range of labour inputs to be considered must reflect the operational realities of the organisation. Hence, routine information on these inputs should include the range of staff with social care responsibilities, such as social services home care and residential staff, but could also include nursing and occupational therapy support. The extent to which inputs also include the contribution made by NHS staff would depend on how these are thought to impact on outputs in a particular local area and the degree of integration in the local configuration of services.

These inputs have costs attached to them and these have been studied in relation to social care services. PSSRU's work on residential care for older people has studied costs as one element in the calculation of efficiency. The more consistent measurement of costs and the use of techniques to explore the wide variations in costs between units or authorities have been pursued in this work (Darton and Knapp, 1984; Darton et al., 2003). In order to examine efficiency more thoroughly, account has been taken of not only the cost inputs into the process of care but also how these influence client outcomes, such as well-being, morale and satisfaction. There are other factors that will also influence costs — such as, for example, the characteristics of homes, resident dependency and the nature of any other services provided.

The insights from this academic work have been influential in the use made of cost data in some of the national indicator packages. Costs, particularly unit cost data, have been outlined for a number of services. Unit costs are usually taken to be an indicator of efficiency, so that a low unit cost represents the more efficient use of resources. However, many other factors might influence the costs of such things as staff, residential places and so on. The considerable variation around the national average in the costs of services such as residential care, day care and domiciliary care, may reflect other factors at work such as variations in definitions; local labour markets; and the local balance of care (SSI/Audit Commission, 1998c). These difficulties notwithstanding, unit cost data can be used to ask questions of individual authorities such as: are the local systems of monitoring service costs consistent and effective? Are cost increases inevitable for particular services? Which unit costs are rising and falling and are there good reasons for this? (Department of Health, 1997a).

This research work is traditionally not seen as a part of PI development in terms of nationally collected data. However, much can be learned from it. It helps to make clear some of the potential problems of using PIs in comparing social services authorities. For example, the assumption that low unit costs are necessarily indicative of good performance can be seriously questioned. This questioning is implicit in the Best Value approach (Cm 4014, 1998). Cost data must be supplemented with information regarding client dependency, characteristics of the service in question, staff characteristics and indicators of outcome. In judging their influence on costs these variables, when considered together, permit a more sustained analysis of efficiency.

Non-resource inputs

Non-resource inputs relate to aspects of the care environment, such as the characteristics of clients and attitudes of staff. They are the less tangible determinants of intermediate and final outputs (Davies and Knapp, 1981; Challis and Davies, 1986). In this sense, *quality of care* — an aspect of the environment in residential and community settings — is more properly considered a non-resource input. It can be measured indirectly by indicators such as staff-client ratios. There are some difficulties of definition in the literature and it is often not easy to see how staffing characteristics such as these relate to the overall output of services. Non-resource inputs are best reflected in indicators such as those of dependency, client and staff characteristics. They are important indicators as they may have cost raising consequences, such as the higher costs in meeting the needs of more dependent clients. They are thus in dynamic relationship with the resource inputs into care and their associations with resource use and cost may be explored to provide insights into how care processes operate (Darton and Knapp, 1984). Indicators of non-resource inputs are, however, often difficult to operationalise.

Need indicators

Early indicator systems included little in the way of judgements concerning client need, even though this is an important characteristic increasingly used to guide decisions. Various need definitions have been described in the social work and academic literatures. Need is an expression of an individual's state of welfare, often with some future focus, so that it expresses how resources should be deployed to cover an individual's future circumstances. It may be considered as a shortfall from an identified appropriate state of well-being (Davies, 1977). It is thus a statement about relative priorities and should therefore guide action. It also must take into account some notion of the expected benefits from services to clients in different circumstances.

There has long been an acknowledgement that service provision within a local area may not match the needs of the local population. It can help an authority enormously if some explicit criteria of need can be established by which to guide the distribution of service resources. The comprehensive study of service provision in social care services for children and older people undertaken by Davies (1968) was a first attempt at confronting this problem. Until that time, there had been a lack of academic work exploring techniques for the measurement of need in social care. No national data were available that could give an adequate indication of the proportion of older people likely to need particular services.

Bebbington and Davies (1980) discussed previous need indicators used to describe variations in the need characteristics of areas. These were imprecise in their ability to predict resource allocation and policy decisions. They described an alternative approach for social care of the elderly based on need judgements for target groups of individuals, that is, groups similar in the circumstances that might relate to their needs for services. This approach is drawn from a survey tradition in social research (Duncan et al., 1974; Brearley, 1975). Some definitions drawn from this approach include need-related groups who might potentially need residential care and others categorised on the basis of personal care, social isolation and independence. Some examples of their need indicators are listed in Box 3.4.

Some broad indicators of need within an evaluative context were highlighted by Davies et al. (1990). These consisted of the probability of admission to residential care, disability, degree of 'diswelfare' of both users and carers, and adequacy of informal support. They modelled the associations between types of services and the need-circumstances of clients in order to examine targeting issues. Need was classified into independent (low need),

---

Box 3.4
*Need indicators for social care of the elderly based on target groups
(after Bebbington and Davies, 1980)*

- Age groups over 75
- Living alone
- Lack of basic household amenities
- Lack of household member to give assistance
- Health hazards at home
- Difficulty with stairs
- Need for assistance with mobility

---

long interval, short interval, and critical interval need (Isaacs and Neville, 1976). These were subdivided into whether the client was supported by a carer.

Other need-related categories, seen as important in research studies, would be difficult to devise and analyse based on routine data and include the impact of life events and social networks (Brown and Harris, 1978; Henderson et al., 1980). It would be difficult to use this type of indicator to determine population-based allocation and expenditure estimates for local authority areas. However, the general theoretical approach can be adapted for local use. Definitions and estimates of need from the survey literature can be translated into indicators, which can help to define need for different groups of clients.

Need indicators are important in pointing to an initial judgement concerning allocation decisions. They assume importance under recent policies where the deployment of services is meant to be based on need as opposed to the supply of services already existing in a locality. If need indicators are combined with those concerning actual service provision, such as output indicators, it is then possible to estimate the extent of under provision, overprovision or correct provision of services in any particular area. This may help to establish whether targeting and allocation of services is adequate in relation to specific policies.

Intermediate outputs

Intermediate outputs relate to the services actually provided by care agencies, that is, what is being done for the client (Institute of Municipal Treasurers and Accountants, 1972). Some see them solely as indicators of performance although, in our terms, they are more correctly interpreted as indicators of service activity, or the means by which policies are achieved. They are probably the easiest of indicators to specify and measure and are relatively easy to use in the planning process (Knapp, 1983).

Data relating to service outputs are possibly the easiest to collect in the context of routinely available information. Most national collections have concentrated quite heavily on intermediate outputs. However, this was not always the case. Davies (1968) cites a number of problems with the early collection of basic output data on older people's services. For example, it was not until the ten-year plans for social services that data on numbers of staff in old people's homes were collected. A further example is that in 1968, when he completed his study, the provision of meals-on-wheels was the only voluntary sector service for which data were available nationally. In his early study, Davies classified outputs as indicators of resource allocation, or the 'number of units of service performed' (p. 52). These included visits per 1000 population and numbers of meals-on-wheels served. It is interesting that, at the time, these indices were classified as 'measures of performance', rather than — in the scheme proposed here — merely one aspect of it.

Knapp (1983) distinguished the broad types of intermediate output in relation to residential care as *levels of provision* and *throughput* measures. Levels of provision are often outlined in national data. They have included the numbers of residents in homes supported by the local authority, the proportion of residents in different age or dependency bands, and the proportion of short stay as against long stay placements. Levels of provision can be a guide to the extensiveness of service. They are useful in comparison with other data, such as staffing levels and expenditure, in order to judge service activity in relation to policy. Throughput measures, on the other hand, relate to indicators such as the number of admissions, discharges, occupancy or turnover in a defined period, perhaps broken down by type of admission such as emergency admissions. The earlier health indicators, relying almost exclusively on hospital provision, made extensive use of throughput measures. Care must be taken in analysing throughput in services like residential care, as this may be a function of mortality rate, which is more properly considered as outcome. Throughput measures are important as they express the rate of production of a service. This has theoretical and empirical links with other indicators of input, expenditure and costs. Knapp (1983) has reviewed some of the more detailed calculations of these measures for the residential care of older people.

Intermediate outcomes represent the achievement of service-level objectives. In discussion, a field social worker, for example, might signal the success of an intervention by reference to the fact that all relevant services were provided for a client. The impact these services had on the welfare of a client would rarely be articulated in an explicit and verifiable way. This is the issue of final outcome, which will now be considered.

Care outcomes

A complete evaluation of how social care agencies benefit their clients is only made possible by considering the final outputs of care; outcomes that are valued in their own right. The fact that the measurement of final outcome defines the organisation's success in pursuing its objectives is stressed by several commentators (Institute of Municipal Treasurers and Accountants, 1972; Brody and Krailo, 1978; Martin and Kettner, 1996). It is a measure of the ultimate effectiveness of a programme of care and must be considered on a wide range. It is here that we find the most difficulty in devising routine measures.

In the PSSRU's work on the Kent Community Care Scheme and its derivatives (Challis and Davies, 1986; Challis et al., 1995; Challis et al., 2002) a number of different outcome domains considered important in the care of older people have been outlined. Destinational outcomes are important, such as the likelihood of entering residential care as against staying at home. Other outcomes are more concerned with the quality of life of older people themselves. These can be expressed by a range of standardised instruments that attempt to explore these domains for social care. Challis (1981), for example, discussed the domains in which to operationalise outcome measures that relate specifically to social care services for the elderly. These include: nurturance, or basic physical care which includes activities of daily living; compensation for disability, including the activities involved in maintenance at home such as food preparation and shopping; maintenance of independence, including the felt independence of the older person in retaining control over their own life; morale, which includes personal growth, life satisfaction and the presence or absence of psychopathology, such as depression; social integration, referring to boredom and loneliness and the presence of confiding relationships; and family relationships and informal sources of help, focusing on the problems of stress and difficulties experienced by family and informal carers. To these can be added Goldberg's (1970) assertion that improvements in safety and comfort, amenities and income, self-care, diet and activities constitute the measurable objectives of domiciliary services for older people. Knapp (1983) has discussed how the measurement of final outcomes relate to the objectives of residential care, stressed in both national policy statements and research studies throughout the post-war period. These are inevitably more narrowly defined than for community-based forms of care. They include: the psychological well-being of residents; their physical, mental and sensory state; the home's mortality rate; and outcomes of significant others in the resident's life. Many of these are further elaborated in Davies and Knapp (1981).

These outcome domains represent judgements regarding the criteria of success for social care services, viewed from the perspectives of clients and professionals. The extent to which they can be translated into routine use as part of indicator sets remains an open but important question. Some outcome measures used in research would be difficult to interpret if used as part of routinely collected data. The collection of information comparable in scope to that of research instruments would also place undue demands on those collecting the data, both in terms of time and expense. There are also further problems connected with the concept of outcome itself. For older people, the outcome of services is difficult to measure routinely as it usually relates to long-term care and is difficult to define and expensive to monitor in practice (Linn et al., 1977). There are a host of factors that may affect outcome, ranging from the personality and lifestyle of the older person to other support available in the immediate environment. It is therefore difficult to assess, to any reliable degree, the extent to which services have contributed to final outcome without recourse to complex multivariate analysis. This kind of examination of routine data is presently beyond the scope of most social services authorities.

The pursuit of such a level of measurement in this context is probably a chimera. There probably is an inherent weakness in translating levels of measurement commonly expressed in standardised research instruments into routine indicator sets. In research studies, instruments are usually only administered at particular points in time. This reflects the wish to test hypotheses concerning the operation of certain aspects of services. They can often fail to detect subtle changes in a client's well-being as a result of specific interventions and may, therefore, fail to reflect service consequences in the real world. If outcome is to be measured more routinely as part of the actual operation of social care services it must, instead, enable actual effects upon the client to be monitored more regularly. However, as we have seen in the discussion of Chapter 2, the problems are not insurmountable. Various types of information that are more easily available can act as proxies for final outcome.

Outcome data that are more routinely available can be used to judge the effects of services or programmes of care on the client. Mortality is one such measure, particularly in residential care, and its relevance is considered to be important for the way it reflects the influence of other inputs and processes. For example, there is the evidence of the higher rates of mortality and morbidity immediately after admission to a home (Wittels and Botwinick, 1974; Bowling et al., 1993; Dale et al., 2001). Indicators of low mortality after admission could therefore reflect a reasonable degree of success in the care offered. Morbidity too can reflect outcome indirectly. Variations in rates of morbidity reflect, in part, the operation of other parts of the care system such as non-resource and resource inputs (Davies and Knapp, 1981). Degree of physical incapacity, for instance, has been shown to relate to the way in which older people in residential care are encouraged to make use of their capabilities

(Lawton and Cohen, 1974). It may therefore reflect the effective operation of staff programmes and routines within the home. A range of other, diagnostic related, data may be used in such routine assessments. These can include: urinary tract infections; immobility; the inability to feed unaided; and the incidence of falls and fractures. Such data have already been used as part of the evaluation of nursing home quality in the US (Zimmerman et al., 1995, 2003) although care has to be employed in the interpretation of these data where there are relatively small numbers of cases with particular needs within homes (Mor et al., 2003).

Generally available indicators of mortality and morbidity, while reflecting outcomes in a more indirect sense, also reflect a number of influences, not just those connected with the care setting. Mortality rates, for instance, are influenced by the personal circumstances of the older person. Morbidity levels too may reflect the influence of certain diseases and biological processes which are difficult to disentangle from the effects of general health services provision. Estimates of case-mix must be included when comparing levels of mortality and morbidity across units or facilities. Outcomes considered in measuring social care performance must also be attributable to social rather than health care.

Attempts at exploring outcome from routine data have included work into the quality of care in residential settings. Shapiro and Tate (1995) used routinely collected administrative data on 15,501 older people admitted to nursing homes in Manitoba, Canada. They analysed outcomes, in terms of mortality rates and diagnostic data, controlling for age, sex, and dependency level using survival analysis techniques. Their outcome indicators were compared across regions and by type of nursing home over a four-year period, firstly at admission and subsequently at yearly review. Due to the nature of the analysis, it was possible to estimate the relative risk of occurrence of factors dependent on resident characteristics, dependency, type and location of home, taking the contribution of each factor into account separately. They state that these outcome indicators should not be treated as definitive signs of the quality of care, rather they could act as 'triggers' for the routine evaluation of outcomes in residential care. For instance, a high relative incidence of falls and fractures in a particular region or home type could reflect inadequate staffing levels, poor supervision of residents, inadequate precautionary safeguards, or a combination of these factors. Exploring routine outcome indicators in this way may therefore point to particular facilities or areas of operation which require further investigation. For example, information from standardised assessments repeated through time can provide evidence of change across large groups of people receiving services, providing scope for routine data to act as a relatively inexpensive starting point for judging the outcomes of care. The most well known example of this is the Minimum Data Set Resident Assessment Instrument (Morris et al.,

1990), which has been translated for use in the UK (Challis et al., 2000). A community version has also been developed for use in the UK (Carpenter et al., 2002). In the community setting, outcome is arguably more wide-ranging, inputs and processes more variable, and needs more heterogeneous, so that both measurement issues and analytic methods become more complex. The introduction of the Single Assessment Process with its emphasis on more standardised assessments should facilitate the production of more readily available data for use in community settings (Department of Health, 2002c).

The concept of outcome emerging from the academic literature runs into problems when we attempt to use it as part of the performance process. It requires special data collections, which do not easily transfer to routine information collections undertaken on a day to day operational basis. Numerous difficulties arise in translation. There are difficulties in expressing the changing circumstances and needs of older people as they receive services. There are also problems in coming to conclusions regarding the influence of particular services on outcome, as so many other factors are of influence, both directly and indirectly. It may be mistaken to attempt to measure outcome in as direct a sense as that contained within evaluation instruments. If a more comprehensive picture of the outcomes for the client is needed, then special studies or consumer surveys will need to be undertaken. In the absence of these, measures of intermediate outputs, such as forms of service provision or throughput, can act as proxies for outcome.

This is the basic dilemma in attempting to translate research measurement into routine indicator information. Intermediate outputs are routinely collected, both nationally and by departments themselves. They are easier to measure than final outcomes, yet it is final outcome measures that provide us with an indication of success in achieving objectives. Standards are therefore relatively easy to set for the outputs of services. However, these rely on the values of planners and professionals about what constitutes acceptable and adequate levels of care. In this way, intermediate outputs do not really measure effectiveness but only the constraints of policy and procedure (House of Commons, 1972). Direct effectiveness measures present problems in availability and cost which militates against their use as routine performance indicators.

The significance of these arguments lies in the insights they give for the further development of indicators. Although much of the academic work, drawn from social policy, management and social work perspectives, has assisted in clarifying some conceptual difficulties (such as the wider definition of efficiency), this has not fed through fully to work on performance indicators. There has been a marked tendency for indicators in social care to concentrate merely on inputs and outputs. The fact that this approach expresses too simplistically the operation of social care services seems to have been overlooked. The issue at present is how these insights can be translated into the measurement and analysis of routine data from social services departments' records.

Applications to social services practice

Some research approaches have applied efficiency concepts to the measurement of performance, drawing on data collected within social services authorities. Gorbach and Sinclair (1989) examined how indicators derived from a computerised client information system were used to monitor the home help service in Gateshead. They analysed how far the service complied with specific policies such as those to provide a targeted, flexible, integrated and equal service. Indicators of need (such as numbers of older people in different age bands, percentage living alone or those lacking use of a bath or WC) were derived from census data. These were related to levels of provision in each area of the department to enquire into whether different patterns of service were related to need. To examine how far the service was targeted towards those with greatest disability, they examined the rate of use of home helps amongst those aged over 75 – a target group seen as at greater risk of entering residential care. Receipt was also broken down by disability level (examined by ability to undertake tasks of daily living). The flexibility of the service was examined with reference to the number of hours per week of home help as against a 'standard package' (judged to be 3-4 hours per week). Hours of receipt were also analysed against disability levels and were compared by home help organiser. To assess how far the home help service was integrated into the pattern of other services, indicators of the number of clients assessed for other domiciliary services were examined by area.

In all, the indicators were used to enable identification of anomalies in service provision that could be discussed with staff so that any changes in policy and procedures could be justified. The authors suggest that their indicators did not provide a comprehensive management system for the service. Only a small part of the available information was used. However, their work illustrates the potential of PIs in monitoring the provision and use of social care services. The possibility of using further indicators to support specific policy objectives was also mentioned. Overall, the indicators were used to raise questions which could be checked against any apparent deviation from policy.

Llewellyn (1994) used efficiency indicators in residential care for the elderly. A ratio of costs (inputs) to quality of care (outputs) was used to analyse data from 100 homes in different sectors of care. Quality of care was measured along eight dimensions: building quality; procedures; regime; medical services; promotion of continence; dementia care; general services; and interviewer observations. The variables chosen followed the SSI guidelines on service standards in homes (Social Services Inspectorate, 1989). The cost inputs were measured both in terms of running costs (costs per bed per week) and standardised costs (total resource inputs, including finance charges). Due to the high quality of care within the homes studied, much of the variation in efficiency ratings could be explained by the wide range of running costs between the homes. The differences between the homes were not as great if standardised costs were used, owing to the greater burden of finance charges on the private homes. This study is a useful one as it discusses some important methodological difficulties inherent in applying such indicators to care settings. These include: the difficulties in quantifying both cost inputs and the valuation of outputs; the effects of confounding factors, such as the inclusion of items that have cost consequences within quality of care measures; and the different efficiency concepts on offer, each of which raises specific issues. The use of efficiency in this study corresponds closely to that of 'input mix efficiency' (Davies and Challis 1986, p. 20), in that it examines the range of inputs in the different sectors of care and how these relate to outputs, in terms of the quality of care provided.

Gibbs and Smith (1989) used data envelope analysis to study value for money in private nursing homes. They studied the expansion in public funding for residential care, prior to the *Caring for People* reforms. Specifically, their analysis was directed towards evaluating whether variations in nursing home charges were related to differences in the quality of provision. The quality dimension included measures of the quality of facilities and upkeep, staffing and management efficiency and quality of care and quality of life of residents. Thus, the study sought to identify the influence of inputs (using charges as a proxy) upon multiple outputs (the quality of overall provision). It attempted to compare charges in a sample of 72 nursing homes in relation to quality of provision in order to determine a 'reasonable charge' for a given quality of care. Best performing homes, in terms of quality in relation to charges, were used as benchmarks by which other homes were evaluated. A reasonable charge for nursing home care could then be based on a comparison with other homes in the area offering similar levels of care. This study is important for the use it makes of a particular procedure for measuring performance. However, the study failed to include measures of residents' dependency, which could be a major determinant of their quality of life in relation to charges for care. This, again, underlines the importance in taking account of possible confounding factors in devising any indicator set.

A small-scale study was undertaken by Hall (1993) in examining the benefits of introducing a performance measurement scheme into the work of a local authority social services department. Some recommendations for good practice in management were also provided. The measurements analysed were not really performance indicators in the true sense, but were derived from a study of individual practitioners' views of performance. The analysis was a situational one, in that it attempted to highlight, through documentary evidence, aspects of performance identified by staff. Thirty performance measures were generated and an exploratory analysis was undertaken to assess their usefulness. Changes in performance levels identified by staff were highlighted as were some problems with the process of performance measurement itself.

These insights, although set in the context of specifically designed research studies, have much to offer the design of any PI system for local use. Efficiency has been a key element and differing ways in which the concept has been operationalised offer different perspectives on the use of indicators in providing comparative information at a more conceptual level. The measurement of efficiency, as stressed in the host of initiatives and policy reports throughout the 1980s, remains ambiguous. Its use has been unclear in public pronouncements and, before a judgement can be offered as to the performance of an authority, the particular type of efficiency measured needs to be made clear.

Measuring achievement in social care

There needs to be a sound theoretical underpinning to work on performance measurement. One of the reasons for the muted development of performance appraisal in social services is the long-running difficulty in measuring the success of social care. Clear statements as to the goals, aims and objectives of social services were sadly lacking throughout the 1980s. In fact, problems in devising measurement schemes by which objectives can be judged have bedevilled social work for many years. There has been a lack of clarity in promoting the setting of goals and in setting out sufficient evidence of effectiveness, in both individual social work practice and the practice of long-term care (Sheldon, 1978; Goldberg, 1981). In contrast to health care, where research endeavour is part of professional training and development, social care has operated in an environment which does not tend to support the need for evidence-based learning (Macdonald, 1999). While individual practitioners necessarily formulate specific aims in relation to individual cases, these have not tended to fit into a coherent theoretical framework (Giller and Morris, 1981). What counts as improvement or success for a whole unit or department has therefore seldom been set out in a satisfactory way. This inherent difficulty in defining objectives precisely has meant that evaluating performance against these objectives is often contested.

There is a sense in which the personal social services share with the health service a number of problems in evaluating performance, which have already been considered in Chapter 2. Klein (1982a) summarises these with reference to the fact that these organisations exhibit: a high degree of complexity, with large numbers of staff involved in a wide range of service provision;

heterogeneity, with many different activities being carried out; and uncertainty, as to the precise relationship between inputs and outputs. For any form of service there are a number of types of objectives which can be articulated. Some can relate to the training and supervision of staff, some to the actual running of services and others to the eventual outcome of the service for clients. So, for example, translating the language of 'output budgeting' into a social services department presents many difficulties. The main one being the variation in services received by a typical client-base. Each one of these services will have its own objectives and relating these to indicators that can express the performance of the whole department is difficult.

This myriad nature of objectives in social care has meant that it is difficult to devise PIs which adequately reflect the nature of the service under review. Much of the information routinely used in departments is chosen for its availability rather than its appropriateness in judging the success of objectives. A variety of performance information is usually needed and it is necessary for many SSDs to supplement their routine management information with service review data or commissioned research. However, theoretical models which could assist in formulating and measuring the achievements of social services have been slow to develop.

Indeed, as far back as the late 1960s this was recognised by Davies (1968, p. 55) who, in investigating the concepts used to distinguish service elements, pointed to an absence of theoretical work by which achievements could be judged. This lack of theoretical specification has also had an effect on the types of data collected centrally from local authorities. A vicious cycle of data paucity has developed; authorities, not guided by any coherent framework, have failed to collect data of relevance to their day to day operations. Central government, in turn, has not always requested relevant information which could fit into an overall scheme for judging the effectiveness of social services on a national level.

More recently, a number of authors have examined the difficulties in setting objectives and measuring achievement in social care services. Bamford (1982) has spoken of a management by objectives approach to social services. This involves clarity in setting objectives and the processes by which they will be measured. Objectives must be defined behaviourally, such as targets for an increased volume of service, rather than by global statements that cannot be observed directly. This type of approach has been used on a case-by-case basis in some teams (Parsloe and Stevenson, 1978). However, these authors questioned the extent to which it has been used more widely in measuring performance at a local departmental level.

Bovaird and Mallinson (1988) outlined a hierarchical approach to the setting of objectives in social care whereby certain activities within a service unit were logically related to one another in order to explain the eventual impact of the service on the user. This eventual outcome objective may be difficult to define precisely and it is also difficult to establish how activities necessary to bring this about relate together in a coherent way. It is important to measure objectives on a broad level such as this, as the achievement of objectives on one level may not follow for the achievement of objectives on another.

These considerations are part of a general hierarchical model of evaluation outlined by many writers (see St Leger et al., 1992). So, for example, the overall goals of social care for the elderly (the ends to which we aspire) are ultimately very difficult to define with any precision other than by broad statements of intent, such as maintaining an acceptable quality of life for users in the face of disability (Challis et al., 1996). The aims of services (the ends through which goals may be realised) need to be more concrete and relate to specific targets, such as supporting older people to remain in their own homes or, if this is not possible, to safeguard their rights within a residential environment. Service objectives, however, are operational tasks which must be completed to ensure the achievement of aims and goals. So, for example, an objective of social services for older people might be to divert users away from residential care if this is at all possible. Because objectives are part of the operational tasks for any department they are often set as policy standards. These standards can be operationalised quite precisely within an individual department. PIs can comment on these objectives by the comparison of one indicator with another or over time. For example, an indicator measuring the proportion of clients assessed at home according to dependency can be compared with the proportion of long-term residential placements by dependency, as a measure of the success of a diversion objective.

Although PIs will mostly be used to comment on objectives, they can also be used to measure the achievement of wider aims, although their use in this context is more contentious. For example, the respect of individual independence and rights in residential care can be measured by more qualitative measures or residents' perceptions of the care processes at work. It is extremely difficult to identify PIs for overall goals as there is often no comparable yardstick to measure their achievement.

Performance indicators can be used as tools to define service objectives more clearly and to measure achievement in relation to specific targets. In this context, they must relate to observable results which can be expected from the pursuit of particular policies (Bovaird and Mallinson, 1988). In other words, they should signal the intentions of specific policy. This is not merely a technical exercise. Providing linkages such as this to enable performance measurement to take place may help staff in a department to become more acquainted with the objectives of the organisation. Defining objectives in a hierarchical manner is an approach which has been used in the broader local authority context (National Consumer Council, 1983). This approach has several advantages but may be difficult to implement in social care agencies owing to the differing interpretations of valued objectives voiced by various stakeholders such as staff, users and carers (Ritchie, 1992).

A major theme in devising indicators of performance for social care is therefore how these can be placed within an integrative framework which enables all relevant aspects to be monitored. Such a framework would help to structure the design, collection and interpretation of indicators so far discussed (Kendall and Knapp, 2000). The Production of Welfare model, described earlier, has permitted some theoretical developments to take place. It has provided the framework to structure some of the academic material on social services indicators. Of further importance is structuring an indicator scheme for social care which reflects the particular nature of social services activity. This involves going beyond existing business models (for example, Cummings and Worley, 1993; Pugh and Hickson, 1968), or those derived from local government described in the last chapter. The Production of Welfare framework provides a possible starting point for this. However, further areas need to be addressed.

Problems in measurement

The difficulties inherent in the measurement of performance in the public sector mentioned by many commentators (Carter, 1989; Carter et al., 1992; Pollitt, 1986; Ranson and Stewart, 1994) are no less true in social care services. The problems are more than conceptual ones and reflect practical problems and difficulties in the perceptions of key players towards the measurement of effectiveness. The fact that the developments in PIs, reviewed earlier, happened at different times and in varying contexts means that there is considerable variety in their form and operation. This, in itself, poses problems in presenting any firm guidelines for the use of PIs in social services agencies. A number of problems have been highlighted in the measurement of performance indicators and are reviewed below with their particular relevance for social care:

• There are multiple, often conflicting, objectives in social care. Care for an older person for example, has numerous components and sometimes implies protection and occasionally control.
• There is a difficulty in measuring the quality of service delivery. How should this be expressed?
• There is organisational complexity within social services departments. There are many service units which are often dependent on each other for fulfilling the functions of the department. This presents difficulties with the ownership of performance, as the ability of one unit to deliver a good

service is dependent on how other units perform (Carter, 1989).

- The criteria by which social care is evaluated are wide-ranging. Efficiency is important but so too are equality of access, standards of care and so on.
- There is a difficulty in finding indicators that are both relevant and operational (Arvidsson, 1986).
- There can never be what may be regarded as a complete set of PIs in public services. There will always be dispute and political compromise. Indicators are not neutral but can be used as a tool for control.
- There is a problem in defining and measuring the final output or outcome of social care services. The reality of this problem should be faced. Proxy indicators of outcome should be used in the absence of individualised markers of client improvement.

The answer to these difficulties is not to abandon the pursuit of PIs in social care but resolve to accept their limitations and make use of imperfect or uncertain indicators until the benefits of their use can be judged.

The limitations of existing information

As opposed to conceptual problems in translating PIs into use for social care, there have also been very real problems in the quality of information sources. Nationally collected data concerning social services activity have shown a number of weaknesses which have hampered the development of performance indicators. As mentioned, there have been technical measurement problems with the national data routinely collected from local authorities. There are few checks on accuracy and, as data sets such as those of the SSI rely on the data of other agencies, there is often a delay between collection and publication. Data drawn up by CIPFA, for example, have become inadequate to monitor the increasingly complex pattern of service provision and are also not directly related to the policies of most SSDs. Miller (1986), in his review of management information, pointed to many of the limitations of nationally collected data for social services:

- There has been difficulty in ensuring client-level measurements of need as opposed to population-level measures.
- There has been an absence of policy priorities adopted by social services.
- Indicators adopted so far have not differentiated between similar services in terms of their functions and quality of provision.
- There has been a lack of integration of information on manpower, service level and expenditure in the CIPFA data.
- Particularly in the CIPFA data, there is a stress on financial information. Factors such as client dependency, service quality and effectiveness can all

contribute to cost variation, but are poorly represented.
- Little account has been taken of complementary services, such as NHS and voluntary agencies, particularly in Department of Health and CIPFA data. Indicators relating to rates of provision are compromised by this fact.
- There is a lack of guidance on how data such as costs are collected, for example for CIPFA returns. There is substantial diversity in the way SSDs allocate staff to different functions which will dictate how this information is collected.
- Indicators have failed to measure aspects of importance to the service user such as accessibility of services, information available, speed of response, flexibility and quality. The concerns of carers too have been under-represented.

The limitations of local social services databases have also been well recognised, especially in relation to the NHS. Targets for the provision of services have not been routinely set so compliance with a standard is difficult to measure and evaluate. Other limitations of routinely generated data were pinpointed by Barnes and Miller (1988) in their review of performance measurement in social services:

- Most management systems provide only static information —for example, occupancy figures in homes rather than dynamic information concerning turnover.
- Information systems concentrate on activity levels and finance to the neglect of information on service users and the impact of services on them.
- It is difficult for information from different sources, say staffing, service characteristics and service user information to be brought together in a coherent system.
- The outputs of existing information systems do not relate to the policies of a department or to management processes.
- Motivation for staff to input into the system is low due to the lack of adequate feedback to them of the uses of the information.

These limitations lead to the requirement to develop information systems more in line with current service arrangements and policy objectives. Information needs to be more integrated at the local level to include financial, service and staffing data within a system which can reflect the fluid nature of the demands and priorities within social care. It would be helpful also if PI systems could be integrated into operational systems to prevent duplication of effort by staff charged with inputting the data.

More recent developments

The monitoring of community care

A number of more recent developments have led to a review of existing indicator packages and made it necessary to refine the information on offer. Not least, the implementation from April 1993 of the community care reforms had a profound effect on the management and delivery of social services for adult client groups. The Key Indicators for social services may make it possible to monitor the implementation of the reforms by providing comparative data over time. However, the change in focus consequent on the reforms called for a thorough review of indicators to more faithfully reflect the reality of current service arrangements.

In the early 1990s, some authors made a start in attempting to relate performance indicators more closely to the reforms. Hoyes et al. (1992) conducted a small-scale study to evaluate the ways in which four social services departments had responded to the changes. They discussed some of the issues in performance measurement and began to highlight some of the ways in which indicators could be related to performance criteria in social care. Their study collected baseline data for eleven social services departments with data collection for four authorities after the reforms. Much of this was from existing national data collected from CIPFA and the DH but data were also collected locally from the authorities concerned. The study also referred to the level and sophistication of the information systems in the authorities with some common deficiencies being identified. Information concerning inputs, such as numbers of staff and expenditure, and that of outputs, for instance number of day care places, was more readily collected. There were, however, difficulties in producing information on processes of assessment and service delivery due to limitations in information technology. The study concluded that while there might be evidence of improvements in some of the technical aspects of performance measurement, inadequacies in social services information systems at the time may have prevented a full assessment of the impact of the reforms.

Murphy and Stroud (1996) likewise pointed out that data sets existing at the time did not make it easy to match up the health and social care delivered to one population. They concluded that centrally collected data did not enable the assessment of service deployment and outcomes against individual needs assessments. There was seen to be considerable room for innovation and inquiry in the way relevant data are defined and linked together in order to respond to the reforms.

The management of care management

Allied to the broad changes brought about by the reforms of community care, there has also been a growing need to consider how best to monitor the performance of the core tasks of care management at the local level. Much debate has focused on the information needs of care managers themselves in defining eligibility and levels of service. However, managers in departments will also require information with which to monitor the progress of assessments and packages of care across areas and also over time. The guidance available for managers (SSI/SSWG, 1991) discussed some of the changes in the culture of information gathering necessary to support these changes. The information required is not only that which is readily available, such as costs and the supply of services, but also the quality of the care that is provided; a focus more on outcome than on traditional inputs and outputs. There also needs to be a greater willingness to engage in the systematic recording of a department's activities and the extent to which care plans are implemented.

Thus, since the community care reforms managers have needed to discover ways to monitor the process of care management itself. This could call for quite sophisticated data to provide indicators of client need that can feed back into the service planning system. Indicators other than those traditionally examined were necessary such as response times, user and carer involvement and explicit criteria for decision making in each case.

Social services performance measures – the Department of Health revised framework

In 1994, the Department of Health undertook a review of its Key Indicators of social services performance in order to make them more relevant to changing service arrangements, particularly the community care reforms (Department of Health, 1994b). The working group involved in this review developed a framework for indicators for adult services. This aimed to reflect the context of the reforms, in particular new procedures for staff and the extent of the achievement of aims relating to improvements in services and in the welfare of clients and carers. An outline of the framework is set out in Table 3.5. From this, a number of examples were put forward of indicators which would permit the monitoring of the aims and objectives of current service provision.

The Department of Health's revised framework set out the aims and objectives of social care services in relation to the *Caring for People* reforms. Some examples of possible indicators of performance are listed in Table 3.6 against the aims and objectives supported by this policy. While offering real improvements, many of these succumb to similar problems as the indicators already outlined, particularly the difficulty in establishing final outcome measurements for social care services.

Table 3.5
Department of Health revised framework for adult Key Indicators (Department of Health, 1994b)

Policy issues

Community care reforms
Supply led services–Needs led services
   Institutional care–Community care
         Public sector–Mixed economy
      NHS auspices–Local government auspices

SSD policy
Local issues

Policy on provision for specific client groups
Procedures / mechanisms:
Assessment and care management
Planning
Promotion of independent sector
Arms length inspection
Involvement of other agencies
Development of multidisciplinary services
Development of complaints services
Training

Aims supported by objectives:

Improved targeting in relation to needs by:	Proper assessment of need and good care management
	Effective discharge arrangements
Improved range and mix of services by:	Development of domiciliary, day and respite services
	Practical support for carers
	Development of flourishing independent sector
Improved provision for specific client groups by:	Implementation of care programme management
Improved efficiency by:	Promotion of greater competition
	Clarification of role of agencies
	Introduction of new funding structure
	Management of the market
	Joint commissioning
	Value for money
Improved quality by:	Improved response times
	Improvements in training and qualifications of staff
	Delivery of agreed care packages
	More homely residential care
	Complaints procedure

Managing departmental performance

During the 1990s there were attempts by the Department of Health to set a context and provide performance information to better serve the needs of social services managers according to local priorities and procedures. Much of the context for this was the community care reforms and their effects on service delivery.

A review of performance trends for social services in England was produced in 1997 (Department of Health, 1997a). This attempted to provide feedback to individual department managers from the statistical returns they send to the Department, as part of the Key Indicators package. It aimed to provide information on service trends, quality improvement and costs for all social services departments. The intention of the document was not to provide comparative data but to enable local authorities to ask their own questions about service development in line with national trends. The publication stressed expenditure, costs and outputs. Questions concerning service quality were raised through indicators such as staff-client ratios in residential care. Those concerning efficiency and effectiveness were raised by the use of indicators of service activity and spending. Analysis of the numbers of people supported by the local authority in residential care and comparisons of unit costs between the local authority and independent sectors were used to investigate the operation of the community care reforms by treating balance of care as an aspect of performance. Thus the extent of service provision to help people remain in their own homes, the use made of the independent sector and the costs to local authorities of residential placements in the different sectors were all analysed by the use of appropriate indicators.

Earlier, in conjunction with Social Information Systems, the Department of Health had produced a workbook outlining how some of the principles of performance management could be implemented locally (Bernstein, 1994). It was intended to draw on the experience of departments that had already put in place mechanisms for performance management. The intention was for the workbook to be used by management to provide a review of all management activities, to act as a tool for planning by the setting of standards and as a stimulus to reflection by individual managers. The workbook also contained an audit checklist which enabled management to review their planning in relation to specific services. The management principles in the document were set out around the need for everyone in a department to be aware of evaluative activity and to respond to changes in policy. The document also discussed the wider structure for performance management activity, which is outside the scope of this book. Some of the issues in the implementation of such a structure are outlined in Chapter 7, where the use made of indicators within a social services department is discussed.

Table 3.6
Examples of social services performance indicators with reference to community care policy (Department of Health, 1994b)

Aims and objectives	Indicator information
Improved targeting in relation to need	
Proper assessment of need and good care management	Number of assessments, referral times, number of packages agreed, unmet need, eligibility criteria, outcomes. Dependency levels (age as proxy?)
Effective discharge arrangements	Destination on discharge from hospital, care packages agreed for discharges, re-admission rates.
Improved range and mix of services	
Development of domiciliary, day and respite services and practical support for carers	Volume of day and domiciliary services provided, intensity (no of clients), Change in balance between day and residential care, improved mix of services, number of packages of care, respite care.
Development of a flourishing independent sector	Balance between LA and independent provision, change in balance, number of new businesses.
Improved efficiency	
Promotion of greater competition	Unit costs/prices for LA/independent provision, Overall expenditure on services, expenditure in relation to population.
Management of the market	Overall provision of residential and day/domiciliary care in relation to population, occupancy rates of residential care, creation and closure of businesses.
Introduction of new funding structure	Overall costs including DSS expenditure, Unit costs.
Joint commissioning	Number of people receiving NHS and SSD care, cost of 'joint' care packages.
Value for money	Cost of care packages, unit cost of residential care, charges to users.
Improved quality	
Improved response times	Time from referral to assessment, time from assessment to service delivery or decision not to provide service.
Improvements in training and qualifications of staff	Range and qualifications of LA employed staff, Qualifications of residential staff and domiciliary staff.
Delivery of agreed care packages	Review procedures, measurement of successful outcome.
More homely residential care	Match of accommodation to assessment and user wishes, resident/staff ratios/ other measures of quality?
Complaints procedures	Number of complaints – response times.
Improved provision for specific client groups	
Reducing role of long-stay hospitals	Provision of residential/nursing care for each client group.

The social services White Paper – 'Modernising Social Services'

The White Paper, *Modernising Social Services* (Cm 4169, 1998) set out the government's plans for the improvement of social services for the new century. Many recurring problems with management of services were discussed including the need for better service co-ordination, more flexible responses to need, a greater clarity of roles and objectives, and better consistency and efficiency of services. Performance was a central issue, linked to the setting of new regulatory standards. These standards were set down nationally but a National Commission for Care Standards was established to regulate a wide range of local social services activity including domiciliary care, staff training and, for the first time, local authority residential homes.

The White Paper set out the themes for modern performance measurement, the justification and details of which were drawn from the Joint Reviews by the SSI/Audit Commission (SSI/Audit Commission, 1998a,b). Benchmarking was a central theme – to 'drive up standards to match those of the best'. The government planned to honour best practice authorities with 'beacon status' as providing centres of excellence. The establishment of criteria to measure outcomes was also an important imperative with the establishment of satisfaction surveys as one element. The White Paper drew on the Department of Health's *National Priorities Guidance* (Department of Health, 1998b) in setting national targets and standards for social services departments to achieve in the medium term. These are set out in general in Box 3.5. These targets established the mechanism by which local social services authorities are accountable to government.

The responsibilities of local authorities were set out with a clear role for central government to intervene to ensure that defined standards are met. The government was to produce an annual report detailing the performance of each social services authority in relation to these targets. A departure from prior performance initiatives was the linking of performance targets to finance, whereby a condition of receiving extra funds was the achievement of these desired objectives.

Another theme of the new proposals was a greater integration of health and social care services within a new performance management structure, setting standards and targets for quality and efficiency. A national set of performance indicators was established, after consultation, including some which examined the interface between health and social care. These were emergency admissions for older people; emergency psychiatric admissions; delayed discharge; and discharge from hospital. These were common to both the social services and health performance frameworks. The consultation document (Department of Health, 1999a) included these within a set of 46 performance indicators for social services. These indicators were intended for local use as well as to comment on the performance of social services nationally.

Box 3.5
National objectives for social services (Cm 4169, 1998)

In general
- To actively involve users and carers in planning services and tailoring individual packages of care. To ensure effective mechanisms for the handling of complaints.
- To ensure through regulation that adults and children in regulated services are protected from harm and poor standards.
- To ensure that workers are appropriately skilled, trained and qualified and to promote the uptake of training.
- To maximise the benefit to service users of the resources available. To demonstrate the effectiveness and value for money of care. To allow for choice and different responses to different needs.

For adult services
- To operate a charging regime which is transparent, consistent and equitable; one which maximises revenue without providing distortions or disincentives affecting the outcomes of care.
- To promote independence for those assessed as needing social care support, respecting dignity and furthering social and economic participation.
- To enable clients to live as safe, full and normal a life as possible, in their own home wherever feasible.
- To ensure that people of working age are provided with services in ways which maximise their and their carers' capacity to take up, remain in or return to employment.
- To work with the NHS and other agencies to avoid unnecessary admission to hospital and inappropriate placement on leaving hospital. To maximise health status and independence.
- To enable carers to care for as long as they and the service user wish.
- To plan, commission, purchase and monitor an adequate supply of appropriate, cost-effective and safe social care provision for those eligible for support.

The arguments in the White Paper reinforce one of the central themes of this book. Proposals for initiatives whereby social services can monitor their performance at a local level were put forward but these were set within the context of new national legislation and policy. A national Performance Assessment Framework (PAF) sought to establish national objectives for social care. In the shorter term, many of these key objectives were set out as targets, through the *National Priorities Guidance*. It was intended that performance would be more clearly managed by linking it to financial resources thereby rewarding authorities who exhibit good practice. Where there were shortfalls or failures in performance, it was intended that the government could intervene directly, using statutory powers if necessary (Cm 4169, 1998). This was to overcome an earlier objection to performance measurement, particularly from observers of the Citizen's Charter initiative, namely that it was not stated explicitly what consequences would arise as a result of not satisfying a standard (Pollitt, 1994). Hudson (1999) draws a more insidious conclusion from the proposals. The White Paper redefines the organisation of central-local relations for social services with more centralised control of social services along with a national focus on the performance of each authority.

The White Paper built on and set out many of the arguments already reviewed on the structure of performance assessment. In particular, it placed performance review in social services within the perspective set out in the Best Value system for other parts of local authority services (Cm 4014, 1998). The Performance Assessment Framework modified Best Value to some extent, in order to take into account social services concerns. The system by which performance was monitored is described in Table 3.7. Some examples of the performance indicators with particular relevance to older people are given under each of the areas identified.

The Performance Assessment Framework was designed to guide the regulatory powers set out in the White Paper. It was intended to provide authorities, central government and the regulatory bodies with the measures needed to assess performance across a range of service activity. It was also intended to enable the performance of one authority to be compared with another. The framework brought together other key indicators of performance as well as those of Best Value in a scheme that could comment particularly on social services provision. The indicators were based on data currently available or already planned in order to provide information on a comparable basis for all authorities (Department of Health, 1999a).

After consultation with local government interests, the first release of the new set of PIs against the Performance Assessment Framework was published (Department of Health, 1999b). This showed average figures on each aspect of performance identified in the framework according to Audit Commission groups. These allowed tentative conclusions to be drawn concerning authorities' compliance with government objectives nationally. It was intended that the framework would enable authorities to develop their own performance measurement systems in line with these objectives.

This set of PIs was intended as a first step to developing a coherent suite of indicators to examine the performance of each social services authority. The consultation document stressed that improvements would need to be made in the light of further information. The performance framework related indicators to current national objectives, thus offering the potential to develop other indicators when more local concerns and information came to light. There are certain objectives nationally for which no useable indicators were provided, for example to measure whether referral and assessment procedures

Table 3.7

The social services Performance Assessment Framework, with examples of national performance indicators for older people

Area of performance	Interpretation	Example of indicators
National priorities and strategic objectives	Extent to which local social services are delivering the national priorities for social care – set out in National Priorities Guidance, national objectives and their own local strategic objectives	A5 Emergency admissions to hospital of people aged over 75 per head of population 75 plus
Cost and efficiency	Extent to which local social services provide cost effective and efficient services	B9 Unit costs of residential and nursing home care B13 Unit costs of home care
Effectiveness of service delivery and outcomes	Extent to which services are appropriate to need; in line with best practice; to agreed standards; timely; delivered by appropriately trained staff The success of an authority in using services to increase self sufficiency and social and economic participation and provide safe and supportive services	C22 Supported admissions to residential/nursing home care per head of population 65 plus C24 Number of households receiving Intensive home care per head of population 75 plus C28 Older people receiving community-based services per 1000 population 65 plus C30 Injuries by accidental falls/ admissions for hypothermia, per head of population 65 plus
Quality of services to users and carers	User/carer perceptions and experiences of services, responsiveness to individual need, continuity of provision, involvement in assessment/review	D33 Proportion of single adults allocated single rooms in residential care D35 Percentage of people receiving statement of needs and how they will be met D37 Delayed discharge from hospital of older people 75 plus against per 1000 75 yr olds not in hospital D42 Waiting times from referral to care package D41 Number of carers receiving an assessment against number of clients identified as having a carer
Fair access	Fairness of provision in relation to need Existence of clear eligibility criteria Provision of accessible information about service provision	E45 Number of households receiving non-intensive home care per head of population 65 plus

Source: Department of Health (Cm 4169, 1998) and consultation document (Department of Health, 1999a).

discriminated in an effective way between different types and levels of need. There were also no indicators to assess whether social care workers were adequately trained and qualified. The consultation document makes reference to the fact that measures are to be developed to help fill these gaps (Department of Health, 1999a).

The range of statistical measures available

An integration of the available statistical information concerning social care services at a national level has recently taken place. This is published from departments' returns and there are improvements to both the scope of published information and its collection. Again, the data are available for use by social services managers, academics and government to compare aspects of performance across authorities. For instance, the Department of Health has issued key statistics of local authority personal social services (Department of Health, 1998d). This reports activity and expenditure data for 1997–98 and budget data for 1998–99. It is intended to provide important summary information on a fast track basis. The data contained in this package are used to form key indicators that concentrate on budgets for key client groups (to provide a measure of overall resource commitment), expenditure, and the number of contact hours per 1000 population for home care services. Some of this reflects wider service provision such as the gross expenditure per week in independent homes per supported resident. This can be used to compare provision across sectors.

The Key Indicator package continues to be produced and has recently become available as a web-based system. The most recent package, at the time of writing, contains around 300 indicators, including all data contained within the Performance Assessment Framework (Department of Health, 2005). Where relevant data are available, this package also includes output for the indicators going back to 1990–91, enabling comparisons to be made across time for each local authority. The Key Indicator Graphical System (KIGS) supports the ability to examine performance through line charts and bar charts so that clusters of authorities can be identified by which to compare particular indicators. The package also provides a full list of indicators by indicator category such as those of need, expenditure, budgets and those specifically designed for children's and older people's services. An overview of those indicators for older people's services included in a recent package is set out in Table 3.8.

The Referrals Assessments and Packages of Care (RAP) Project

This was a major development project intended to provide a national information collection in the area of adult community care. It was intended to

Table 3.8
*Selected indicators for older people contained within the Key Indicators
Graphical System (KIGS)*

Indicator	Description
BU02	PSS budget for older people per population 65 plus
EX21	Gross expenditure on older people per population 75 plus
EX22	Gross expenditure on residential care per population 75 plus
EX23	Gross expenditure on nursing placements per population 75 plus
EX24	Gross expenditure on meals services per population 75 plus
EX25	Gross expenditure on day centres per population 75 plus
EX26	Gross expenditure on home support per population 75 plus
EX27	% residential expenditure on older people recouped in fees and charges
OA01	Residential places in homes for older people per 1000 population 75 plus
OA02	% residential places in independent homes
OA03	% residential places in homes for older people in single rooms
OA06	Nursing care places in residential and nursing homes per 1000 population 75 plus
OA51	Number of weekly places in day centres per 1000 population 65 plus
OA63	Households receiving home care where oldest client aged 85 plus per 1000 population 85 plus

Source: Department of Health (2002b)

provide a framework for defining and collecting person based information locally on the main aspects of community care provision and assessment processes. It thus stressed process aspects in contrast to existing central returns, which concentrated primarily on resources and service delivery. Information from the RAP return was intended to monitor care management aspects such as the number of initial contacts and procedures for screening and assessment. The type of information requested from authorities includes: the number of contacts at screening and the actions taken after screening; sources of referrals; numbers of assessments completed; and type of service, for example home care, day care or professional support. This information may be compared by local authority and aggregated to a regional and national level. It can be used to monitor community care activity against important legislative requirements such as that for independent carers' assessments (House of Commons, 1995) and the Fair Access to Care initiative (Department of Health, 2002a). Local authorities will also be able to use the information to monitor their internal provision and develop PIs to make comparisons with other like authorities.

Completed forms were returned by authorities in respect of the RAP project's first dress rehearsal covering the first quarter of 1999 (Department of Health, 1999c). A second dress rehearsal took place in the financial year 1999–2000. Full implementation of this annual collection took place from April

2000. Individual social services departments are expected to complete annual returns and the information required from these coordinated with that demanded from the Department of Health and the Audit Commission.

Overall, the indicators provided as part of the recent initiative are eventually intended to take account of:

- All aspects relevant to the national objectives.
- All key aspects of social services work.
- Outcomes, rather than merely inputs and activity.
- National Service Frameworks (NSFs) for specific groups, setting standards and national service models to guide best practice. The NSF for Older People was published in 2001 (Department of Health, 2001a).
- Each dimension of the national framework, in order to provide accurate and useful performance measures. In particular, local surveys of users and carers will be undertaken to monitor the quality of provision. Further measures of fair access may include indicators on the availability of information.
- The timeliness of data, which will be reported on much more quickly, using data relating to the period immediately before publication.

The modernisation initiative will be judged by its ability to deliver on these and other key principles. During its implementation, individual councils with social services responsibilities may employ some of the contextual information contained in the preceding sections in order to develop and modify their indicators to reflect current demands. The work reviewed in subsequent chapters offers a focus for ways to develop local data which can be set against these national objectives.

Summary

The arguments in this chapter provide a context for material in later chapters concerning the information needs for performance measurement at the local level. However, the wider processes and arguments concerned with a performance management structure for social services have not been extensively reviewed here. Much of the literature concerned with quality assurance and continuous quality improvement in social care addresses aspects of performance improvement, such as shared vision, which can be differentiated from the more technical issues of measuring performance per se. There is an intimate relationship between the activities of measuring performance and undertaking appropriate corrective action but the two processes need to be clearly delineated. This chapter has mainly focused on the design and collection of the measures themselves. Wider debates have been touched on whenever they offer a focus for the development of useable indicators.

Locally managed social services departments need coherent mechanisms by which to measure their performance in meeting the needs of their local populations. There is a long history of performance indicators devised by central government in planning the provision of social care across the country. Some of these were appropriate for their time but now need to be modified to take account of present conditions. In particular, the collection of relevant data failed to keep up with changes in the world of social care throughout the early 1990s, particularly the community care reforms and care management. Although showing some notable refinements, for example the better collection of information on costs, the data still reflect the concerns of output (particularly numbers of staff and facilities) and structure (the resources available and expended on care) rather than wider process and outcome considerations.

In the early 1970s, little was known about which clients were in receipt of what types of services and the outcomes achieved as a result (Goldberg, 1980). The attempts of central government to implement planning mechanisms, by requesting information returns on the nature of services, called for a deeper and more sophisticated awareness of measurement issues than had hitherto been the case. The operation of these initiatives was seriously compromised by the variability in response across authorities and the limitations in some of the data provided. In this earlier period, a framework did not exist to guide the collection of relevant information concerning the operation of social services at a national level. Improvements were forthcoming and reference has been made to many of them, drawing on management, policy and academic approaches. However, indicators in this period can be considered to be imperfect reflections of service activity.

To be effective and have utility, performance indicators for social care need to relate to the particular problems addressed by social services. They should be able to both express the objectives of individual programmes and the wider aims of social care in general. If this is the ideal, we remain some way off it. Historically, the indicators developed specifically within social care have concentrated more heavily on intermediate outcomes (such as the provision of certain types of service) and resource inputs (such as costs and expenditure). While measures such as these have been the easiest to collect, they may fail to express wider processes and objectives. More recent developments have attempted to consider indicators of need and proxies for final outcome which may better serve an integrated system of performance measurement.

Although performance indicator development in social care has contained some major steps forward in approach, there has been little in the way of a substantial review which could claim to mirror that of the Korner committee in its review of NHS information. However, a caveat should be entered here. Despite the Korner data providing a large number of indicators, there was no conceptual framework into which they could be placed. Therefore, although emerging from a thorough review of information requirements, the indicators were not acted upon by many health authorities and there was resistance in some quarters. St Leger and colleagues (1992) have termed such an approach as based on a 'shopping list' principle of data collection:

> '...whereby information is to be gathered because it is believed to be useful, but there is little reference to how it should flow within the organisation, be interpreted or inform decision making. Moreover, this opportunistic and atheoretical approach does not encourage systematic determination of information requirements and thereby tends towards that which is traditionally or readily available'. (St Leger et al., 1992, p. 190)

A point to emerge is the necessity for indicator systems to be part of the planning process rather than divorced from it and also for them to be based on an explicit framework for data collection. There are some lessons for the development of indicators in social care here, some of which are confronted in Chapter 5.

The recent period has witnessed a substantial growth in performance management initiatives. At a national level, the government has conducted a large scale review of its indicators for social care. Clearer objectives, national guidance and targets, monitoring systems and resources are all priorities stemming from the social services White Paper (Cm 4169, 1998) and other guidance. The RAP project in particular has increased both the quality and standard of process measures (Department of Health, 1999c). These initiatives are an attempt to overcome some of the limitations in earlier schemes, such as the original Key Indicator package and that from other academic sources reviewed here. There have also been attempts to measure outcome, in particular, more coherently. The recent range of initiatives also attempt to promote performance indicators for use at a local level rather than merely for use by central government departments. These indicators are placed within the context of a national performance framework to permit some control from the centre in the future running of local social care services.

Many social services departments have made use of nationally available information, such as that of the Audit Commission's performance indicators, those of the Department of Health, and locally produced indicators to monitor their performance. Departments also collect a range of local management information that can be used in monitoring. The measures set out as part of Best Value (Cm 4014, 1998) specify a number of national indicators by which authorities can set targets for their performance. However, despite the increased demand for performance data, there is a danger that local authorities may not devise thoroughly thought-out measures which can comment on the more effective operation of services. In order to develop local data to suit particular requirements, authorities will need to take note of conceptual as well as technical work, much of which has been considered here. Despite the advances reviewed in this chapter, a systematic body of performance indicators for social care, which could evaluate the output, receipt and outcome of care between authorities and for local use, still requires further development. The work outlined in the following chapters is an attempt to rectify this situation. We present the fieldwork conducted in one social services authority, which reviewed local policies and information systems designed to monitor its performance. This work is then placed within a conceptual framework, enabling a more comprehensive approach to performance measurement to be developed. The book then goes on to offer some concrete examples of how performance indicators can be used and from this draws some conclusions for the future.

Chapter 4

The Cheshire Study

Setting national developments in performance indicators within a framework which can be used by local social services authorities is one of the main tasks of this book. This chapter traces the work undertaken by PSSRU in conjunction with Cheshire Social Services Department in developing and implementing a set of performance indicators for use in the department. It outlines the results of staff interviews, which were conducted in Cheshire for the purposes of eliciting views concerning existing mechanisms and how these could be used within a system for measuring performance in a number of areas. This review was set in the context of the overall aims and objectives of the department in serving its older people. The key issues described here are pertinent both to the past development of PIs, outlined earlier, and to the work of other social services departments who might wish to review their own performance measurement systems.

During the 1990s, Cheshire Social Services Department (SSD) commissioned the Personal Social Services Research Unit (PSSRU) to recommend and then help to implement and monitor a set of performance indicators for services to older people. It was intended that the performance indicators would meet eight criteria. They would:

- Fit within relevant theoretical approaches to the Production of Welfare and care management;
- Draw on best practice approaches to the development and use of indicators;
- Relate to Cheshire SSD's policies and objectives for older people and in particular the shift towards community-based as opposed to institution-based responses;

- Be set in a wide local context to reflect the policies and practices of other Cheshire County Council departments and other key agencies towards older people;
- Relate to relevant service standards and quality assurance mechanisms in Cheshire;
- Rely on data and other information from a variety of sources, including user/carer feedback;
- Be set within a managerial system for taking remedial action to exceptions; and
- Be developed to be valid, reliable, timely and effective over time.

The first two of these criteria, relating to theory and conceptual issues, have already been considered. Relevant theoretical approaches will be further detailed in Chapter 5. The rest of these broad intentions were initially agreed and discussed in a series of meetings, which will now be described in the context of Cheshire SSD at that time.

The Cheshire context

The county of Cheshire

Cheshire was at the time one of the larger shire counties with (before local government reorganisation in 1998) a population approaching 1 million people. It has a growing population, a buoyant economy and, with an expected 30 per cent increase in the over 85s in the next 10 years, a need for a wide range of social care services for older people. The provision of community care increasingly needs to take account of the needs of people with different cultural or racial backgrounds. Approximately 2.8 per cent of Cheshire's population were born outside the UK.

At the time of the study, Cheshire Social Services was devolved to six operational Social Services Districts through district managers. Financial resources were allocated to districts to take account of broad population figures for relevant age groups and also indicators of social stress and deprivation. Planning for community care in Cheshire has taken account of various national data in predicting the likely levels of need for key groups. For instance, using Audit Commission figures based on the number of high dependency older people likely to require residential or nursing home care, the department estimated that there was an overprovision of this type of care in Cheshire as of April 1992. There was thus found to be great scope for enabling more people to stay at home through its community care policy.

The Cheshire Community Care Plan, along with local District Plans, published the information about services, priorities and resources in the development of current and future services. Much had been accomplished in the preparation for the changes in service delivery consequent on the community care reforms of April 1993.

Quality assurance

In Cheshire's Community Care Plan of April 1992, it was stated that service quality is consequent on a commitment by all relevant agencies in the provision of community care to organise and deliver services which are effective in meeting the needs of consumers. Quality in this context meant 'fitness for the agreed purpose'; if it could be demonstrated that services were actually meeting the purposes for which they were intended, then quality is assured. This requirement for quality services meant that the local authority needed to set clear objectives for its services. Performance outcomes, indicators and targets needed to be outlined and agreed by service users and ways found to measure them in order to ascertain how they were being achieved. In developing service quality, Cheshire SSD set store by 'building in' ideas about quality into its framework of services, rather than seeing it as an abstract entity imposed from the outside. Cheshire SSD produced its own 'Cheshire Standard' in order that all its contacts with service users could be governed. It is within this context that performance indicators were needed.

Current information systems and developments

Cheshire SSD has a long-standing commitment to the use of information systems and appropriate technology in support of policy and practice development. At the time of the study, within Cheshire, aggregated information about community care and care services to older people was fed back from computerised systems in a number of ways, notably:

a. Routine financial tables generated from the Financial Information System for Cheshire (FISC) showing spending in the financial year compared with estimates, and predictions about final outturn expenditure. Monthly financial data were also available showing spending in the financial year.
b. Monthly 'Mapping the Market' reports, showing numbers of people with different dependency levels placed in different types of homes per district, and also showing spending on placements per district.
c. A considerable number of routine reports from the department's mainframe *Client Record and Resources Information System (CRRIS)*. Examples of these are listed in Box 4.1.
d. Surveys with other north west authorities on activity in residential and nursing homes reporting on admissions, turnover, respite provision and occupancy levels.

Box 4.1
Cheshire CRRIS information

- Routine print out of home care referrals, open cases, closed cases, reasons for referral and reasons for closure.
- Monthly caseload lists on a ward basis showing referrals, priority cases, cases closed and placements in residential care homes and nursing homes.
- Monthly referral statistics to each team and unit showing referrals open at the start of the period, referrals opened and referral reasons in the period, and referrals closed in the period.
- Monthly feedback on screening and assessment activity from a recently added CRRIS module.
- Monthly feedback from planning forms completed on cases where service gaps are identified giving information on the types of services needed and where.
- Routinised six-monthly feedback of formal complaints made about services or the way services were assessed, provided or charged for.
- Annual reports from the Inspection Unit which includes figures and commentary on complaints made on public sector homes and independent sector homes in each district and details of registered residential care homes for adults.

Another information initiative was the development of a 'Care Planning' module for CRRIS to complement the screening and assessment module. The care planning module was designed to apply to all adult service users, covering their age; social services' aims, objectives and timescales for intervention; case category and dependency/care band; how reviews were to be achieved and the form of monitoring; whether residential care was appropriate and various placement needs and other details; and whether community-based care was appropriate and which services were to be provided.

In addition, business management was introduced in Cheshire in an attempt to develop a more business-like approach to the purchase and provision of services. The tasks of business management included monitoring internal and external market activity, validating purchasing behaviour to ensure resources were effectively managed, planning for the future, and providing performance management information and analyses to purchasers so that performance targets could be set, assessed and monitored. The tasks of business management and purchasing support are set out in Box 4.2.

Box 4.2
Business management in Cheshire

- Mapping the market for social care services.
- Monitoring internal and external market activity, validating purchasing behaviour to ensure resources are effectively managed, and planning for the future.
- Carrying out market research.
- Providing business and other information to purchasers to help their decision-making.
- Providing performance management information and analyses to purchasers so that performance targets can be set, assessed and monitored.
- Providing information to purchasers so that contracts can be monitored effectively.
- Managing, resourcing and coordinating the district's community care planning and resource planning processes.
- Developing and managing customer reception facilities so that local communities can have ready access to information about their eligibility for council services.

Aims and objectives of services for older people

While the goal of long-term care for older people is often the maintenance of as high a quality of life as possible in the context of chronic disability, it is difficult to measure whether this is achieved in practice. In line with earlier arguments about the proper use of performance indicators, it was thought necessary first to place this work within the context of the SSD's overall aims and objectives for services to older people. Cheshire SSD's aims for services for older people were located in two key documents, a statement of intent (undated) and community care plans for 1992/93 and onwards.

In the statement of intent some broad principles were laid down. They are summarised in Boxes 4.3 and 4.4 with a distinction made between outcome aims and process aims.

To implement its statement of intent, Cheshire SSD set store by establishing appropriate and effective financial and information systems on the administrative side and assessment and care management systems on the practice side. The objectives of the financial and information systems were to inform purchasers and providers about activity, performance and development needs so that informed decisions could be made. Services were planned and delivered in such a way that needs identified through the assessment and care management process were met. It was declared that financial and information systems should produce analyses of current spending, and should inform each

---

Box 4.3
Principles of older people's services – outcome aims

- Cheshire County Council will provide older people and their carers with necessary and appropriate support to meet their specific needs in terms of care, protection and independence.
- The Council will strive wherever possible to ensure that older people are supported to remain in their own home.
- Where care in accommodation other than the old person's home is required, it will be in a homely setting which continues to respect independence and rights.
- The objective will be to sustain the full potential of every older person regardless of their abilities and with due consideration of their needs.

---

principal officer in reviewing and assessing the need for future spending in relation to budget heads relevant to them.

The *objectives* of the assessment and care management systems were to achieve needs-based assessments within resource constraints and to deliver services to meet need. In the Statement of Intent, it was declared that assessment and care management systems should ensure that:

- Assessments are appropriately available and consistently identify need.
- All users have a care plan within a specified time period, according to their assessed priority.
- All care plans have a named worker.
- All care plans are reviewed within a specified time period, according to their assessed priority.
- Mechanisms are in place to record service gaps and deficiencies.

Within this framework a number of user-focused and service-focused objectives, tasks and targets were set. These may be broken down into seven related components:

Targeted – ensuring the right services go to the right people at the right time, with a focus on high dependency groups and the use of 'promotional ' funding to enable other agencies to provide appropriate care.
Timely – referring to the need for assessment and service processes to support care through timely actions and responses.
Efficient – referring to the best use of resources, and the need to ensure that spending is appropriate to the current resource position, spending decisions are continually reviewed, and unit costs are kept at reasonable levels.
Diversion – by diverting older users from institutional care to community-based care, striking a balance between what is desirable and what is possible.

Box 4.4
Principles of older people's services – process aims

- Interventions will be timely.
- Decisions taken by the Council will recognise and take into account the different needs which may exist between older people and their carers.
- The Council will actively involve families and carers in discussions about service requirements.
- In providing care, the privacy and dignity of users will be respected.
- In providing care, factors such as gender, race, religion, culture, sexuality and social background will be recognised but will not adversely affect users or jeopardise the services they may receive.
- The Council will support, and in situations of risk, intervene to help and protect, older people and carers who are threatened by abuse, neglect and exploitation; and;
- In carrying out its responsibilities, the Council will: identify measurable standards; provide information to users, carers and the public; monitor and review services; and ensure open access to the complaints and appeals process.

Individual – within a context of diversion, referring to non-institutionalised services tailored to individual needs, the range of care plans, the diversity of care packages, and service flexibility.

Involved – increasing users' and carers' involvement in assessment, care management, and related decision making.

Choice – covering the range of services available to users and carers, and the number of options actually offered to them.

The 1994/95 community care plan for the department summarised the principles and objectives described in the statement of intent. The plan covered other issues relating to principles and values that are relevant to the development of performance indicators. These were statements about service principles, financial implications, medical care, equality, joint objectives, reprovision, GP and social work liaison, complaints, and user and public information. These are shown in Box 4.5.

The analysis of these broad values, intention statements and organisational goals provided the PSSRU with a framework for developing performance indicators. The types of performance indicators that were identified referred to outcomes, processes, need and supply. These different aspects of performance were likely to be relevant to different constituencies or stakeholders in the organisation. In order to unravel the complexity of these different perspectives, a series of interviews was undertaken with a range of staff in Cheshire SSD. The findings are discussed below.

Box 4.5
The Community Care Plan for Cheshire (1994/95)

Key service principles which confirm the right of people to:
   Lead a normal life;
   Be treated as individuals;
   Maintain and develop local roots;
   Participate in decision making; and
   Be protected where this is necessary.

Financial implications of services. A commitment to keep users and carers fully
   informed, prior to decisions being made, of any personal financial implications
   of care plans.

Continuing medical care. Where an individual's continuing need for medical care
   remains, that care should be provided free of charge.

Equality. A commitment to provide appropriate services to all sections of the
   community and to foster attitudes and understanding that confront
   discrimination in all its forms. An emphasis that service provision is about
   meeting the needs of individuals rather than fitting people into existing
   circumstances. The department works to the County Council's Statement of
   Intent regarding equality, which covers issues of individual equality,
   distribution, equity, access and equality of involvement.

Joint objectives. A joint commitment to provide social and health care through a
   single streamlined service which is flexible and responsive, and will help
   people live at home or in a homely environment for as long as possible. To
   help achieve this objective, there should be effective multidisciplinary
   assessment, care management and team working for people in greatest need,
   and feedback from users. Other joint objectives echo the Statement of Intent,
   summarised above.

Reprovision. The department and health authorities in Cheshire agree that
   decisions concerning individuals leaving hospital must be based on joint
   agreements, and that each discharge arrangement must identify sufficient
   resources to support the care plan.

GP / social work liaison. To continue to develop and monitor the success of
   individual liaison with practices and the use of a GP referral form.

Complaints. The department enables people who wish to complain about
   services to do so, and provides information and advocacy to facilitate people
   wishing to make complaints. It is intended, among other things, to review the
   information which supports the complaints procedure and to ensure that every
   person undergoing the assessment and care management process is given a
   copy of the complaints leaflet at an early stage.

User and public information. The department is committed to providing a *Guide
   to Community Services* and to review and update any other information
   leaflets.

Method: process of deriving indicators

Information review

In order to help design a set of indicators, PSSRU worked with members of staff in Cheshire to look at the information currently available in the department's systems and its strengths for future development. This part of the project involved 13 semi-structured discussions with staff at varying levels within Cheshire SSD and in various locations. The interviews covered the information staff need to know so that they can do their job, the information they actually receive and examples of recent uses of information.

According to staff, there was broad agreement that information was needed for a number of reasons. Some of the main reasons highlighted in the consultation are reviewed in Box 4.6.

Box 4.6
Information needs of staff

- To assess whether policy and practice goals have been achieved, and whether goals or actual practice need reviewing.
- To help monitor the shift from residential care to community based services, associated costs and safety risks taken.
- To assess and plan for users' needs.
- To manage work, workloads and caseloads.
- To monitor and assess service performance.
- To set out parameters and monitor spending.
- To set out what providers are offering.
- At the time, to prove to the independent sector that STG spending was appropriate and that the 85 per cent rule was being followed.
- To provide comparisons between districts and units on key policy and practice areas.

Information shortfalls and inadequacies

There were comments and criticisms by staff of the reports and routinely generated information systems currently in use. These have been divided into general comments that apply to several or all reports or systems and comments about specific reports or systems. They are summarised here to indicate their general validity about information systems then in use. It must be remembered that these comments were made in the setting of a relatively 'information rich' organisation at that time. The situation in many local authorities was likely, therefore, to have presented greater difficulties.

General issues

Staff considered that the implementation of the NHS and Community Care Act and other initiatives had taken up much of their energy and resources. Therefore information was often given lower priority. Little information was collected – directly or indirectly – about the views or wishes of users and carers about the services they needed and the service they actually received; an area where many staff would have liked to see positive development on a systematic basis. There was little information about users' service careers, outcomes and time taken to deliver services.

A focus on spending controls was seen by some as diverting thinking about service aims and indicators. Attention was seen as more properly focused on service performance in pursuit of departmental aims such as diversion and choice.

None of the routine reports clearly addressed equity issues, such as ethnicity. This was not a mandatory field on the computer.

Exceptions were hard to identify as there were no pre-set limits or levels which, if breached, might signal shortfalls in performance. The only exceptions to this were financial reports where there were financial estimates (and hence targets) for each budget head. Although reports compared districts, there were no pre-set guidelines to tell managers when they might be out of step with other districts.

Performance data on other local authorities were available from the usual sources – Audit Commission, Department of Health, and CIPFA – but little use was made of them. Principal reasons were their broad-brush nature and lack of timeliness. Some staff did not see it as their role to be concerned with such comparative data.

The information provided rarely came with interpretation, generated many questions, provided few answers, and did not seep down into the department. Information was disseminated within the department according to status and hence did not always reach those who needed to see it on a timely basis. In particular, there was limited dissemination of budgetary information. Some staff trying to manage budgets had to pro-actively request financial information from the system.

Comparative data were produced, and senior managers and principal officers invested considerable time in exploring inter-district comparisons; yet the implications of the figures were rarely discussed between districts, teams and units below senior management levels. Little or no systematic data about the activities of other County Council or local NHS services were routinely received.

There was often duplication of information from both manual and computer systems. The computerised systems failed to collect and/or feed back key information for local management and there was therefore a need for localised manual systems. Manual systems, while laborious to analyse, are at least under the control of their keepers, and can be amended to reflect new demands for information in less time than department-wide computerised systems.

Specific issues

Specific comments fell naturally into those dealing with financial information and those which dealt with purchasing/commissioning and care management information.

Financial information

Financial information ensures probity and facilitates the financial management of a department's affairs. While this information did not directly address the shift from residential care to community-based options, it highlighted scope for flexibility. Below service manager levels, little budgetary information was made directly available. For example, team leaders did not receive monitoring information about their purchasing activities and hence would have to carry on purchasing until a line manager formally told them to stop.

Purchasing information

Reports which mapped the care market were considered to be very useful to those who received them, although direct circulation was limited. The existence of linkages between placement and dependency levels was seen as crucial in examining care decisions. This information suggested useful inter-district comparisons. Policy and practice issues were picked up and explanations requested. A suggestion was that quarterly feedback on placements would allow for trends to be discerned more easily and remedial action to be more appropriate.

Care management information

Problems were reported with both the input and output sides of the computerised information system. On the input side, the system was said to be very demanding of practitioner time due to hardware scarcity and need for staff training. The system was a client index and did not collect data on the work done and the help given to service users. It was reported not to reflect the reality of hospital social work as there was not scope for the system to amend assessment information other than to artificially commence a fresh episode, even when the assessment was being updated in changing medical situations. On the output side, routine feedbacks from CRRIS were very limited in scope. Routine caseload lists were seen not to reflect workload and to be inappropriate to settings, such as hospitals, where the turnover of cases was high.

Staff felt that the screening and assessment activity reports lacked information on service levels. They considered that, for hospital social work, more detailed information needed to be collected so the various response or activity times could be calculated.

It was found that care plan extract and service intention information was only analysed in respect of placement, whereas in fact the information was collected on all cases. It was seen as potentially useful to encourage practitioners to supply care plan and service information on all their cases, and for the material to be analysed both for people in homes and at home.

Furthermore, a 'planning form system' (that reported on service gaps) did not operate in all areas. In theory, service deficiency forms were completed on all cases that were assessed. However, in practice the forms were not consistently completed, rendering analysis partial and not particularly helpful.

Future information requirements

Detailed comments were also made by staff about information requirements for the future. Some comments related to general data issues, others related to specific pieces of information and the need for new forms of information and feedback. These are presented below separately.

Managing and data

There was general acceptance among managers that the department needed to manage through evidence and to secure value for money. Managers at all levels needed to be committed to their policy and service objectives and to using information to review those policies and objectives.

It was also considered that purchasers needed to be systematically made aware of the impact of their purchasing activities on providers, and providers needed to have a systematic means of telling purchasers about service performance and shortfalls between purchasing intent and provider reality.

Providers also needed to be aware of market opportunities and for this to happen they needed information about services being provided (or not being provided) by other agencies or sectors.

District comparisons needed to be augmented by team comparisons and unit comparisons so that purchasers and providers could be aware of the patterns of variation in the local market. However, these comparisons needed to be understood in their local context as variations could be due to contextual factors requiring different strategies.

For first line managers to manage it was thought that there must be easy access to meaningful financial and cost data which could guide their resource allocation decisions. Assessment, care planning and review activities could all generate helpful information for case decisions and, when aggregated, provide helpful information for strategic planning.

Home care team leaders were very clear in their determination to receive feedback from users in order to assess the quality of the service they were providing. A checklist was developed to ask a dozen or so questions about home care. It was simply and effectively designed for users to self complete. In addition to the checklist, the leaflet asked for complaints and comments. In one district a user panel met regularly with staff to discuss service standards, problems and development.

Aims, targets and indicators

Information and indicators needed to be related to broad service aims and the operational requirements of these aims. Targets or 'exception levels' needed to be set for each indicator.

Information and indicators were required on key departmental aims for services for older people – such as diversion from residential care, choice, support for carers, accountability to the public, and individuality of users. There should be a small number of performance indicators with detail available when required rather than mountains of routine information.

Standards and targets or exception levels needed to be set for services and information should have been collected to monitor and illuminate these standards, targets and levels.

Future information and feedback needed to address equity issues, but for practical not presentational reasons. For example, information on race was seen as useful, but information on language was crucial if users and carers who prefered to speak in languages other than English were to receive adequate help with interpretation and translation.

Qualitative aspects

Formalisation of existing contacts with informal groups and interested parties could provide useful feedback of service progress. User and carer feedback should be incorporated into routine systems of monitoring. A sampling procedure should be attempted to cover all user groups and all districts in a phased and planned way. Softer data on quality of life for users in care homes or supported at home could also be employed in this respect.

Systems of collection and feedback

It was felt that more training should be given to staff on how to use computer systems efficiently and more terminals should be available.

Consistent, timely, standardised, formatted and interpreted feedback was needed to reach all relevant parties at the same time, with pre-determined systems for taking action. A standard needed also to be established for the production and interpretation of information, with time built in so that exceptions could be investigated and explained.

It was seen that information production and analysis could be based around four foci: purchasing activity; internal service performance; staff turnover, recruitment and other issues; and a specific theme for the year. For the first three foci there should be a limited number of indicators.

The dissemination of aggregated information should follow a path through the department that engages the policy makers and professionals who need to see the data and can comment on it. The interpretation of information and subsequent action needed to feed into the planning process.

Special studies

Ad hoc studies on specific issues were seen as desirable to complement indicator data and feedback from users and carers, perhaps with a different theme for the studies each year.

Some staff reported special information exercises they had initiated in this regard. One team leader spoke of measuring contact time, showing how user-contact time had decreased due to increased administrative time. The findings were reported to the Social Services Committee as part of the argument for more administrative resources in order to free up social workers to increase direct contact time with service users.

Quality assurance

Much quality assurance activity was already ongoing. A key need was to integrate this information. Line management, inspection unit and member visits to different facilities helped to develop services, yet no aggregated or comparative data were produced. In fact, there were aggregated figures reported about complaints in the community and in care homes, yet few staff knew of these reports. As only formal complaints were officially recorded, this was considered a poor source of information.

Summary

It is important to point out that a number of criticisms of these existing systems had already been recognised by senior managers and principal officers in Cheshire, at the time of the PSSRU commission to work with them, and developments were in train to address them. In this way, the review of existing information systems and requirements, which formed part of the development of performance indicators, was linked to an ongoing commitment from the department to pursuing refinements to its information system.

The concerns identified locally in Cheshire relate to many elements discussed in Chapters 2 and 3 regarding the development of performance indicators. At issue is the extent of coverage of local information and the way in which this is used to monitor the performance of key areas of social services activity for older people. The initial review of currently available systems in Cheshire highlighted a number of key points, which could later be taken forward in defining a set of performance indicators, specifically for use in older people's services. It was important first to examine ways in which indicators could be designed to complement existing information where this was working well and to look at ways in which drawbacks in the existing system could be overcome by the use of indicators which more faithfully reflected current information needs. It was also deemed important to place the use of indicators within the specific objectives of the department's services for older people and for these to be stated clearly.

In order to develop appropriate PIs, a framework was required which could integrate the levels and stages of activity in the social care of older people with relevant indicators, directives and policy guidance. 'Causal process' frameworks which were dynamic, such as those of Donabedian (Donabedian, 1980) and the PSSRUs own 'Production of Welfare' (Davies and Knapp, 1981) approach, were seen as particularly appropriate. To this end the Performance Indicator Analytical Framework (PIAF) was developed and this is discussed in the next chapter.

Chapter 5

The Performance Indicator Analytical Framework

Supervisors like explorers, must know where they have been to know where they are so that they can plot the course to get where they want to go. To put it another way: Unless you know how you are doing as you move along, you'll never know when you're done or if you have succeeded. Each characteristic that makes up your project must be considered...We must be able to identify these component parts and measure them before we can know how our schedule, cost and quality are doing.

(Crosby, 1979, p. 101).

The criticisms of performance indicators outlined by many commentators, including the staff interviewed in this work, have pointed to the failure to place PIs within an integrated framework which permits us to use them more profitably. The debate around the development of performance indicators and the development of community care, with a greater emphasis on themes such as individuality and customer care, calls for fresh thinking on the development and use of indicators.

The work developed at PSSRU attempted to bring together the logic of past and recent academic, administrative, professional and financial approaches into a framework for performance measurement that could be used locally. Such a framework should offer a structure for performance indicators in social care which could improve substantially their *design*, *collection* and *interpretation*. These three aspects are important as they help to underscore many of the debates and technical aspects of PIs:

- Design, because a structure is needed in order to categorise statistical information;
- Collection, as without a framework for shaping the relevant questions, useful data are often not collected; and
- Interpretation because the array of routine information generally available is virtually useless without a means of logically linking items of information together.

The underlying organising framework is described below.

A performance indicator analytical framework

In order to provide an overarching framework which could shape the development and utilisation of performance indicators, the PSSRU developed a Performance Indicator Analytical Framework. Throughout the rest of this book, this framework is referred to as the PIAF. The design of this reflected national performance indicator developments over the last two decades and a range of theoretical and policy based material. Particularly salient were the community care reforms with their emphases on care management processes, the emergence of standards and charters for customer care, and a growing emphasis on the concept of quality.

The PIAF draws on and develops as source material the Social Services Inspectorate's *Key Indicators* package, initially reported by Warburton in 1988 (Warburton, 1988) and the Social Services Research Group's performance management framework described by Barnes and Miller in the same year (Barnes and Miller, 1988). Both of these provide a range of indicator domains and indicator types. However, both are essentially cross-sectional and static categorisations of a range of indicators. What was also required was a more dynamic element to the framework which could articulate the inter-relationship and causal connections between indicators.

Two sources provided this sense of causal relationships between domains within which indicators were devised. The first was the well-known work of Donabedian in providing the framework of structure, process and outcome (Donabedian, 1980) as key domains for the evaluation of interventions and services. The second was PSSRU's own Production of Welfare (POW) model (Davies and Knapp, 1981; Challis et al., 1988; Challis and Darton, 1990). The Production of Welfare approach distinguishes between inputs (including costs), non-resource inputs (such as the quality of staff or styles of working), intermediate outcomes (such as receipt of a needed service) and final outcomes (such as improvement in well being). This provides a dynamic causal framework which permits the investigation of how the relationship between the provision of services, delivered in certain ways to certain types of individual may lead to positive impact upon older people or their carers. In short, it is the key set of questions required of a service agency, whether for evaluation or effective management – namely 'Who gets what services provided in what way, at what cost and with what effect?' These questions underlie the approach to performance indicator development described herein.

The PIAF distinguishes seven broad domains within which to measure social care performance. Along with a consideration of the policy context as one domain, there are six broad types of performance indicator:

- *Need indicators* (NI) refer to numbers and types of potential and actual users and carers, and the help they want or need. In other words, *who is served or in need* of care. An analysis of need is the first step to examining the performance of social care services. The established literature on need outlines a number of indicators and routine information that could be usefully used in local planning. In social care services for the elderly, it is important to have information both on the existence of priority groups likely to be in need of services as well as the circumstances of different local areas. Social need indicators are used as part of the Department of Health's *Key Indicator* package, where they are presented by local authority, by class of authority and for England as a whole. Needs indicators can usefully be combined with data concerning referrals and screenings to show any potential mismatch between potential need and expressed need.
- *Contextual and policy factors* are used to frame and structure the collection of performance information, at both local and national levels. They determine the way in which social services departments provide for a range of needs. These wider contextual factors include such elements as central government policy and guidance, the wider local authority policy in relation to older people and the social services' own policies and objectives. These factors can be seen to act as a filter between existing needs, the expression of those needs and the service response. Included in this are the range of policy priorities for community care outlined by central government and other local authority policies, for example those regarding housing and community development, which may influence or constrain an authority's ability to meet the needs of its elderly population. Included among the relevant social services policies are their competing priorities as to whether to provide care in institutional settings or at home, the range and mix of services provided in-house or by independent agencies, and the mechanisms for assessing and delivering care: eligibility criteria, contract type, liaison with other health and social care agencies and the conduct of provider services, including their own quality assurance mechanisms (Wistow et al., 1994; Knapp et al., 2001). These polices should stem from, or be related closely to, the social services department's objectives for the care available to older people.
- *Supply indicators* (SI) refer to the service system in a broad sense – expenditure, facilities, staffing in all sectors of provision, service charges, and unit costs. In other words, *what is available*? This type of information is traditionally readily available in social services departments. It has also been the easiest to pinpoint and collect on a national basis (House of Commons Social Services Committee, 1982a). Such indicators include: the numbers of social work and other staff; the number of home care hours available from different providers; and the number of delivered meals provided. Other supply data are also relevant, such as unit costs, although

these remain problematic to collect for many social service departments (Department of Health, 1999c). Supply indicators give a global picture of community care provision. Comparing these indicators by authority or between areas within an authority will highlight differences in provision as well as differences in service flexibility. This may include the extent of home care provision, the extent to which there is a choice of home or residential care for users, and the extent to which there is an adequate independent sector for day, domiciliary and residential care.

- *Practice process indicators* (PPI) cover all stages of care management from case finding to closure, and describe the ways in which people are assessed for services, how things are done, and the quality of what is done, both by way of individual practice and service delivery. They examine the *quality of the care management process* and the performance of the core tasks themselves. Although the Department of Health offered a revised framework for their Key Indicators in line with post-reform changes to the community care system (Department of Health, 1994b), there still remains a lack of indicator information dealing specifically with the monitoring of care management processes. This is an important aspect of the recent scene as such indicators enable an assessment of the quality and efficiency of the whole process and the primacy of users and carers in the provision of care.

- *Service process indicators* (SPI) cover deployment of staff, service patterns, service usage, and cost of packages of care. They examine the *quality of the services provided as a consequence of care management practice.* These indicators consider such things as the extensiveness and mix of provision, the optimal use of staff time and the distribution of resources across different levels of need. These can be used to measure the efficiency with which available resources are used as well as how they are used. Service process indicators can be used to express judgements about the quality of care available. Indicators such as staff/resident ratios have already been used as proxy indicators of quality in residential care (Gibbs and Sinclair, 1992a,b), through the effect on such factors as security as well as upon the feasibility of positive activities to promote quality of life. Similar indicators may be used to indicate the quality of provider services in community-based care.

- *Outcome indicators* (OI) describe the effects of service intervention upon the user or carer which are valued in their own right. They describe achievement or the 'impact' of provision. The purest form of outcome may be described as a *final outcome* and refers to the direct impact on users' and carers' welfare and subjective well-being arising from the services they receive. Other outcomes, still valued in their own right, are defined as *intermediate outcomes* and refer to experiences expected to lead to final outcomes, such as the impact of provision of community-based services or admission to a care home. Many indicators devised as part of this domain will be of the intermediate outcome variety – volumes of services produced – rather than final outcomes. They represent the end-points in the process of care, but do not directly measure the effects of care on the user. For this, some form of special study or survey will need to be undertaken. Outcome indicators can be used to express areas of policy and practice related to the attainment of objectives. These objectives can be specified in terms of achieving a satisfactory coverage of services, or in terms of statements of intensity and quality (Knapp, 1984). For example, a major objective throughout the history of community care has been the diversion of users away from institutional care. Outcome indicators, such as the numbers of admissions to long-term residential care, can signal the extent to which institution-based care is being substituted for home-based care in support of such policy objectives.

Within the model, these indicator types will at times interact so that, for example, some process indicators will be user- or carer-focused, and others supply-focused. They should therefore be interpreted accordingly, as shown in Figure 5.1. This diagram may be interpreted as a causal process where local demand or need factors impinge upon or are influenced by both national and local policies and context, which in turn influence the supply of services available in the locality. The two sets of process indicators refer to how that supply is translated into forms of practice and styles of service provision. In turn, the service outputs will work through into effects experienced by users and carers to generate outcomes.

Figure 5.1
The Performance Indicator Analytical Framework (PIAF) at different levels of analysis

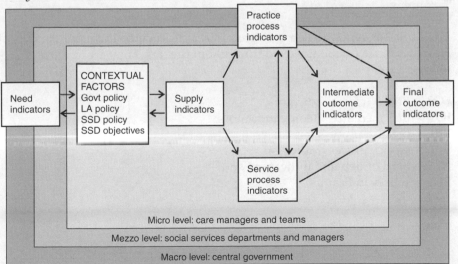

Although developed locally, in conjunction with the work detailed in the last chapter on the design of local information systems, the PIAF can be interpreted at a number of different levels (Clarkson and Challis, 2000). At the broad macro level of government regulation, the PIAF may be used to structure the relationship between existing national indicators, such as those contained in the government's Performance Assessment Framework (Department of Health, 1999b). Many of the developments outlined in Chapters 2 and 3 have occurred at this level and, recently, national performance data have been structured around key government objectives, such as the diversion of older people from residential care. Below this, at the mezzo level, the PIAF can be used to structure the collection and analysis of information used to evaluate performance at the managerial level within individual social services departments or similar organisations. The framework was originally developed to facilitate work at this level in developing a suite of indicators within one particular social services department. In this context, indicators can be devised to take into account service delivery processes within departments and these are linked to local objectives. At the micro level, of individual practitioners and teams, indicators have hardly been used at all. However, the PIAF can be used to enable practitioners to monitor the progress of cases with reference to assessment and practice standards, some of which are now being developed (Geron and Chassler, 1994; Department of Health, 2000; Clarkson and Challis, 2003). Figure 5.1 represents the PIAF as a 'nested' design, permitting the collection of performance information at these different levels.

Taxonomy

The indicator types, which constitute our Performance Indicator Analytical Framework are frequently used throughout the text. They are abbreviated as follows:

FOI – final outcome indicators;
IOI – intermediate outcome indicators;
PPI – practice process indicators;
SPI – service process indicators;
NI – need or demand indicators; and
SI – supply indicators.

The PIAF and performance dimensions

Once the multidimensional nature of performance is recognised, it is possible to locate dimensions, judged as significant in the history of performance measurement, within the analytic framework proposed here. The domains of the PIAF framework can be used to judge social care performance against criteria already described as important in an appraisal of performance. These include the criteria of economy, efficiency and effectiveness, as set out in key policy documents such as those of the Audit Commission and Department of Health. Additional criteria, contained in much of the social services development work on indicators, can also be considered using this framework. Included here are the domains of equity and quality to show how combinations of measures, derived from the framework, relate to particular concerns of social care.

Other performance dimensions, judged important from the community care reforms of the early 1990s, could also be included in the framework. These would include criteria of service responsiveness such as involvement, user choice and timely service delivery. Some of the dimensions of performance that may be identified within the framework will now be described:

- *Economy* relates to resource savings at the simplest level. Indicators of resources employed are useful to judge whether these are minimised. For example, a stand-alone indicator such as that in the social services *Key Indicators* package (Department of Health, 2002b) – 'total gross expenditure on older people per population 65 plus' – can be used to measure economy.
- *Efficiency* can be defined as the ratio of supply indicators (predominantly costs) to outcomes. In many cases, the costs of units of service provided will be a simple measure of efficiency: for example, unit costs such as the cost per place in a residential home. In this case, cost efficiency expresses the wish to provide the maximum possible output per unit of input and so a lower unit cost will denote relative cost efficiency. However, in a broader context, efficiency considerations will be based on the relationships between costs and benefits. Benefits can be interpreted on a wider level to include the positive value of services received such as the quantity and quality of care, responses to need and the way in which care is delivered. These aspects relate more to final rather than to intermediate outcomes of care. They express the notions of allocative efficiency described earlier.
- *Effectiveness* is seen in the relationship between supply/process indicators and outcomes. It investigates how far objectives have been accomplished. Effectiveness has two elements which dictate the measures to be used. There is effectiveness at the service delivery level, which includes a consideration of intermediate outcomes; and there is that at the client-

impact level, which concentrates on final outcomes. Effectiveness is more difficult to measure routinely and may require special studies such as user satisfaction surveys to fully establish final outcomes. In the absence of these, the effectiveness of service delivery can be studied by the use of proxy outcome indicators such as reasons for entry to care homes.

- *Equity* is usually defined with reference to whether services are appropriately targeted towards those in need, according to broad philosophical considerations of fairness and justice (Rawls, 1972). It can be subdivided into *equality of care* – whether care is provided on an equal basis according to the level of need; and *equality of access* – whether services are available to those in need, regardless of whether they are actually used. Both equity considerations are best evaluated by observing the relationship between need, process and intermediate outcome indicators.

- *Quality* has been defined in a number of different ways. The term can express the totality of performance or a specific component thereof, more usefully referring to those elements closely related to the experiences and preferences of consumers (Pollitt, 1990; Walsh, 1991). In this respect, it can be explored by a ratio of outputs *that meet a quality standard* to inputs (Martin, 1993). In the present context, this would refer to intermediate outcomes of quality in relation to their supply such as the number of meals delivered on time. This expresses the quality dimension of responsiveness in relation to the supply of this service.

Figure 5.2 outlines some of the ways in which the framework can be explored to inform the way indicators are designed and used. In this, relevant performance criteria such as efficiency and quality are superimposed upon the PIAF framework. Combinations of different measures from each of the domains in the model can be used in measuring performance against these criteria. This not only enables a clearer view of how performance criteria and service aspects fit into the framework but also allows us to devise appropriate indicators in a more coherent fashion.

It is important to be aware of the dynamic nature of the PIAF model in attempting to operationalise indicators to measure performance according to these criteria. Indicators derived from the model should be seen as interrelated sets of measures which bring into focus aspects of performance judged against important supply or policy considerations. This is due, in large part, to the fact that there will often be conflicts and negative relationships between objectives. It is possible to comment on these by investigating the relationships between different elements of the model in judging overall performance. For example, the differing types of efficiency already identified in the PSSRU work, and outlined in Chapter 3, use different combinations of indicators in assessing differing aspects of performance.

Figure 5.2
The PIAF and performance criteria

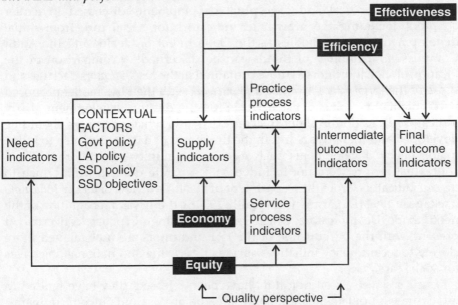

The relationships between performance criteria and the components identified by PIAF are not static. Policy development will alter the content of the domains and particular questions may alter the focus; for example, if it were desired to evaluate aspects of the wider care system, such as how social services provision links with health or the voluntary sector (Kendall and Knapp, 1998). Again, an examination of performance in an integrated health and social care system would require change in the contents of the domains but their inter-relationship would remain broadly the same.

The benefit of using the PIAF framework in this way is that it helps to ask the right questions of the service system by drawing attention to which indicators, either alone or in combination, are important in any analysis. The absence of well defined measures that reflect the service system as it actually operates is one reason for past difficulties in measuring performance within both social and health care. The framework also enables the construction of indicators to be kept to a minimum; only those indicators from which the right questions can be formulated need to be produced. This avoids the potential risk of excessive information, often of doubtful relevance, crowding the system.

From theory and past developments into current practice

From the theoretical and conceptual developments discussed in earlier chapters, including the growth of indicators for social care from initial developments by such bodies as the Department of Health and the Audit Commission, a number of trends can be discerned. A comparison of the location of such indicators as those contained in the *Key Indicators* package and those of the *Performance Assessment Framework* with the PIAF model proposed here, highlights some deficiencies in past indicator development. Early indicator sets said little about the context within which measures should be developed and there was a drift in the timeliness of data with which to judge major policy developments such as the community care reforms. Thus, contextual factors were not included as a separate domain from which to devise indicators. From the Department of Health's review of its *Key Indicators* package in 1994 (Department of Health, 1994b), there was a recognition of the need to devise indicators which reflected changing policy concerns. At present, with the introduction of the PAF, indicators are now aligned more closely to recent policy initiatives such as Best Value and national objectives for social care.

As successive sets of indicators have been released, they have tended to increasingly populate the right hand side, the process and outcome domains, of the PIAF model. In particular, process indicators have recently begun to be included to judge care management processes, such as the conduct of assessments. The Referrals Assessments and Packages of Care (RAP) project (Department of Health, 2001b) includes indicators comparable to the practice process indicators of the PIAF. These include indicators of the number of contacts at screening, the action taken after screening and the number of assessments completed. The PAF is to be adjusted in the light of the indicators collected as part of this project.

Indicators have also begun to populate the final outcome domain with proxies for final outcomes, such as cases of avoidable harm, being included in the PAF. User satisfaction, more clearly located within the final outcome domain, is also forming part of the performance assessment arrangements for social services departments with the requirement for local authorities to carry out user satisfaction surveys stated in the *Modernising Social Services* White Paper (Cm 4169, 1998, para. 2.62). In the medium to long term, the aim of the Department of Health is to have nationally comparative data on the experience of all social service user groups in England.

Past national developments

An examination of the framework enables comparison to take place between the indicators developed in the work described in this book and those in previous national developments. In terms of the PIAF, previous collections have stressed only a limited range of indicators. For instance, the original Department of Health and CIPFA information outlined in Chapters 2 and 3 mostly related to supply indicators (costs, staff hours etc.) and 'intermediate outcomes' (places in establishments, occupancy, attendance days etc.), rather than 'final outcome' measures. In Table 5.1, a range of national indicator sets, both past and present, are listed along with their intended performance dimensions according to the components identified in the PIAF. General examples of the types of indicators used are also described in parentheses. This enables the reader to have a clearer grasp of the indicator sets devised so far and their similarities and differences to those provided in this work, which are described in the following chapters. The limitations in previous schemes can be clearly identified in that many fail to provide indicators to measure outcome and most do not provide a policy context in which to place their indicators. This latter attribute is essential for a suite of indicators to be useful at both a national and a local level.

Academic contributions

Other contributions to the development of indicators for older people's services such as those provided by the SSRG (Barnes and Miller, 1988) can also be placed within the framework in order to judge their usefulness for further work. While many of the SSRG indicators widened the scope and context for performance measurement, some were intended to express more qualitative aspects and so precise indicators were not included for every component of their model. These indicators were, however, linked to statements of policy and service objectives and so included contextual factors from which to devise measures. The SSRG's indicators were significant in expressing the full range of domains likely to be important in judging social care performance. In terms of the PIAF, their indicators covered need, supply and outcome information. Process indicators were also included with links to the quality of assessment practice, such as the time interval between referral, assessment and service delivery. Client satisfaction surveys were mentioned as one indication of final outcome. Although not including all indicators within a model to describe the service system, the SSRG work was a significant development in devising indicators with relevance to policy and local objectives.

In order to place these developments into a context for current practice, there is a need to recognise both the strengths and limitations of previous indicator developments. Like any framework, the usefulness of the PIAF can only be judged by the extent to which it offers an effective guide to the collection and interpretation of data according to the present functions of the service system.

Table 5.1
Rationale and functions of national PI systems and links with the PIAF framework

Indicator system	Intended audiences	Performance dimensions	Components identified in PIAF
Department of Health[a] Health Service Indicators (HSIs)	NHS management, central government	Economy, efficiency timeliness	Supply (unit costs, staffing, expenditure), service process (length of stay, turnover, treatment intensity), intermediate outcome (discharges home)
Department of Health[b] Social Services Key indicators	Social services management, central government	Economy, efficiency	Need (population / age groups), supply (expenditure, unit costs, staffing), service process (home help receipt), intermediate outcome (no. of residential places)
Audit Commission[c] Local Authority Profiles	The public and service users	Economy, efficiency, effectiveness, equity, timeliness	Need (numbers of elderly), supply (expenditure), practice process (needs assessments), intermediate outcome (provision of service), final outcome (customer satisfaction)
National Consumer Council[d] Guideline indicators	The public and service users	Quality, timeliness effectiveness	Need, supply (charges, numbers and type of services) service process (costs to user), outcome (customer satisfaction)
CIPFA Personal Social Services Statistics[e]	Social services management, central government	Economy, efficiency	Supply (expenditure and unit costs)
Department of Health[f] National Performance Assessment Framework	Social services management, central government	Efficiency, effectiveness, quality, equity	Context, supply (unit costs), practice process (quality dimensions), service process (service useage), intermediate outcome (supported admissions)

Sources: a Department of Health (1989)   d National Consumer Council (1986)
            b Department of Health (1991b)   e CIPFA (1999)
            c Audit Commission (1998)   f Department of Health (1999b)

Performance dimensions and indicator sets

For developments in theory to influence current practice, the performance dimensions previously identified need to be linked to indicator sets; sets of measures that can provide more precise evidence on aspects of performance. Examples of such sets of measures are summarised in Table 5.2. Indicator types are listed against some of the important criteria commonly used in performance appraisal (such as the four Es). Examples are also given of possible social care indicators based on different combinations of components in the PIAF. Many are thus ratio measures, reflecting the combination of different PIAF elements. Some, like those referring to final outcomes, are, however, of a more qualitative nature and can be collected from consumer surveys or special studies.

Table 5.2
Performance dimensions and indicator sets

Performance dimensions	Indicator types	Examples
1. *Economy*	Resource inputs (levels employed), expenditures, average costs	Vehicle miles, residential space, total expenditure
2. *Efficiency* Intermediate outcome efficiency Final outcome efficiency	Service volume/budget Comparative assessment (special studies)	Cost/ unit of service Cost benefit/effectiveness analysis
3. *Effectiveness*	Intermediate outcomes Final outcomes Quality of outputs	Volume of outputs/inputs Quality of life surveys Customer satisfaction surveys
4. *Equity* Service targeting Procedural equity	Intermediate outcome/need Service access Supply/service process Supply	 Number of clients receiving care
5. *Quality* Responsiveness	Practice process	Time between referral and first response

Defining indicators in this way promotes clarity in deciding what information to collect when devising indicators for local use. It also makes it possible to identify some of the components currently being proposed in national indicator sets, as these are often implicit.

The PIAF framework and the SSD requirement

In the present work PSSRU sought to develop a set of indicators for services to older people. A full list of indicators for each of the PIAF components is provided in Appendix 1. This can be used as a reference point to guide the material described in later chapters. There is a need to unpack the PIAF to enable this to take place. Reference has already been made to the policies and national priorities which structure the ways in which indicators are used at present and in the near future. These include, importantly, the development of community-based care, the quality agenda (Department of Health, 2000) and central government priorities such as the pursuit of efficiency, Best Value (Cm 4104, 1998) and closer integration of health and social care (Department of Health, 2001a; Cm 4818-I, 2000). Furthermore, there are specific objectives relating to the individual SSD policies, which were outlined in Chapter 4: those relating to services which are targeted, timely, individual and involved and offer diversion and choice. In the work with the SSD, these were seen as important in providing a basis for performance measurement and in structuring subsequent work. In Chapter 6, the PIAF is used in framing some of the indicators provided to the department and these are related to national policy.

All these developments provided a solid platform on which to establish a full suite of performance indicators for services to older people. Unlike previous sets of indicators which were lists of relevant measures, the PIAF provided a dynamic model which helped to pose questions about the links between different indicators and which indeed helped to shape the curiosity of staff in their use of indicators, and to raise questions so as to improve the quality of care provided. Therefore, the different components of the department's information systems – both historic and recently developed – dovetailed with and complemented the joint SSD/PSSRU work. In response to the department's needs, the PSSRU identified a set of performance indicators for services for older people that fitted into the PIAF framework. These are now described in Chapter 6.

Chapter 6

Constructing and Using Indicators in Practice

This chapter outlines the application of the PIAF framework to the local authority's information about older users and services as part of the construction of key indicators of performance. As performance indicators need to be developed in context, the starting place was the social services department's aims for its services for older people. Many of the wider aims of the department have already been described in Chapter 4. This chapter provides a sharper focus by bringing together these aims within the analytical framework described in the last chapter. Using this framework, and following the information review described earlier, a small development group of staff in the social services department was involved in a series of intensive meetings to devise appropriate indicators as described in Chapter 4.

This chapter summarises the development process and considers some exemplar indicators for each PIAF domain and provides interpretative commentary on them. It also considers issues of the relationship between national and local performance, the format of indicators, and makes links between the indicators devised and the Best Value framework (Cm 4014, 1998).

Local service objectives in a national framework

From the framework of service objectives outlined from the various social services department policy documents, a number of user-focused and service-focused objectives, tasks and targets were identified. These broadly reflected the national objectives for social services departments from *Caring for People* (Cm 849, 1989) which are outlined in Box 6.1. The local objectives are grouped under five topics in Box 6.2, which capture the general service principles of the

---

Box 6.1
National objectives in Caring for People

- To promote the development of domiciliary, day and respite services to enable people to live in their own homes wherever feasible and sensible.
- To ensure that service providers make practical support for carers a high priority.
- To make proper assessment of need and good case management the cornerstone of high quality care.
- To promote the development of a flourishing independent sector alongside good quality public services.
- To clarify the responsibilities of agencies and so to make it easier to hold them to account for their performance.
- To secure better value for taxpayers' money by introducing a new funding structure for social care.

Source: Cm 849 (1989 para. 1.11)

---

department. A marker showing what type of information or indicator these relate to, using the PIAF, is included in parentheses. This enabled staff to be clear in searching for what type of information could support each target.

Focusing on these objectives provided a starting point for the generation of indicators that were relevant to local policy and could guide the practice of the department. Some examples of the indicators provided in support of the general objectives of the department are set out below. These are grouped according to each domain of the PIAF. Hence, the indicators can be linked to the social services department's key areas for services for older people as described in the department's Statement of Intent, and subsequently to the service objectives as agreed by the Special Interest Group for Older People. They can reasonably be generalised to most social services departments.

Staff perceptions on need for indicator development

In order to generate indicators, material was identified from the information review on specific future requirements or improvements that needed to be made. These requirements were also located within the PIAF model described in Chapter 5, which provided a focus as to how indicators might be improved in the future. A summary of these is contained in Table 6.1 around six core themes: User/carer level needs; service activity; budget/finance; care management activity; service effectiveness; and any interrelations between these elements. Staff at all levels, from service managers through principal officers to team leaders, provided comments as to the types of information they considered would be useful in assisting the generation of effective

Table 6.1
Staff comments used to set background for indicator development

Themes	Comments
User/carer level needs	Information required on the characteristics of users including race and language, sensory impairment, cognitive impairment and continence problems. Information should include the needs that interventions are aimed at meeting. Changes in dependency bands over time should be included and comparison of dependency in different settings. Information needed on the factors which precipitate referral. Data on service gaps and under-resourcing to help commissioners and in-house providers to respond to unmet need, including bed turnover and bed blocking.
Service activity	Data are needed on cover and intensity for home care, contact time with users, travelling time, home care visits and rotas, staff sickness, and contributions users make to the costs of services. Information needed on contract compliance: hours purchased by teams compared with hours actually provided to users. Information needed on the use of independent sector provision compared with council provision. Information needed on home care hours planned and provided during weekdays, evenings and at weekends or where users refuse service. Information needed on the turnover of allocated cases and for working out how to allocate rotating short-term care.
Budget / finance	Information needed on cost comparisons between providers, both in-house and the independent sector. Appropriate budget needed to monitor, control and plan spending and discriminate between assessment and provision.
Care management activity	Information needed on how assessment activity measures up to quality standards, user satisfaction and complaints. Information needed on throughput of hospital social work and allocated and unallocated cases per team. Response times are needed to show the lapse between referral and initial action, initial action and assessment and between completed assessment and service plan. A caseload weighting system is needed. Information needed on cases jointly assessed and worked by SSD and NHS.
Service effectiveness	Placement data need to be developed showing year on year comparisons, and seasonal trends. Information needed on the number, scope and costs and effectiveness of care packages for people at home.
Integrating data	Data needed to help with resource allocation decisions; linking needs and costs.

Box 6.2
Local objectives, tasks and targets

Avoiding breakdown and protecting users and carers
- Avoid breakdowns and emergencies (IOI);
- Protect people at risk and manage their situations (IOI);
- Intervene with appropriate speed and in appropriate ways (PPI);
- Reduce carer breakdown (IOI);
- Increase the number of emergencies supported at home (IOI); and
- Ensure that there are contingency plans for all cases at high risk of breakdown (PPI).

To reduce admission to long-term residential care by providing alternative accommodation
- Reduce admissions to long-term residential care for all priority categories of users (IOI);
- Ensure consistently high standards of care within each form of accommodation (SPI);
- Establish an information centre at each community support centre, which will provide users and carers with useful information (SI); and
- Establish a carer support group at each community support centre (SI).

Developing and using respite care, for the benefits of both users and carers
- Map alternative accommodation and respite care facilities available to the department (SI);
- Integrate respite care facilities into support at home according to risk and dependency factors (SPI);
- Gauge the need for alternative accommodation including respite care (NI);

Care at home
- Map the extent, purpose, balance and standards of services and facilities available to the department to enable people to stay at home (SI);
- Ensure that tasks needing to be performed for users are described in care plans (PPI);
- Increase the numbers in each priority band who are cared for at home, and in particular the number of priority 2 cases supported at home over 24 hours (IOI);
- Ensure standards of care are applied within the home care service (SPI).

Networks of support
- Mobilise agencies, carers and communities to support vulnerable older people (SI);
- Identify how the department can encourage vulnerable older people to use the support services that are available (PPI);
- Develop the service level agreement approach for voluntary agencies (SPI);
- Stimulate and support carer support activity in each district (SI);

Box 6.2 continued

- Ensure other agencies know the department's community care procedures, and where appropriate have their own procedures (SI);
- Raise awareness about the nature of elder abuse (PPI and SI); and
- Ensure that information is available to enable people to seek advice/ assistance from an independent advocacy function (SI).

---

indicators. Despite the length of this list, not everyone who was interviewed was very clear about their information needs and some had to be encouraged to discuss issues such as feedback on user needs and outcomes. Staff members differed in their perceptions of and needs for information. For example, no senior staff gave ideas for specific indicators. Conversely, social workers' comments were mainly about information on practice process, with no comments on outcomes. This relates to the earlier discussion of different audiences for performance measurement, and different training required by different groups, each with an interest in different types and levels of information.

A distinction needs to be made between information and performance indicators, where the performance indicator is a specific sub-set or combination of relevant information designed to highlight concerns covered by a richer, wider range of information. Hence, the presence of information is a precondition for the effective creation and interpretation of performance indicators. Information requirements were therefore specified that may not have proved to be performance indicators in their own right, but which were essential to create and interpret them. In addition, not all information could be readily collected within existing systems but was still essential if performance was to be effectively analysed and understood.

Specific performance indicators

The new indicators were developed from a range of sources. These included the social services department's policy documents and statements of intent; existing local performance indicators; interviews with staff; available national indicators and associated thinking; charter requirements; and international material. These indicators were shaped according to the PIAF framework. It was recommended that indicators should be broken down for comparison by district at the very least. For a number of indicators, particularly those relating to practice process and service process aims, disaggregation to unit, team or even individual worker, if not essential, was considered desirable. In such cases, comparison of the most disaggregated unit of analysis would need to be interpreted in the light of an overall norm as well as comparison with similarly disaggregated units. However, it was essential for teams and units to have performance indicators of relevance to them at different levels such as district, team or worker level in a nested design. In the next section, some examples of the range of indicators are discussed along with commentary as to appropriate sources of information.

Content and interpretation of indicators within PIAF domains

A number of indicators were devised covering important areas of policy and practice, both locally and nationally. Their relevance and relatedness to national indicators was kept in mind, as were their links with the mainstream academic literature. The approach to their construction is described below with a number of factors stated within each PIAF domain. For each domain, these factors focus upon: a definition of the scope of each domain; the availability of data; local sources from which to derive indicators; devising indicators; and using them.

Need indicators

Indicators in this domain were intended to cover information on the nature of different catchment areas within a social services authority. They include a number of need indicators relevant to general social care issues as well as others relating to specific issues in the care of older people. These indicators provide a context through which need and demand are expressed. They can take at least three forms: prevalence indicators of the estimated level of illness or morbidity; incidence measures of the numbers of new cases referred or assessed for services; and social needs indicators of the general elderly population. Within the local authority, these need indicators can provide contextual material at an area or district level. Social needs indicators can show the degree of deprivation or affluence of an area or the age-mix of its population, and inferences can be drawn about the ability of people in an area to support those who are personally in need, and about the ability of individuals in need to cope given deprived circumstances. These social need indicators can be aligned with other incidence type need indicators of referrals and screenings to indicate the degree of mismatch between potential need and expressed need. Inferences can also be drawn about comparative need between areas, the visibility of social services, the strength of local referral systems and the relevance of social services as perceived by user groups and local communities.

Social need indicators are widely used at both national and local levels, as part of routine and special studies. They are used in a variety of ways by government, academic institutions and other bodies. The Department of Health include them as part of the Key Indicators package, where they are presented by local authority, by class of authority and for England as a whole (Department of Health, 2002b). Specific incidence type indicators, relating to referrals and screenings, are contained in the government's RAP returns (Department of Health, 1999c, 2001b). Other prevalence type indicators are used within social services departments to estimate the level of disability or morbidity within an authority by relating the results of field surveys to local data (Holmes et al., 1995; Cooper, 1997). The prevalence of limiting longstanding illnesses is also contained in the national *Key Indicators Graphical Package* (Department of Health, 2002b).

The local sources from which to devise such need indicators include for social needs indicators, the national census, mid-year population estimates, population changes, local population data and standardised mortality ratios; for incidence needs indicators, the numbers of referrals and screenings (monthly through the client information system); and for prevalence type indicators, specially commissioned studies, for example to identify impairment, immobility, instability, and incontinence within an authority and in defined geographical areas.

In devising local need indicators, as well as general measures of social need which may be derived from national sources, there are specific areas of importance in the community care of older people. Indicators of specific circumstances and difficulties are needed in order to judge the performance of care on a range of criteria; such indicators might include numbers of screenings in different ethnic or user groups (by impairment or dependency), those older people with and without carers, or those experiencing abuse or neglect. The 'Five I's' of intellectual (or cognitive) impairment, immobility, instability, incontinence and a (lack of) informal carer have been identified by research as being key predictors of need for help among older people, and as potential determinants of entry to care homes (Isaacs, 1981; Challis et al., 1995, 2002). Hence, areas with higher proportions of referred users with one or more of the 'Five I's' are likely to have more complex needs, often associated with admission to hospital or care homes or both. Some of this information may be difficult to collect and is often not available nationally. For instance, due to problems of detection and diagnosis at referral, identification of those with cognitive impairment at the referral stage is likely to be poor. It is also difficult on occasions at referral or screening for valid information about detailed and very personal aspects of disability such as immobility, instability and incontinence to be collected. Within the locality, screening data could be compared with data from a number of national research studies to calculate the expected numbers of people within different categories. Comparisons between national and local data would allow for analysis of expected with actual prevalence.

The determination of risk and the appropriate response to it constitutes another important element in the assessment of need. An indicator was therefore devised focusing on the consistent application of risk and response categories to cases of similar types with similar needs across the authority. Proportions in four different priority bands (High, Medium, Low and None) could be compared across individual districts and teams. These could highlight different levels of need and risk faced by each area. They could also, in fact, highlight different approaches taken to risk or different understandings of what constitutes risk between areas. There are no national data currently available on these aspects.

A key yet contentious aspect of the Caring for People (Cm 849, 1989) reforms was the provision of information on service gaps or unmet need. Most social serves departments have not collected information on unmet need in a consistent way, despite clarification (Department of Health, 1997c), and likewise on eligibility for social care (Department of Health, 2002a). There are no consistent national data, yet many local and national research studies have highlighted service gaps (Challis and Davies, 1986; Challis et al., 2002). An indicator of this aspect of need can be compared across individual districts and teams. Comparisons may highlight different approaches to assessment and the identification of unmet need and service gaps. They can also focus attention on the resources available to districts and teams and pinpoint new service developments. They can also highlight potential risks to users coping with less than adequate or inappropriate services.

At the time these indicators were developed, the interface between the NHS and social services, and the withdrawal of the NHS from long-stay provision for older people were contentious areas (Wistow, 1995). An indicator was devised looking at the proportions of users for whom there was a continuing medical need after assessment, but for whom that need was not met through NHS provision. This draws attention to continuing care policies and practice, and the ability of users to meet the costs of care from their own resources. Comparisons across districts could show whether this burden is spread evenly or not and will reveal the demands upon both users and social services resources. It is likely that there are no local systems capable of collecting these data on a routine basis. However, data can be compared with emerging research findings about this topic (Glendinning, 1998; Heaton et al., 1999; Simmons and Orrell, 2001).

The uses of these needs indicators include making comparisons between areas such that the indicators can show which areas are receiving high levels of referrals and which low levels. They can also show the differences in social need between different areas. Where there are high levels of social need it is reasonable to expect relatively high levels of referrals. Combining these two types of indicators can therefore be used to measure Horizontal Target

Efficiency (the extent to which those in need of services are in touch with them) (Davies and Challis, 1986).

Supply indicators

Indicators derived from this domain give a global picture of provision. Comparisons between areas will highlight differences in levels and types of provision as well as differences in service flexibility. This may include the extent of home care provision, the extent to which there is a choice of home or residential care for users, and the extent to which there is a flourishing independent sector for day, domiciliary and residential care. These together provide a measure of the local balance of care.

A number of supply aspects are reported routinely in national data. There are limited national indicators on some aspects, such as field social work and the provision of day, domiciliary and residential care by different providers. There are no national Key Indicators on residential places for the cognitively impaired. However, the Department of Health have recently reported on a regular basis on the extent of the independent market for day and domiciliary care. Social services departments also report on delivered meals through their returns to the Department of Health. The Department of Health produce information on places in nursing homes for older people. At the local level, most social services departments routinely collect information on the services they provide. These include: the numbers of social work staff; the number of purchased home care hours available from different providers; the number of delivered meals provided; and the number of day care places available to the elderly population. Information on the mix of residential and nursing care is also reflected in indicators relating to numbers of care home beds, both in total and according to different sector providers. Some of this information is not routinely provided, such as the number of home care hours provided out-of-hours and at weekends. Much of it, however, is included in national packages such as the *Key Indicators Graphical Package* (Department of Health, 2002b).

The sources from which to devise such indicators locally might include quarterly reports through the client information system, provider data, national and local population data using the census, and commissioning information.

Some of these indicators report on specific and detailed concerns about the supply of services. For example, the proportion of single rooms by residential care provider was intended to express the extent of privacy and choice within care home provision. The document Home Life (Centre of Policy on Ageing, 1984) recommended that 80 per cent of all places in residential care homes should be in single rooms (see also, Department of Health, 2002d). It may be desirable to demonstrate whether or not it has been possible to encourage the development of more single room accommodation. An indicator was also devised to report on the number of care places designed specifically for elderly people with cognitive impairment (EMI) by residential and nursing home providers. This indicator shows whether care homes, including those of the local authority, set aside places for cognitively impaired users. Some evidence (Evans et al., 1981) has suggested that mixed homes become dysfunctional once more than a third of residents are cognitively impaired. Comparisons between areas will therefore highlight differences in designated provision as well as differences between providers within areas. They may also indicate when there is cause for concern in the running of a home.

For some aspects of provision, different age groups for the denominators were identified. These are intended to reflect the different populations served by different forms of provision. For example, the number of weekly lunch club places is expressed per 1000 population aged 65 years and over. The age group for the population is lower for this indicator because there are a significant proportion of younger elderly users who attend lunch clubs.

Practice process indicators

These indicators were intended to monitor the stages and core tasks of care management, from case finding to closure (Challis and Davies, 1986; Challis et al., 1995). They are potentially one of the more difficult areas to measure on a routine basis. Practice process indicators are intended to measure the efficiency and quality of the whole care management process and to give a primary focus upon users and carers. Not dissimilar efforts at improving the quality of care management practice have emerged in a number of countries despite differences in the definition, organisation and funding of services. For example, quality assurance procedures have been developed in the US using appropriate indicators with which to measure the performance of the core tasks of care management (Geron and Chassler, 1994; Applebaum and McGinnis, 1992). In the UK, the development of the RAP returns represents the first national initiative to systematically capture these types of data. Such strategies, along with the use of these process indicators, have much to offer care management practice in the UK (Clarkson and Challis, 2003). These indicators are considered below, grouped under the core care management tasks.

Case finding and screening
Case finding or screening is intended to define a target population of older people requiring long-term care services (Kane, 1990; Challis, 1992). Indicators used to measure aspects of practice in this regard therefore concentrate on aspects of a department's referral and initial screening activities in relation to the older population. Therefore, such measures of the screening process will cover activity prior to the formal assessment stage in the care management

process. The degree to which the screening of referrals identifies an at-risk population of older people can be monitored by the use of measures of such activity.

On a national basis, indicators available in the RAP returns (Department of Health, 2001b) identify the number of contacts which result in a further assessment of need or the commissioning of an on-going service by assessment priority; the number of contacts whose needs were attended to solely at the point of contact; and the source of referral for these events. Such indicators are designed to monitor screening processes across local authorities.

The sources from which such indicators could be devised locally include: special studies and monthly and three monthly reports through the client information system.

In devising the PIAF indicators, reliable and valid information was needed on such factors as the time of initial contact, the time of first response, the numbers of referrals that resulted in a formal assessment and the actions taken after screening. These types of information are now close to that required in the RAP returns (Department of Health 2001b). A key indicator here is the time interval between acceptance of referral and a subsequent first contact by the social services department for people with varied levels of need. Such data are frequently used to measure the efficiency of case management systems in the US. In the state of Washington Department of Social and Health Services, for example, the time standard is five days following initial screening (Department of Social and Health Services, 1986). Since April 1993, many social services departments monitor this interval, particularly in relation to hospital patients. It is a recommended Citizen's Charter indicator taken from the Department of Health's Local Community Care Charters (1994a). Problems in definition are particularly crucial here. What was meant by initial response is likely to vary between areas due to important factors such as variations in intake systems and staffing patterns and levels. The indicator provides a measure of response time for the different priority bands. Although for some cases it will be likely that referral, contact and commencement occur almost simultaneously, for others intervals between these points will occur. It would be expected that on average the intervals should be shorter for higher priority cases.

Other indicators were devised to measure the efficient operation of care management at the screening phase. Aspects of Vertical Target Efficiency (the extent to which those who receive services are those for whom they were designed) could be measured by combining practice process with need indicators. An indicator of the number of ongoing cases (in different age bands and different user categories) was used to monitor aspects of targeting in relation to the aged population with a higher propensity to use services. This indicator should be ranked alongside social need indicators in different districts in relation to departmental targeting policy. Questions which could thereby be addressed would include: Is there variation across districts? Does the pattern of provision exhibit variation across age bands? Why is this so? Differences between areas might reflect differential targeting interpretations across areas. However, social need characteristics such as the availability of carers and housing circumstances might influence area proportions of cases. In addition, agency factors may be important, such as the policy of community nursing services and hospital discharge patterns between areas.

Assessment

It is important for departments to provide a consistent response to need across areas in response to initial referrals. Indicators in support of this area of practice were intended to assess to what extent these differences are of sufficient magnitude to be of concern. They could help to identify whether differences are real (due to differences in need/demand) or artifactual (due to inconsistency in reporting systems). Assessment related indicators included: the total numbers of assessments, the proportion of assessments that were comprehensive, and the distribution of assessment types across different types of priority level and degree of dependency. Successful targeting is likely to be associated with more intensive assessments being devoted to the more dependent and higher priority groups. The Single Assessment Process (SAP) categories (Department of Health, 2002c) could be usefully employed in this fashion.

National data available on assessment are contained in the Department of Health's RAP returns (Department of Health, 2001b), which include the number of clients for whom an assessment was completed or terminated, the number of clients for which care plans and reviews have been scheduled or carried out, the number of informal carers recorded in assessments, and the length of time between first contact and completed assessment by priority level and referral category.

The sources from which such indicators could be drawn locally include monthly and three monthly reports through the client information system. The RAP project (Department of Health, 2001b), has developed much informaiton in this area, although not in the degree of detail indicated here. The current national RAP returns contain comparable indicators to those devised locally in this work. For instance, an indicator of the proportion of carer assessments undertaken in cases where there was a carer involved was intended to reflect the extent to which carers received an assessment as a separate process, part of the older person's assessment or not at all. This was particularly relevant owing to the requirement to assess the needs of carers in the Carers (Recognition and Services) Act 1995 (House of Commons, 1995, c12).

The time taken for the completion of assessment and the implementation of a care plan was another indicator of a timely response in care management. Speed of completion is not necessarily a virtue in itself, particularly in complex cases. However where problem formulation and therefore required response are unclear, then testing care plans and revising them is probably more helpful than continued assessment. In the Case Management Program of King County, Seattle, for example, in general the assessment would be completed within five working days following receipt of a referral (King County Division on Aging, 1986). Similar approaches are employed in the State of Wisconsin Community Options Program (WDHSS, 1991). This is a complex area and special studies could be mounted to get behind the detail of when assessment ends, care planning begins and implementation commences (Glastonbury et al., 2000). Delay on this indicator could be attributed to ongoing assessment; ongoing care planning; partial or non-implementation of a care plan. This area is important as it measures the balance of time devoted to assessment activities compared with other aspects of care management and provision (Stewart et al., 2003). Some concern was noted in Department of Health monitoring that the demands of assessment activity are reducing continuity of involvement with carers and the neglect of reviews (Department of Health, 1993, 1994c).

Care planning and arranging services
Inevitably, early care plans can be like testing hypotheses: services are tested to see if they have the desired effect. Lengthy intervals between assessment and service provision may indicate such issues as lack of suitable available service responses, difficult liaison between assessors and providers, or contract problems. Therefore, the indicators relating to this area are ones such as the time taken between the completion of assessment and the start of services (by priority level). This indicates the degree of responsiveness in setting up services to meet identified need in relation to the complexity of cases.

Assessment and setting up of care plans need also to be related to clear aims and objectives for care. Indicators of the distribution of care plan aims and objectives were devised that could develop a clear link between assessment and care plans. The need for such clarity has been specified in Department of Health special studies (Department of Health, 1993, 1994c). It would be expected that care plans will be distributed across the different aims and objectives and excess focus on any one category or similar variability across areas might be indicative of a narrower focus of intervention.

The number of home care hours arranged per case (by dependency) was an indicator relating to the intensity of provision where the expectation of policy changes has been that, per case, intensity will increase as a result of targeting processes. This has been made clear by past work such as that in *From Home*

Help to Home Care (SSI, 1987). Comparison across time periods, districts and teams will indicate trends in intensity and also variations between areas. Again, this is a more subtle indicator of intensity than those used nationally since it links provision with dependency (Audit Commission, 1996b; Department of Health, 2001b).

Effective hospital discharge arrangements have been a longstanding concern to provide effective community care (Department of Health, 1994d; Styrborn et al., 1994; House of Commons, 2003). Two main factors underlie this: concern that assessment arrangements could increase length of stay in the acute sector for elderly people and the known consequences of poorly planned hospital discharge. An indicator of the percentage of patients discharged from hospital where social care services were not provided at home when required, according to the discharge plan, and the reasons for this was therefore included. Where a relatively high level of cases discharged without suitable services is found, consideration of the following factors would be relevant: Which hospital settings were involved? Are social services staffing levels adequate? Would changing the organisation of hospital based work assist? Service developments such as specialised hospital discharge services can be considered in the light of this indicator.

The sources from which such indicators could be devised include monthly and three monthly reports through the client information system, special studies and audit.

On-going contact, monitoring and review
Monitoring and review is part of the care management process from which attention is often diverted (Stewart et al., 2003). Assessment and care planning are tasks which probably receive greater attention in the literature and probably also in the time of practitioners (Department of Health, 1994c; Weinberg et al., 2003). This imbalance in focus was identified in the White Paper *Modernising Social Services* (Cm 4169, 1998).

The national data contained in the RAP returns include indicators designed to comment on the ongoing contact phase of the care management process. The returns include: the number of clients receiving services, the number of clients involved in service starts, transfers and finishes by service category, the number of clients receiving services by ethnic group, the length of time between first contact and first service and the length of time between first contact to the provision or commissioning of services. These indicators are comparable to the ones developed for the department in this local work.

The sources from which such indicators could be drawn locally included three-monthly reports through the client information system and special studies.

Indicators were designed to comment on various aspects of the on-going contact phase. Regular review of cases has been seen as one means of ensuring resources are used to best effect (Cm 4169, 1998). However, faced with a pressure of new assessments, agencies may be unable to conduct the reviews they would have wished. Consequently, there may be a degree of slippage of reviews, as assessment becomes a priority activity. A resource conflict may occur which requires monitoring. The implications of this conflict for a policy focusing resources upon high priority cases are particularly great. An indicator of the proportion of overdue reviews for people receiving home based care was devised to monitor this.

The follow up of elderly people in homes following placement and the balance of work of care managers between community-based and setting-based work is also important. An indicator of the proportion of overdue reviews in residential and nursing care was devised. This balance of activity is likely to influence the capacity of care managers to offer alternative home support to nursing and residential care. A high level of institution-based work is likely to reduce the ability to create and maintain extensive packages of home-based care. This was the experience in one Canadian province (Challis, 1994).

It was also judged important to monitor the style of practice of care managers/social workers in the light of debates about changing patterns of practitioner workload and optimal balance. An indicator of specific user-related time as a percentage of all time spent by community care workers was used to assess this. The balance of time spent by community-based workers between 'direct work' involving face-to-face contact with clients and carers may be expected to shift in care management with a greater degree of reliance upon 'indirect work' (Weinberg et al., 2003). However, insufficient time in direct work may be associated with a more administrative style of work with a correspondingly less 'clinical' approach (Challis, 1994; Huxley, 1993).

Case closure
Case closure is an important aspect to monitor since balance of workload may only be maintained with a balance of new cases and closed cases. A failure to achieve this is likely to lead to the inability to undertake reviews and an assessment-oriented mode of practice.

Data relating to case closure forms a part of the on-going contact phase for the purposes of the national RAP returns (Department of Health, 2001b). Indicator P3, which requests data on the number of clients involved in service starts, transfers and finishes, can be used to devise comparable indicators to the ones advanced here.

The sources from which such indicators could be drawn locally include three-monthly reports from the client information system on a routine basis.

Case closure indicators that were devised concentrated on a quarterly count of cases through the system and the duration of care provided both at home and in care homes. From this, a measure of turnover was devised focusing on the proportions of current cases opened and closed during each quarter and the switches between caseload types. This addresses issues such as potential 'silting up' of caseloads, and the capacity to manage assessment activities. Maintaining an appropriate balance between long-term cases and assessment/short-term work will depend on the specific role of the worker/team and the setting in which they are located. All these aspects can be monitored using this indicator.

Service process indicators

In contrast to practice process indicators, which are designed to comment on the quality of the care management process itself, service process indicators comment on the quality of services provided as a consequence of care planning by care managers (Geron and Chassler, 1994). In tandem, these two types of indictors offer a comprehensive selection of quality measurements intended to monitor care management performance. Indicators in the area of service process consider such things as the extensiveness and mix of provision, the optimal use of staff time, staff turnover ratios and the distribution of resources across different levels of need. These indicators can be used to measure the efficiency with which available resources are used as well as how they are deployed.

Nationally available information such as that in the Department of Health's *Key Indicators Graphical System* (Department of Health, 2002b) contains some indicators which relate to this domain, although not as extensively as those devised locally here. The Key Indicators include those relating to the number of households (rather than individual users) receiving home care and attendances by older people at day centres. However, these indicators are not broken down into types of specialist services received, such as the numbers receiving equipment or adaptations, those receiving teleshopping or community alarm systems. A number of issues of local relevance, such as the number of staff reporting problematic incidents or the number of older users reporting complaints, are not addressed in national data. Staffing patterns and ratios are also not included in the national package.

The sources from which such indicators could be drawn locally include three-monthly reporting through the client information system, special studies and staffing statistics.

An indicator of the number of older users of home care (per 1000 population aged 75 and over) was devised to examine the proportion of home care users as a proportion of the population at risk. This indicates the degree of spread of provision. On the one hand, spread has been valued in terms of preventative cover of vulnerable elderly populations. On the other, public sector provision of domiciliary support may have a particular niche in the overall pattern of care, such as supporting the most dependent and at risk groups. In such a scenario a relatively low level may be desirable and considered appropriate. High levels may be an indication for further development of the non statutory sector.

An indicator of specific user-related activity time as a percentage of all time spent by home care staff provides an indication of the optimal use of staff time, minimising the time spent in travel and administrative duties. The higher the proportion of time that can be spent on direct service-related activities in general, the better in terms of efficiency. However, where there are differences between areas these may be attributable to contextual factors such as rurality, or to style of operation such as attention to the details of matching the elderly person with their domiciliary care worker. Comparison of an area or district level on this indicator should be made with that of the authority as a whole and with available studies in other authorities for evaluation.

Other staff-related indicators were provided such as staff leaving rate, vacancy rates and sickness rates by staff group type. These are relevant to concerns about recruitment and retention (Department of Health, 2000). These were intended to cover such things as morale but vacancy rates may indicate areas of staff scarcity and also potential pressure points in the organisation which may impact upon morale and effective functioning. National information on vacancy rates and turnover would provide comparative information. In a social services organisation, higher levels of sickness might be seen as a measure of occupational stress and indicate where personal support interventions may be required.

Resource costs are a main element of care packages that require careful monitoring. The *total average weekly costs to the social services department of care packages in the community (in cost bands by dependency)* (SP9) covers the distribution of resources across different levels of need. The policy objective has been to focus resources upon those with higher levels of need, reducing the tendency to offer relatively fixed levels of service to people in different circumstances. Overall, it would be expected that a clear gradient of cost by dependency should be observed. Variations in this across the authority may suggest areas where there is room for further examination of the degree to which resources are reflecting differences in needs. A further indicator – *the proportion of older users at home whose gross weekly cost to the social services department is greater than a series of cost thresholds of residential care for older people* (SP10) was concerned with the balance of expenditure between residential and home-based care. The extent to which significant numbers of home care packages can exceed the cost of residential care is limited, and early warning of these cost pressures is required. This type of measure was previously used as an indicator of expenditure implications requiring review in the Kent Community Care Scheme (Challis and Chesterman, 1985).

Aspects of service usage were included in indicators so as to measure service efficiency. *The proportion of units of different care services actually provided to older people, as a proportion of the units purchased* (SP11) was an indicator concerned with the efficiency with which the available resources are actually used. This measures the extent to which allocated resources are used for the purpose of direct care for individual elderly people. The indicator will produce scores between zero and 100. Most services will be in the upper end of this distribution, where 100 indicates full utilisation of purchased/contracted resources. The extent to which an area, district or sector has less than optimal deployment of its home care resources may provide an indication of relative organisational slack (Hay and Morris, 1979). However, an indication of 100 may also be achieved where insufficient home care has been contracted and the under-supply has been fully used. For each service, multiplication of the indicator by 100 thus provides a percentage efficiency factor.

Efficiency in the use of residential beds and day care facilities was also expressed in indicators of occupancy (weekly and daily). In general, it would be believed that a higher occupancy rate would be indicative of a more efficient use of resources. However, some additional factors need to be considered in interpretation, which might distort this relationship. The length of time that a facility is open during the day and whether it is open at weekends, as well as the client group for whom it is designed, and whether it offers routine or back up/crisis services are important elements. In residential care, the higher the proportion of beds used for respite or short-term care, the greater the turnover and therefore the greater probability that there will be more vacancies and a consequently lower occupancy rate.

A variety of indicators in the service process domain were used to assist in judgements about the quality of care available. This aspect was measured in terms of user and staff ratios: home care staff per home care manager; users per home care staff; and residents per member of staff in local authority homes. Staff/resident ratios in residential care are an important proxy indicator of quality of care through the effect on such factors as security as well as upon the feasibility of positive activities to promote quality of life (Gibbs and Sinclair, 1992b; Mozley et al., 2004). This indicator is most appropriately employed on a comparative basis both longitudinally and cross-sectionally. Variations in staffing ratios across homes may occur due to differences in resident dependency and this must be considered as a possible explanatory element in examining variations.

The average number of current cases per social worker/community care worker, by dependency (SP21), was related to the capacity of care management to offer the possibility of greater residential independence as indicated in several policy documents (Cm 849, 1989; Cm 4169, 1998; Department of Health, 1998b). Caseload size has long been an indicator of the capacity of a service to offer an intensive approach to care management (Challis et al., 2001). In examining this indicator, caution is required when only considering averages, which may conceal key aspects of the distribution. For example, a high average caseload may consist of a small number of staff with relatively small caseloads, undertaking intensive approaches and a larger number with higher caseload sizes undertaking less intensive work. Hence, the indicator is also banded to permit distributions to be examined.

Outcome indicators

Many of the indicators in this domain represent intermediate outcomes – volumes of services produced – rather than final outcomes. They represent the end-points in the process of care but do not directly measure the effects of care on the client. They can be used to express areas of policy and practice related to the attainment of objectives. These objectives can be specified in terms of achieving a satisfactory coverage of services, or in terms of statements of intensity and quality (Knapp, 1984). All of these should be based on clearly articulated principles. For example, a policy objective – identified by many local authorities – was that of preventing unnecessary admissions to care homes. Where admissions have occurred it is important to attempt to identify the extent to which these causes might be remediable. Indicators of the reasons for admission and discharge to and from long-term residential and nursing home care make it possible to do this.

Nationally available information also tends to concentrate on indicators of intermediate outcome, such as the numbers of older people in residential and nursing homes. However, these data do not report on the numbers of users who subsequently leave such facilities nor their reasons for admission. These data are also not broken down to reflect the different dependency characteristics of service users. The sources from which such indicators could be drawn locally include monthly and three-monthly reports through the client information system and special studies.

The number of residents in long-term residential care for older people aged 75 and over, expressed as a proportion of the over 75 population (O1), covers the extent to which institution-based care is being substituted for home-based care. The Audit Commission has used a similar indicator, albeit not standardised on the higher-risk population. The advantage of this indicator is that it provides an index of admissions standardised on the main at-risk group rather than losing sensitivity to the influence of the 65–74 age group. The main focus of interpretation needs to be upon inter-area variation compared to the overall pattern of variation. A number of factors are important to provide contextual information. The historical legacy of provision sets the level of variation across areas and the base from which changes may take place. Hence, current trend data must also be examined. This is provided by the indicator of the *proportion of high dependency screenings supported at home after different time periods* (OI10). This focuses upon the community tenure of those seen as high risk on entry to the social services department's system. Area variations in this indicator may have longer-term expenditure implications which may be detected early through the proportion of high priority placements.

The proportion of new long-term placements by dependency bands (OI7) focuses upon the policy objective of 'downward substitution' of institutional by community care. It permits analysis of variations between subunits of the authority in terms of placement patterns. It can be compared with pre-existing levels of residential and nursing home places and of home-based care.

The indicator of the *proportion of older people discharged from hospital and helped by the social services department who are re-admitted within two weeks* (OI11) provides an indication of possible failures in discharge planning and support. Where variations are observed in proportions of patients discharged from hospital and admitted soon after, this may be attributable to a variety of factors. Some may be associated with over-early discharge, others with inadequately intensive home care. Of course, to formulate a coherent understanding and response requires other information such as hospital data on variations in re-admission rate, inter-agency consultation and possibly local joint commissioning decisions.

The use of indicators in this domain would focus on assisting managers in judging the attainment of objectives. For example, the objective of diverting inappropriate admissions from institutional care might be measured against indicators of the reasons for admission to residential and nursing home care. Variation in patterns of reasons for admission might indicate areas for local policy and practice initiatives: for example, where carer breakdown is higher in one area than another, or where housing factors are more prevalent, or where physical illness predominates. Carer factors might indicate a within department initiative for carer services whereas housing or illness factors might suggest a housing or community nursing initiative.

To provide a clearer grasp of the indicators that were produced, a summary is included in Table 6.2. These are abbreviated descriptions of the full suite of indicators which are set out more fully in Appendix 1. They are summarised according to the PIAF domains along with their reference numbers to assist interpretation.

The national/local performance interface

These performance indicators developed at the local level articulate local objectives in a national context and vice versa. Overall, the department's aim was to arrange effective, individual packages of care, involving users and carers. Services were to be timely and targeted on those most in need. Older people were to be offered choice from a range of services to meet their unique needs and to help divert them from institutional care by enhancing their ability to remain at home. In so doing, the authority strove to make the most

Table 6.2
Performance indicators for older people's services

PIAF domain	Indicators
Need	
N1	Social indicators of need – general
N2	Social indicators of need – older people
N3	No. of screenings per 1000 population 75 plus
N4	No. of screenings per 1000 population 75 plus with carer
N5	No. of screenings per 1000 population 75 plus in different user groups
N6	No. of re-screenings within 6 months per 1000 population 75 plus
N7	No. of screenings by assessment teams per worker
N8	No. of screenings by hospital social work departments per worker
N9	No. of referrals for assessment per 1000 population 75 plus
N10	No. of referrals for assessment per 1000 relevant age group
N11	No. of referrals for assessment per 1000 population 75 plus living alone
N12	No. of referrals for assessment per 1000 population 75 plus with carer
N13	No. of referrals for assessment per 1000 population 65 plus by ethnic group
N14	No. of referrals for assessment per 1000 population 75 plus in different user groups
N15	No. of referrals for assessment per 1000 population 75 plus involving abuse
N16	Screening source and consent of user
N17	No. of referrals for assessment in priority for response bands
N18	No. of cases for which there are service gaps
N19	Types and frequency of service gaps
N20	Users with continuing medical needs provided with substitute services
N21	Users with continuing medical needs charged for substitute services
Supply	
S1	No. of field work staff (generic/elderly user group) per 1000 population 75 plus
S2	Ratio of social workers to community care workers
S3	No. of OT staff per 1000 population 75 plus
S4	Percentage of OT staff who are qualified
S5	No. of home care hours per 1000 population 75 plus purchased by authority
S6	No. of independent sector providers of domiciliary care
S7	No. of home care hours provided by independent sector by source
S8	% of home care hours purchased by SSD provided in evenings or weekends
S9	No. of night sitting sessions purchased by SSD per 1000 population 75 plus
S10	No. of delivered meals per 1000 population 75 plus arranged by SSD
S11	No. of weekly day care places and family placements per 1000 population 65 plus
S12	% of weekly day care places for older people available at weekends
S13	No. of weekly lunch club places per 1000 population 65 plus by provider
S14	No. of people receiving daily intensive home care per 1000 population 75 plus
S15	No. of residential care beds per 1000 population 75 plus by provider

Table 6.2 continued

PIAF domain	Indicators
S16	No. of nursing beds per 1000 population 75 plus
S17	% of care beds in single rooms in total and by home
S18	No. of care beds for cognitively impaired elderly per 1000 population 75 plus
S19	No. of care beds for minority ethnic elders per 1000 population 75 plus
S20	No. of care beds for short-term/respite care per 1000 population 75 in total
S21	Expenditure on residential care placements per 1000 population 75 plus
S22	Expenditure on new residential care placements per 1000 population 75 plus
S23	Expenditure on nursing home placements per 1000 population 75 plus
S24	Expenditure on new nursing home placements per 1000 population 75 plus
S25	Expenditure on day care per 1000 population 65 plus
S26	Expenditure on home care per 1000 population 75 plus
S27	Expenditure on meals at lunch clubs per 1000 population 75 plus
S28	Expenditure on equipment and adaptations per 1000 population 75 plus
S29	Expenditure on all services for older people per 1000 population 75 plus
S30	% breakdown of total expenditure – long-term res/nursing home care
S31	% breakdown of expenditure on older people in support of promotion
S32	Unit cost of SSD residential care homes
S33	Unit cost of SSD home help hour
S34	Unit cost of SSD day centre attendance
S35	Unit cost of SSD delivered meals
S36	User contributions to costs of care packages as % of total expenditure
S37	Charges levied by private and voluntary sector homes

Practice process

Case finding and screening

PP1	Time between initial contact/referral and first response by priority band
PP2	Distribution of referrals for assessment within priorities
PP3	% of actions taken after screening
PP4	No. of ongoing cases per 1000 population 75 plus by proportion who are active
PP5	No. of ongoing cases per 1000 relevant age group by proportion active
PP6	No. of ongoing cases per 1000 population 75 plus in different user categories
PP7	No. of ongoing cases of people living alone per 1000 population 75 plus
PP8	No. of ongoing cases per 1000 population 75 plus with carers and status
PP9	No. of ongoing cases per 1000 population 65 plus in different ethnic groups
PP10	% of screenings from primary/secondary health care using special form

Assessment

PP11	No. of assessments per 1000 population 75 plus
PP12	% of assessments which are full
PP13	% of assessments in priority for service bands and dependency
PP14	Proportion of carer assessments undertaken
PP15	Time between first response and start of assessment by priority/setting
PP16	Time for the completion of assessment by assessment type

Table 6.2 continued

PIAF domain	Indicators
PP17	% of cases at home where assessments jointly carried out by NHS/SSD
PP18	% of cases assessed where mental health assessment undertaken

Care planning and arranging services

PP19	Time between completion of assessment and the start of services
PP20	Distribution of Care Plan Aims
PP21	Distribution of Care Plan Objectives
PP22	No. of home care hours arranged by SSD per case by dependency
PP23	Proportion of people admitted in emergency not reviewed within 72 hours
PP24	% of patients discharged from hospital where social services not provided
PP25	% of patients discharged from hospital, subsequently referred to SSD
PP26	Proportion of service users and/or carers not taking up a service
PP27	Proportion of people receiving domiciliary services by dependency
PP28	Proportion of people in each dependency category receiving services
PP29	No. of users receiving service packages by new/existing users
PP30	No. receiving services from different providers by new/existing users
PP31	No. of older people on supervision register per 1000 population 75 plus

Ongoing contact, monitoring and review

PP32	Proportion of overdue reviews for people receiving home-based care
PP33	Proportion of users referred for re-assessment prior to review
PP34	Proportion of reviews overdue in residential/nursing homes
PP35	Specific user-related time as % of all time spent by social workers

Case closure

PP36	Turnover – proportion of current cases opened/closed during each quarter
PP37	Duration of care at home by cost and dependency
PP38	Duration of care in care homes by cost and dependency

Service process

SP1	No. of older users of home care per 1000 population 75 plus
SP2	No. taking up and no longer needing home care service per 1000 population 75 plus
SP3	No. of older users of delivered meals per 1000 population 75 plus
SP4	No. of older users of day care per 1000 population 65 plus
SP5	No. of users with equipment/adaptations per 1000 population 75 plus
SP6	No. of teleshopping accounts used per 1000 population 65 plus
SP7	No. using the central alarm system per 1000 population 75 plus
SP8	User-related activity time as % of all time spent by home care staff
SP9	Total average weekly costs to SSD of care packages in the community
SP10	Proportion of users whose gross weekly cost is greater than cost thresholds
SP11	Units of different services provided as a proportion of units purchased
SP12	Proportion of users in different types of short-term care and reasons
SP13	Proportion financially supported in residential/nursing care by type of care

Table 6.2 continued

PIAF domain	Indicators
SP14	No. of older users reporting complaints
SP15	Number of staff reporting problematic incidents with users and carers
SP16	Home care staff per home care manager
SP17	Users per home care staff member
SP18	Day care users per care staff in day centres
SP19	Residents per member of care staff in local authority homes
SP20	Care staff per managers in local authority homes
SP21	Cases per field work staff member by dependency
SP22	Occupancy of local authority residential care facilities
SP23	Occupancy of local authority day care facilities
SP24	Staff leaving rate by staff group type
SP25	Staff vacancy rates by staff group type
SP26	Staff sickness rates by staff group type

Outcome

O1	No. of users in long-term residential care per 1000 population 75 plus
O2	No. entering/leaving long-term residential care per 1000 population 75 plus
O3	No. in long-term nursing home placements per 1000 population 75 plus
O4	No. entering/leaving long-term nursing homes per 1000 population 75 plus
O5	Reasons for admission to long-term residential /nursing home care
O6	Reasons for discharge from long-term residential /nursing home care
O7	Proportion of new long-term placements by dependency bands
O8	Proportion of current long-term placements by dependency bands
O9	Proportion of residents in placements possessing cost-raising attributes
O10	Proportion of high dependency screenings supported at home
O11	Proportion discharged from hospital and helped who are re-admitted
O12	Proportion of full assessments placed in homes and staying at home
O13	Proportion of older people supported in their own homes by dependency
O14	%. of screened carers attending carer support groups
O15	%. of screened carers attending training and information sessions
O16	% of older users accessing independent advocacy services
O17	No. of users and carers participating in community care planning process
O18	% of users satisfied with assessment and care management processes
O19	% of carers satisfied with assessment and care management processes
O20	% of users satisfied with services
O21	For closed cases, reasons for closure

efficient use of available resources. In Table 6.3, each of these objectives is highlighted with explanatory information and examples of useful indicators in support of them. Each indicator is accompanied by a number relating to abbreviated descriptions in the Appendix. This enables us to see how the recommended indicators were used to highlight areas of particular concern.

Table 6.3
Indicators within the local authority's key objectives

Local objective	Explanatory information	Examples of indicators[a]
Targeted	Services to right people at right time; services distinguish between dependency groups	PP2 – proportion of cases allocated to each priority category after screening
Timely	Ensure that the processes support good care	PP1 – Time between initial contact/referral and the first response by priority band
Efficient	Best use of resources; review of balance of spending in light of current resource position	SP9 – Total average weekly costs to the SSD of care packages in the community in cost bands by dependency
Diversion	To work out whether diversion from institutional care is efficient or effective; balance between diversion and what is possible	S14 – No. of elderly people receiving intensive personal care on a daily basis
Individual	Service response tailored to individual need; flexibility; care package diversity; volume and type of provision	S8 – % of home care hours purchased by SSD for older people provided in evenings and at weekends by sector
Involved	Client involvement in assessment, care management and decision making	N16 – Proportion of older users who self-refer or who are referred for screening by others
Choice	Range of services available; number of options offered to user	O5 – proportion of users falling into the main reasons for admissions codes defined by authority

Note: a Numbers relate to the indicators contained in the Appendix.

Levels and types of indicators

The PIAF indicators were broken down into three types. There are those which are 'core' (so important that they need to be produced and analysed routinely at all levels of management and practice) those which are non-core, and those requiring special studies. Core indicators could be produced monthly, quarterly or every six months. Non-core indicators could be produced quarterly or less frequently. Special studies could be six-monthly or annual. From special studies, it could be possible to identify ways to routinise information that proved to be valuable and worth producing on a regular basis.

As described earlier, developmental work was being undertaken in the authority to ensure that the social services department increasingly managed through information and evidence. Hence, some of the indicators that were recommended had already been produced; other indicators could be readily generated because the basic information was already collected and further indicators could be generated through slight modifications of existing information collections. However, some of the core indicators proposed presented challenges to the social services department and had to be accorded 'special study' status until ways of readily generating the basic information could be found. It is likely that in a developing environment this would always be the case.

Defining the indicators

Based on the developmental work with the department a number of indicators were identified of which 41 are core indicators. These are outlined fully in the Appendix. For each indicator listed there, the details were provided as shown in Box 6.3.

Comparable national indicators

There were several national sources containing some indicators comparable to those developed locally at the time of this work. These included:

CIPFA Personal Social Services Estimates (CIPFA-E);
CIPFA Personal Social Services Actuals (CIPFA-A);
Department of Health's Key Indicators of social services (DH-KI);
Department of Health's Community Care statistics (DH-CCS);
The Audit Commission's Citizen's Charter indicators (AC-CCI);
Community Care Charter requirements (CCC);

Box 6.3
Definition of indicators for social care

- *An Indicator number and title.* The numbering is based on the different types of indicator. Hence N4 is the fourth mentioned of the Needs Indicators, and PP16 is the sixteenth Practice Process Indicator.
- A full *Definition.*
- The Key Area to which the indicator relates. Sometimes an indicator can relate to more than one Key Area. Where an indicator provides essential contextual information for interpretation the Key Area is given as 'Context'.
- The component of the *Service Objective* to which the indicator relates. Sometimes an indicator can relate to more than one Service Objective. Where an indicator provides essential background information for interpretation the Service Objective is given as 'Background'.
- The *Indicator Status*, which says two things: first, whether the indicator is Core or Non-core or requires a special study; and second, how frequently the indicator should be generated.
- The *Benchmark* which states the comparator for indicator values at different levels of aggregation (e.g. district or team). The county average was the most usual benchmark.
- The *Level of Aggregation* which gives the various structural levels at which the indicator should be presented. Usually, it is suggested that each indicator should be given for the county as a whole, each district, and each team.
- *Notes* are given to elaborate on particular points of interest.
- *'Comparable national statistics'* sources are given whereby these indicators can be compared with indicators from other authorities.

The Association of Directors of Social Services' routine reports of referrals and assessments for adults, post- April 1993 (ADSS);
NHS Executive's Health Service Indicators (NHSE-HSI).

In addition to these annual booklets of indicator data, relevant national bodies have updated the types of indicators and revised definitions on a regular basis. Additionally, national indicators of immediate relevance to the recent government modernisation agenda are also reflected in the present work. The sources containing comparable information to that outlined here are:

Department of Health's Personal Social Services Performance Assessment Framework 1998–99 (DH-PAF)
Department of Health's Key Indicators Graphical System 2002 (DH-KIGS)
Department of Health's Referrals, Assessments and Packages of Care (RAP) in Adult Social Services (Department of Health, 2001b) (DH-RAP).

Sometimes a national indicator was defined in exactly the same fashion as the present indicators; at other times there were differences in definition. Where the differences are slight, the national indicator is clearly referenced as comparable, although a note of caution is given. Where the difference is more substantial, the text first states that no national comparisons can be made, after which the existence of the national information is noted.

In additional to information that is generated in indicator format by national bodies, there is a substantial amount of information collected and published in the public domain, not as indicators but as straightforward information. For example, the Department of Health produces statistical information about social services provision, staffing and usage which is not published in the Key Indicators or the Community Care statistics documents. Such additional information needs to be studied along with the indicator data to provide a context for interpretation.

It needs to be noted that not all the local authority's indicators are reproduced at the national level. Similarly, not all the national indicators are included in the local set of indicators. There are four reasons for this: first, the authority's indicators were specifically developed with staff in the authority for local purposes. Second and linked to the first point, the definitions of some national indicators do not enable social services staff to explore policy and practice issues that are important locally. Third, because of the nature of local authority information systems, not all the material that could be generated in an authority, either immediately or in the near future, can be generated at the national level. While social services staff develop their own indicators, they will need to ensure that their information systems remain capable of generating all the indicators required by national bodies, irrespective of their importance to the authority (Clarkson and Challis, 2002). Fourth, the level and degree of detail required at a national level is more general than that required for effective local management.

PIAF indicators within the Best Value framework

With regard to national indicators, a particularly salient area is the Best Value Framework (Cm 4014, 1998). This framework is now an important focus for local attempts at measuring performance. In this section, therefore, a number of the present indicators are located within the Best Value framework to provide further illustration of their contextual relevance. There may be more than one way of structuring the information provided and therefore social services departments need to consider the range of current legislative duties and national guidance in ordering their indicator information. Table 6.4 lists the performance aspects identified in the Best Value regime with examples of indicators derived from the PIAF model. Identified here is one of the authority's key objectives, *diversion*, and examples are given of indicators that

Table 6.4
Performance aspects of the Best Value regime with PIAF indicators

Aspect of performance	Indicators
Strategic objectives	Diversion objective
Cost and efficiency	Expenditure on home care per 1000 population 75 plus (S26 Expenditure on nursing home placements per 1000 population 75 plus (S23)
Effectiveness	Proportion of screening in high dependency band supported at home after different time periods (010) Proportion of current long-term placements by dependency bands (08)
Quality	Proportion of people admitted to homes in an emergency and not reviewed within 72 hours (PP23) % of patients discharged from hospital and required home services not provided according to discharge plan (PP24)
Fair access	No. of ongoing cases aged 65 and over in different ethnic groups (PP9) No. of care beds designated for minority ethnic elders (S19)

can be used to support it (reference numbers for these indicators relate to those in the Appendix). Examples of at least two indicators, reflecting both home care and residential care, are given for each aspect. This is in order that indicators may express the balance between residential and home-based care in judging this policy objective. This may be helpful for authorities in looking for ways forward to ensure their compliance with the duty to undertake fundamental performance reviews as part of Best Value (Cm 4014, 1998, pp. 69–74).

In setting local indicators alongside the Performance Assessment Framework and the government's objectives, work needs to be undertaken as to sources of information. For example, ethnic origin is not collected on a consistent basis by most social services departments. However, it is an essential indicator as a measure of equity and Horizontal Target Efficiency. Thus, there is a common finding that black people are under-represented among referrals and service users. From the indicators of fair access chosen from this suite of indicators, questions could be asked such as: to what extent does the actual proportion of ethnic minority referrals reflect the age-specific proportion? To what extent does the pattern of cases reflect the pattern of referrals? Are there places in homes set aside for minority ethnic users? Comparisons between areas will highlight differences in designated provision, as well as differences between providers within areas. There could be choice issues for black users who could prefer homes with a high proportion of other black users.

Setting out the material in this way enables authorities to see how their own local objectives may fit into the new framework. It may also be used as a guide to sources of relevant information in the package of indicators we have provided.

Standardisation and aggregation of Indicators

Before evidence can be utilised as an indicator of performance, there are some simple points which need to be borne in mind. These involve ensuring that there are valid comparators, that information is appropriately standardised and that it is suitably aggregated.

Underlying many indicators is the assumption that there is an expected level or rate against which the actual level or rate for any level of aggregation should be compared. For example, one indicator (N10) relates the referrals for assessment to the elderly population in terms of broad age bands. The actual age groups of the cases in any one district or team can be compared with the actual age groups of cases in the authority as a whole. Everything else being equal, one might expect the proportions for the authority, the districts and teams to be roughly the same. Where differences occur, they need to be explained.

Many indicators comprise a numerator and a denominator. The numerator always refers to older users aged 65 and over. The denominator will often be different, most referring to the population aged 75 and over. This is because most service users are aged over 75 and it is sensible to relate the number of users (albeit including some 'young' old people) to the main groups in the population (that is, those aged 75 and over) from which older users are drawn. However, for day care, lunch clubs and a handful of other services, higher proportions of users aged between 65 and 74 are to be expected. Therefore, for indicators relating to these services the denominator is the population aged 65 and over.

Measures of dependency are not frequently available for cases living in the community. To permit comparisons between users of community-based care and residential settings, measures of dependency for all cases are required. It is important to distinguish between measures of dependency or potential need for care, and priority for service response, which might reflect the need for immediate action rather than the long-term nature of the care required.

Some indicators, for example certain needs indicators (N4 and N5), comprise a number of sub-indicators, relating to different types of information. Social services departments may wish to retain these composite indicators as single indicators, but may prefer to break them down into different indicators using their component parts.

Summary

This chapter has considered the design and collection of relevant indicators within the PIAF model. These indicators were linked to the local objectives of the social services department in planning its services for older people. By devising a suite of indicators located within each domain of the PIAF, this approach exemplifies a dynamic, logical and planned method for the design and collection of indicators. Such an approach represents an improvement on earlier approaches to indicator development in that it enables linkages to be discerned between indicators, thus enabling more complex dimensions, such as efficiency, to be monitored. Having used the model advanced here in order to guide the design of measures, indicators of relevance to particular objectives can then be drawn from the suite of potential indicators. This facilitates the analysis of indicators against appropriate standards. The next chapter moves on to consider the implementation and use of such indicators in the local context of one social services department.

Chapter 7

Implementing Performance Measurement

It will be apparent from previous chapters that a diffuse and voluminous literature has developed on performance measurement, throughout many parts of the public sector. Despite this, there is a lack of empirical work in social care concerning the translation of these principles into practice. Without this, we are unlikely to see the benefits of performance measurement systems for the future practice of social care. While the conceptual refinements so far discussed are important, they need to be grounded within an understanding of how performance information can be used within the setting of an individual department. Two questions emerge as central: can the performance mechanisms so far discussed be applied to the routine work of social services? Moreover, what actions and benefits result from this?

A start was made in the last chapter in discussing the content of some of the suite of indicators which are shown in the Appendix. However, the construction of logical, coherent and theoretically consistent indicators is only one part of the effective monitoring of performance. The other component is the process of implementation. Although implementation of performance systems is not the central thrust of this book, this chapter describes some of the processes employed to engage staff in the activities of using information, systematic examination of patterns of variation across units of organisation, formulating questions or hypotheses and deploying available information to answer those questions. The focus is on ways in which indicators can be used and the utility of the information they provide in assessing the objectives of social care services for older people.

Interviews were held with a range of senior staff in the social services department who had played key roles in the planning, development and implementation of performance indicators for older people. The rest of this chapter is concerned with outlining key issues which emerged from these interviews, which were conducted once the performance system had been operational within the department.

Introduction: the experience of implementation

The implementation of the indicators in the social services department was very much a case of 'designing the system' of performance measurement (Jackson and Palmer, 1989). Thought had to be given as to who was to collect the necessary information; who was to receive it and in what form; how data were to be presented; and what action was to be taken as a result of the information. One important aspect to emerge was the matching of indicators to specific objectives and activities for which particular staff had responsibility. So, performance information may be understood as being devised at different levels, according to the use that is to be made of it and its importance and relevance. Two particular issues became important: the frequency and form of reporting performance information; and how it was presented. In the rest of this chapter, the processes involved in implementing the PIs recommended by PSSRU are highlighted. The systems in place within the department, which described aspects of routine work and how these systems were used to feed information back to staff, were outlined earlier. The initial interviews with social services staff also looked at their future information requirements. During 1999, further visits were made to the department in order to look retrospectively at how these performance systems had developed and question key managers who were involved in the initial process to review the problems involved in implementation. Outlining the problems and prospects for performance measurement described here may go some way in providing information of use to other departments experiencing difficulties with the current performance agenda.

When the work began, normal practice in the department, as in most at the time, was one where social work activity was not systematically measured and management of budgets near to the front line was relatively new. It was a period of change necessitating a huge culture shift within the department, the success of which was viewed as attributable, in part, to the performance framework being developed with PSSRU. The process of implementation followed an iterative process involving a staff group and their internal knowledge of the organisation. This was a group of enthusiastic staff who were not just 'inputters' to the development process but also 'message takers' to the rest of the organisation. This was a challenging position for the group: a recognition by practitioners of a need for external input in order to improve services. PIs had been commissioned earlier in children's services and this existing model was helpful as, within older people's services, the volume of work overwhelmed people and left staff with a lack of grip on what was happening. The children's model thus provided an example of prioritisation and helped staff to be clear about current policy issues.

Although the authority was well placed to begin this work at the start of its commission to PSSRU, owing to its effective use of information technology and the development of a performance measurement system in children's services, there was still a need to engage staff in the principles and methods for using PIs and in some of the ensuing debates. The work therefore focused on organisational as well as technical aspects of implementation (Walsham, 1993). Much recent evidence (SSI/Audit Commission, 1998c) has also reinforced the view that more consistent performance measurement systems require not only improvements in technology but also a shift in culture and attitudes on the part of staff. The implementation of performance measurement is thus as much a management issue as a technology issue (Warburton, 1999). A strategy was therefore needed in order to engage staff in the use of information and to clarify what this meant for their day-to-day work. The involvement of a wide range of staff in the evaluation of community care services, because of the complexity of the system and the number of people involved, was seen as the way to take this work forward. Staff at different levels in the organisation were involved in reviewing performance information, raising questions about how services worked and then formulating further questions so as to sharpen understanding. In time, this was described as having brought about a 'mini-research culture' in the organisation.

The interviews with managerial staff who had been involved in the implementation process covered the following domains: an explication of the process of implementation and an evaluative judgement by the staff concerned of the perceived strengths and weaknesses of the approach. The chapter follows this pattern. In the next two sections, the development and implementation processes are considered, followed by discussion of specific issues relating to the whole process concentrating on the lessons learned: measurement issues; the role of the PIAF framework; barriers to implementation; staff factors; dissemination; and staff involvement.

Development process

The process of development described here was an iterative process between PSSRU and the staff involved. This focused firstly on specification and clarification of the measurement approach. Different types of indicator were designated and some of these were to be collected as core, others as non-core indicators and some as the focus of special studies. Secondly, relevant national policy and local goals were considered as an environment within which to locate relevant indicators. After an initial presentation of the framework and draft indicator format to a group of management staff, there was a series of intensive meetings whereby each proposed indicator was considered in the light of feasibility of data collection, relevance, clarity of specification and means of standardisation. This led to the final set of indicators described earlier and listed in the Appendix.

The initial development of the PI system began with the linking up of the authority's key objectives such as Diversion and Timeliness with possible indicators from each domain of the PIAF (Chapter 6). In many ways, these objectives represented a local formulation of national policy. From this point, indicators were reviewed and developed in detail as part of an ongoing process of refining information and feeding it back to staff. As a start to the process, a mission statement outlining a number of key principles was clarified and agreed by staff as part of the process of operationalisation of what Algie (1975) has termed 'banner goals' into day-to-day indicators. Such a statement of key principles appeared essential to underpin any performance measurement system. The statement of key principles developed in the department is outlined in Box 7.1.

Moving on from this, key initial elements were debates about the role of proxy indicators (whether correlations were evidence of causality and the relationship of process to outcome); and whether modes of recording and definitions were accurate. Focusing upon these issues through intensive periods of activity in events such as 'away days' proved very helpful in sustaining this process.

The work eventually engaged a wider range of staff through a series of workshops. The authority's key objectives provided a set of locally derived 'output' domains; indicators were operationalised so as to reflect the impact of the way in which services were provided. The work was therefore not primarily viewed as measuring performance in the abstract but was about using information to influence styles of work in order to improve the quality of service delivery.

Implementation

There were many views about what would constitute the most effective means of implementing the performance measures within the social services department. A number of issues had to be taken into account. First, there was a need to spread information and understanding across a wider range of staff, in terms of both numbers and levels, from the core group of predominantly middle managers who had invested in shaping and planning the indicators. Secondly, there was the classic debate between 'big bang' versus 'stockade' modes of implementation (Fisher and Kenny, 2000). The former would consist of attempting to make a large number of indicators operational on a particular

---

Box 7.1
The social services department's key principles of performance measurement

- There is a need to recognise the fundamental difference between information systems and the raw data they produce and key performance management information which is derived from this.
- Raw activity data are essentially neutral as they cannot be interpreted without explanation or evaluation by senior managers.
- Strategic performance data must incorporate trends in activity over time as well as enable fair comparisons to be made across the county by standardising activity data (such as rate per 1000 population).
- Performance data must link directly to the measurement of agreed policy objectives and targets.
- There should be one overall performance management system which is corporately commissioned by lead senior managers and which is delivered via the business management function.
- The data which drive the performance system must be accurately and uniformly inputted across the group and system outputs should similarly be consistent on a county and district basis.
- Performance data should be routinely fed back to all staff at the appropriate level of detail and at agreed intervals.

---

date in the near future with the concomitant risk of poor data and insufficient staff understanding but the advantage of scale of effect. The latter would consist of taking forward a limited number of indicators for which data could be reliably collected in a planned and focused way, with the risk that implementing the larger group of indicators would be postponed for a long period due to technical and organisational factors.

Thirdly, there was the debate about whether a 'top-down' or 'bottom-up' strategy should be employed. The former would have the benefit of fast implementation but might be received less than wholeheartedly by staff. The latter might engage a larger number of staff but would risk the process of implementation being both lengthy and costly. Fourthly, it was debated whether changes should be made to information systems prior to moving ahead, or whether those changes should be made as part of and in response to the process of implementing the indicators.

Of course, there is no optimal or easy solution to balancing these dilemmas but it was decided to take the indicators forward on the basis of a few key indicators for each of the then prevailing policy objectives, such as timeliness and diversion. The focus on this limited number of indicators made it more feasible to pursue a second goal, that of developing a more information orientated approach to decision making in social care.

The means chosen for implementing these indicators was a series of workshops. The first of these, as already stated, focused upon the framework within which the indicators were based, the PIAF, and upon sample indicators within different domains of this framework. This provided an opportunity for a wider group of staff to familiarise themselves with the indicators and the underlying rationale for their development. The later workshops focused upon the presentation of data from the limited number of indicators chosen for each of the key objectives shown on a comparative basis by district and the average for the county as a whole. This comparative approach was deliberately designed so that staff could begin to examine the reasons behind variations in different districts and consider whether remedial action was required. Other levels of aggregation could also be used for analysis. For instance, similarities and difference in service response between teams could be compared. Even variations between individuals within teams could be compared against variations between teams. Again, performance, particularly financial performance, could be compared over time. Finally, comparison of actual performance could be compared against expected performance. The interpretation of data is dependent on the benchmark chosen, so that if the comparator is the departmental average, analysis will be different than if the comparator is by year or against some external standard, drawn from research or best practice approaches.

Examples from these presentations, focusing on three objectives, those of Targeting, Efficiency and Timeliness, follow. Firstly, the objective of *Targeted* services was set to focus priorities for service delivery on the most vulnerable older people. Initially, the achievement of this objective was difficult to measure. A standardised measure of dependency was needed that could be integrated into the assessment process in order to signal those cases who were most vulnerable and in need of more intensive care. A dependency scale was thus developed for use in all assessments where residential or nursing home care might be considered. The scale relied on professional judgement as to a person's functional ability in domains such as personal hygiene, mobility, night attention, continence, memory and mood. In addition to covering many of the criteria required for an assessment tool (Stewart et al., 1999), the scale was intended to inform care managers' judgements and provide consistency across workers and teams. Dependency scores from the scale were aggregated into five 'bandings' that were also used to assist with payments for residential and nursing home care. Inspection of indicators relating to both home care and placement activity by dependency bands was thus used to comment on the targeting objective. Figure 7.1 outlines output on one indicator examining the distribution of current long-term placements of older people by dependency bands. This intermediate outcome indicator measured the prevalence of placements in both residential and nursing home care at the end of each month. An interesting difference occurred in the distribution of care banding across districts. The highest dependency placements (dependency 5) were the most expensive for the department to fund but one district, district 1,

Figure 7.1

Intermediate outcome indicator – distribution of current long term placements by dependency bands (one month figure 1997/98)

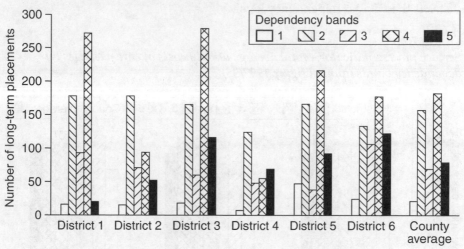

had fewer proportionately than other districts. Management enquiry found several reasons why this might be so. Of most importance was the existence of health practitioners within care management teams in the district. This had the effect of moderating nursing assessments and identifying more accessible health service provision in the area, both factors that reduced the need for high dependency nursing home admission in the district. The dependency profile of placements across the County did not show a smooth gradient of placements against dependency. Further action was therefore required in order to target resources more precisely, in particular domiciliary services, towards the more vulnerable elderly. Of particular note were the high numbers of placements in particular districts in dependency band 2, which reflects those older people needing a high level of assistance or supervision that could, nevertheless, be provided at home. The characteristics of such cases warranted further attention and, in this way, the system was seen as useful in directing attention to areas of concern.

The department's *Efficiency* objective was measured in a number of ways. Firstly, efficiency relates to the best use of resources and to ensuring that spending decisions are continually reviewed in light of the current resource position. Therefore, appropriate indicators to measure the success of this objective were those relating to cost and particularly the cost of care packages, with a reference point being the limit on care packages at home (£185 per week at the time of the study). Care packages costing more than this were signalled for special attention from team leaders and management. In order to monitor the overall efficiency of home care, a service process indicator was devised showing the total average weekly costs of care packages by dependency (see Figure 7.2). This indicated more variation of costs across districts than across dependency levels.

Figure 7.2
Service process indicator – total average weekly costs of care packages by dependency bands (annual figure 1997/98)

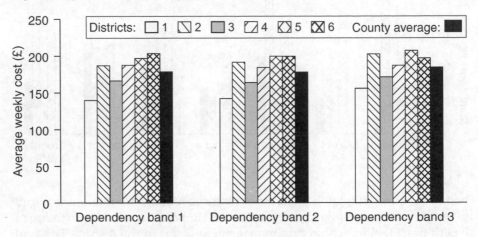

At one point, the department set targets for a five per cent reduction in costs overall with a ten per cent reduction in the costs of high cost packages. Increases in income collection through charges were also planned to achieve this objective. The information in Figure 7.2 enabled managers to see the variation across districts in the cost of care packages compared with the County average. The average cost of care packages differed across districts although within districts this average cost was consistent over time. Two districts whose care package costs were consistently lower than others, districts 1 and 3, were signalled for special attention. It was found that their staffing levels were similar, as were their purchasing patterns. In both districts, most care packages costing less than £100 per week were composed of single services, such as home care. Certain factors were seen as contributing to these purchasing patterns: both districts had a larger supply of day care in their localities and were smaller geographic areas, leading to efficiencies in travel costs of home care staff. Similarly, the consistently high average cost of care packages in district 6 was thought to be attributable to the greater proportion of the population aged 85 and over in this district. Further analysis was undertaken (not shown), plotting the average cost of care packages by age band where a clear gradient of costs by age was found. However, a similar relationship was found in other districts. It was considered that further analyses were required in order to seek explanations for these variations and that these would have to involve appropriate statistical analysis. An optimal statistical model might have to be a multivariate one rather than an analysis along single indicators. This would help to explain to what extent dependency was a determinant of cost variation as opposed to other sources, such as levels of supply, the influence of local hospitals or health care providers, or factors such as rurality and population across districts.

Another strand to the efficiency argument was the need to judge whether in-house home care was cost effective in comparison with the independent sector. Indicators of unit cost were therefore employed to examine differences between the two sectors. It was found that the cost of in-house home care appeared to be expensive. Drawing on these comparisons, efficiencies in in-house home care were made in a variety of ways: first, savings were made by the use of appropriate technology such as teleshopping for those clients requiring this type of assistance; second, by reducing travel costs of home care staff by locating of teams nearer to the clients served; third, through the introduction of flexible working practices to respond to a rapid rise in packages that required frequent short visits throughout the day and night. In these ways, the management information produced by the department was beginning to show benefits in terms of monitoring costs and outputs in a more detailed fashion. The more precise measurement of unit costs was essential to this process. At the time of implementing the approach, efficiency was very much linked to the current policy concern of consistency (Cm 4169, 1998): examining the costs of services across districts and across clients with similar dependency profiles in order to learn from these possible sources of variation.

Some of the indicators identified for use at the workshops were ones with high policy relevance in terms of the quality of service delivery but for which data systems did not permit available information. The best example of this was an examination of the time between screening and assessment and assessment and service provision for older people at different levels of priority (indicators PP15 and PP19). While the outputs of such indicators were presented to the workshops, it was already apparent that collecting data on the care management process in this way presented a number of difficulties. The presentation of findings from these indicators stimulated debate as to when assessment begins and ends, when care planning begins and implementation commences. Such debates need to inform the design of information systems supporting the collection of these kinds of data. These indicators were used to measure the *Timeliness* objective. Figure 7.3, for example, outlines data on one indicator measuring the time taken to complete assessments from initial intake for priority 1 (high risk) cases. For higher priority and complex cases such as this, the required response may be unclear but continued assessment is not helpful as it inhibits testing of the care plan.

Figure 7.3
Practice process indicator – time for completion of assessment from initial
intake (in days) for priority 1 (high risk) cases (annual figure, 1996)

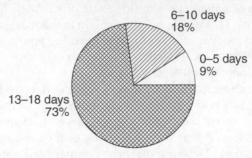

The timeliness of response in completing assessments can be compared to an external standard: in this case, the minimum requirement that assessments be completed within ten days of intake used in some US states (Justice, 1993). This may be a useful yardstick on this indicator, and delay may be attributable to ongoing assessment or partial or non-implementation of the care plan. In presenting these preliminary data in the presentations, it was found that over nine per cent of assessments for this priority group took longer than ten days to complete. This generated further questions as to whether investigations should be planned to enquire as to the characteristics of those cases that showed delay on this indicator. Were there particular circumstances, for example, that led to delay in assessing high priority cases across the county or in particular districts?

Approximately fifty staff would attend each of the workshops. Initially the management group led the discussion on the key domains and how to collect the relevant information. The format of the workshops developed with time but would always commence with a presentation of these comparative data and interpretation of the relevance of some of the variation identified. The summarising of information in this way meant that different people in the organisation were examining the same data at different levels of aggregation salient to their operational concerns. Thus the Director could see activity levels across districts; Senior Managers in charge of districts could see activity levels between districts; Principal Officers (who direct the purchasing) could identify similarities or differences between teams. Most importantly, teams could monitor their own performance against that of their peers, not as a competitive mechanism but as a means of judging their own performance.

Ongoing sub-groups were formed focusing on indicators relevant to each of the policy domains and, for those indicators which lacked available data, the working groups would plan, and in-between workshops execute, special studies to provide data for these indicators. A breakdown of the rationale for these sub-groups is provided in Table 7.1 as an example in time, where the purpose, source of information and style of analysis of each specific study are

Table 7.1
Outline of sub-groups investigating indicators relevant to each policy domain

Sub group	Methods of investigation		
	Identify a target for area of activity	Review in light of changing purchasing guidelines	Identify any additional areas to measure and report on
Timely	A need to define different categories of response before setting targets.	Indicator would not require adjustment; it will highlight problems that should be responded to.	Measuring timely reviews could provide insight on the impact of reviews upon assessments.
Efficient	5% reduction (County) in average cost of care packages. 10% reduction in proportion of high cost packages. 5% improvement in income collection.	Current principles are in line with activity on this indicator.	There is an urgent need to establish dependency bands for people receiving community care packages. Average costs could then be set for each band.
Targeted	Targets set for percentage increase within established priority bands. But problems with this.	Current pressure to respond to priority 1 and 2 but to delay priority 3 responses.	A better measure of targeting would use priority for service categories.
Choice	Difficult to set targets for reason for admission to care homes. The use of this PI has declined.	Degree of choice limited by financial constraints and a revised aim ought to be the extent to which, once assessed as needing residential care, people are given a choice as to establishment.	None.
Involvement	100% of users giving their consent for referral.	Good practice to maximise involvement and legislation requires this.	Monitor involvement of carers in the process.
Individualised	16% SSD home care purchased on weekends. 1% independent provision to be used after 11 pm.	Major conflict in individual current policies.	Different systems have operated to measure Independent sector and SSD home care. This needs to be clarified.
Diversion	Many assumptions underlie diversion policy. Target could be proportion of people/spend between high and low cost care not exceeding x% of total.	Problems in system as receipt of day care alone can put users in the category of intensive home care.	Target not only for those residing in community but also needs to be set between bands and between agencies.

presented. Targets were set for each policy objective and these were revised in the light of changing policies. This approach was different to that of the county-wide comparisons, which used the county average as a yardstick to enable staff to question and explain variation. Instead, targets sought to establish an expected level of performance to inform staff whether they were 'on-line' to achieve policy intentions. The conclusions from some of these special studies would then inform the presentation of data. For instance, one conclusion of these studies was the very real need to develop dependency and priority bands for community care activity so as to adjust for 'casemix' in any comparison of activity. These adjustments were, as already shown, included in the data presented to workshops.

A subsequent session in the workshops would examine the relationship between practice, local policy developments and national policy issues so as to make explicit closer linkages between individual practice, the activities of individual units of organisation, the social services department and national policy. Finally, the PSSRU would contribute an external perspective on the process of development and possible ways forward to develop the indicator process. Box 7.2 shows a sample workshop agenda. Workshops took place initially on a three-monthly basis over an eighteen-month period from whence the frequency reduced to a four to five month period.

Although at this stage staff involvement was very high and was quite analytical, there were still a number of problems to overcome. The first problem was a technical one, where the information required to provide some of the proposed indicators was simply not available. Often, there had to be special data collections to answer key questions such as the indicator for timeliness of response – identifying the passage of time between referral, assessment and receipt of care package. Much discussion ensued concerning the difficulties in collecting information on the assessment process, for instance, where does it begin and end? Links between resource and activity information were also not common. Other problems centred on the continued development of the information system. Work was identified in making links between the main information suites of Workforce, Finance, Children's services and Community Care. There was the task to eventually process and store all data pertaining to community care activity centrally so that differing information needs could be catered for from the same location.

Lessons from the implementation process

Some of the strengths and weaknesses in the implementation process were highlighted during interviews with key staff involved in the work. Firstly, the manner in which the whole process of implementation was conducted was seen by staff as particularly helpful. It served to clarify the goals of the

---

Box 7.2
A sample workshop agenda

9.0 **Arrival**

9.20 *Introduction*
Aims of the day

9.30 *Key issues from last workshop*
District feedback

10.30 **Coffee**

10.45 *Home care monitoring*
Current priorities
Reports
Unit costing

11.15 *Information suite*
Presentation of indicators

11.45 *District groups*

12.30 **Lunch**

1.30 *Feedback from groups*

2.00 *Community care plan 1997/2000*

2.20 *Groups – to consider key issues*

2.55 *Feedback*

3.15 **Tea**

3.30 *District assessment service*

3.45 *Comments from an academic perspective – PSSRU*

4.0 *What else is going on?*

4.30 **Close**

---

organisation for the staff involved – what they did and why. In retrospect, some managers were of the view that the process could have benefited from a clearer specification of the goals of the implementation at the outset. However, in contrast, the involvement of the university and social services department staff together was perceived as making sense of the whole process. These different standpoints were used to ensure theory and practice were being continually scrutinised. Although this seemed, at times, more untidy and time-consuming, the process was perceived as offering a greater degree of gain than otherwise would have been the case. Practitioners and first line managers were confronted by the need to be more disciplined in their use of information and being required to link theory to practice – the need to test ideas against relevant, external criteria rather than merely trusting professional judgement.

In retrospect, the local authority staff considered that it would have been helpful to have placed more explicit prioritisation in relation to the process of implementation. The overall process raised the question of 'satisficing' with regard to indicators. That is, was information asked for that was more easily obtained, but which had relatively low value on its own, or could more appropriate indicators have been demanded that meant new systems and processes had to be put into place? Speed presses for the former while quality for the latter. An example of this was the ready availability of financial information at the outset due largely to the culture of financial management existing in the department at the time. A continuing learning process was therefore important to deliver a suite of wider indicators in keeping with the organisational concerns of the department.

Linking indicators to the existing departmental key objectives, in retrospect, was perceived as more relevant to managers than to practitioners. A large number of indicators were initially designed and from these a few were chosen. This incremental approach was seen as being the right method at the time. The organisation was changing its culture and getting people to move their thinking by simplifying processes into a number of smaller indicators was seen as valuable. This pragmatic approach worked because it focused upon indicators with multiple purposes in contrast to managers' traditional focus on financial aspects alone. The aim was to focus upon the most defensible indicators in terms of what staff had routinely reported during the course of their work. The success of this also gave positive feedback to staff. A key turning point was the enthusiasm of one particular business manager who had substantial control over information and could bring together activity and cost data and was able to disseminate it in a usable and coherent form.

The process of implementation was characterised by a number of different elements. Each of these is discussed below as a way of expanding on the issues raised by staff concerning the strengths and weaknesses of the approach.

Measurement issues

As the work progressed, these examples of output from the system began to be seen as limited. Building on the model developed in the department, measuring social care performance was seen as more complex than originally supposed. The comparative information produced so far related to individual indicators chosen for their salience to important organisational objectives with the benchmark chosen as the County average. At first, this approach was seen as essential in terms of building competence in examining data and in developing an information culture within the organisation. However, it was increasingly seen as important to employ external benchmarks derived from research or good practice. It was also realised that to monitor performance in a more detailed and sophisticated fashion required combinations of indicators and statistical techniques that could examine when differences between areas were of sufficient magnitude to be worthy of investigation. In this respect, links with an academic environment were viewed as crucial in aiding staff attempts at monitoring performance in a more faithful way than perhaps current national collections, such as the PAF, allow.

The process of formulating relevant questions also led staff to consider the need for more complex multivariate techniques for examining particular aspects of performance. For example, in considering the average costs of care packages, staff commonly identified other factors that could have been important in explaining the variation across districts. In order to control for these factors, multivariate procedures could have been used to assist managers to judge which factors contributed most to costs and which did not. Multivariate procedures, cited earlier, used in some research studies examining performance information within social services departments have much to offer work at this level (Gibbs and Smith, 1989; Llewellyn, 1994). However, these methods rely on extensive and good quality data and it may be some time before the right conditions for analysing such data are available within authorities.

The PIAF

The PIAF framework was seen as a valuable tool in helping staff to move towards forming explanatory causal hypotheses and questioning the environment in which they worked. It enabled people to move from relatively simplistic single causal models to the evaluation of the inter-connectedness of several features. It was seen as a way of ordering information, in the first instance, against relevant criteria, permitting performance indicators to be developed around them. The framework was seen as very helpful in that it was simple, easy to identify with, and it therefore provided an anchor for the subsequent development of indicators. Practitioners were able to use it to integrate the material and to see performance as a production process moving from local demand to the impact of services on the individual client, or the aggregation of individual impacts within a district. The link between activity and outcomes was viewed as particularly useful along with the distinction between intermediate and final outcomes. This latter element was a particularly important distinction as most staff were locked into focusing upon the immediate outcomes of their activity: namely, users receiving a service. The PIAF was therefore seen as helping staff to recognise that there was also a final goal to their activity. It enabled staff to see how all the components of the department's work fitted together. Once it was explained to the staff involved, the framework was seen as beneficial in organising the thinking process.

However, the framework was more difficult for fieldworkers to grasp, and the capacity to look at the final parts was very limited since there was a lack of readily employable outcome measures available. There was also a danger in these staff viewing it as a linear model. The interactions between the elements in the PIAF were presented as a two-way process, but this may not have been sufficiently grasped by field level staff working within their particular area of responsibility. In addition, most of the work using the framework focused on need (on the left side of the model) rather than outcome and it was harder to collect 'true outcomes' routinely. For this, managers felt that specific measures were probably needed, such as institutionalisation, morbidity and mortality data. They considered that, in the future, outcomes could be linked into the client review process. It would then be possible to ask if the client had got better or worse, even by employing simple 'same-better-worse' categories and including these in coded form within the computerised system. This same issue was recently found to be true in a review of the department's Community Care processes and procedures. There was evidence of well-developed assessment and care plan activities but poor information supporting monitoring and review, which has also been observed on a national basis (Weiner et al., 2002; Stewart et al., 2003). It was interesting to speculate whether the development of the review process could contribute to improved outcome measures, such as user-defined outcomes.

The selective implementation process did not permit indicators to be developed for every domain of the PIAF as would have been desirable. However, significant advances were made following completion of the initial work, and the staff subsequently became more familiar with the concepts included in the framework. The PIAF, which set operational processes in a structured fashion, was seen as highly useful. It was also seen to have utility across all client groups. Although much of the community care research and evidence has focused upon the greater numbers of older people, this was also felt to be a helpful framework in adult services such as those for people with disabilities. However, the patterns and trends involved in work with these client groups deal with much smaller numbers so it is much more difficult to see how some of the indicators could be interpreted. As PIs are now becoming more a part of everyday work within social services departments, the framework and model adopted here could thus be usefully applied in several different contexts.

Staff factors

There were two important issues prevalent amongst staff during the implementation process. One key issue was to get practitioners to understand and own the broader picture: namely, the question of where work with individual clients fits into the wider activity of the department, or how individual staff relate their activities to overall organisational goals. The workshop meetings were seen as leading to a 'mini-research process' with staff leaving the meetings committed to a small project with a responsibility to feed back at the next meeting. This created a view that a proper analysis of issues was needed before moves to implement change could be considered. It fuelled an information or evaluative culture within the department. Indeed, one manager observed that staff remained engaged in this with, for example, current analysis being undertaken of Team Leaders' workloads and of patterns of placements.

A second key issue was for managers to see that performance management was not a simple business of relating inputs to outputs in a technical fashion. It was also seen as necessary to use performance information to challenge a management culture of depersonalisation which had developed due to an overspend in the department during one year. Due to managers being faced with budgetary deficits, management targets and resource pressures predominantly concerned with control, this had led to fundamental values and broader policy goals not being addressed. Budget management was a single indicator and easily measured and, in the management climate of the time, financial indicators had assumed priority. Consequently, activity was mainly examined in a financial context, with the deleterious effect that broad policy goals such as the balance of care and diversion were not always pursued to the same extent. These became secondary to the issue of whether cases were less expensive to serve in one area than another. In short, the financial focus at senior management level tended initially to undermine the broader perspective. These two agendas were linked in that staff felt the individual professional focus was undermined by too narrow a focus on finance. Implementation of the indicators with a broader group of staff enabled these linkages to be made and ensured a commitment to these wider goals and objectives.

Barriers to implementation

Several barriers to implementation were experienced: technical, human and organisational. The technical barriers included a lack of consistency or reliability of information and problems of definition. There was seen to be a serious need to enable definitions to be understood and shared by staff in the organisation. In this respect the RAP project (Department of Health, 2001b) has now moved thinking a substantial way forward. However, much hinges upon whether computer systems are adequate and data are available. Hence the incremental approach to developing the indicators was seen as appropriate. Additional data demands caused by implementing new systems from scratch would have raised too great an opposition.

There were additional human barriers. Certain types of staff were perceived as information resistant, particularly social workers. Some staff also had to be guided about the types of information required to ensure consistent data entry. This led to a specific role for administrative staff in managing information. However, it was seen that managers became more involved in this process and showed greater diligence since the growth of Central Government demands for information and the development of a more information orientated culture within social services departments. People now appear to understand information as an essential tool for their day-to-day work and can more easily handle elements such as charts or tables than before. There is now a growing tendency for staff such as team leaders to interrogate agency information.

A major organisational barrier was dilution of effort through Local Government Reorganisation, which took place in the department during the period of implementation. This led to the loss of 18 months' energy and also a loss of key middle managers and insufficient senior management involvement. This had a major impact in separating the key actors involved in the initial development work. It was thought that there should, in retrospect, have been a return to the original work to identify the key indicators empirically and to have gained more reliable and valid information. It was believed that this should have been prioritised, however difficult the task. Further progress might have been achieved with a subsequent 'top down' process, but changes in the directorate/Senior Management Group as a result of reorganisation made this development unlikely.

Dissemination/Involvement

As the commission from the department to PSSRU was to devise and produce the measurement product – including the framework and rules for the analysis of information – implementation was largely viewed as the task of management. In this regard, the workshops were seen to be of considerable utility. They involved a large group of staff and, while a smaller group of staff could have managed the process of shaping and evaluating information more speedily, a larger change effect was achieved by involving a wide range of staff. The workshops brought staff together to examine information at the same time and in the same way and raised awareness of the significance of information reliability. They facilitated a 'bottom-up' strategy for the collection of information and they were the only forum that brought people together from all the districts.

As involvement progressed, information increasingly focused upon more personalised questions, such as what degree of variation is considered appropriate and for whom? Staff of the local authority would go away to study particular information and bring back a report following discussion of differences and perceived reasons for this variation. A very positive view emerged of social workers as informed questioners. There was an interest in the link between information and changes in behaviour. For example, an admission to residential care form was changed to examine more clearly reasons for entry as a consequence of social worker involvement in collecting information.

There were some initial difficulties in moving the workshops forward. At first, there was some suspicion that the process was all rather theoretical, but subsequently the meetings began to help staff to frame an agenda for the collection of relevant information. For example, home care staff needed to find indicators of proxy outcome to justify more explicitly the level of in-house pro-vision. Linking indicators to the needs and requirements of certain staff groups was a key factor in implementation. The increasing involvement of a wider range of staff was also viewed as making the process more organisationally relevant.

Exposure of staff to the degree of variation between areas generated competitive interest and began to engage all levels of staff. The quantification of service elements began to raise questions of what precisely staff did and the reasons why certain activities could be considered more effective than others. The analysis of differences gave the process credibility as the whole process of service delivery was made real and relevant to practitioners and managers. The meetings across the organisation enabled people to move from observation of variation to an examination of the reasons why this occurred. It may not have been possible at first to exactly measure the phenomena of interest, but once the process had begun, staff were able to quantify both activity and components of service in useful ways. The variation, of itself, threw up issues such as why things were done in a certain way and offered opportunities for learning from the way other districts operated. Interestingly, staff were able to avoid these investigations becoming value- laden, such as a view that one district was 'wrong' in their level of activity or that a certain point was the optimum level of performance that could be expected. Thus, competition between districts was avoided.

Such an analytical approach to service delivery has been identified as still rare in social services departments (SSI/Audit Commission, 1998c). The way in which information from the initial period of implementation was dissemi nated was viewed as offering staff a framework to enable them to ask constructive questions and to set these in a broader context. Colleagues in the NHS were also involved and, since social services are seen as historically less rigorous in their use of information, this gave strength to the department's liaison with the NHS.

Quarterly meetings were arranged, with feedback from the indicators as a way of disseminating the ideas worked upon in the initial implementation process. These dissemination meetings were seen as very valuable in developing consistency. They engaged people in understanding and evaluating information and bringing their own information for discussion and consideration. The meetings were seen as contributing significantly to developing an attitude of using information as a problem-solving tool. It was noteworthy that the meetings were always well attended and had a degree of continuity. For example, issues would be identified at one meeting and key elements from the previous meeting would be researched in the interim and the results of investigation and information gathering or evaluation would be fed back at the subsequent meeting. It was felt that the presence of external persons (PSSRU staff) at the meetings provided a valuable critique enabling participants to consider where the development process was heading. As a result of the meetings, staff appeared to became more analytic in their approach to problem solving.

Longer-term impact

In examining the longer-term impact of this work, staff identified a number of issues, many of which have recently been recognised at a national level (SSI/Audit Commission, 1998c; Warburton, 1999). Amongst these were the development of a culture of using information as a management tool; using routinely collected data to monitor the outcomes of service activity; and a greater acceptance of day-to-day monitoring. Also important is the marrying of central government demands for data with local requirements for management and service development information. Recognising the need for integrating these two elements into a policy for the use and dissemination of performance information locally is now a task facing most social services departments. The rest of this section considers these issues in terms of work to be done in formulating more coherent performance measurement systems.

Central and local foci

Any strategy to implement a set of PIs has to link to central government requirements, particularly since these have grown since the indicators described here were originally devised. Most of the indicators employed at the workshops were so grounded wherever possible. Indeed, the subsequent government indicators cover many areas included in the set of indicators devised for the local authority — for example, timeliness — and the Audit Commission covers many of the local indicators considered here, or these could be modified or be updated with little loss. Recent indicator development, such as that contained in the RAP Project — undertaking work on indicators linking the time between referral, assessment, and provision of care (Department of Health, 1999c) — also has close links with the work developed in this joint PSSRU performance work. Ways need to be found to integrate the two processes so that the indicators being collected from central returns are compatible with those demanded locally as part of the strategic management function. This is not without its problems. Not every national indicator reflects practice in the way that local departments would like. Similarly, locally devised indicators run the risk of responding to idiosyncratic concerns and may therefore not be valid for wider evaluation. However, the process of implementing the present suite of indicators was a start to the integration process. The confidence of staff in responding to a Department of Health consultative document (Department of Health, 1999a) was enhanced through the indicator development process. Their responses were seen as more thought-through and critically aware as a consequence of the process of PI development and implementation.

Dissemination of performance information

Once indicators have been designed within locally produced objectives which recognise national policy concerns, they must then be disseminated to staff. This has to be done in a way that identifies the particular need of staff to understand and use information relevant to their own concerns. One recent element in the dissemination of information in the local authority is the 'Balanced Scorecard' developed from the Business Excellence model (Kaplan and Norton, 1993, 1996). This provides key objectives for each actor within the organisation, with a particular focus upon an indicator of relevance to that actor. Business activity figures are produced monthly aggregated down to the level for which particular staff are responsible; the coverage of information is tailored towards the particular responsibilities of staff, becoming more detailed as one goes down the organisation. For example, information is limited for senior managers to help them to act strategically. However, more comprehensive information is available at team manager and practitioner levels. This approach avoids a major difficulty with past performance work, namely, the over-aggregation of performance data (Wholey and Hatry, 1992). In other words, managers only need detailed information related to their own area of responsibility, not that relating to the organisation as a whole. This approach could be linked into the PIAF model with good effect.

It appeared that staff involvement in and understanding of the importance of adequate data for performance measurement led to a move towards greater consistency in recording. Another outcome from the process was seen to be a sharpening of people's perception of the contribution of their activity to the organisation. They were more likely to employ the analysis of information as the first stage of changing patterns of work activity. Overall, it could be seen as a move towards an evidence-based approach with the development of what was described as 'meaningful activity data'. The social services department had previously looked at different elements of performance but not at the totality. Key areas of recent concern are unit costs, workload, consistent practice (differences in practice style by district), and workforce indicators.

Along with developments associated with RAP, the Department of Health's Key Indicators, Quality Protects (children's services) and other externally determined indicators (Department of Health, 2001b, 2002b), the department also planned to bring in more personal feedback to individual workers. However, data quality remained a major issue, and there was a need for data quality training and the development of a shared understanding of the need for high quality data.

There has recently been a greater consistency in central government approaches to performance. To some extent, local and national objectives can be seen to be running in parallel since the White Paper *Modernising Social Services* (Cm 4189, 1998). For social services departments, there are attempts to integrate information demands, for example for the RAP project and Joint Review material (Department of Health 2001b; Social Services Inspectorate/Audit Commission, 1998b). Within the local authority in question, a staff group was involved in examining links between process and outcome in information terms so that indicators could provide evidence for Joint Reviews. This identified gaps in the required information. Special studies were employed to provide information for service development, an activity which would have been more difficult but for the PI culture which had been created. A similar methodology might usefully be exploited by other departments to integrate central and local demands for performance information.

Changes in information systems

A national study of social services departments (Challis et al., 1998) found a considerable variation between authorities in their capabilities and use of information technology to support systems for monitoring performance. Throughout the work described here there was continued development in the information system supporting the indicators which were devised. This development occurred in response to conceptual issues raised in the workshops as well as capability issues around the storage of relevant data.

There continue to be changes in information systems within the department. A replacement for the client information system was being designed as it had been in operation for a number of years and, although more sophisticated than most, a more modern system was seen as needed in order to store client-level data. More sophisticated data storage was also needed, for example, to provide longitudinal data that can offer evidence on care pathways for older people. Small studies continued to address system validation and to collect relevant information for key areas such as timeliness. The development of outcome measures was planned, based on six-week review and every subsequent review. An idea of the costs of certain client packages, such as those approaching designated cost ceilings, was also envisaged to act as a 'red light' to managers.

It is important to stress that such changes to the design of information systems in the department were guided by the ongoing development of measures and staff feedback. This was assisted by the input from PSSRU staff in commenting on the eventual use of indicators. Technical developments need, therefore, to go hand in hand with advances in academic work, to guide the interpretation and use of indicators.

Change in practitioner's views of using information

There continues to be a debate as to the use of indicators and other performance related mechanisms on the part of social care practitioners. This debate often centres on a contrast between traditional casework practice and post-reform practitioner behaviour, particularly in respect of care management (Payne, 1995; McDonald, 1999). Performance measurement is characterised as one part of the managerial assault on social work, a monitoring technology that ignores the role of traditional values in practice. In contrast, acknowledged skills, such as counselling, are held as examples of client-centred practice focusing on needs and outcomes for users – more in keeping with the value base of social work. However, there is something of a 'naive contrast' in this since the two traditions are not mutually exclusive. There is a recognition that care management can be seen as the point at which client-based objectives, emphasising user choice and service flexibility, meet with the economic criteria of resource constraint and budget management (Challis, 1992). Practitioners are well placed to explore information at the interface of need and scarcity. In this sense, information drawn from assessments can be used for the benefit of the service user to measure outcome and, at a sufficient level of aggregation, can be useful in monitoring services at the managerial level. The approach adopted within the department was to enable practitioners to fit their individual goals and activities into a broader set of local authority goals. In a similar vein, managers were encouraged to view the work as involving an analysis of community care activity related to client-centred goals rather than financial targets alone. In this way, both approaches are integrated at the service planning level through the appropriate use of information systems thereby enabling practitioners to recognise this was useful in modifying established assumptions concerning the use of information.

One way of approaching the integration of these approaches was to link certain indicators together in the pursuit of shared aims. For example, combining Efficiency and Diversion indicators was a means to enable Team Leaders to focus on options for addressing financial issues while also maintaining long-term policy goals. This was done by examining which cases could experience a marginal reduction in care hours without reducing their capacity to continue living at home. In short, staff were seeking those cases where marginal productivity was lowest in relation to well-being and community tenure. Where this occurred it enabled one district to save rather than overspend. The combination of indicators in this way enabled both Team Leaders and managers to visualise trade-offs between the efficiency and diversion objectives. Thus, staff in different positions in the hierarchy, both practitioners and managers, were able to use data to support their own practice.

A positive feature from this work was the desire of staff to move further into issues of performance such as why there appeared to be considerable variance in social worker behaviour across districts. Such a study would, in an earlier period, have been characterised by a degree of anxiety about the whole process. However, the recognition, on the part of all staff, of the different uses to which indicators may be put and the benefits of receiving information at different levels in the organisation appeared to guard against this danger. It is perhaps the case that the involvement of staff is a real protection against 'gaming' in performance measurement: namely, the production of material which appears to deliver what is required. This process of staff involvement was often exciting as one witnessed the emerging information culture beginning to inform and modify the informal and case-based approach often characterising work in social care.

Using performance indicators

Performance indicators have a range of uses. From the examples of indicators given here and the earlier review, a number of guidelines can be outlined in order to ensure more consistent reporting. The key principles adopted in the local authority (Box 7.1) underpinned the operation of the performance system. Central to this was a recognition that, in order for data to act as a guide to action in community care planning, it must first be interpreted by senior managers. For this to happen the raw data need to be put into a form that can be used to support the enquiries made of it. Within the local authority, a number of outputs from the PI system were adopted. These included:

- A comparison of activity between districts (using rates per 1000 population or percentages).
- A comparison of activity between other adults' and older people's services.
- A time series comparison to show key trends.
- A comparison of district activity against a county average.

Initially, these outputs were in the form of charts, at the top of which was described the overall objective to be achieved along with a commentary outlining the demonstrated performance described by the data. Suggestions for further analysis and the sorts of questions which could be asked were also included.

Using performance indicators on a comparative basis such as this need not be limited to comparisons at such a high level of aggregation. Within a relatively large local authority, comparisons may also be undertaken across smaller units of organisation. For instance, one worker or type of worker can be compared with another; teams such as social work or home care teams can be compared; units such as day centres or care homes can be compared as well as comparisons across authorities. In making comparisons, there are two key things to bear in mind. Firstly, like should be compared with like. For example, a shire county would probably compare itself with other shire counties, possibly of similar size, demography and levels of social deprivation. Secondly, it must not be assumed that these differences reflect something wrong. For example, suppose that one team closes more cases than another in the same authority. There can be many possible explanations other than those to do with efficiency: some may be based on artefact (closure may be operationally defined in different ways by the two teams); some may be based on different populations served (one team may be dealing with a more dependent population); and others based on team styles (one team may close cases in the knowledge that many cases will be re-referred in due course).

Comparative information can also be used in an innovative fashion to record such elements as patterns of case activity in screening, assessment and, ultimately, care outcomes including changes in 'care careers'; unit costs of providing screening and assessment; the use of resources in residential and domiciliary care; the market availability of different care providers and placement decisions. All these uses of information characterised the earlier work.

Comparative performance data can also be used in other ways:

- To compare between a standard that is hoped for and actual practice. For example, based on 'Home Life' recommendations, it is now universally accepted that at least 80 per cent of accommodation in residential care homes should be in single rooms (Centre for Policy on Ageing, 1984). Using an indicator of this standard, local authorities can see how they compare, and possibly how the different sectors (namely, council, private and voluntary) operating in their areas compare. Such an indicator was included in the set of PIs recommended for the local authority (indicator S17) and is also included in the Department of Health's PAF framework (Department of Health, 1999b, indicator D37).

- To compare expected frequency patterns with observed frequency patterns. For example, the percentage of older people in an authority area who are from minority ethnic communities can be compared with the percentage of older people from such communities who are referred for help. Differences between expected and observed frequencies need to be interpreted with caution, but they can be effective indicators of both good or bad screening processes and service access. Currently, there are major difficulties in this type of analysis across social services departments (Warburton, 1999) and there is scope for further thought to be given to this.
- To compare performance with that set by government policy and linking this up to local concerns with variation and comparative analysis. For instance, the work across the local authority could have concentrated on the history of consistency across sectors of the County such as the reasons for one district appearing 'deviant' to the rest of county owing to its distinct culture. At the time of the initial work analysis did not focus upon ensuring consistency of service across different geographical areas. Consistency is now a very important theme stemming from the White Paper (Cm 4169, 1998), but was not considered as significant an issue for the department then. However, the analysis of variation across the county has emerged as even more relevant alongside the government's equity issues.

Overall, these comparisons very much depend on the differences in characteristics between the areas or units being considered; factors such as demography, deprivation and crime levels may all contribute to variability. A serious question of method is how to take account of these factors while, at the same time, presenting information in a useable form. Statistical adjustments, allowing for factors such as poor housing, single person households, and need for residential care, would enable better judgements to be made from the data.

A changing policy context also requires data to be used in different ways. The early work in the local authority focused on differences between areas and assumed that this variation was legitimate to some extent. However, the modernisation White Paper (Cm 4169, 1998) encourages standardisation. In encouraging consistency, the government has set a yardstick for performance, and authorities will need to investigate the characteristics of their different areas to ensure coherence with these policy aims. This may be done by exploring the extent to which variability is appropriate or not by recognising local concerns and needs indicators when making judgements from the data.

Technical issues

There are a number of more technical issues around the use of PI systems, which involve the way data are held and processed. A number of principles have proved useful in the design of systems, many of which can be translated into the way social services departments manage their records. Within the local authority, a number of these were taken into account in managing data. They included the need to ensure the accurate and uniform inputting of data across the system. The system outputs needed similarly to be consistent on a county and a district basis. Staff were also aware that technical requirements tended to define the parameters of the possible in terms of available and extractable information.

A number of problems in the way social services departments currently extract and manage data have been identified in the Department of Health's information special study (Warburton, 1999). Of particular importance is the capacity to relate user to activity to cost data on a case-level basis. Many departments currently do not have the technical capability to achieve this. Even if they do, there are often problems with the manner in which such data are stored. These data are often held on different files or even in different parts of the department or local authority. This makes extraction of relevant data and the linking up of different sources of information problematic. This is important as the ability to relate referral information to that on assessment, service delivery, care packages and costs is crucial in being able to track cases over time, essential to monitoring community care activity. Within the local authority, a number of such problems were identified. Managers mentioned that there was often a lack of available data and a slowness to be able to change data collection systems. For example, to insert a new box onto the client information system so as to enable routine recording of an aspect of need took eight to nine months. There was thus a cost involved in development as well as inputting and extracting relevant information, which needed to be borne in mind. Nevertheless, the system in the local authority was able to relate information from different sources together, store it in one location and disseminate it in different formats dependent on the recipient of the information. The information suite had therefore already begun to conform to the principles outlined in recent reports.

Some broader principles have been set out for the way information is collected, which can assist departments in the management of their data. One aspect is the form in which information is stored. As many ratio measures are made up of a smaller number of data items, it first of all makes sense to store the data originally in the form of absolute values rather than as ratios (Jackson and Palmer, 1989). This is a simple point, but holding data in this form then enables checks for accuracy to be made and ratios can be readily modified if demands on the system change. It also enables staff to go back and check whether anomalies in the output may be attributable to the values of numerators or denominators rather than as a signal of true differences in performance.

There are also a number of principles to bear in mind for investigating performance comparisons, such as the distributions of values between districts or units. A number of factors may influence the eventual output and these must be taken into account. These factors might include: missing values, when a unit does not return a value or if the value is zero but this has not been recorded; data error, which may produce abnormal results of its own accord; abnormal distributions, which might be skewed around a particular value causing difficulties in interpretation; and reliability of the data source, where definitions of the data to be collected are of the utmost importance (Jackson and Palmer, 1989). The likely presence of these factors mean that the output from the system will often need to be cross checked perhaps with reference to other comparable indicators. For instance, extreme values may show up consistently on some measures. However, before jumping to any conclusions, reasonable hypotheses must be formed in the light of the behaviour of other indicators and contextual data. Extreme values may be due to one event or the underlying distribution of one other indicator in each area, such as one of need. In the interpretation of ranked tables or distributions of indicators, it also needs to be borne in mind that those units of provision with values at the top or bottom of a distribution are not necessarily poor performers. There may be special reasons why these units are there. These must be investigated rather than conclusions being reached on limited information. Also, the overall distribution and scale of differences between the units of provision need to be examined. In a simple rank ordering broken into, say, two groups the difference between the lowest unit in the upper group and the highest unit in the lower group may be extremely small (Mor et al., 2003).

Summary and conclusions

There were a number of beneficial aspects to the implementation process summarised here. Central to these was the structuring of the performance management system around the seven key performance areas or dimensions described in Chapter 4. These were Targeted, Timely, Efficient, Diversion, Individual, Involved and Choice. These linked local policy goals for older people with broader national policy objectives. The Diversion objective, in particular, was seen as very useful as this focused on areas for greater investigation by field staff. The key dimensions enabled staff across the department to judge whether intentions and objectives were being realised. This was done through the analysis of system outputs relating to each dimension, drawing on indicators from relevant domains of the PIAF.

As a consequence, through this process staff became more focused upon the big picture: the impact of their own work and the effects of different ways of working upon the strategy of the whole department. Staff also became more skilled in the collection of data. As the work progressed, a more evidence based orientation to social care emerged, with staff seeing the value of proper data collection as an essential part of their practice. In the sections that follow are outlined, under appropriate headings, some of the conclusions reached by managers on the whole process of implementation in consultation with PSSRU staff. Where appropriate, links are made with wider debates to inform the conduct of future work.

Implementation is as important as design

Much work has examined the design of PIs which, although important, is only one element in the whole process of performance measurement, from the conceptualisation of the system to its implementation and subsequent evaluation. Implementation can be seen as a process of social change (Walsham, 1993), involving changes in values on the part of participants in the process. There is therefore a need to reach agreement with key parties and ensure that information development recognises the diverse views of different groups. One successful method for accomplishing this is to undertake implementation in such a way that it is owned by staff rather than being seen to be imposed by experts (Audit Commission, 2000). The process of implementation is therefore as important as the content of indicators and the technical methods for refining and using them. Reasons for this include issues of data quality and the human issues of becoming more information oriented. Within the department, the process of the workshops and staff enquiry was seen as crucial in ensuring that the product was owned by the organisation.

Successful implementation also requires such elements as coalition building between stakeholders, ideological training in the value of measurement, and political tactics, such as the defusing of conflict (Walsham, 1993). These factors help to build support for information systems and their use within the organisation. Considerable effort was expended by managers in seeking to include a wide range of staff in the process. The translation of strategic objectives into measurable indicators was undertaken in a creative fashion, with broad policy goals being related to the local setting and, to reduce ambiguity, the information was carefully specified.

Phasing is crucial

The incremental process to implementation of the indicators was seen as valuable. Initially, the indicators seemed separate from day-to-day activity, but the key dimensions were important in focusing upon the core business of the department and rendering the indicators relevant to agency policy. A reasonably comprehensive set of indicators initially was developed for each of the department's key objectives. The use of single indicators in isolation from other measures was considered quite dangerous as it risked misinterpretation. The incremental approach to implementation meant that a suite of indicators could be developed, which were seen as relevant and assisted staff in making informed decisions. In retrospect, it was felt that perhaps the phasing of activity could have been more planned and structured. Managers felt that the whole process would have benefited from a project planning approach. In addition, there was a view that within an organisation there needs to be a product champion to ensure consistent direction, but resources did not permit this to be achieved in any consistent way. Incremental build was an appropriate strategy, but it was also important to see that the whole organisation was buying into the development. A phasing process was therefore seen as sensible and correct, with direction coming from the focus on key indicators. Subsequently, there was a need to move from process indicators to sharpening up and improving the outcome indicators.

Involvement important

The importance of both senior management support and staff involvement are seen as key issues for successful implementation in the management literature (Walsham, 1993). The support of senior management is seen as providing the contextual elements of a shared vision and authority for the dissemination of information (Leigh, 1988). Over and above this, other staff-centred objectives need to be identified and heeded. Within the department, the involvement of staff at all levels was seen as absolutely central in making performance measurement work. The mechanisms for involving a wide range of staff included the way in which the indicators themselves were designed. Drawing from each domain of the framework and linking into each of the local policy objectives meant that the indicators had relevance to staff with different levels of responsibility. Practitioners as well as managers were therefore included in the process, from its initial development, through the design of indicators and their eventual dissemination throughout the department. This approach gave feedback to staff, about their activities as part of an organisational process and helped them to feel included as part of the work. Interestingly, the Department of Health's PAF has relatively few indicators of immediate interest to practitioners. Central government indicator sets are mostly concerned with aspects of immediate concern to middle management, such as the commissioning and monitoring of services. In contrast, the approach adopted in the present work sought to devise indicators of relevance to the full range of staff who might need to judge the effectiveness of and produce changes in service delivery. The method of dissemination was also important. Tailoring the workshops in response to the views expressed by participants was one reason for the high level of involvement amongst staff.

Participation in the planning forums was valued by those who attended, which was evident in their regular attendance. It was also important in ensuring their commitment to the programme and to guarantee data quality. In retrospect, it was felt that this should have occurred to a greater extent across the then existing purchaser/provider divide. This was important since the indicators provided information across the divide and NHS staff should also have been involved in key issues such as hospital discharge. This would be easier in the present climate than was possible then.

Developing an information culture

In broadening the discussion of key factors in implementation, cultural aspects were also deemed to be of importance in fostering what has been termed a 'learning organisation' (Garvin, 1993) whereby collective learning takes place across the whole spectrum of work. A 'mini-research culture' developed in the department, with hypothesis testing from indicator information emerging along with a critical appraisal of patterns of differences. The PI work was seen as having sponsored the development of a learning culture within the department as a whole. This was at the time unique for many social services departments, with people becoming 'knowledge hungry'. Managers saw this as a desirable outcome of the PI workshops. Ideally, such developments should be linked to the broader research world. Thus, local concerns and issues need to be set into a broader national framework and related to broader evidence and knowledge in order to ask the right questions of the information. This would be likely to require more complex analyses than were undertaken routinely at the time.

Evaluation of differences – variance comparison

The exploration of differences between areas was seen as a totally valid strategy for asking questions. The main focus was exploration of variation from the county norm and the pattern of variability between individual districts from this. As a result of this work, geographical mapping by postcode was being planned to provide more information about the population in a particular area, linking information about demand in a particular area to its socio-demographic features. Elements here could include the population base served, trends in clusters of known service users, or links with health and education data to gain further insights into trends. The system in use only recorded variations in demand over time. There was little attempt to move towards expected rates of demand which can be compared with actual rates. Census data also could be investigated in order to explore true need, which is based on the numbers of older people who have not yet come into contact with services.

The analysis of differences provided a comparison with a central benchmark: the county average. There were also cross-sectional comparisons and 'time series' comparisons (Carter et al., 1992). However, these approaches had certain limitations. A further step, making more effective use of the framework, would be to move towards a more outcome-focused set of analyses, which was seen as being feasible in the longer term. Strategic outcomes or targets could have been developed within the performance framework, which might be specified by different players such as elected members, managers or team-level staff. Another area of concern is the use of external comparators, providing a benchmarking of performance with practices elsewhere, although there are difficulties in finding the appropriate local authorities with which to compare. Also, managers stated that the department needed to move further towards more consistent targets for PIs and indicators of 'final outcome' such as quality of life. Evaluation of variance in the original work was not in terms of final outcomes but in terms of 'intermediate outcomes' (Davies and Knapp, 1981). This was inevitable given the available data. In part, this was entirely appropriate given the focus upon consistency in the recent agenda (Cm 4169, 1998).

Of wider application, work with a group of local authorities would have meant the development of consistent definitions of indicators across authorities. Indeed, even European data would have been valuable, though of course it must be remembered that service-level data are always context-specific whereas client-level data may permit trans-system comparisons.

Areas for further development

The discussions with managers who had been involved in the process of implementation raised issues concerning the prospects for the future. Recently, there have been a number of significant initiatives from the Department of Health, for example the RAP exercise, KI graphical system and the PAF framework (Department of Health, 1999a,b,c). However, ways have to be found for supplementing, or more correctly complementing, this information with more locally derived indicators which can comment on local priorities. The suite of indicators recommended by PSSRU, suitably modified, could act as a best-practice model for this development to take place. They could also be used to evaluate national policy developments.

Methods of analysis of performance indicators also need to be investigated more fully. The missing element in the initial work with the local authority was proper analytical skills in computing to address issues derived from wider questioning of the data. Indeed, in the absence of sophisticated data analysis, performance measurement in social care will tend to rely on routine descriptive data and standard outputs. Other specific studies may be needed to concentrate attention on particular issues and these will require the development of specific methodologies. For example, special studies might move from primary data collection to secondary analysis, examining issues such as 'critical pathways' through different care environments (Leininger and Cohen, 1998; Myers et al., 1996). Proper links to academic environments may be needed for work such as this to take place. In addition, project planning and a greater commitment to information technology changes is needed to provide indicators of lasting value.

Other dimensions of community care practice are beginning to be of importance to the national picture (Department of Health, 1997c; Cm 4169, 1998) and could be further understood and evaluated by the use of indicators. For example, the government includes interface indicators to monitor joint priorities with the NHS. There is thus considerable room for further development. The social services department involved in the work considered here has moved away from a relatively narrow focus on community care, which was initially built around levels of placement activity and cost of care packages and how these can be managed, towards a focus on the whole agenda of prevention and rehabilitation. This is an area recently advocated by government (Department of Health, 1997c, 2001a, 2001c; Cm 4169, 1998) and needs to be enhanced in future indicator work. However, these aspects present greater measurement challenges and information linkage problems, particularly in respect of information sharing with the NHS.

Condition specific indicators for particular circumstances affecting the lives of older people in receipt of social care services are also a potential future development. These could include conditions such as dementia, the burden of which contributes to costs of £4,684 million annually (at 1992 price levels). Around 17 per cent of these costs are borne by social services departments (Schneider et al., 1993). Currently there are no national indicators which examine these aspects. Also, a housing dimension, an important but neglected area of community care planning, was not built in to the work and could be an area of development.

Chapter 8

Conclusions

In this book we have provided a framework in which performance indicators may be related to one another in a causal pathway; developed a series of performance indicators for local use in social care for older people; and examined processes of effective implementation of a local performance culture. Many of the conclusions to be drawn from such an exercise mirror those of other commentators who have studied the growth of performance indicators in other areas of public sector activity (for example, Pollitt, 1984; Flynn, 1986; Jowett and Rothwell, 1988; Carter et al., 1992). Some of the models and processes we describe have also been reviewed from a US perspective (Anthony and Herzlinger, 1980; Martin and Kettner, 1996). The need is for a system of indicators that can review important aspects of a social care organisation's work in a meaningful way. At issue, however, are wider debates concerned with who defines performance, and the criteria to be used in measurement. There have been political, conceptual and technical arguments associated with the analysis of performance indicators, and we have drawn attention to many of these throughout this book.

In the development of indicators for social care, account needs to be taken of not only the measurement and conceptual work discussed here, but also the way in which existing indicators have been devised and implemented. The lessons from history need to be learned and translated into a perspective for social care that includes a consideration of theoretical models, so permitting the more sophisticated use of indicators. Due weight needs to be given to practitioner concerns, derived from the wider political debates touched on throughout our discussion and also to the perspective of service users, perhaps most effectively captured in indicators of intermediate and final outcome. We conclude this book by offering, first, some arguments and debates that touch on many of the themes we have reviewed. Second, we discuss what we think are the beneficial aspects to bear in mind when using a PI system. We end with our recommendations for the further development of PIs for social care, building on much of our work with Cheshire Social Services Department.

Indicators: argument, rhetoric and development

It will by now be apparent, from the earlier chapters, that performance measurement is not a static or uniform subject. The development and use of performance indicators has been open to debate and sometimes hostile criticism from a number of writers, drawing on a number of perspectives. Many in public management have sung their virtues, arguing that only technical refinements are needed in order for them to be used more widely. Some, writing about particular initiatives, have cast doubts but have welcomed their use overall (for example, Pollitt, 1984). Others have been scathing in their attacks on the whole edifice of performance measurement, particularly from the health service side (Davies and Lampel, 1998). The whole notion of evaluating progress towards goals has also been questioned. Long ago, Etzioni (1960) argued that mechanisms by which we hope to measure the achievement of goals may not be an adequate depiction of reality. He saw goals as sets of cultural meanings or 'target states', often imposed by observers outside the organisation. The decision to measure achievement in pursuit of these goals often results in an organisation being found to be ineffective. This is not necessarily due to failure on the part of the participants concerned, but is because goals sometimes express ideal states that are not meant to be realised. Stewart and Walsh (1994) have stated that because performance assessment is dependent on values, it is necessarily a matter of judgement. They suggest that we may never be able to fully define satisfactory indicators of performance, and a search for technical methods for doing so ignores the special character of public services. Within welfare services, Cutler and Waine (1997) have termed the notion of performance measurement a 'bogus prospectus' and have warned against the uncritical acceptance of performance measures in the management of services. They argue that there are many difficulties with performance indicators, both in their conception and in their use. These difficulties include: their centralised nature, their use in the control of expenditure and people, and their manipulation in order to reflect performance in a more favourable light. They argue that 'the plethora of information on public sector performance is effectively part of a presentational politics where, often, increases in activity and claims regarding quality are tendentious.' (Cutler and Waine, 1997, p. 166).

What are we to make of these criticisms? Just as many commentators criticise PIs for their links with certain ideologies and values, they are usually doing so from their own particular viewpoint. Jackson (1993) warns of the folly in the logical conclusion to these debates: either public service performance should not be measured at all, or that performance is always impossible to measure. Both these conclusions are, in themselves, value-laden and seem unworkable in practice. The idea that we should never measure performance is a naive reaction to a technical style that characterised much earlier managerial writing. Indicators of private sector performance are now at a level of complexity far removed from the traditional view. Values and quality processes are now included that stand outside simple measures of profitability. If public services are ever to serve the needs of their populations in a more comprehensive way, some of these arguments will be relevant. Notwithstanding some conceptual difficulties, the arguments set out here also go against the idea that performance is impossible to measure. There are established criteria that can be used to measure social services performance. Owing to the variety of objectives and players in the social care market, some of these arguments are complex. This should be recognised, and the approach adopted here has been to include indicators as part of a department's strategic management function. This recognises complexity and the difficulties in measuring competing objectives and claims on resources.

It is important to recognise, however, that while the virtues of performance indicators often seem self-evident, they are intimately tied up with the political process. In the UK this process began with the arguments of the new managerialists in the mid-1980s and has continued in the emphasis on Best Value and national measures of performance. It is therefore impossible to divorce these measures from wider questions concerning who defines satisfactory performance and the kinds of ends which are to be served by using measurement in the delivery of services. Evaluating how performance measurement might work in a social care organisation therefore takes us beyond a search for the right data. It is necessarily a part of the political environment. Many of the technical problems with PIs may, in fact, reflect the uncertainty in ascribing numerical values to what is an evaluation of people's responses to the policy and guidance before them. However, performance measurement is also an approach which seems particularly suited to social care at this stage in its development. It seems valuable to pursue assessment methods that can comment on important aspects of our services. However, rather than rely totally on performance measures, we need to recognise them as a means of supporting judgement (Stewart and Walsh, 1994).

In order to permit further work to occur on performance indicators, we need to take note of the criticisms that have been levelled at them, from various quarters. The opportunities afforded for manipulation of the data need to be recognised, as does the political context for the use of performance measures. However, we have concentrated here on ways of devising coherent measures and on the way these measures can be used, as well as some of the conceptual issues, which are important to consider. We have approached the work in this way, as it is now increasingly a requirement that social services departments have available to them, a range of data to make performance review possible. The wider issues are important, and much can be learned from them, but unless questions of design and technical methods are advanced, we may learn little of how to respond to these recent demands.

Refinements to some of the complex measurement issues involved in the use of indicators could make possible real changes in the way they are used. Particularly in social care, we need to ensure that we are measuring what we intend to measure and that comparisons are not made on a simplistic basis. The variety of performance information which is needed should be recognised, and considerable inventiveness is required in translating this into workable data. If the benefits of using PIs cannot be seen directly by the impact they make on the service, then they risk being viewed as political tools with which to control and regulate staff. We must also guard against perverse incentives within performance systems which lead an organisation into pursuing goals in order to justify the measures themselves, rather than seeing them as tools for assessing the organisation against its priorities and objectives. From the work reviewed in this book, we remain less sceptical than some commentators. It is our contention that performance information offers very real benefits to social care organisations in pursuing their objectives and in underpinning the more general aims of older people's services.

A number of measurement issues and practices are useful to review here. In this work we draw a distinction between using PIs in comparative league tables, where the aim may be to avoid demotion or relegation, and in using them to reflect on and evaluate practice at a local level. The present use of indicators nationally, such as those of the Audit Commission and Department of Health, can only touch on areas of public interest, for example regarding expenditure and service patterns across the country. They are limited to offering national comparisons which local authorities can use in their own work. They cannot really assist individual organisations in their planning and monitoring of community care activity. For this, measurable local objectives and policy have to be set against local indicators used to inform and review policy on a regular basis. From the entire range of uses to which PIs have been put, we would argue that this offers the potential of greatest benefit to the efficiency and effectiveness of social care organisations. Not only managers but also practitioners can assess their activities by the use of relevant tools of analysis, such as those we have described here.

The uncertainties about whether we can ever measure performance at a technical level have been accompanied by conceptual difficulties. These may be summed up as uncertainty about whether the measures chosen can, in any real sense, reflect the dimensions of performance that are seen as important for any particular activity. Some of the detractors in the performance measurement debate have argued that, despite the best efforts of those developing measures, the notion of performance always eludes attempts at measuring it. Cutler and Waine (1997), for example, argue that the different dimensions of performance are not commensurate with one other. There is a plurality of measures needed in order to serve a plurality of consumers of performance information. But, in extending these measures, it becomes ever more difficult to say exactly what characterises good or bad performance. The dimensions of performance constantly escape the attempts of indicator sets to measure them. If we attempt to remedy this by including all relevant dimensions of performance, then this leads to an indeterminate set of measures that cannot really offer any precise notion of what it is we are attempting to evaluate.

We have attempted, in the work reviewed in this book, to tackle some of these conceptual issues and offer clearer definitions of the various dimensions of performance. It is apparent from our review of the definitions of performance and its various elements that these dimensions could conceivably be extended to include almost every possible area of performance. This would be unhelpful as, for social care, a number of dimensions would be seen as more important than others. Efficiency and equity are important dimensions in the debates, as are quality and choice for users. A degree of parsimony is therefore needed. It is important for indicator sets to concentrate on the performance dimensions that are relevant to present concerns, and that are commensurate with particular objectives. We believe that the PIAF framework developed in our work with Cheshire Social Services Department assists in drawing attention to the most important dimensions to consider. The framework supports the integration of levels and stages of activity in the social care of older people, providing relevant indicators that can be linked to wider government directives and policy guidance. It helps to place indicators in context and assists in the search for relevant information, as well as offering an aid to interpreting many of the issues involved.

Much has been said about the difficulties in measuring the final outcomes of social care. Most indicator sets do not exhibit a comparable level of measurement to research instruments, traditionally used as outcome indicators. There is a sense in which we perhaps should not search for this as the distinction between routinely generated data and special collections of information, in such areas as user satisfaction, made in the present work helpfully distinguishes between outcome information and intermediate outcomes. Of course, more empirical work needs to be done on the relationship between levels of output and final outcome in order to address this relationship. In particular, the extent to which levels of service outputs can act as proxies for final outcomes is an issue deserving of further examination.

Levels of performance

The main thrust of our work on performance indicators stemmed from a recognition that performance can be considered on a number of different levels. The great body of performance indicator work has been developed at the central government level, and this was responsible for a number of the initiatives described in Chapter 1. Here, performance has been described nationally, in seeking to regulate the conduct of a range of government departments and agencies and to assist in the regulatory functions at the centre. Most of the national indicator sets now available are meant to assist health or social services districts and authorities monitor their performance as a whole, often in comparison with others, in order to support accountability to elected officials and the public. The history of performance indicators and performance monitoring as a centralised development continues with the introduction of the government's Performance Assessment Framework (Department of Health, 1999a). The centre has imposed strict monitoring requirements on social services departments to ensure that their performance reaches defined standards. This is backed up by financial incentives to improve performance. At a lower level, mechanisms by which a local authority can pursue its own targets, in relation to central government policy and its own objectives, have been less evident. Hopefully, the work considered here forms part of a wider recognition that schemes for measuring performance must have relevance at the local level, if they are to offer benefits in terms of the improved meeting of need.

Another sense in which the notion of levels of performance is important is in respect of the different levels within an organisation itself. At the higher management level, performance information is used to monitor the overall functioning of large-scale organisations. However, at the lower level associated with first line management and individual practitioners, indicators can also aid the process of appraisal by offering a focus on the benefits of individual care planning activity. Staff can use indicators to examine how their work fits in with the activity of the wider department and this may enable them to see more clearly the wider benefits of their activity to individual clients. These are laudable aims, but considerable inventiveness needs to be invested in devising systems that include a place for the individual member of staff.

In our work with Cheshire SSD, for example, data were analysed at different levels of aggregation within the organisation to reflect patterns of variation which could merit further investigation. Such investigation would sometimes take the form of local data collection to inform more fully differences in practice and thereby engaged practitioners in enquiry as to the most effective modes of working rather than a more centrally driven focus upon simply achieving greater consistency.

A new approach to measuring performance

The wider economic and political changes that were discussed in the opening chapter have advanced a particularly centralised approach to performance measurement in this country. Most of the developments discussed, ranging from those of the civil service and government executive agencies to those of the Audit Commission and the Social Services Inspectorate, have come from the centre. Even the consumer initiatives promulgated through the Citizen's Charters involved setting targets from the top-down, and users are usually left out of the process of devising indicators (Cutler and Waine, 1997). This development is likely to continue with the broad changes in setting standards for public services as part of the government recent prospectus. There are however, some seeds of potential development in seeking to measure performance at a more local level. The Best Value framework, highlighted in Chapter 2, attempts to establish national standards against the local priorities and objectives of each local authority, and authorities will be expected to use their own performance measurement systems in producing their performance reviews. Local performance measurement schemes have been developed in many authorities for some time (Warburton, 1993). This is now explicitly recognised and authorities will now have to ensure that their local schemes support and recognise not only their own local concerns, but also those national objectives and priorities published in the range of documents to which we have referred. The work advanced here will hopefully go some way towards enabling local social services authorities to devise their own performance measurement systems better.

Performance indicators must be placed in their proper context. It is not sufficient for indicators to be used only as the end points in service investigations. Thus, an organisation that is serious in its intentions for continuous evaluation ought to 'build in' ideas about the quality of its services from the start of the performance appraisal process. The likelihood of certain outcomes and service directions should be tested in a continuous process of performance review. In support of this, it is striking that the movement away from strict value for money and efficiency measures towards quality and Best Value, comes at a time of corresponding change in the operations of the private business sector. Formal control mechanisms, which characterised much of the early development of PIs, are being replaced in business organisations by participative learning and a philosophy of continuous improvement by concentrating on the culture of the organisation (Whitney, 1993). These changes have been characterised as a movement towards the 'learning organisation' (Senge, 1990; Garvin, 1993). In such an organisation, front-line staff are involved in sharing knowledge concerning best practice and learning from the testing of hypotheses about which particular processes bring about the best results. This fosters a systematic approach to problem solving through using information to assess the organisation's past experience critically and learning from the best practices of others.

From this perspective, the use of PIs is less about control than about all staff benefiting from a range of information placed at their disposal. Within the learning approach, as stated by Pedler et al. (1991), performance information is used to inform and empower staff, rather than to control and disempower them. This necessitates a different approach. It requires data supporting performance to be made available as widely as possible, perhaps in a form specific to the individuals receiving it, and to be used as an aid to understanding rather than for reward or punishment. Staff need to be encouraged to understand the nature of performance data, and that all systems of output show inherent variation and that this variation needs to be understood rather than merely controlled. In interpreting the data, an investigation of the possible causes of unusual variation will assist in coming to conclusions about the likely steps needed to change current practice. Only after this is done can any changes be made to the output of the organisation.

Translated into social care, this use of information raises questions for managers about why services deviate from planned targets, or whether these targets are achievable or justified. For practitioners, information enables cases to be monitored with reference to key objectives. However, for an organisation to learn about its practices requires a change in behaviour as a precondition of the use of performance measures. Staff need to understand the relevance of the information that is to be generated and its likely beneficial effects for themselves. A good deal of re-thinking may be necessary in order that all levels of a social care organisation understand the purposes to which information may be put and how this will be communicated throughout. Therefore, the technical issues in developing PIs should not obscure the changes which initially need to be made in organisational culture, in order for an indicator scheme to be workable in practice.

Within Cheshire, the use of regular workshops which involved the participation of staff at all levels in the organisation was helpful in creating what was later described as a learning organisation. In many ways, staff became engaged in the use of information to pursue explanations of patterns of variation which had hitherto been understood only on the basis of historical assumptions and speculation. In many ways, this returns us to the arguments, stated at the beginning of Chapter 1, concerning the use of a locally-based case review system in monitoring performance (Goldberg and Warburton, 1979; Challis and Chesterman, 1985).

Conceptual and theoretical refinements

The work contained herein has involved some improvements to the models we can use to help define and measure performance. The performance models used more traditionally in public sector services have been expanded to include wider service-related aspects. These include: the processes and activities of staff who are performing the core tasks of care management; local and national policy and guidance; and quality dimensions with particular relevance to social services activity. The PIAF framework is intended to inform and assist in the selection and interpretation of data. It should now be easier, for those implementing a performance management scheme, to decide where in the production of services to place relevant indicators that can comment on performance.

In setting our work in context, we have also offered definitions and conceptual work on indicators. Some of our wider definitions of efficiency permit social care services to be appraised more comprehensively than hitherto. Indicators derived from these concepts, particularly those related to targeting and assessment, reflect more complex judgements regarding service allocation. They offer a more rounded view of performance than do those indicators devised for social care through the later half of the 1980s. Indeed, some writers have pointed to a previous imbalance in the concept of value-for-money audit (Jackson, 1993). The indicators generated during the 1980s informed judgements concerning whether greater service outputs were produced, as against the inputs required. Since the community care reforms, however, social services departments have had to think more strategically. Services have had to be consciously modified in order to reflect changes in needs, and the impact of other factors, such as the mix of services available to respond to these needs. These factors reflect the concerns of allocative rather than technical efficiency. Indicators have failed to keep up with these developments. It is our intention that some of our indicators relating to process aspects in assessment and care planning will lead to a more careful evaluation of what is currently provided and the value which users place upon it.

Principles for the use of indicators

In looking through the indicators devised in our work with Cheshire and the review of measurement issues (Chapter 2), it is possible to provide some pointers to their use in practice. The initial development of PIs in business also gives us some material from which to work (see, for example, Helfert, 1965, pp. 66-75). Useful principles to remember are:

- Be mindful in the selection of data. Only use indicators which are relevant to the purposes of a particular analysis.
- If possible, performance indicators should be related to measures available from outside sources (Anthony and Herzlinger, 1980). Not only will these offer a context for measurement but they may also call for data collection on a similar basis, thus avoiding duplication of effort.
- Different measures should be developed for different purposes. Indicators can be tailor-made for the specific needs of staff. This is made easier if there is an explicit framework to guide the selection of indicators, dependent upon their place in the service system.
- Caution should be expressed in devising too many indicators as this will lead to information overload. This can quickly lead to suspicion of the whole enterprise.
- Performance data are best analysed over previous time periods as well as the present in order to detect any trends that can help to answer questions later.
- Attempt to look at variations from standards by cross-checking with other indicators and contextual data. Be wary of over-simplistic comparisons and deviations from the norm. These may be symptomatic of other underlying trends, which are important in their own right.

Considerations of design should precede both questions of measurement and analytic methods (Arvidsson, 1986). Choosing carefully those indicators that offer the best hope of commenting on identified service aspects is the first step in evaluating performance. This is made easier if the indicators are ordered by a framework which is logical, coherent and fits the real world of service provision.

Examination of indicators

In using performance indicators for social care, a number of techniques have been reviewed making it possible to identify aspects of the service system that are in need of amendment. Some of the more complex methods we have reviewed (see Chapter 2) depend on the sophistication of the routine information available and may be difficult to undertake in many social care organisations. These techniques are designed to provide summary measures of performance, often against a theoretical ideal, such as that of technical efficiency. Practitioners and managers may require simpler tools, to assist them in their use of performance management systems. Much can be learned from initial comparisons across units or areas. However, as stated, the limitations and dangers in comparing against the organisational average must be borne in mind. Such techniques used in the presentation of existing national packages, such as those of the Department of Health, are readily applicable to the work of individual local authorities (see Day, 1989, for an examination of some of these). In our work with them, Cheshire SSD presented and used the indicators we describe, in a comparative fashion.

The performance data we have described here may be used for a number of purposes: to review success in pursuing the aims of policy; to judge the achievement of standards; the judgement of services according to allocation criteria (such as those of targeting or eligibility); or to explore wider efficiency considerations. We have made it clear that different methods may be needed to support these different functions of performance indicators. Due caution has been emphasised regarding the interpretation of the results of analysis; taking care in comparison; examining like with like; and being mindful of the way results are presented.

Characteristics of a good PI system

It is also important to take account of the comments made by observers of recent PI systems in the NHS, social services and local government, for advice as to their best practical use. These can be used as criteria against which to assess the suitability of indicators generated for social care. Carter (1991) states that a good PI system should contain a number of attributes. It should be *relevant* to the needs and objectives of the organisation; it should not be open to manipulation by staff who might be assessed; it should be based on a *reliable* and *accurate* information system; and the PIs generated should be *unambiguous*. To be usable, PIs should also be relatively *parsimonious*; too many indicators can quickly overload the system and get in the way of intelligent inference by staff using them. Performance indicators should provide, if at all possible, an *accessible* and *comprehensible* picture of performance. To do this they should also be *timely*; they must provide information quickly enough for it to guide action. Lastly, PI data should be *designed* for the purpose for which it is intended. Many criticisms of the original NHS and social services performance indicators were that they were created in response to political pressures and were therefore constructed hastily from existing statistics. PIs are more likely to be useable if they are constructed for a specific purpose with one eye on how they might eventually be used. This 'custom built' design is made more possible if a comprehensive data system already exists in the organisation.

A Department of Health consultation document on performance makes reference to five major criteria for judging the suitability of social services indicators (Department of Health, 1999a, Annex B, p. 79). These include the fact that indicators should:

• Be readily attributed to social care
• Cover aspects that are relevant and important;
• Avoid perverse incentives;
• Be robust enough to cover all relevant data;
• Be responsive to change, to enable trends to be monitored;
• Be useable and timely.

On the whole, performance evaluation is easier and less expensive if good quality service data are already being collected (Wholey and Hatry, 1992). Part of the aim of this work was to enable performance indicators to work within an integrated system which clearly demonstrated the achievement, or not, of agreed community care objectives. Cheshire subsequently developed a 'Community Care Performance Management System', which scrutinised some of the indicators developed so far and enabled the department to monitor its progress in key service areas. It is clearly important, therefore, to develop performance data on the back of existing well-designed information systems.

We would do well to remember the comments made by Gray and Jenkins (1983), who have argued that, in order for any evaluative scheme to prosper, a number of criteria must be satisfied. These include not only conceptual and technical requirements, but also those relating to organisation and politics. The formulation of indicators within a coherent framework is, therefore, but the first step in a lengthy process. First and foremost, staff at all levels need to understand what indicators are about and must want to use the indicators to monitor and review policies and practice. For this reason, those developing indicators need to do so in partnership with staff, and with an appreciation of the policies and goals of the agency. Information systems will inevitably require modification to generate indicators reliably and validly on a routine basis with least feasible additional demands upon agency staff. Managers and practitioners at all levels need to develop their capacity to utilise information to enhance their decision-making.

Thus, it is not enough just to generate indicators and contextual information items; considerable thought needs to be given as to how the information is collected, when it should be fed back, to whom and how. Also, consideration needs to be given to what existing systems are in place for either carrying out further investigations or taking remedial action should the indicators reveal potential problems.

Problems of implementation

In our work with Cheshire, a number of problems were identified that had less to do with the technical problems in devising indicator systems and more to do with the attitudes of those implementing them. A number of these problems were related to the training and guidance of staff in developing a critical awareness of information. Key issues that emerged for effective implementation included:

- Involvement of staff at all levels in the implementation and utilisation of indicators;
- An exploratory rather than a punitive culture of investigation;
- A phased approach to the development and utilisation of indicators;
- Investment in developing an information culture among staff.

Recommendations for the future development of PIs

In the light of both national developmental work on performance indicators, and the experience of the present work in relation to local information systems, there are several principles that need to be acknowledged and a number of processes and systems that need to be in place for the effective generation and use of performance indicators:

- Performance indicators should be derived from agency policies and objectives and serve as a check on their achievement.
- Performance indicators should be part of the process of good management, ranging from senior management decision making to casework supervision.
- There should be transparent systems for the review of indicators and the taking of remedial action.
- Performance indicators should be part of a broader review and evaluation process, as by themselves indicators often raise more questions than they provide answers.
- Performance indicators should be divided into core indicators or a minimum data set of greatest immediacy and other indicators which, while important, are not required so regularly or are difficult to generate frequently.
- Sensible and appropriate timetables should be established for the generation of core and other indicators, with some indicators being produced monthly, others quarterly, and some annually. Where appropriate, some of the less immediate indicators can be collected via special surveys, perhaps organised on particular themes.

- Performance indicators should be based on information which is complete, valid and reliable and which, if needs be, can be routinely and readily collected.
- Performance indicators should be based on different types of data – both quantitative and qualitative – covering different service aspects to provide a whole picture of agency goals, activities, resources used and available, and impact on users.
- When analysed, performance indicators need to be set in the context of not only agency history, policies and funding, but also the policies and practices of other agencies.
- Performance indicators can be most useful when one service unit or one team or one worker is compared to another. However, if like is not being compared with like or if key features about one unit, team or worker are overlooked, the comparisons can be rendered meaningless.

Staff within social services departments, such as Cheshire, will of course have systems in place to generate the information required on an annual basis by the Department of Health, the Department of the Environment (for Revenue Out-turn and Capital Account returns) and CIPFA. It will also have arrangements in place for assembling the indicators required by the Audit Commission for the Citizen's Charter, and it will think of what information to collect for the local Community Care Charter initiative.

Much of the interest in Cheshire SSD in performance indicators arose from the local need to monitor and compare community care developments across the districts, and between the various units and teams operating in the county. However, Social Services Departments are also encouraged to make appropriate comparisons between themselves and other similar authorities using the Department of Health's Key Indicators, the CIPFA Actuals and Estimates, and other sources. The inspection of these national indicator sources should be systematic and part and parcel of the overall move to an information culture in social care organisations.

This work has been about statistical indicators of performance. However, only a partial view of performance can be expressed by hard data. More qualitative descriptions and statements may be needed to fully express some of the performance dimensions currently advocated (Arvidsson, 1986). Clear references to the performance elements contained within this book will, however, facilitate more informed discussion concerning the procedures and mechanisms necessary to comply with current guidance.

A local performance measurement system

To date, performance measurement in social care in the UK has been a relatively top-down process and has, on the whole, been based on discrete items of information which are not part of a broader framework. For example, the PAF represents a pragmatic collection of items, each highly salient to government concerns. It does contain several discrete indicators of sensitivity to the local impact on national goals, such as consistency, the health and social care interface and care provided at home. However these are predominantly descriptive indicators permitting comparison of inter-authority variation, but none of these relates structure, process and outcome in ways that permit the causal processes occurring within organisations to be unravelled and understood. The Best Value framework, common to all departments of local authorities, is not specific to social care or older people. It generates a process which authorities must follow and, as such, indicators derived from this framework do not permit the relationship between activities and outcomes, and the possible trade offs that may be made between different outcomes or goals, in social care to be specifically evaluated. Furthermore, it does not enable the user of the wider information collection contained in the KIGS (Department of Health, 2005) such as an individual manager in a social care organisation, a researcher or a citizen, to enquire as to a specific aspect of performance with which they might be concerned. In contradistinction to the recent monitoring of performance in the UK, work in Japan following the implementation of the Long-term Care Insurance System (Ikegami et al., 2003; Campbell and Ikegami, 2000, 2003) has been dependent on developments undertaken at the local level. These developments have the enormous advantage of producing more detailed information of specific relevance to older people, which can be aggregated for local managerial and performance review as well as providing information for more broad brush monitoring at the local authority level. Interestingly, in Japan over 60 per cent of municipalities, which are responsible for administering the Long-term Care Insurance System, have adopted a common performance measurement software program in order to analyse and benchmark the implementation process (Community Care Policy Network, 2001; Institute of Health and Economic Programmes, 2002). This bottom-up approach has arisen precisely because the responsibility for variations between areas in implementation is the legitimate purview of the municipalities as insurers and national monitoring is, by contrast, relatively undeveloped.

For the UK, there are important lessons from the Japanese context. In particular, the locally administered information relating to a common system of insurance makes possible the generation of client-level data in a similar format, facilitating the development of a shared perspective of effective performance between similar municipalities, thereby permitting local benchmarking. In the UK, such a shared approach is hampered by the lack of appropriate common information other than those items of information prescribed from the centre. Perhaps the way in which such a development could move forwards in the UK is through shared client-level data approaches, such as the Electronic Health Record (Department of Health, 1998e), and the SAP (Department of Health, 2002c) to produce more standardised information.

However, addressing questions of data design is a necessary but not sufficient condition to developing a coherent locally-based performance measurement system. Other factors, considered in the present work, are also important. These include the attitudes and perceptions of those charged with actually collecting the data required at this level, namely front-line staff and their immediate managers. More generally, we would conclude three other factors are of importance. First, there is the need for an overall integrative framework linking the individual indicators with one another and more broadly with the activities and goals of the organisation. Second, we need to use or have access to appropriate analytical techniques so that the data may be used to its full potential in addressing key questions for the organisation. Third, for performance review to have an effect in shaping, developing and changing the host organisation, there is a need to develop an inclusive learning culture within the organisation.

There are some recent developments that appear to seek a reconciliation between the top-down approach adopted by governments in the UK to performance measurement and the bottom-up approach described in this book. The document *National Standards Local Action* (Department of Health, 2004) suggests ways in which such a rapprochement might take place:

A ... shift is now required in the way improvements in people's health and care are planned and delivered. This means moving away from a system that is mainly driven by national targets to one in which:

- *standards* are the main driver for continuous improvements in quality;
- there are *fewer national targets*;
- there is greater scope for addressing *local priorities*;
- incentives are in place to support the system; and
- all organisations locally play their part in *service modernisation*

(Department of Health, 2004, p. 7).

This is designed to permit the development of local targets within a framework of national core and developmental standards.

It is hoped that some of the technical and conceptual problems with devising such a measurement system may have been helped by this book. Our motives for doing this have been to assist in the development towards a 'new performance measurement' which links individual activities to wider organisational goals and which can positively facilitate adaptive change and development within social care organisations.

In conclusion, it is possible to examine the use of performance indicators from a range of perspectives and offer many criticisms of them. However, it seems likely that they and other measurement systems, designed to monitor performance in social care, will profoundly influence service provision throughout the current century. The duties of the Best Value performance framework will continue to put greater demands on social services departments to routinely monitor their performance in relation to objectives and standards for these. Hopefully, the argument and information provided in this book will be of benefit to authorities who will need to monitor their performance locally and relate this to the wider national framework. It is hoped that this book will contribute to this being accomplished in a clearer and more coherent way than in the past, thus avoiding some of the pitfalls in earlier approaches to routine monitoring.

Appendix

Indicators – Detailed Descriptions

We list here the suite of indicators developed in this study. The total number of indicators in each domain of the PIAF model as well as those that are considered core indicators are outlined. We also outline particular indicators, with their reference numbers, under each service objective.

PIAF and service objectives

Totals of indicator types

	No.	Core
Needs:	21	7
Supply:	37	9
Practice process	38	7
Service process	26	6
Outcomes	21	12
Totals:	143	41

Service objectives

Note: Core monthly indicators are shown by *
Core quarterly indicators are shown by +
Core six-monthly indicators are shown by #
Some indicators relate to two or more service objectives

Background
N1 N2
S1 S3 S10 S13 S15 S16 S27 S28 S29+ S37
PP10

SP15
Total: 14
Core: 1 (no monthly)

Targeted
N3* N4 N5+ N9* N10 N11 N12 N13 N14+ N15 N17*
S14+ S18 S19
PP2* PP3 PP5 PP6+ PP7 PP8 PP9 PP11* PP12* PP13+ PP14 PP22+ PP27 PP28
   PP29 PP30 PP31 PP37 PP38
SP1 SP2 SP3 SP4 SP5 SP6 SP7 SP9* SP21
O7* O8* O9+ O10+ O13+
Total: 47
Core: 18 (9 monthly)

Timely
N17*
PP1 PP15 PP16 PP19 PP32 PP34
Total: 7
Core: 1 (1 monthly)

Diversion
N6* N20
S5+ S7 S9 S11 S12 S14+ S20 S21* S22* S23* S24* S25 S26+ S30+
PP17 PP20+ PP21 PP23 PP24 PP37 PP38
SP1 SP2 SP4 SP10* SP13#
O1+ O2+ O3+ O4+ O5+ O6+ O7* O8* O10+ O11 O12* O13+ O21
Total: 41
Core: 23 (9 monthly)

Efficient
N6* N7+ N8 N18 N19 N20 N21
S2 S4 S21* S22* S23* S24* S30+ S32 S33 S34 S35 S36
PP4 PP5 PP6+ PP11* PP12* PP13+ PP18 PP20+ PP21 PP23 PP24 PP25 PP32
   PP33 PP35 PP36 PP37 PP38
SP8 SP9* SP10* SP11 SP13# SP16 SP17 SP18 SP19 SP20 SP21 SP22+ SP23+
   SP24 SP25+ SP26
O2+ O4+ O5+ O6+ O11 O18 O19 O20 O21
Total: 62
Core: 22 (9 monthly)

Involved
N16
PP26
SP14
O14 O15 O16 O17 O18 O19 O20
Total: 10

Core: 0

Individual
N18 N19
S8 S12 S14+ S17 S31
PP20+ PP21 PP27 PP28 PP29 PP30
SP2 SP12 SP13#
O15
Total: 17
Core: 3 (0 monthly)

Choice
N18 N19 N21
S6 S7 S8 S17 S31 S36
PP20+ PP21 PP26 PP29 PP30
SP2 SP12 SP13#
O2+ O4+ O5+ O6+ O21
Total: 22
Core: 6 (0 monthly)

The indicators

Needs indicators

N1   Social indicators of need – general

Definition: Proportion of the total population in age bands 0 to 4, 5 to 9, 10 to 17, 18
    to 64, 65 to 74, 75 to 84, 85 and over; (DH-KI: SN1 to SN7);
% economically active residents who are unemployed; (DH-KI: SN50);
% people in households that are not self-contained; (DH-KI: SN51);
% people in households in overcrowded accommodation; (DH-KI: SN52);
% households renting flats in residential buildings; (DH-KI: SN53);
% people from different ethnic groups; (DH-KI: SN54 approximately);
Standardised Mortality Rates. (DH-KI: SN34; NHSE-HSI).

PIAF category: NI
Key Area(s): Context
Service Objective(s): Background
Indicator status: Non-core, annual – but some special studies required
Benchmark: Equivalent authorities – Group A Shire Counties (Shaw Classification)
Level of aggregation: Authority, district, team
Comparable national statistics:
CIPFA-E
CIPFA-A
DH-KI: SN1 to SN7; SN50 to SN54; SN32 (see above for which indicator matches
    which national indicator)

NHSE-HSI: this set of indicators contains a variety of SMRs and other morbidity statistics that provide useful contextual information

DH-KIGS: contains comparable indicators to those defined in earlier packages which may be referenced differently

N2   Social indicators of need – older people

Definition: Growth in the elderly population aged 65 to 74, 75 to 84, and 85 and over, in recent years and / or projected for the coming 5 years; (AC-CCI: for growth of population aged 65-74, and 75 & over);

% of those of pensionable age and over living alone; (DH-KI: SN60);

% of those of pensionable age in rented accommodation; (DH-KI: SN61);

% of those aged 65 and over with a limiting long-standing illness; (DH-KI: SN62; NHSE-HSI);

% of those of pensionable age from different ethnic groups.

PIAF category: NI
Key Area(s): Context
Service Objective(s): Background
Indicator status: Non-core, annual – but some special studies required
Benchmark: Equivalent authorities – Group A Shire Counties (Shaw Classification)
Level of aggregation: Authority, district, team
Comparable national statistics:
AC-CCI
DH-KI: SN60; SN61; SN63; SN70 (see above for which indicator matches which national indicator)
NHSE-HSI: this set of indicators contains a variety of morbidity statistics that provide a useful context for interpreting local social care indicators
DH-KIGS: contains comparable indicators to those defined in earlier packages which may be referenced differently

N3   No. of screenings per 1000 population aged 75 and over

Definition: Proportion of the very elderly population who are screened by social services.

PIAF category: NI
Key Area(s): Context
Service Objective(s): Targeted
Indicator status: Core, monthly
Benchmark: Authority average
Level of aggregation: Authority, district, team
Notes: In this and most other indicators the population denominator is elderly people aged 75 and over. This is because the vast majority of users are aged 75 and over. They are some exceptions. For day and lunch clubs, a large proportion of users are aged under 75; hence it makes sense to relate usage to the population aged 65 and over
Comparable national statistics:

AC-CCI: the Audit Commission ask local authorities for the numbers of adults referred for assessment

ADSS: at a regional level the ADSS collects information from local authorities on referrals and assessments

N4   No. of screenings per 1000 population aged 75 and over with carer and the status of that carer

Definition: Proportions of the very elderly population at risk through a lack of informal carers, or carers who are under considerable pressure and likely to withdraw or reduce their effort, who are screened by social services.

PIAF category: NI
Key Area(s): Breakdown
Service Objective(s): Targeted
Indicator Status: Special study – six monthly:
Benchmark: Authority average; within district internal differences between carer / non-carer
Level of aggregation: Authority, district, team
Comparable national statistics: none

N5   No. of screenings per 1000 population aged 75 and over in different user groups where visual impairment, auditory impairment, cognitive impairment, depression, physical impairment (including immobility, instability and incontinence) have been identified

Definition: Proportions of the very elderly population at risk through impairments who are screened by social services.

PIAF category: NI
Key Area(s): Context
Service Objective(s): Targeted
Indicator status: Core, quarterly
Benchmark: Authority average
Level of aggregation: Authority, district, team

Notes: In this and similar indicators, the proper identification of these impairments is crucial to the quality of the data. Where clinical diagnoses are available, these should be used. Annual Public Health reports can be checked for comparable data. Proper mechanisms need to be in place to capture these data.
Comparable national statistics: none

N6   No. of re-screenings within six months per 1000 population aged 75 and over

Definition: Proportions of the very elderly population for whom repeat requests for screening by social services are made within a relatively short time following a previous screening.

PIAF category: NI
Key Area(s): Care at home, Breakdown, Assessment and care management
Service Objective(s): Diversion, Efficient
Indicator status: Core, monthly
Benchmark: Authority average
Level of aggregation: Authority, district, team
Comparable national statistics: none

N7   No. of screenings by assessment teams per assessment worker

Definition: The number of screenings by each assessment team divided by the number of whole time equivalent assessment staff.

PIAF category: NI
Key Area(s): Assessment and care management
Service Objective(s): Efficient
Indicator status: Core, quarterly
Benchmark: Authority average
Level of aggregation: Authority, district, team
Comparable national statistics: none

N8   No. of screenings by hospital social work departments per assessment worker by ward

Definition: The number of screenings by each hospital team divided by the number of whole-time equivalent assessment staff per ward (specialty), and of these the percentage in, out and closed.

PIAF category: NI
Key Area(s): Breakdown, Alternative accommodation
Service Objective(s): Efficient
Indicator status: Special study – annual
Benchmark: Authority average
Level of aggregation: Authority, district, team

Notes: The degree to which 'specialty' is broken down needs to be clarified.
Comparable national statistics: none

N9 No. of referrals for assessment per 1000 population aged 75 and over

Definition: Proportion of the very elderly population who are referred for assessment.

PIAF category: NI
Key Area(s): Assessment and care management
Service Objective(s): Targeted
Indicator status: Core, monthly
Benchmark: Authority average
Level of aggregation: Authority, district, team

Notes: It is important to compare screenings and referrals for assessment to understand filtration processes.
Comparable national statistics:
ADSS: at a regional level the ADSS collects information from local authorities on referrals and assessments

N10 No. of referrals for assessment per 1000 relevant age group in different age groups (65 to 74, 75 to 84, 85 and over)

Definition: Proportion of the elderly population in three broad age groups who are referred for assessment.

PIAF category: NI
Key Area(s): Assessment and care management
Service Objective(s): Targeted
Indicator status: Non-core, quarterly
Benchmark: Authority average
Level of aggregation: Authority, district, team
Comparable national statistics: none

N11 No. of referrals for assessment per 1000 population aged 75 and over living alone or with others

Definition: Proportions of the very elderly population either at risk by virtue of living alone or potentially benefitting from informal care, who are screened for a service

PIAF category: NI
Key Area(s): Breakdown
Service Objective(s): Targeted
Indicator status: Non-core, quarterly
Benchmark: Authority average; within district differences between alone / not alone
Level of aggregation: Authority, district, team
Comparable national statistics: none

N12   No. of referrals for assessment per 1000 population aged 75 and over with carer and the status of that carer

Definition: Proportions of the very elderly population at risk through a lack of informal carers, or carer who are under considerable pressure and likely to withdraw or reduce their effort, who are referred for assessment by social services following screening.

PIAF category: NI
Key Area(s): Breakdown
Service Objective(s): Targeted
Indicator status: Special study – six monthly
Benchmark: Authority average; within district internal differences between carer / non carer
Level of aggregation: Authority, district, team
Comparable national statistics: none

N13   No. of referrals for assessment per 1000 population aged 65 and over in different ethnic groups

Definition: Proportion of the elderly population in broad ethnic groups who are referred for assessment. The ethnic groups can be based on the OPCS' Census of 1991: White, African, Caribbean (including Black British), South Asian, Other Asian, and other.

PIAF category: NI
Key Area(s): Assessment and care management
Service Objective(s): Targeted
Indicator status: Non-core, six monthly
Benchmark: Authority average; proportion in screenings compared with relevant population
Level of aggregation: Authority, district, team

Notes: Local relevant definitions of ethnic groups need to be produced.
Comparable national statistics:
DH-PAF: E47 asks for the proportion of users in different ethnic groups who are receiving an assessment

N14   No. of referrals for assessment per 1000 population aged 75 and over in different user groups where visual impairment, auditory impairment, cognitive impairment, physical impairment (including immobility, instability and incontinence) have been identified

Definition: Proportions of the very elderly population at risk through impairments who are screened by social services following referral.

PIAF category: NI
Key Area(s): Assessment and care management

Service Objective(s): Targeted
Indicator status: Core, quarterly
Benchmark: Authority average
Level of aggregation: Authority, district, team

Notes: In this and similar indicators, the proper identification of these impairments is crucial to the quality of the data. Where clinical diagnoses are available, these should be used. Annual Public Health reports can be checked for comparable data. Proper mechanisms need to be in place to capture these data.
Comparable national statistics: none

N15   No. of referrals for assessment per 1000 population aged 75 and over involving physical abuse

Definition: Proportions of the very elderly population at risk through apparent physical abuse by those living with or caring for them, who are referred for assessment by social services following screening. Abuse may also mean systematic neglect.

PIAF category: NI
Key Area(s): Breakdown
Service Objective(s): Targeted
Indicator status: Special study – six monthly
Benchmark: Authority average
Level of aggregation: Authority, district, team

Notes: Aim to routinise to 'Non-core, quarterly' status
Comparable national statistics: none

N16   Screening source and consent of user

Definition: Proportions of the older users who are self refer or are referred for screening by others including their families, GPs and other sources, including hospital. If referred for screening by others, the extent to which users gave their consent for the referral to be made.

PIAF category: NI
Key Area(s): Assessment and care management
Service Objective(s): Involved
Indicator status: Non-core, quarterly for the proportions of screenings by source. Annual special study for consent.
Benchmark: Authority average
Level of aggregation: Authority, district, team

Notes: Surveys of care plans can be carried out to analyse the extent to which users give their consent to referrals for screening.
Comparable national statistics: none

N17   No. of referrals for assessment in priority for response bands

Definition: Proportions of the older users who at referral for assessment are assigned to each of the relevant four priority bands used.

PIAF category: NI
Key Area(s): Assessment and care management
Service Objective(s): Targeted, Timely
Indicator status: Core, monthly
Benchmark: Authority average
Level of aggregation: Authority, district, team
Comparable national statistics:
AC-CCI: the Audit Commission ask for the percentage of assessments recommending no service, service by a single agency and service by more than one agency. This could help put indicator N17 in context.

N18   No. of cases for which there are service gaps

Definition: Proportions of older users for whom following a standard or full assessment there are service gaps identified by assessing staff, based on users' expressed preferences and staff's professional judgements.

PIAF category: NI
Key Area(s): Networks of support
Service Objective(s): Efficient, Individual, Choice
Indicator status: Non-core, quarterly
Benchmark: Authority average
Level of aggregation: Authority, district, team

Notes: This indicator while measuring need, also provides insight into process issues. In part, an SSD might derive this indicator by the inclusion of questions about user preferences which the SSD is not able to meet.
Comparable national statistics: none

N19   Types and frequency of service gaps

Definition: Proportions of older users for whom following a standard or full assessment there are identified specific service gaps identified by assessing staff, based on users' expressed preferences and staff's professional judgements.

PIAF category: NI
Key Area(s): Networks of support
Service Objective(s): Efficient, Individual, Choice
Indicator status: Non-core, quarterly
Benchmark: Authority average
Level of aggregation: Authority, district, team

Notes: Categorisation of the likely major service gaps is required. Routine information for this indicator can be derived from the an amended Green Card – see previous indicator.
Comparable national statistics: none

N20   No. of service users with continuing medical care needs who are provided with substitute social services

Definition: Proportions of older users for whom following a standard or full assessment there are continuing medical needs which are met not through the NHS.

PIAF category: NI
Key Area(s): Breakdown, Alternative accommodation
Service Objective(s): Diversion, Efficient
Indicator status: Special study – annual
Benchmark: Authority average
Level of aggregation: Authority, district
Comparable national statistics: none

N21   No. of service users with continuing medical care needs who are charged for substitute social services

Definition: Proportions of older users for whom following a standard or full assessment there are continuing medical needs but provision is through charged social services.

PIAF category: NI
Key Area(s): Breakdown, Alternative accommodation
Service Objective(s): Efficient, Choice
Indicator status: Special study – annual
Benchmark: Authority average
Level of aggregation: Authority, district
Comparable national statistics: none

Supply indicators

S1   Number of field work staff (with generic or elderly user group focus) per 1000 population aged 75 and over

Definition: The number of field work staff (in areas or hospital-based) that are available to serve the elderly population. The types of staff covered in this indicator comprise social workers and community care workers. The number is based on whole-time equivalents.

PIAF category: SI
Key Area(s): Context
Service Objective(s): Background

Indicator status: Non-core, quarterly
Benchmark: Authority average, Equivalent shire authorities
Level of aggregation: Authority, district, team
Comparable national statistics: none

S2　Ratio of social workers to community care workers (with generic or older user group focus)

Definition: The ratio of social work staff to community care workers (in areas or hospital-based). The number is based on whole-time equivalents.

PIAF category: SI
Key Area(s): Context
Service Objective(s): Efficient
Indicator status: Non-core, quarterly
Benchmark: Authority average
Level of aggregation: Authority, district, team
Comparable national statistics: none

S3　Number of OT staff per 1000 population aged 75 and over

Definition: The number of OT staff working for the SSD, who are qualified or not, to serve the elderly population. The number is based on whole-time equivalents.

PIAF category: SI
Key Area(s): Context
Service Objective(s): Background
Indicator status: Non-core, quarterly
Benchmark: Authority average, Equivalent shire authorities
Level of aggregation: Authority, district, team
Comparable national statistics: none

S4　Percentage of OT staff who are qualified

Definition: The proportion of OT staff working for the SSD who are qualified. The number is based on whole-time equivalents.

PIAF category: SI
Key Area(s): Context
Service Objective(s): Efficient
Indicator status: Non-core, quarterly
Benchmark: Authority average
Level of aggregation: Authority, district, team
Comparable national statistics: none

S5   No. of home care hours per 1000 population aged 75 and over purchased by the SSD

Definition: The total amount of home care hours that are purchased by the SSD per head of population.

PIAF category: SI
Key Area(s): Care at home
Service Objective(s): Diversion
Indicator status: Core, quarterly
Benchmark: Authority average, Equivalent shire authorities
Level of aggregation: Authority, district, team
Comparable national statistics:
DH-KI: AA65 but note that the KI is about contact hours, and is for all user groups
DH-CCS: Table 1.7 gives contact hours per 10,000 households for all cases and by sector of provider
DH-KIGS: AA65 requests contact hours per 1000 population aged 75 plus

S6   No. of independent sector providers of domiciliary care

Definition: self explanatory.

PIAF category: SI
Key Area(s): Care at home, Networks of support
Service Objective(s): Choice
Indicator status: Non-core, quarterly
Benchmark: Authority average
Level of aggregation: Authority, district
Comparable national statistics: none

S7   No. of hours provided by independent sector providers of home care by source

Definition: The amount of home care hours that are actually provided by different independent providers – private or not-for-profit.

PIAF category: SI
Key Area(s): Care at home, Networks of support
Service Objective(s): Diversion, Choice
Indicator status: Non-core, quarterly
Benchmark: Authority average
Level of aggregation: Authority, district
Comparable national statistics:
DH-KI: AA6 but this KI is only an approximation as it is about '% of contact hours provided by the independent sector'
DH-CCS: Table 1.1 gives contact hours by sector of provider, for all users not just elderly users

DH-KIGS: AA66 request percentage of contact hours provided by independent
sector

S8   Percentage of home care hours purchased by SSD for older people provided in evenings and at weekend by types of provider

Definition: The number of home care hours that are provided 'out of normal' hours
as a proportion of all home care hours by type of provider – SSD, private and
not-for-profit.

PIAF category: SI
Key Area(s): Care at home, Networks of support, Respite
Service Objective(s): Individual, Choice
Indicator status: Non-core, quarterly
Benchmark: Authority average
Level of aggregation: Authority, district
Comparable national statistics: none

S9   No. of night sitting sessions purchased by SSD per 1000 population aged 75 and over arranged by SSD

Definition: The number of night sitting sessions – as distinct from home care or
nursing input – that is provided to maintain surveillance on elderly services users
during the night, per relevant population.

PIAF category: SI
Key Area(s): Care at home, Respite
Service Objective(s): Diversion
Indicator status: Non-core, quarterly
Benchmark: Authority average
Level of aggregation: Authority, district
Comparable national statistics: none

S10   No. of delivered meals per 1000 population aged 75 and over arranged by SSD by type of meal

Definition: The delivered meals – whether chilled / frozen or hot – that are provided
to the elderly population in total. Excluded from this indicator are meals which are
prepared by home care staff as part of their responsibilities, and food bought by
home care staff when they shop for users.

PIAF category: SI
Key Area(s): Care at home
Service Objective(s): Background
Indicator status: Non-core, quarterly
Benchmark: Authority average, Equivalent shire authorities
Level of aggregation: Authority, district
Comparable national statistics:

DH-KI: AA81 but this KI covers all users of delivered meals
DH-CCS: Table 2.4 gives delivered meals per 10,000 population, but covers all
  users
AC-CCI: the Audit Commission ask for the number of meals provided by the
  authority per elderly person aged 65-74, and aged 75 & over
DH-KIGS: AA81 number of delivered meals per 1000 population aged 75 & over

S11 No. of weekly day care places and family placements – per 1000 population aged 65 and over available from SSD, voluntary and private providers

Definition: The number of potential day care places and family placements that are
  available to the elderly population from different providers. The types of day care
  covered in this indicator comprise day centres for older people, places for older
  people in multi-user centres, day care places in resource centres, day care
  places in residential settings, drop-in facilities, and family placements. The
  definition of 'weekly' places is taken from the Department of Health's Key
  Indicator publication for 1994. (The age group for the population is lower for this
  indicator, compared with others, as there are significant numbers of younger
  elderly users who attend day care.)

PIAF category: SI
Key Area(s): Respite
Service Objective(s): Diversion
Indicator status: Non-core, quarterly
Benchmark: Authority average, Equivalent shire authorities
Level of aggregation: Authority, district
Comparable national statistics:
DH-KI/ DH-KIGS: OA51 covers no. of weekly places in day centres only
DH-CCS: Table 3.3 for day care only, and per 10,000 population per 1000 population
  aged 65

S12 Percentage of weekly day care places for older people available at the weekend

Definition: The number of day care places that are available to the elderly population
  at the weekend as a proportion of all weekly day care places. The types of day
  care covered in this indicator comprise traditional day centres for older people,
  places for older people in multi-user group centres, day care places in resource
  centres, day care places in residential settings, and drop-in facilities. The
  definition of 'weekly' places can be taken from the Department of Health's Key
  Indicator publication for 1994.

PIAF category: SI
Key Area(s): Respite
Service Objective(s): Diversion, Individual
Indicator status: Non-core, quarterly
Benchmark: Authority average

Level of aggregation: Authority, district
Comparable national statistics: none

S13   No. of weekly lunch club places per 1000 population aged 65 and over available from SSD, voluntary and private providers

Definition: The number of potential lunch club places that are available to the elderly population in total, and from different providers. The definition of 'weekly' places can be taken from the Department of Health's Key Indicator publication for 1994. (The age group for the population is lower for this indicator, compared with others, as there are a significant proportion of younger elderly users who attend lunch clubs.)

PIAF category: SI
Key Area(s): Networks of support
Service Objective(s): Background
Indicator status: Special study – annual
Benchmark: Authority average
Level of aggregation: Authority, district
Comparable national statistics: none, although CCS: Tables 2.1 onwards give information on people attending lunch clubs and meals served there. DH-KIGP asks for number of weekly meals served at lunch clubs per 1000 population aged 75 & over.

S14   No. of elderly people living at home who in the last quarter received at least 4 hours of personal/day care on a daily basis each week per 1000 population aged 75 and over

Definition: The number of elderly people at home who receive intensive personal care or surveillance amounting to at least 4 hours. The personal care help can include all forms of domiciliary care and day care. It can be provided at any time throughout the day and night, in small or extended units of time.

PIAF category: SI
Key Area(s): Breakdown, Care at home, Respite
Service Objective(s): Targeted, Diversion, Individual
Indicator status: Core, quarterly
Benchmark: Authority average
Level of aggregation: Authority, district

Notes: One of the most important indicators in the whole package; difficult to produce but essential for the evaluation of community care. Initially the indicator can be set up to capture users receiving more than 4 hours a day. However, the hours might need to be modified upwards or downwards depending on how many users and what types of users the indicator casts light on.
Comparable national statistics:

DH-KI: AA70 but this KI is only a close approximation and deals with households receiving help who receive at least six visits in the week with total contact hours of five or more

DH-CCS: Tables 1.3 to 1.5 show contact hours and numbers of visits for all home care users. This information can approximate to S14.

DH-PAF: C28 requests the number of households receiving intensive home care. Defines intensive as 10 or more contact hours and six or more visits in the week (this is DH-KIGS indicator AA71).

S15   Within the authority, no. of residential care beds for elderly people per 1000 population aged 75 and over, and % provided by council, voluntary and private providers

Definition: The number of residential care places in either residential care homes or dual registered homes available to the elderly population, in total and from different providers.

PIAF category: SI
Key Area(s): Alternative accommodation
Service Objective(s): Background
Indicator status: Non-core, quarterly
Benchmark: Authority average, Equivalent shire authorities
Level of aggregation: Authority, district
Comparable national statistics:
DH-KI: OA01 gives the number of places in residential homes in total; OA02 gives the percentage of places that are in independent homes
DH-KIGS: AA01 for number of residential places in total; AA02 for percentage of places in independent homes; AA03 for percentage of places in voluntary homes

S16   Within the authority, no. of nursing beds for elderly people per 1000 population aged 75 and over

Definition: The total number of nursing beds in either nursing homes or dual registered homes available to the elderly population.

PIAF category: SI
Key Area(s): Alternative accommodation
Service Objective(s): Background
Indicator status: Non-core, quarterly
Benchmark: Authority average
Level of aggregation: Authority, district
Comparable national statistics: the District Health Authority should be approached for access to some data.
DH-KIGS: OA06 asks for nursing places in residential and nursing homes for older people per 1000 population aged 75 and over.

S17   Percentage of care beds for elderly people in single rooms for residential care providers in total, for each residential care home, for nursing home providers in total, and for each nursing home

Definition: The proportion of residential care places in either residential care homes or dual registered homes or nursing homes available to the elderly population, in total and for individual homes which are in single rooms.

PIAF category: SI
Key Area(s): Alternative accommodation
Service Objective(s): Individual, Choice
Indicator status: Special study – annual
Benchmark: 80%
Level of aggregation: Authority, each home

Notes: The benchmark derives from Centre of Policy on Ageing's study 'Home Life'.
Comparable national statistics:
DH-KI: OA03 which gives the percentage of residential places in residential care homes for older people that are in single rooms
AC-CCI: the Audit Commission asks for the percentage of adults going into residential care who are offered single rooms. This indicator can act as a proxy for S17.
DH-PAF: D37 asks for percentage of people in residential and nursing home care offered single rooms (this is DH-KIGS indicator OA03). This is the same as the Audit Commission indicator L6.

S18   No. of care beds designated for cognitively impaired elderly people per 1000 population aged 75 in total and by broad type of provider

Definition: The number of care places specifically designated for elderly people with cognitive impairment (EMI) available to the elderly population, in total and by residential care bed providers (that is, the council or others) and nursing home providers.

PIAF category: SI
Key Area(s): Alternative accommodation
Service Objective(s): Targeted
Indicator status: Non-core, annual
Benchmark: Authority average
Level of aggregation: Authority, district
Comparable national statistics:
DH-KIGS: OA07 requests the % of residential places for mentally infirm older people

S19   No. of care beds designated for minority ethnic elders per 1000 population aged 75 from those respective groups, in total and by broad type of provider

Definition: The number of care places specifically designated for elderly people of African, Caribbean, South Asian, Other Asian, Mid and East European descent and from other minority ethnic groups available to the elderly population from those groups, in total and by residential care bed providers (that is, the council or others) and nursing home providers.

PIAF category: SI
Key Area(s): Alternative accommodation
Service Objective(s): Targeted
Indicator status: Non-core, annual
Benchmark: Authority average
Level of aggregation: Authority, district
Comparable national statistics: none

S20   No. of care beds designated for short-term episodes and respite care per 1000 population aged 75 in total

Definition: The number of care places specifically designated by all types of provider for short term or respite care, available to the elderly population.

PIAF category: SI
Key Area(s): Respite
Service Objective(s): Diversion
Indicator status: Non-core, quarterly
Benchmark: Authority average
Level of aggregation: Authority, district
Comparable national statistics: Audit Commission asks each local authority to specify how many nights of respite are they provide or fund
DH-KIGS: AA22 asks for short term admissions to residential care; AA23 for the percentage of short term admissions to independent homes

S21   Expenditure on residential care placements for older people per 1000 pop aged 75 and over

Definition: Gross expenditure in the month, and to date in the financial year, on SSD and other residential care placements in relation to the elderly population broken down by long-term care and short-term care (less than 6 weeks).

PIAF category: SI
Key Area(s): Alternative accommodation, Finance
Service Objective(s): Diversion, Efficient
Indicator status: Core, monthly
Benchmark: Authority average, Equivalent shire authorities
Level of aggregation: Authority, district

Notes: This helps to monitor STG spending. There are a number of indicators in the
    PIAF package about people or care homes of one kind or another, and
    expenditure / activity related to these placements.
Comparable national statistics:
DH-KI: EE2 for gross spend in the year
DH-KIGS: EX22 asks for expenditure on residential care for older people aged 75
    and over

S22   Expenditure on new residential care placements for older people per 1000 pop aged 75 and over

Definition: Gross expenditure in the month on new SSD and other residential care
    placements in relation to the elderly population broken down by long-term care
    and short-term care (less than 6 weeks).

PIAF category: SI
Key Area(s): Alternative accommodation, Finance
Service Objective(s): Diversion, Efficient
Indicator status: Core, monthly
Benchmark: Authority average, Equivalent shire authorities
Level of aggregation: Authority, district

Notes: This helps to monitor STG spending. There are a number of indicators in the
    PIAF package about people or care homes of one kind or another, and
    expenditure / activity related to these placements.
Comparable national statistics: none

S23   Expenditure on nursing home placements for older people per 1000 pop aged 75 and over

Definition: Gross expenditure in the month, and to date in the financial year, on
    nursing home placements in relation to the elderly population broken down by
    long-term care and short-term care (less than 6 weeks).

PIAF category: SI
Key Area(s): Alternative accommodation, Finance
Service Objective(s): Diversion, Efficient
Indicator status: Core, monthly
Benchmark: Authority average
Level of aggregation: Authority, district

Notes: This helps to monitor STG spending.
Comparable national statistics:
DH-KIGS: EX23 asks for expenditure on nursing placements for older people aged
    75 and over

S24 Expenditure on new nursing home placements for older people per 1000 pop aged 75 and over

Definition: Gross expenditure in the month on new nursing home placements in relation to the elderly population broken down by long-term care and short-term care (less than 6 weeks).

PIAF category: SI
Key Area(s): Alternative accommodation, Finance
Service Objective(s): Diversion, Efficient
Indicator status: Core, monthly
Benchmark: Authority average
Level of aggregation: Authority, district

Notes: This helps to monitor STG spending.
Comparable national statistics: none

S25 Expenditure on day care for older people per 1000 pop aged 65 and over

Definition: Gross expenditure in the quarter on SSD and other day care in relation to the elderly population.

PIAF category: SI
Key Area(s): Respite, Finance
Service Objective(s): Diversion
Indicator status: Non-core, quarterly
Benchmark: Authority average, Equivalent shire authorities
Level of aggregation: Authority, district
Comparable national statistics:
DH-KI: EE3 for gross spend in the year for day centres for elderly and mixed user groups
DH-KIGS: EX25 asks for expenditure on day centres for those aged 75 and over

S26 Expenditure on home care for older people per 1000 pop aged 75 and over

Definition: Gross expenditure in the quarter on SSD and other domiciliary care in relation to the elderly population.

PIAF category: SI
Key Area(s): Care at home, Finance
Service Objective(s): Diversion
Indicator status: Core, quarterly
Benchmark: Authority average, Equivalent shire authorities
Level of aggregation: Authority, district
Comparable national statistics:
DH-KI: EE4 for gross spend in the year on all home help users

DH-KIGS: EX26 asks for expenditure on home support services for those aged 75 and over

S27 Expenditure on meals – delivered and served at lunch clubs – for older people per 1000 pop aged 75 and over

Definition: Gross expenditure in the quarter on SSD and other meals in relation to the elderly population.

PIAF category: SI
Key Area(s): Care at home, Finance
Service Objective(s): Background
Indicator status: Non-core, quarterly
Benchmark: Authority average, Equivalent shire authorities
Level of aggregation: Authority, district
Comparable national statistics:
DH-KI: EE5 but note that the KI relates spending to population aged 65 and over
DH-KIGS: EX24 asks for expenditure on meal services for those aged 75 and over

S28 Expenditure on equipment and adaptations for older people per 1000 pop aged 75 and over

Definition: Gross expenditure in the quarter on SSD equipment / adaptations in relation to the elderly population.

PIAF category: SI
Key Area(s): Care at home, Finance
Service Objective(s): Background
Indicator status: Non-core, quarterly
Benchmark: Authority average, Equivalent shire authorities
Level of aggregation: Authority, district
Comparable national statistics:
DH-KI: EE6 but note that the KI relates spending to population aged 65 and over
DH-PAF: C38 requests percentage of items of equipment costing less than £1000

S29 Expenditure on all services for older people per 1000 pop aged 75 and over

Definition: Gross expenditure in the quarter on all SSD and other services in relation to the elderly population.

PIAF category: SI
Key Area(s): Context, Finance
Service Objective(s): Background
Indicator status: Core, quarterly
Benchmark: Authority average, Equivalent shire authorities
Level of aggregation: Authority, district
Comparable national statistics:

DH-KI: EE1 but note that the KI relates spending to population aged 65 and over
AC-CCI: the Audit Commission asks for net expenditure per head of population on
social services for elderly and physically disabled people
DH-KIGS: EX21 asks for expenditure on services to older people aged 75 and over

S30 % breakdown of total expenditure on older people in long-term residential care and nursing home placements

Definition: Percentage of gross expenditure in the quarter devoted to long-term
institutional care placements in relation to all expenditure on elderly service
users.

PIAF category: SI
Key Area(s): Alternative accommodation, Breakdown, Care at home, Assessment
and care management, Finance
Service Objective(s): Diversion, Efficient
Indicator status: Core, quarterly
Benchmark: Authority average
Level of aggregation: Authority, district
Comparable national statistics:
DH-KI: DE6 shows the expenditure on non-residential care as a % of gross
expenditure on older and physically disabled service users

S31 % breakdown of expenditure on older people in support of promotion

Definition: Percentage of gross expenditure in the quarter devoted to supporting
voluntary organisations and other agencies in support older people, where the
SSD does not carry out a formal assessment.

PIAF category: SI
Key Area(s): Care at home, Networks of support
Service Objective(s): Individual, Choice
Indicator status: Non-core, annual
Benchmark: Authority average
Level of aggregation: Authority, district

Notes: This indicator is about funding of voluntary organisations and other agencies
to address social care issues. It excludes contracts placed with such bodies
following formal SSD assessments. In some ways 'promotion' relates to
'prevention'
Comparable national statistics:
DH-KI: C24, but this KI is only an approximation of indicator S31, and measures the
breakdown of SSD net current expenditure in support of voluntary organisations
with a focus on older people

S32 Unit cost of SSD residential care homes

Definition: Self explanatory.

PIAF category: SI
Key Area(s): Alternative accommodation, Finance
Service Objective(s): Efficient
Indicator status: Non-core, quarterly
Benchmark: Other homes, Authority average, Equivalent shire authorities
Level of aggregation: Authority, each home
Comparable national statistics:
CIPFA-E: Col 73
CIPFA-A: Col 69
DH-KI: HE1 & HE2
DH-PAF: B13 unit costs of residential and nursing home care

S33 Unit cost of SSD home help hour

Definition: Self explanatory.

PIAF category: SI
Key Area(s): Care at home, Finance
Service Objective(s): Efficient
Indicator status: Non-core, quarterly
Benchmark: Authority average, Equivalent shire authorities
Level of aggregation: Authority, each home care management unit
Comparable national statistics:
CIPFA-E: Col 85
CIPFA-A: Col 91
DH-KI: HE6 but these unit costs apply to all user groups

S34 Unit cost of SSD day centre attendance

Definition: Self explanatory.

PIAF category: SI
Key Area(s): Respite, Finance
Service Objective(s): Efficient
Indicator status: Non-core, quarterly
Benchmark: Other centres, Authority average, Equivalent shire authorities
Level of aggregation: Authority, each day centre
Comparable national statistics:
CIPFA-E: Col 79
CIPFA-A: Col 76

S35 Unit cost of SSD delivered meals

Definition: Self explanatory.

PIAF category: SI
Key Area(s): Care at home, Finance
Service Objective(s): Efficient
Indicator status: Non-core, quarterly
Benchmark: Authority average, Equivalent shire authorities
Level of aggregation: Authority, each kitchen / round
Comparable national statistics:
CIPFA-E: Col 93
CIPFA-A: Col 100 but CIPFA do not separate delivered meals from lunch club meals
DH-KI: HE7 for delivered meals only

S36 Financial contributions users make to costs of packages of community-based services as a % of total expenditure

Definition: The proportion of costs recouped in charges in the quarter.

PIAF category: SI
Key Area(s): Care at home, Finance
Service Objective(s): Efficient, Choice
Indicator status: Non-core, quarterly
Benchmark: Authority average, Equivalent shire authorities
Level of aggregation: Authority, district, team

Notes: The denominator in this indicator are will be the accounted costs on particular services, in line with RO3 and CIPFA definitions. As such it will not represent the real and full costs. This indicator may be shown for the care package as a whole; but might also be shown for individual services where user contributions are sought.
Comparable national statistics:
DH-KI: DE8 is the % of SSD gross expenditure on home help for all user groups recouped through feed and charges, and hence approximates indicator S36

S37 Charges levied by private and voluntary sector homes

Definition: Gross charges actually levied in the independent sector.

PIAF category: SI
Key Area(s): Alternative accommodation, Finance
Service Objective(s): Background
Indicator status: Non-core, quarterly
Benchmark: Authority average
Level of aggregation: Authority, district, home
Comparable national statistics: none

Practice process indicators

a) Case Finding and Screening

PP1   Time between initial contact /referral and the first response by priority band

Definition: The interval (in working days) between the acceptance of a referral by the SSD and subsequent first action-oriented contact by SSD professional for people with varied levels of need. This first contact can be arrangement of a visit, or a letter or telephone contact as well as a home visit. Delaying letters do not constitute a response; the first contact must be action-oriented which may include despatching an OT self assessment form.

PIAF category: PPI
Key Area(s): Assessment and care management
Service Objective(s): Timely
Indicator status: Non-core, annual
Benchmark: Care at home
Level of aggregation: Authority, district, team

Notes: This indicator is a requirement of the Community Care Charter. It is possible to produce it based on sample weeks and sample sites.
Comparable national statistics:
CCC – a Community Care Charter requirement

PP2   Distribution of referrals for assessment within priorities

Definition: The proportion of cases allocated to each priority category after screened in for assessment.

PIAF category: PPI
Key Area(s): Assessment and care management
Service Objective(s): Targeted
Indicator status: Core, monthly
Benchmark: Authority average
Level of aggregation: Authority, district, team
Comparable national statistics: none

PP3   % of actions taken after screening

Definition: The proportion of cases who receive a SSD assessment after screening.

PIAF category: PPI
Key Area(s): Assessment and care management
Service Objective(s): Targeted
Indicator status: Non-core, quarterly
Benchmark: Authority average

Level of aggregation: Authority, district, team
Comparable national statistics: none

PP4   No. of ongoing cases per 1000 pop aged 75 and over, by the proportion who are active to social workers or on team caseloads

Definition: Proportion of aged population becoming ongoing cases broken down into those allocated to individual social workers, and those on team caseloads.

PIAF category: PPI
Key Area(s): Assessment and care management
Service Objective(s): Efficient
Indicator status: Non-core, quarterly
Benchmark: Authority average
Level of aggregation: Authority, district, team
Comparable national statistics: none

PP5   No. of ongoing cases per 1000 relevant age group in different age bands – 65 to 74; 75 to 84, 85 and over – by the proportion who are active to social workers or on team caseloads

Definition: Proportion of aged population becoming ongoing cases with care plans, broken down into those allocated to individual social workers, and those on team caseloads.

PIAF category: PPI
Key Area(s): Assessment and care management
Service Objective(s): Targeted, Efficient
Indicator status: Non-core, quarterly
Benchmark: Authority average
Level of aggregation: Authority, district, team
Comparable national statistics: none

PP6   No. of ongoing cases per 1000 pop aged 75 and over in different user categories – visual impairment, auditory impairment, cognitive impairment, depression, physical impairment

Definition: Proportions of the very elderly population at risk through impairments who become ongoing cases with care plans.

PIAF category: PPI
Key Area(s): Assessment and care management
Service Objective(s): Targeted, Efficient
Indicator status: Core, quarterly
Benchmark: Authority average
Level of aggregation: Authority, district, team

Notes: This information will need to be recorded on care plans in a systematic
    fashion.
Comparable national statistics: none

**PP7   No. of ongoing cases of people living alone per 1000 population aged
75 and over**

Definition: The proportion of cases accepted as ongoing which comprise one person
    elderly households.

PIAF category: PPI
Key Area(s): Breakdown
Service Objective(s): Targeted
Indicator status: Non-core, quarterly
Benchmark: Authority average
Level of aggregation: Authority, district, team
Comparable national statistics: none

**PP8   No. of ongoing cases per 1000 population aged 75 and over with carers
and the status of the carer**

Definition: The proportion of cases accepted as ongoing which have (or do not have)
    identified informal carers; and of these cases, the number where carers are
    under considerable pressure and likely to withdraw or reduce their effort.

PIAF category: PPI
Key Area(s): Breakdown
Service Objective(s): Targeted
Indicator status: Special study – six monthly
Benchmark: Authority average; within district differences
Level of aggregation: Authority, district, team
Comparable national statistics: none

**PP9   No. of ongoing cases per 1000 population aged 65 and over in different
ethnic groups**

Definition: Proportion of the pensionable population in broad ethnic groups who are
    accepted as ongoing cases by social services following assessment. The ethnic
    groups can be based on the OPCS Census of 1991: White, African, Caribbean
    (including Black British), South Asian, Other Asian, Mid and East European
    descent and from other minority ethnic groups.

PIAF category: PPI
Key Area(s): Assessment and care management
Service Objective(s): Targeted
Indicator status: Non-core, six monthly
Benchmark: Authority average; proportion on caseloads compared with relevant
    population

Level of aggregation: Authority, district, team

Notes: This indicator should be considered alongside that for screenings, and data on local prevalence of ethnic groupings.
Comparable national statistics:
DH-PAF: E48 asks for the proportion of users in different ethnic groups who are receiving services following an assessment, to be developed as part of the RAP return

PP10   % of screenings from primary and secondary health care sources where special form used

Definition: The proportion of referrals for screening from these health sources where the special referral form was used to secure access to care.

PIAF category: PPI
Key Area(s): Assessment and care management
Service Objective(s): Background
Indicator status: Special study – annual
Benchmark: Authority average
Level of aggregation: health care sources

Notes: Primary health care teams should monitor the receipt of feedback information from social services following referral action.
Comparable national statistics: none

b) Assessment

PP11   The number of assessments per thousand population aged 75 and over

Definition: The total number of assessments, both full and standard, undertaken for the 75 and over age group.

PIAF category: PPI
Key Area(s): Assessment and care management
Service Objective(s): Targeted, Efficient
Indicator status: Core, monthly
Benchmark: Authority average
Level of aggregation: Authority, district, team
Comparable national statistics:
AC-CCI – the Audit Commission ask local authorities for the numbers of adults referred for assessment
ADSS – at a regional level the ADSS collects information from local authorities on referrals and assessments
DH-PAF: E49 requests number of assessments per head of population aged 65 and over, to be developed from the RAP return

PP12   % of assessments which are full

Definition: The proportion of assessments undertaken which are full assessments.

PIAF category: PPI
Key Area(s): Assessment and care management
Service Objective(s): Targeted, Efficient
Indicator status: Core, monthly
Benchmark: Authority average
Level of aggregation: Authority, district, team

Notes: There is an urgent need to establish adequate, reliable definitions of assessment types.
Comparable national statistics: none

PP13   % of assessments in priority for service bands and dependency

Definition: The distribution of assessment types across different types of priority level and degree of dependency covering all cases, both community and residential.

PIAF category: PPI
Key Area(s): Assessment and care management, Breakdown
Service Objective(s): Targeted, Efficient
Indicator status: Core, quarterly
Benchmark: Authority average
Level of aggregation: Authority, district, team

Notes: The categorisation of dependency should be established in a simple fashion. The Isaac and Neville categorisation of potential need is recommended.
Comparable national statistics: none

PP14   Proportion of carer assessments undertaken

Definition: Where carers are present, the percentage of cases where carer's needs are assessed using a separate form, and the percentage where standard form used.

PIAF category: PPI
Key Area(s): Assessment and care management, Breakdown
Service Objective(s): Targeted
Indicator status: Non-core, quarterly
Benchmark: Authority average
Level of aggregation: Authority, district, team
Comparable national statistics:
DH-PAF: D42 requests the numbers of carers receiving a separate assessment as a proportion of total numbers of assessments

PP15 Time between first response and the start of assessment by priority and by setting

Definition: The interval (in working days) between the first action-oriented contact by SSD professional and the start of the assessment for people with different levels of priority and in different settings.

PIAF category: PPI
Key Area(s): Assessment and care management
Service Objective(s): Timely
Indicator status: Non-core, annual
Benchmark: Authority average
Level of aggregation: Authority, district, team

Notes: This first contact can be arrangement of a visit, or a letter or telephone contact as well as a home visit. Delaying letters do not constitute a response; the first contact must be action-oriented which may include despatching an OT self assessment form. This indicator is a requirement of the Community Care Charter. It is possible to produce it based on sample weeks and sample sites.
Comparable national statistics:
CCC – a Community Care Charter requirement

PP16 Time for the completion of assessment by assessment type

Definition: The time between the completion of assessment and implementation of care plans. Assessments are defined as completed when workers record this to be the case, and they are authorised.

PIAF category: PPI
Key Area(s): Assessment and care management
Service Objective(s): Timely
Indicator status: Non-core, annual
Benchmark: Authority average
Level of aggregation: Authority, district, team

Notes: It may be helpful to define this as the initial assessment, since in practice early care plans are likely to contribute to reassessment particularly in complex cases. However some defined end to assessment in its first stage is helpful despite the reality of continued reassessment. This indicator is a requirement of the Community Care Charter. It is possible to produce it based on sample weeks and sample sites.
Comparable national statistics:
CCC – a Community Care Charter requirement

PP17   % of cases living at home where community care assessments were jointly carried out by NHS staff and SSD staff by location and user category

Definition: The proportion of cases where assessment was multidisciplinary carried out in different settings such as hospital services, and category of user – for example, cognitive impairment, physical illnesses. This definition excludes separate sequential assessments; it also excludes the simple provision of information by NHS staff for an assessment.

PIAF category: PPI
Key Area(s): Assessment and care management, Networks of support
Service Objective(s): Diversion
Indicator status: Special study – annual
Benchmark: Authority average
Level of aggregation: Authority, district, team
Comparable national statistics:
AC-CCI: the Audit Commission asks for the number of assessments involving services by more than one agency. This can be taken as a proxy for joint assessments

PP18   % of cases assessed where special mental health assessment undertaken

Definition: Self explanatory.

PIAF category: PPI
Key Area(s): Assessment and care management, Networks of support
Service Objective(s): Efficient
Indicator status: Non-core, annual
Benchmark: Authority average
Level of aggregation: Authority, district, team
Comparable national statistics: none

c) Care Planning and Arranging Services

PP19   Time between the completion of assessment and the start of services by priority service band

Definition: The interval (in working days) between the completion of the initial assessment phase, as defined above, and the beginning of service provision; where care plans are commenced before the completion before assessment, this should be noted in the system.

PIAF category: PPI
Key Area(s): Assessment and care management
Service Objective(s): Timely
Indicator status: Non-core, annual

Benchmark: Authority average
Level of aggregation: Authority, district, team

Notes: This indicator is a requirement of the Community Care Charter. It is possible
  to produce it based on sample weeks and sample sites.
Comparable national statistics:
CCC – a Community Care Charter requirement
DH-PAF: D43 requests waiting time for care packages to be developed under the
  RAP return

PP20 Distribution of Care Plan Aims

Definition: The proportion of care plans distributed across different aims relating to
  restoring stability/alleviating crisis; reducing social isolation; maintain in own
  home; achieve independence and so on.

PIAF category: PPI
Key Area(s): Assessment and care management, Breakdown, Respite, Alternative
  accommodation, Care at home, Networks of support
Service Objective(s): Diversion, Efficient, Individual, Choice
Indicator status: Core, quarterly
Benchmark: Authority average
Level of aggregation: Authority, district, team, worker
Comparable national statistics: none

PP21 Distribution of Care Plan Objectives

Definition: The proportion of care plans distributed across different objectives
  relating to improving / maintaining user's functioning, skills, relationships,
  securing appropriate placement and so on.

PIAF category: PPI
Key Area(s): Assessment and care management, Breakdown, Respite, Alternative
  accommodation, Care at home, Networks of support
Service Objective(s): Diversion, Efficient, Individual, Choice
Indicator status: Non-core, six monthly
Benchmark: Authority average
Level of aggregation: Authority, district, team, worker
Comparable national statistics: none

PP22 Number of home care hours arranged by SSD per case by dependency

Definition: The average number of hours received per case to whom home care was
  provided within dependency bands.

PIAF category: PPI
Key Area(s): Care at home
Service Objective(s): Targeted

Indicator status: Core, quarterly
Benchmark: Authority average, Equivalent shire authorities
Level of aggregation: Authority, district, home care management unit

Notes: This is an important targeting indicator – referred to as 'cover'. Dependency
    categories need to be devised to facilitate use of this indicator.
Comparable national statistics:
CIPFA-E: Col 84 but CIPFA indicators are not by dependency
CIPFA-A: Col 90 but CIPFA indicators are not by dependency
DH-KI: AA68 but not by dependency and this KI is about contact hours
DH-CCS: this source gives information that approximates to indicator PP22. Table
    1.1 shows both the number of contact hours and households being helped, so
    hours per household can be readily calculated. Table 1.3 shows the percentage
    of households receiving home care by sector of provider and various contact
    hour bands. Table 1.5 shows the percentage of households receiving home care
    services by number of visits and various contact hour bands. However, these
    data relate to all user groups including older people.

PP23 Proportion of people admitted to homes in emergency situations and which were not reviewed within 72 hours

Definition: The number of admissions to care homes undertaken in an emergency
    where standard practice was bypassed, as a proportion of the total.

PIAF category: PPI
Key Area(s): Breakdown
Service Objective(s): Diversion, Efficient
Indicator status: Non-core, quarterly
Benchmark: Authority average
Level of aggregation: Authority, district
Comparable national statistics: none

PP24 Percentage of patients discharged from hospital where social care services not provided at home when required according to discharge plan; and reasons

Definition: The percentage of patients discharged home without social care services.
    The reasons will include: premature discharge, lack of warning for carers, late
    response by SSD, and so on.

PIAF category: PPI
Key Area(s): Breakdown, Care at home
Service Objective(s): Diversion, Efficient
Indicator status: Special study – annual
Benchmark: Authority average
Level of aggregation: Authority, district, team
Comparable national statistics: none

PP25 Percentage of patients discharged from hospital, subsequently referred to SSD within two weeks for health related reasons

Definition: self explanatory.

PIAF category: PPI
Key Area(s): Breakdown, Networks of support
Service Objective(s): Efficient
Indicator status: Special study – annual
Benchmark: Authority average
Level of aggregation: Authority, district, hospital
Comparable national statistics: none

PP26 Proportion of service users and/or carers who do not take up a service and reasons by user type

Definition: The proportion of users and / or carers who are seen for assessment but who either refuse all or part of a care plan or do not take up services after they have been agreed, and the reasons why. Reasons for refusal or non take-up can include reaction to charges, inappropriateness of services, user / carer differences over the need for help, lack of service flexibility, and so on.

PIAF category: PPI
Key Area(s): Breakdown
Service Objective(s): Involved, Choice
Indicator status: Special study – annual
Benchmark: Authority average
Level of aggregation: Authority, district, team

Notes: This indicator links to previous indicators on service gaps.
Comparable national statistics: none, although DH-PAF – E50 requests the percentage of assessments which lead to service being provided. PP26 can be deduced from this

PP27 Proportion of people receiving various domiciliary services by dependency

Definition: The distribution of dependency categories within major domiciliary care services – home care, meals, sitting services, day care.

PIAF category: PPI
Key Area(s): Care at home, Networks of support
Service Objective(s): Targeted, Individual
Indicator status: Non-core, six monthly
Benchmark: Authority average
Level of aggregation: Authority, district, unit of provision
Comparable national statistics: none by dependency, but DH-CCS is a good source of information about home care, meals and day care provision

PP28 Proportion of people in each dependency category receiving various domiciliary services

Definition: The distribution of services – home care, meals, sitting services, day care – within each dependency category.

PIAF category: PPI
Key Area(s): Care at home, Networks of support
Service Objective(s): Targeted, Individual
Indicator status: Non-core, six monthly
Benchmark: Authority average
Level of aggregation: Authority, district, unit of provision

Notes: This is another way of looking at the information used to generate the previous indicator. This indicator looks at the distribution of service types in each dependency band. The one above looks the distribution of dependency in each service.
Comparable national statistics: none by dependency, but DH-CCS is a good source of information about home care, meals and day care provision

PP29 The number of all users receiving packages of domiciliary services, with a breakdown between new and existing users

Definition: The number of older users receiving different numbers of services – one service, two to five services, six to 10 services, 11 or more services, with a separate breakdown showing the data for new users in the six months and existing users at the start of the six months.

PIAF category: PPI
Key Area(s): Care at home, Networks of support
Service Objective(s): Targeted, Choice, Individual
Indicator status: Non-core, six monthly
Benchmark: Authority average
Level of aggregation: Authority, district, team
Comparable national statistics: none

PP30 The number of older people receiving services from different types of provider with a breakdown between new and existing users

Definition: The number of people receiving services from different types of provider – one source, two sources, three sources, four or more sources, with a separate breakdown showing the data for new users in the six months and existing users at the start of the six months.

PIAF category: PPI
Key Area(s): Care at home, Networks of support
Service Objective(s): Targeted, Choice, Individual
Indicator status: Non-core, six monthly

Benchmark: Authority average
Level of aggregation: Authority, district, team

Notes: This is another way of looking at the information used to generate the
    previous indicator.
Comparable national statistics: none, although DH-CCS shows the provision of
    home care, meals and day care by sector of provider in relation to both the
    population and users. This information, however, does not usually differentiate
    between user groups

PP31   The number of older people on supervision register per 1000
population aged 75 and over

Definition: The number of older people on the supervision register because of actual
    or suspected abuse or neglect, in relation to the elderly population.

PIAF category: PPI
Key Area(s): Breakdown, Care at home, Networks of support, Respite
Service Objective(s): Targeted
Indicator status: Non-core, six monthly
Benchmark: Authority average
Level of aggregation: Authority, district, team
Comparable national statistics: none

d) On-going contact, monitoring and review

PP32   Proportion of overdue reviews for people receiving home-based care

Definition: Proportion of cases at home whose prescribed review has not been
    undertaken in the time period set for review. Time periods are: up to three
    months overdue, three to six months overdue, and more than six months
    overdue.

PIAF category: PPI
Key Area(s): Assessment and care management
Service Objective(s): Timely, Efficient
Indicator status: Non-core, quarterly
Benchmark: Authority average
Level of aggregation: Authority, district, team
Comparable national statistics: none, although DH-PAF – C40 requests the numbers
    of clients receiving a review as a percentage of adult clients receiving a service

PP33 Proportion of older users on team caseloads who are referred for re-assessment prior to their review, with reasons for referral

Definition: Proportion of cases on team caseloads who are referred from any source prior to the formal review date, and reasons for this including health related circumstances.

PIAF category: PPI
Key Area(s): Assessment and care management, Breakdown, Care at home
Service Objective(s): Efficient
Indicator status: Special study – annual
Benchmark: Authority average
Level of aggregation: Authority, district, team
Comparable national statistics: none

PP34 Proportion of reviews overdue for people in residential care and nursing homes

Definition: Proportion of older users supported by the SSD in residential care or nursing homes whose prescribed review has not been undertaken in the time period set for review. Time periods are: up to three months overdue, three to six months overdue, and more than six months overdue.

PIAF category: PPI
Key Area(s): Assessment and care management
Service Objective(s): Timely
Indicator status: Non-core, quarterly
Benchmark: Authority average
Level of aggregation: Authority, district, team
Comparable national statistics: none

PP35 Specific user-related time as a percentage of all time spent by social workers / community care workers

Definition: The proportion of practitioner time spent in specific user-related contacts as a proportion of total time. These contacts include contacts with carers, colleagues and other agencies.

PIAF category: PPI
Key Area(s): Assessment and care management
Service Objective(s): Efficient
Indicator status: Special study – annual
Benchmark: Authority average
Level of aggregation: Authority, district, team, worker

Notes: Work for this indicator can be based on work by NISW in this field, and can be possibly expanded to include other activities.
Comparable national statistics: none

e) Case Closure

PP36 Turnover – proportions of current cases opened and closed during each quarter and switches between caseload type

Definition: The proportion of cases – both active and team – which were open at the start of the quarter and were subsequently closed during the quarter or went from active caseloads to team caseloads, or vice versa. The proportion of cases – both active and team – open at the end of the quarter which were opened during the quarter, or which went from active caseloads to team caseloads or vice versa.

PIAF category: PPI
Key Area(s): Assessment and care management
Service Objective(s): Efficient
Indicator status: Non-core, quarterly
Benchmark: Authority average
Level of aggregation: Authority, district, team, worker

Notes: This complicated indicator needs to reflect how cases are being handled. It should be developed to show the traffic between active and team caseloads, and the link between closure and re-referral for screening.
Comparable national statistics: none

PP37 Duration of care at home by cost and dependency

Definition: For cases closed during the year, the length of time they were open, and the average cost of SSD care (with sub analyses of dependency).

PIAF category: PPI
Key Area(s): Assessment and care management, Care at home, Breakdown, Finance
Service Objective(s): Targeted, Diversion, Efficient
Indicator status: Special study – annual
Benchmark: Authority average
Level of aggregation: Authority, district, team
Comparable national statistics: none

PP38 Duration of care in care homes by cost and dependency

Definition: For older users dying in or discharged from residential care homes or nursing homes, during the year, the length of time they were in the home, and the average cost of care (with sub analyses of dependency).

PIAF category: PPI
Key Area(s): Assessment and care management, Breakdown, Finance
Service Objective(s): Targeted, Diversion, Efficient
Indicator status: Special study – annual

Benchmark: Authority average
Level of aggregation: Authority, district, team
Comparable national statistics: none

Service process indicators

SP1   No. of older users of home care per 1000 pop aged 75 and over

Definition: Number of older home care users in relation to the elderly population.

PIAF category: SPI
Key Area(s): Care at home
Service Objective(s): Targeted, Diversion
Indicator status: Non-core, quarterly
Benchmark: Authority average
Level of aggregation: Authority, district
Comparable national statistics:
DH-KI/DH-KIGS: AA67 (KI) OA62 (KIGS) but these are about households not
    individual users receiving home care
DH-CCS: Table 1.2 shows the number of households receiving home care per
    10,000 households for users aged 65 and over
AC-CCI: the Audit Commission asks for the percentage of older people receiving
    home help aged 65-74, and 75 & over
DH-PAF: C32 requests the number of those aged 65 and over who are helped to live
    at home, including those receiving day care in residential homes) per population
    of those aged 65 and over

SP2   No. of older users of taking up and no longer needing the home care
    service per 1000 pop aged 75 and over

Definition: Number of older home care users in the quarter who are newly taking up
    the service, and the numbers who are 'leaving' or no longer requiring or needing
    the service' in relation to the elderly population.

PIAF category: SPI
Key Area(s): Care at home, Breakdown
Service Objective(s): Targeted, Diversion, Individual, Choice
Indicator status: Non-core, quarterly
Benchmark: Authority average
Level of aggregation: Authority, district

Notes: This indicator may need to be developed to include reasons why services are
    both being taken up and no longer required. The denominator may need to be
    changed if numbers are too small; an alternative could be the total number of
    home care cases at the end of the quarter.
Comparable national statistics: none

SP3   No. of older users of delivered meals per 1000 pop aged 75 and over

Definition: Number of older users of delivered meals – hot or chilled – in relation to the elderly population.

PIAF category: SPI
Key Area(s): Care at home
Service Objective(s): Targeted
Indicator status: Non-core, quarterly
Benchmark: Authority average
Level of aggregation: Authority, district
Comparable national statistics:
DH-CCS: Table 2.4 shows the number of people of all ages who receive delivered meals per 10,000 population. Table 2.5 shows the proportion of people who receive meals at home who are aged 65 and over, 65-74, 75-84, and 85 and over.

SP4   No. of older users of day care per 1000 pop aged 65 and over

Definition: Number of users of day care in relation to the elderly population.

PIAF category: SPI
Key Area(s): Respite
Service Objective(s): Targeted, Diversion
Indicator status: Non-core, quarterly
Benchmark: Authority average
Level of aggregation: Authority, district
Comparable national statistics:
DH-CCS: Table 3.3

SP5   No. of older users with equipment or adaptations per 1000 pop aged 75 and over

Definition: Number of older user with equipment / adaptations supplied by the SSD in relation to the elderly population.

PIAF category: SPI
Key Area(s): Care at home
Service Objective(s): Targeted
Indicator status: Non-core, quarterly
Benchmark: Authority average
Level of aggregation: Authority, district
Comparable national statistics: none, although DH-PAF – C38 requests percentage of items of equipment costing less than £1000 delivered within three weeks as a quality standard

SP6 **No. of teleshopping accounts used per 1000 population aged 65 and over**

Definition: The number of active teleshopping accounts used on a quarterly basis by elderly service users in relation to the elderly population.

PIAF category: SPI
Key Area(s): Care at home
Service Objective(s): Targeted
Indicator status: Non-core, six monthly
Benchmark: Authority average
Level of aggregation: Authority, district
Comparable national statistics: none

SP7 **No. of elderly people using the central alarm system per 1000 population aged 75 and over, by type of accommodation**

Definition: The number of elderly users who are linked to the central alarm system in relation to the elderly population, by sheltered and ordinary accommodation.

PIAF category: SPI
Key Area(s): Breakdown, Care at home
Service Objective(s): Targeted
Indicator status: Non-core, six monthly
Benchmark: Authority average
Level of aggregation: Authority, district
Comparable national statistics: none

SP8 **Specific user-related activity time as a percentage of all time spent by home care staff, by type of provider**

Definition: The proportion of home care staff time spent in charged for specific user-related contacts as a proportion of total time. These contacts include contacts with carers, colleagues and other agencies. The specific user-related time is broken down into direct contact time, other user-related activities, travel time, and residual time. The indicator is also broken down by type of provider: SSD, private sector and not-for-profit sector.

PIAF category: SPI
Key Area(s): Care at home
Service Objective(s): Efficient
Indicator status: Special study – annual
Benchmark: Authority average
Level of aggregation: Authority, district, home care unit of management
Comparable national statistics: none

SP9 Total average weekly costs to the SSD of care packages in the community in cost bands by dependency

Definition: The average weekly cost to the SSD per case of the care provided in community support, for different dependency groups.

PIAF category: SPI
Key Area(s): Care at home, Finance
Service Objective(s): Targeted, Efficient
Indicator status: Core, monthly
Benchmark: Authority average
Level of aggregation: Authority, district, team, worker

Notes: Ideally such an indicator should include all services that are cost to the public purse; however, it is acceptable only for services both directly provided or paid for by the SSD to be included at this stage. The costing of SSD services may have to be based on formal budget heads, as defined by the RO3 and CIPFA returns, and hence may not show the real and full cost.
Comparable national statistics: none

SP10 Proportion of older users cared for at home whose gross weekly cost to the SSD is greater than a series of cost thresholds of residential care for older people, in dependency bands

Definition: The number of older users at home whose total care package costs to the SSD are more than specified percentages of the cost of residential care for users in similar dependency. The percentages are: less than 75% of the cost of residential care, 76 to 100%, 101% to 125%, 126% to 150%, and 151% and over.

PIAF category: SPI
Key Area(s): Breakdown, Care at home, Finance
Service Objective(s): Diversion, Efficient
Indicator status: Core, monthly
Benchmark: 75% and over, with exception reports for individual cases where costs are equivalent for similar dependency.
Level of aggregation: Authority, district, team, worker

Notes: Ideally such an indicator should include all services that are costs to the public purse; however, it is acceptable only for services both directly provided or paid for by the SSD to be included at this stage. The costing of SSD services may have to be based on formal budget heads, as defined by the RO3 and CIPFA returns, and hence may not show the real and full cost.
Comparable national statistics: none

SP11   Units of different care services provided as a proportion of units purchased by service

Definition: The proportion of units of different care services actually provided to older people as a proportion of the units purchased. The different care service units are: home care hours, day care places, hot meals delivered, teleshop contracts, transport user journeys, and laundry user washes.

PIAF category: SPI
Key Area(s): Care at home, Finance
Service Objective(s): Efficient
Indicator status: Non-core, quarterly
Benchmark: Authority average
Level of aggregation: Authority, district, units of provision

Notes: For each service, multiplication of the indicator by 100 provides a percentage efficiency factor.
Comparable national statistics: none

SP12   Proportion of older users in different types of short-term care, and reasons

Definition: The number of older users in each type of short-term care including NHS facilities, respite care and family placements; and the main reason for the episode: emergency, assessment, treatment, rehabilitation, trial period, and respite.

PIAF category: SPI
Key Area(s): Respite
Service Objective(s): Individual, Choice
Indicator status: Non-core, six monthly
Benchmark: Authority average
Level of aggregation: Authority, district, team
Comparable national statistics: none, although the Audit Commission asks each local authority to specify how many nights of respite are they provide or fund

SP13   Of all people in nursing and residential care homes financially supported by the SSD, the proportion who are there for long-stay, respite, assessment, emergencies by type of provider

Definition: Utilisation patterns of funded care home placements within each type of provider.

PIAF category: SPI
Key Area(s): Alternative accommodation
Service Objective(s): Diversion, Efficient, Individual, Choice
Indicator status: Core, six-monthly
Benchmark: Authority average, Equivalent shire authorities

Level of aggregation: Authority, district, type of provider, home
Comparable national statistics: none

SP14 No. of older users reporting complaints

Definition: A count of the number of complaints broken down into types of complaint.

PIAF category: SPI
Key Area(s): Alternative accommodation, Care at home
Service Objective(s): Involved
Indicator status: Non-core, quarterly
Benchmark: Authority average
Level of aggregation: Authority, district, team

Notes: Need to categorise complaints into main types.
Comparable national statistics: none, although the Audit Commission ask the
    handling of complaints made to local authorities as part of the Citizen's Charter
    information they collect

SP15 Number of staff reporting problematic incidents with users and carers

Definition: A count of the number of staff members who report incidents with users
    and carers which cause the staff member distress, including violence and abuse,
    and racist and sexist insults.

PIAF category: SPI
Key Area(s): Alternative accommodation, Care at home
Service Objective(s): Background
Indicator status: Non-core, quarterly
Benchmark: Authority average
Level of aggregation: Authority, district, team

Notes: Some of the incidents may not be reported directly by staff. but might emerge
    from investigations of users' complaints about staff and services.
Comparable national statistics: none

SP16 Home Care Staff per Home Care Manager

Definition: The number of home care staff per community care team leaders and
    senior home care staff. Both staff groups are based on whole time equivalents.

PIAF category: SPI
Key Area(s): Care at home
Service Objective(s): Efficient
Indicator status: Non-core, annual
Benchmark: Authority average, English shire authorities
Level of aggregation: Authority, district, home care unit of management
Comparable national statistics:

DH-KI: B13

SP17   Users per home care staff member

Definition: The number of current users per whole time equivalent home care staff member.

PIAF category: SPI
Key Area(s): Care at home
Service Objective(s): Efficient
Indicator status: Non-core, quarterly
Benchmark: Authority average
Level of aggregation: Authority, district, home care unit of management
Comparable national statistics: none

SP18   Day care users per care staff in day centres

Definition: The number of users of day care per care staff – but excluding manager, domestic and maintenance staff – in day care centres, based upon weekly attendances and whole time equivalents.

PIAF category: SPI
Key Area(s): Respite
Service Objective(s): Efficient
Indicator status: Non-core, annual
Benchmark: Authority average
Level of aggregation: Authority, district, centre
Comparable national statistics: none

SP19   Residents per member of care staff in local authority homes

Definition: The number of residents divided by the number of whole time equivalent staff actually filling care staff posts in each home.

PIAF category: SPI
Key Area(s): Alternative accommodation
Service Objective(s): Efficient
Indicator status: Non-core, annual
Benchmark: Authority average
Level of aggregation: Authority, district, home
Comparable national statistics: none

SP20 Care staff per managers in local authority homes

Definition: The number of care staff – but excluding domestic and maintenance staff – per manager and deputy manager in each home, expressed as whole time equivalents.

PIAF category: SPI
Key Area(s): Alternative accommodation
Service Objective(s): Efficient
Indicator status: Non-core, annual
Benchmark: Authority average, English shire authorities
Level of aggregation: Authority, district, home
Comparable national statistics:
DH-KI: B14

SP21 Cases per field work staff member, by dependency

Definition: The average number of current cases per social worker and per community care worker, by dependency.

PIAF category: SPI
Key Area(s): Assessment and care management
Service Objective(s): Targeted, Efficient
Indicator status: Non-core, quarterly
Benchmark: Authority average
Level of aggregation: Authority, district, team
Comparable national statistics: none

SP22 Occupancy of local authority residential care facilities

Definition: The weekly occupancy rate in local authority residential care facilities.

PIAF category: SPI
Key Area(s): Alternative accommodation
Service Objective(s): Efficient
Indicator status: Core, quarterly
Benchmark: Authority average, Equivalent shire authorities
Level of aggregation: Authority, district, home
Comparable national statistics:
CIPFA-E: Col 71
CIPFA-A: Col 67
DH-KI: OA04

SP23   Occupancy of local authority day care facilities

Definition: The occupancy rate of day care facilities provided by the local authority.

PIAF category: SPI
Key Area(s): Respite
Service Objective(s): Efficient
Indicator status: Core, quarterly
Benchmark: Authority average, Equivalent shire authorities
Level of aggregation: Authority, district, centre

Notes: For the definition of occupancy use the CIPFA formula.
Comparable national statistics:
CIPFA-E: Col 78
CIPFA-A: Col 75

SP24   Staff leaving rate by staff group type

Definition: The proportion of staff leaving, compared with staff in situ, over a year
    broken down into quarters for each staff group type.

PIAF category: SPI
Key Area(s): Context
Service Objective(s): Efficient
Indicator status: Non-core, annual:
Benchmark: Authority average
Level of aggregation: Authority, district, team, facility:
Comparable national statistics: none:

SP25   Staff vacancy rates by staff group type and location:

Definition: The proportion of posts vacant at the of each three month period for each
    staff group type, and by team / facility.

PIAF category: SPI
Key Area(s): Context
Service Objective(s): Efficient
Indicator status: Core, quarterly:
Benchmark: Authority average, ADSS / LGTB annual data
Level of aggregation: Authority, district, team, facility:
Comparable national statistics: none:

SP26 Staff sickness rates by staff group type: proportion of working time lost through sickness, compared with total hours that staff in post are contracted to work.

Definition: The proportion of working time lost through sickness compared with total hours that staff in post are contracted to work.

PIAF category: SPI
Key Area(s): Context
Service Objective(s): Efficient
Indicator status. Non-core, quarterly
Benchmark: Authority average
Level of aggregation: Authority, district, team, facility
Comparable national statistics: none

Outcome indicators

O1 No. of users in long-term residential care for older people per 1000 pop aged 75 and over

Definition: The number of older users in residential care homes, financially supported by the SSD, in relation to the elderly population.

PIAF category: OI
Key Area(s): Alternative accommodation, Breakdown
Service Objective(s): Diversion
Indicator status: Core, quarterly
Benchmark: Authority average
Level of aggregation: Authority, district
Comparable national statistics
DH-KI/DH-KIGS: OA35 and OA37 to OA40 cover supported older users in residential care in relation to the elderly population. There is, however, no direct equivalent of O1.
AC-CCI: the Audit Commission asks for the percentage of older people supported by the authority in residential care aged 65-74, and 75 & over
DH-PAF: C26 requests the number of admissions of those aged 65 and over to supported residential and nursing care

O2 No. of users entering and leaving long-term residential care for older people per 1000 pop aged 75 and over

Definition: The number of older users, financially supported by the SSD, being admitted to residential care homes, in the quarter in relation to the elderly population; and the number of older residents who for one reason or another leave or are discharged during the quarter in relation to the elderly population.

PIAF category: OI
Key Area(s): Alternative accommodation, Breakdown
Service Objective(s): Efficient, Diversion, Choice
Indicator status: Core, quarterly
Benchmark: Authority average
Level of aggregation: Authority, district

Notes: This is an important outcome and turnover indicator.
Comparable national statistics: none

O3   No. of users in long-term nursing home placements for older people per 1000 pop aged 75 and over

Definition: The number of users in nursing homes, financially supported by the SSD, in relation to the elderly population.

PIAF category: OI
Key Area(s): Alternative accommodation, Breakdown
Service Objective(s): Diversion
Indicator status: Core, quarterly
Benchmark: Authority average
Level of aggregation: Authority, district
Comparable national statistics: Although not exactly comparable, DH-KIGS OA21 details no. of residents receiving nursing care in either residential or nursing homes per 1000 pop aged 75 and over

O4   No. of users entering and leaving long-term nursing homes for older people per 1000 pop aged 75 and over

Definition: The number of older users, financially supported by the SSD, being admitted to nursing homes, in the quarter in relation to the elderly population; and the number of older residents who for one reason or another leave or are discharged during the quarter in relation to the elderly population.

PIAF category: OI
Key Area(s): Alternative accommodation, Breakdown
Service Objective(s): Efficient, Diversion, Choice
Indicator status: Core, quarterly
Benchmark: Authority average
Level of aggregation: Authority, district

Notes: This is an important outcome and turnover indicator.
Comparable national statistics: none

O5 Reasons for admission to long-term nursing home and residential care home placements

Definition: During the quarter, the proportion of users financially supported by the SSD based on the main reason for admission: namely, 'client' choice, physical ill-health, loneliness, absence of appropriate community services, care package in excess of agreed financial limit, loss of main carer, unacceptable risk.

PIAF category: OI
Key Area(s): Alternative accommodation, Breakdown, Finance
Service Objective(s): Diversion, Efficient, Choice
Indicator status: Core, quarterly
Benchmark: Authority average
Level of aggregation: Authority, district, team
Comparable national statistics: none

O6 Reasons for discharge from long-term nursing home and residential care home placements

Definition: During the quarter, the proportion of users financially supported by the SSD who are discharged from care homes back to the community, or who transfer to another long-term facility, or who die there.

PIAF category: OI
Key Area(s): Alternative accommodation, Breakdown, Finance
Service Objective(s): Diversion, Efficient, Choice
Indicator status: Core, quarterly
Benchmark: Authority average
Level of aggregation: Authority, district, team

Notes: It will be important for this indicator to pick up movement between types of residential, nursing home and continuing care facility.
Comparable national statistics: none

O7 Proportion of new long-term placements by dependency bands

Definition: The distribution of new placements, made by the SSD each month, in residential care homes by type of provider and in nursing homes, by dependency bands.

PIAF category: OI
Key Area(s): Alternative accommodation, Breakdown
Service Objective(s): Targeted, Diversion
Indicator status: Core, monthly
Benchmark: Authority average
Level of aggregation: Authority, district, team

Notes: This measures the incidence of placements.
Comparable national statistics: none

O8   Proportion of current long-term placements by dependency bands

Definition: The distribution of current placements supported by the SSD – at the end
  of each month – in residential care homes by type of provider and in nursing
  homes by dependency bands.

PIAF category: OI
Key Area(s): Alternative accommodation, Breakdown
Service Objective(s): Targeted, Diversion
Indicator status: Core, monthly
Benchmark: Authority average
Level of aggregation: Authority, district, team

Notes: This measures the prevalence of placements.
Comparable national statistics: none

O9   The proportion of older residents in long-term nursing home and residential care placements who possess potential cost-raising attributes

Definition: The proportion of older people financially supported by the in residential
  care homes, by type of provider, and in nursing homes with identified attributes
  that significantly raise costs: cognitive impairment, incontinence, terminal illness.

PIAF category: SPI
Key Area(s): Alternative accommodation, Finance
Service Objective(s): Targeted
Indicator status: Core, quarterly
Benchmark: Authority average
Level of aggregation: Authority, district, each home

Notes: This indicator is a measure of case mix. It can also highlight specific
  attributes which may require intervention or identify insufficient community
  services.
Comparable national statistics: none

O10   Proportion of screenings in the high dependency band supported at home after different time periods

Definition: The proportion of those screenings categorised at assessment as high
  dependency, who remain in their own homes after defined periods: three months,
  six months, twelve months.

PIAF category: OI
Key Area(s): Breakdown, Care at home

Service Objective(s): Targeted, Diversion
Indicator status: Core, quarterly
Benchmark: Authority average
Level of aggregation: Authority, district, team

Notes: Dependency indicators need to be developed by the SSD.
Comparable national statistics: none

O11　The proportion of older people discharged from hospital and helped by the SSD who are re-admitted within two weeks

Definition: self explanatory.

PIAF category: OI
Key Area(s): Breakdown, Care at home
Service Objective(s): Efficient, Diversion
Indicator status: Non-core, quarterly
Benchmark: Authority average
Level of aggregation: Authority, district, team, and hospital

Notes: This indicator will pick up a number of issues: the effectiveness of planned discharge, the potential contribution social services can make to care at home, and random health events. Only variation between teams and hospitals is relevant. This indicator needs to be linked to indicators related to the Community Care (Delayed Discharges) Act 2003.
Comparable national statistics: none

O12　Proportion of full assessments placed in homes and staying at home

Definition: Proportion of older users each month who receive a full assessment and who are, as a direct result of that assessment, on the one hand placed in residential care homes or nursing homes or on the other hand stay at home.

PIAF category: OI
Key Area(s): Alternative accommodation, Breakdown, Care at home, Assessment and care management
Service Objective(s): Diversion
Indicator status: Core, monthly
Benchmark: Authority average
Level of aggregation: Authority, district, team,
Comparable national statistics: none

O13　Proportion of older people supported in their own homes by dependency

Definition: Of both standard and full assessments in each quarter, the proportion of people supported in their own homes, as a direct result of the assessment in relation to all people undergoing such assessments. The data are broken down into dependency bands.

PIAF category: OI
Key Area(s): Care at home, Assessment and care management, Alternative accommodation
Service Objective(s): Targeted, Diversion
Indicator status: Core, quarterly
Benchmark: Authority average
Level of aggregation: Authority, district, team

Notes: Dependency indicators need to be developed by the SSD.
Comparable national statistics: none

O14   % of screened carers attending carer support groups

Definition: Of all screened carers, the proportion of carers attending carer support groups, as a direct result of an assessment, where attendance is facilitated by the SSD.

PIAF category: OI
Key Area(s): Assessment and care management, Respite
Service Objective(s): Involved
Indicator status: Non-core, six monthly
Benchmark: Authority average
Level of aggregation: Authority, district, team
Comparable national statistics: none

O15   % of screened carers attending training and information sessions

Definition: Of all screened carers, the proportion of carers attending SSD organised training and information sessions to equip them relevant knowledge and skills about physical or emotional aspects of caring.

PIAF category: OI
Key Area(s): Assessment and care management, Respite
Service Objective(s): Involved, Individual
Indicator status: Non-core, six monthly
Benchmark: Authority average
Level of aggregation: Authority, district, team
Comparable national statistics: none

O16   % of older users accessing independent advocacy services

Definition: The percentage of older users during the six months accessing
   independent advocacy services, which are funded by the SSD.

PIAF category: OI
Key Area(s): Care at home
Service Objective(s): Involved
Indicator status: Non-core, six monthly
Benchmark: Authority average
Level of aggregation: Authority, district, team
Comparable national statistics: none

**O17   No. of users and carers participating in the community care planning
   process**

Definition: For each cycle of the community care planning process, the number of
   users and carers taking part, broken down into relevant stages; namely –
   returning questionnaires, attending open consultations, attending planning
   groups, attending open fora.

PIAF category: OI
Key Area(s): Context
Service Objective(s): Involved
Indicator status: Non-core, annual
Benchmark: Authority average
Level of aggregation: Authority, district
Comparable national statistics: none

O18   % of users satisfied with assessment and care management processes

Definition: During the year, the percentage of users who express satisfaction with
   the way social workers and community care workers have assessed their needs
   and planned services for them.

PIAF category: OI
Key Area(s):Assessment and care management
Service Objective(s): Efficient, Involved
Indicator status: Special study – annual, but with a view to routinely asking and
   rooording uoor'o and oarer'o opinions.
Benchmark: Authority average
Level of aggregation: Authority, district, team
Comparable national statistics: none

O19   % of carers satisfied with assessment and care management processes

Definition: During the year, the percentage of carers who express satisfaction with the way social workers and community care workers have assessed their needs and those of the user, and planned services for them.

PIAF category: OI

Key Area(s): Assessment and care management

Service Objective(s): Efficient, Involved

Indicator status: Special study – annual, but with a view to routinely asking and recording user's and carer's opinions.

Benchmark: Authority average

Level of aggregation: Authority, district, team

Comparable national statistics: none

O20   % of users satisfied with services

Definition: During the year, the percentage of users who express satisfaction with the services they receive.

PIAF category: OI

Key Area(s): Alternative accommodation, Care at home, Respite

Service Objective(s): Efficient, Involved

Indicator status: Special study – annual, but with a view to routinely asking and recording user's and carer's opinions.

Benchmark: Authority average

Level of aggregation: Authority, district, team

Notes: Some studies might focus on users of particular services or sub-groups of users with particular problems.

Comparable national statistics: none

O21   For closed cases, reasons for closure

Definition: For cases closed in each quarter, the percentage falling into pre-coded reasons.

PIAF category: OI

Key Area(s): Assessment and care management

Service Objective(s): Diversion, Efficient, Choice

Indicator status: Non-core, six monthly

Benchmark: Authority average

Level of aggregation: Authority, district, team

Comparable national indicators: none

References

Algie, J. (1975) *Social Values, Objectives and Action*, Kogan-Page, London.

Allen, D., Harley, M. and Makinson, G.T. (1987) Performance indicators in the National Health Service, *Social Policy and Administration*, 21, 1, 70–84.

Anthony, R.N. and Herzlinger, R.E. (1980) *Management Control in Non-profit Organizations*, Richard D. Irwin, Inc, Illinois.

Applebaum, R.A. and McGinnis, R. (1992) What price quality? Assuring the quality of case-managed in-home care, *Journal of Case Management*, 1, 1, 9–13.

Applebaum, R.A., Straker, J. and Geron, S.M. (2000) *Assessing Satisfaction in Health and Long-term Care: Practical Approaches to Hearing the Voices of Consumers*, Springer, New York.

Applegate, W.B., Blass, J.P. and Williams, T.F. (1990) Instruments for the functional assessment of older patients, *New England Journal of Medicine*, 322, 1207–1214.

Arvidsson, G. (1986) Performance evaluation, in Kaufman, F.X., Majone, G. and Ostrom, V. (eds) *Guidance, Control and Evaluation in the Public Sector*, De Gruyter, Berlin.

Ashford, J.R., Butts, M.S. and Bailey, T.C. (1981) Is there still a place for independent research into issues of public policy in England and Wales in the 1980's? A case study from the field of health care: modelling hospital costs, *Journal of the Operational Research Society*, 32, 10, 851–864.

Ashley, J.S.A. (1972) Present state of statistics from hospital inpatient data and their uses, *British Journal of Preventive and Social Medicine*, 26, 135–147.

Audit Commission (1983) *Improving Economy, Efficiency and Effectiveness in Local Government in England and Wales: An Audit Commission Handbook*, Audit Commission, London.

Audit Commission (1985) *Managing Social Services for the Elderly More Effectively,* Audit Commission, London.

Audit Commission (1986a) *Making A Reality of Community Care,* Audit Commission, London.

Audit Commission (1986b) *Performance Review in Local Government: Introduction,* Audit Commission, London.

Audit Commission (1986c) *Performance Review in Local Government: Social Services,* Audit Commission, London.

Audit Commission (1992) *Citizen's Charter Performance Indicators: Charting a Course,* Audit Commission, London.

Audit Commission (1996a) *Local Authority Performance Indicators 1994/95. Volume 1. Education, social services, libraries and expenditure,* Audit Commission, London.

Audit Commission (1996b) *Local Authority Performance Indicators. Appendix to Volumes 1 & 2,* Audit Commission, London.

Audit Commission (1998a) *The Publication of Information Direction 1998. Performance Indicators for the Financial Year 1999/2000,* Audit Commission, London.

Audit Commission (1998b) *Better by Far: Preparing for Best Value,* Audit Commission, London.

Audit Commission (2000) *Aiming to Improve: The Principles of Performance Measurement,* Audit Commission, London.

Balm, G.J. (1992) *Benchmarking: A Practitioners Guide for Becoming and Staying Best of the Best,* QPMA, Schaumburg IL.

Bamford, T. (1982) *Managing Social Work,* Tavistock Publications, London.

Banwell, H. (1959) The new relations between central and local government, *Public Administration,* 37, 201–212.

Barber, B. and Johnson, D. (1973) The presentation of acute hospital in-patient statistics, *Hospital and Health Services Review,* 69, 11–15.

Barnes, M. and Miller, N. (1988) Performance measurement in the personal social services, *Research Policy and Planning,* 6, 2, 1–47.

Barr, A. (1968) Value for money in hospitals, *The Lancet,* 1, 353–355.

Bauld, L., Chesterman, J. and Judge, K. (2000) Measuring satisfaction with social care amongst older service users: issues from the literature, *Health and Social Care in the Community,* 8, 316–324.

Bebbington, A.C. (1979) Changes in the provision of social services to the elderly in the community over fourteen years, *Social Policy and Administration,* 13, 111–123.

Bebbington, A.C. and Davies, B.P. (1980) Territorial need indicators: a new approach. Part II, *Journal of Social Policy,* 9, 4, 433–462.

Beeton, D. (1988) Performance measurement: the state of the art, *Public Money and Management,* Spring/Summer, 99–103.

Bernstein, M. (1994) *Managing for Effectiveness in Social Services – A Workbook*, Social Information Systems/Department of Health, Knutsford.

Bexley, London Borough of (1984) *Annual Review of Service Performance 1983–84*, London Borough of Bexley.

Black, S. (1994) What does the Citizen's Charter mean? in Connor, A. and Black, S. (eds) *Performance Review and Quality in Social Care*, Research Highlights in Social Work 20, Jessica Kingsley, London.

Bovaird, T. (1981) Recent developments in output measurement in local government, *Local Government Studies*, Sept/Oct, 35–53.

Bovaird, T. and Mallinson, I. (1988) Setting objectives and measuring achievement in social care, *British Journal of Social Work*, 18, 309–324.

Bovaird, T., Gregory, D. and Martin, S. (1988) Performance measurement in urban economic development, *Public Money and Management*, 8, 4, 17–22.

Bowerman, M. (1995) Auditing performance indicators: the role of the Audit Commission in the Citizen's Charter initiative, *Financial Accountability and Management*, 11, 2, 171–184.

Bowling, A. (1991) *Measuring Health*, Open University Press, Milton Keynes.

Bowling, A. (1995) *Measuring Disease*, Open University Press, Buckingham.

Bowling, A., Formby, J. and Grant, K. (1993) Factors associated with mortality in national health service nursing homes for elderly people and long-stay geriatric wards in hospital, *International Journal of Geriatric Psychiatry*, 8, 203–210.

Bowns, I., Challis, D. and Sum Tong, M. (1991) Case finding in elderly people: validation of a postal questionnaire, *British Journal of General Practice*, 41, 100–104.

Bradburn, N.M. (1969) *The Structure of Psychological Wellbeing*, Aldine, Chicago.

Brady, R.H. (1973) MBO goes to work in the public sector, *Harvard Business Review*, 51, 2, 65–75.

Bray, A.J.M. (1988) *The Clandestine Reformer: A Study of the Rayner Scrutinies*, University of Strathclyde, Glasgow.

Brearley, C.P. (1975) *Allocating Priorities in Residential Care for the Elderly*, University of Birmingham Clearing House, 7, 101–104.

Brill, P.L., Lish, J.D. and Grissom, G.R. (1995) Timing is everything: Pre-post versus concurrent measurement, *Behavioral Healthcare Tomorrow*, 4, 76–77.

Brody, R. and Krailo, H. (1978) An approach to reviewing the effectiveness of programmes, *Social Work*, 23, 226–232.

Brown, G.W. and Harris, T. (1978) *Social Origins of Depression*, Tavistock, London.

Bullivant, J. (1997) Benchmarking for measurable improvement in social services and health. Part I – the principles, *Management Issues in Social Care*, 4, 2, 29–35.

Burningham, D. (1990) Performance indicators and the management of professionals in local government, in Cave, M., Kogan, M. and Smith, R.

(eds) *Output and Performance Measurement in Government: The State of the Art*, Jessica Kingsley, London.

Burningham, D. (1992) An overview of the use of performance indicators in local government, in Pollitt, C. and Harrison, S. (eds) *Handbook of Public Services Management*, Blackwell, Oxford.

Burns, A., Beevor, A., Lelliot, P., Wing, J., Blakey, A., Orrell, M., Mulinga, J. and Hadden, S. (1999) Health of the Nation Outcome Scales for elderly people (HoNOS 65+), *British Journal of Psychiatry*, 174, 424–427.

Butt, H. and Palmer, B. (1985) *Value For Money in the Public Sector: The Decision-Makers Guide*, Basil Blackwell, Oxford.

Camp, R.C. (1989) *Benchmarking: The Search for Industry Best Practices that Lead to Superior Performance*, Quality Press, Milwaukee, WI.

Campbell, J.C. and Ikegami, N. (2000) Long term care insurance comes to Japan, *Health Affairs*, 19, 3, 26–39.

Campbell, J.C. and Ikegami, N. (2003) Japan's radical reform of long-term care, *Social Policy and Administration*, 37, 1, 21–34.

Carpenter, I., Francis, S., Roberts, S. and Wayman, C. (2002) *MDS Home Care Assessment Instrument for Community Care User's Manual*, InterRAI, York.

Carter, N. (1988) Measuring government performance, *Political Quarterly*, 59, 3, 369–375.

Carter, N. (1989) Performance indicators: 'backseat driving' or 'hands off' control? *Policy and Politics*, 17, 2, 131–138.

Carter, N. (1991) Learning to measure performance: the use of indicators in organizations, *Public Administration*, 69, 85–101.

Carter, N. and Greer, P. (1993) Evaluating agencies: next steps and performance indicators, *Public Administration*, 71, 407–416.

Carter, N., Klein, R. and Day, P. (1992) *How Organisations Measure Success: The Use of Performance Indicators in Government*, Routledge, London.

Cave, M., Kogan, M. and Smith, R. (1990) *Output and Performance Measurement in Government: The State of the Art*. Jessica Kingsley, London.

Centre for Policy on Ageing (1984) *Home Life: A Code of Practice for Residential Care*, Centre for Policy on Ageing, London.

Challis, D.J. (1981) The measurement of outcome in social care of the elderly, *Journal of Social Policy*, 10, 2, 170–208.

Challis, D. (1992) Community care of elderly people: bringing together scarcity and choice, needs and costs, *Financial Accountability and Management*, 8, 2, 77–95.

Challis, D. (1994) *Implementing Caring for People. Care Management: Factors Influencing its Development in the Implementation of Community Care*, Department of Health, London.

Challis, D. and Chesterman, J. (1985) A system for monitoring social work activity with the frail elderly, *British Journal of Social Work*, 15, 115–132.

Challis, D. and Chesterman, J. (1986) Devolution to fieldworkers, *Social Services Insight*, June 21, 15–18.

Challis, D. and Davies, B.P. (1986) *Case Management in Community Care*, Gower, Aldershot.

Challis, D. and Darton, R. (1990) Evaluation research and experiment in social gerontology, in Peace, S. (ed.) *Researching Social Gerontology: Concepts, Methods and Issues*, Sage, London.

Challis, D. and Ferlie, E. (1986) Changing patterns of fieldwork organisation I. The headquarters view, *British Journal of Social Work*, 16, 181–202.

Challis, D. and Ferlie, E. (1987) Changing patterns of fieldwork organisation II. The team leaders' view, *British Journal of Social Work*, 17, 147–167.

Challis, D. and Ferlie, E. (1988) The myth of generic practice: specialisation in social work, *Journal of Social Policy*, 17, 1–22.

Challis, D.J., Knapp, M.R.J. and Davies, B.P. (1988) Cost effectiveness evaluation in social care, in Lishman, J. (ed.) *Evaluation: Research Highlights in Social Work 8*, Jessica Kingsley, London.

Challis, D., Darton, R., Johnson, L., Stone, M. and Traske, K. (1995) *Care Management and Health Care of Older People*, Ashgate, Aldershot.

Challis, D., Carpenter, I. and Traske, K. (1996) *Assessment in Continuing Care Homes: Towards A National Standard Instrument*, PSSRU/Joseph Rowntree Foundation, University of Kent at Canterbury.

Challis, D., Darton, R., Hughes, J., Stewart, K. and Weiner, K. (1998) *Mapping and Evaluation of Care Management Arrangements for Older People and Those with Mental Health Problems*, Focus group, 10 November, PSSRU, University of Manchester.

Challis, D., Stewart, K., Sturdy, D. and Worden, A. (eds) (2000) *UK Long Term Care Resident Assessment User's Manual, MDS/RAI UK*, InterRAI UK, York.

Challis, D., Darton, R., Hughes, J., Stewart, K. and Weiner, K. (2001) Intensive care management at home: an alternative to institutional care? *Age and Ageing*, 30, 409–413.

Challis, D., Chesterman, J., Luckett, R., Stewart, K. and Chessum, R. (2002) *Care Management in Social and Primary Health Care: the Gateshead Community Care Scheme*, Ashgate, Aldershot.

Charnes, A., Cooper, W. and Rhodes, E. (1978) Measuring the efficiency of decision making units, *European Journal of Operational Research*, 2, 6, 429–444.

Chartered Institute of Public Finance and Accountancy (CIPFA) (1987) *Personal Social Services Statistics 1986–87 Actuals*, CIPFA, London.

Chartered Institute of Public Finance and Accountancy (CIPFA) (1993) *Accounting for Social Services in Great Britain*, CIPFA, London.

Chartered Institute of Public Finance and Accountancy (CIPFA) (1999) *Personal Social Services Statistics 1998–99 Actuals*, CIPFA, London.

Clarke, P.J. (1984) Performance evaluation of public sector programmes, *Administration*, 32, 3, 294–322.

Clarkson, P. and Challis, D. (2000) Performance measurement in social care: designing indicators at different levels of analysis, *PSSRU Bulletin*, 12, 30–32.

Clarkson, P. and Challis, D. (2002) Developing and implementing a local performance measurement system in older people's services, *Research Policy and Planning*, 20, 3–16.

Clarkson, P. and Challis, D. (2003) Quality assurance practices in care management: a perspective from the United Kingdom, *Care Management Journals*, 4, 3, 142–151.

Cmnd 9663 (1956) *Committee of Enquiry into the Cost of the National Health Service* (Chairman C.W. Guillebaud), HMSO, London.

Cmnd 1973 (1963) *Health and Welfare: The Development of Community Care*, HMSO, London.

Cmnd 3638 (1968) *The Civil Service. Report of the Committee. Vol 1*, HMSO, London.

Cmnd 3703 (1968) *Report of the Committee on Local Authority and Allied Personal Social Services* (Chairman Frederic Seebohm), HMSO, London.

Cmnd 6453 (1976) *Local Government Finance. Report of the Committee of Enquiry* (Chairman Frank Layfield QC), HMSO, London.

Cmnd 7131 (1978) *The Nationalised Industries*, HMSO, London.

Cmnd 7615 (1979) *Royal Commission on the National Health Service*, HMSO, London.

Cmnd 8616 (1982) *Efficiency and Effectiveness in the Civil Service*, HMSO, London.

Cmnd 9058 (1983) *Financial Management in Government Departments*, HMSO, London.

Cmnd 9297 (1984) *Progress in Financial Management in Government Departments*, HMSO, London.

Cm 555 (1989) *Working for Patients*, HMSO, London.

Cm 849 (1989) *Caring for People: Community Care in the Next Decade and Beyond*, HMSO, London.

Cm 1599 (1991) *The Citizen's Charter: Raising the Standard*, HMSO, London.

Cm 3588 (1997) *Social Services: Achievement and Challenge*, HMSO, London.

Cm 3807 (1997) *The New NHS. Modern. Dependable*, The Stationery Office, London.

Cm 4014 (1998) *Modern Local Government: In Touch with the People*, The Stationery Office, London.

Cm 4169 (1998) *Modernising Social Services*, The Stationery Office, London.

Cm 4818-I (2000) *The NHS Plan: A Plan for Investment, A Plan for Reform*, The Stationery Office, London.

Community Care Policy Network (2001) *Software for Analysis of Long Term Care Insurance Performance: Application and Examples*, Community Care Policy Network, Tokyo.

Connor, A. and Black, S. (1994) *Performance Review and Quality in Social Care*, Research Highlights in Social Work 20, Jessica Kingsley Publishers, London.

Cooper, D. (1997) Principles of service provision in old age psychiatry, in Jacoby, R. and Oppenheimer, C. (eds) *Psychiatry in the Elderly*, Oxford University Press, Oxford.

Coote, A. (1994) Performance and quality in public services, in Connor, A. and Black, S. (eds) *Performance Review and Quality in Social Care*, Research Highlights in Social Work 20, Jessica Kingsley, London.

Crail, M. (1994) Blinking indicators, *Health Service Journal*, 4 August, 10–11.

Crosby, P. (1979) *Quality is Free*, McGraw-Hill, New York.

Cummings, T.C. and Worley, C.G. (1993) *Organisation Development and Change*, West Publishing Company, Eagan, Minnesota.

Culyer, A.J. (1980) *The Political Economy of Social Policy*, Martin Robinson, London.

Cutler, T. and Waine, B. (1997) *Managing the Welfare State: Text and Sourcebook*, Berg, Oxford.

Dale, M.C., Burns, A., Panter, L. and Morris, J. (2001) Factors affecting survival of elderly nursing home residents, *International Journal of Geriatric Psychiatry*, 16, 70–76.

Darton, R. and Knapp, M. (1984) The cost of residential care for the elderly: the effects of dependency, design and social environment, *Ageing and Society*, 4, 157–183.

Darton, R., Netten, A. and Forder, J. (2003) The cost implications of the changing population and characteristics of care homes, *International Journal of Geriatric Psychiatry*, 18, 3, 236–243.

Davies, B. (1968) *Social Needs and Resources in Local Services*, Michael Joseph, London.

Davies, B. (1977) Needs and outputs, in Heisler, H. (ed.) *Fundamentals of Social Administration*, Macmillan, London.

Davies B. (1987) Equity and efficiency in community care: supply and financing in an age of fiscal austerity, *Ageing and Society*, 7, 2, 161–174.

Davies, D.P. and Knapp, M. (1981) *Old People's Homes and the Production of Welfare*, Routledge and Kegan Paul, London.

Davies, B.P. and Challis, D. (1986) *Matching Resources to Needs in Community Care*, Gower, Aldershot.

Davies, B.P., Bebbington, A. and Charnley, H. (1990) *Resources, Needs and Outcomes in Community-Based Care*, Gower, Avebury.

Davies, H.T.O. and Lampel, J. (1998) Trust in performance indicators? *Quality in Health Care*, 7, 159–162.

Day, C. (1989) *Taking Action with Indicators,* Department of Health, London.

Day, P. and Klein, R. (1987) *Accountabilities: Five Public Services,* Tavistock, London.

Dence, R. (1995) Best practices benchmarking, in Holloway, J., Lewis, J. and Mallory, G. (eds) *Performance Measurement and Evaluation,* Open University/Sage, London.

Department of Education and Science (DES) (1970) *Output Budgeting for the DES: Report of A Feasibility Study,* HMSO, London.

Department of the Environment (1972*) The New Local Authorities: Management and Structure,* HMSO, London.

Department of the Environment (1981) *Local Government Annual Reports, A Code of Practice,* HMSO, London.

Department of Health (1988a) *A Report on Korner Indicators,* Department of Health, London.

Department of Health (1988b) *Comparing Health Authorities: Health Service Indicators 1983 to 1986,* Department of Health, London.

Department of Health (1989) *Health Service Indicators Guidance Dictionary,* Department of Health, London.

Department of Health (1991a) *The Patient's Charter,* Department of Health, London.

Department of Health (1991b) *Key Indicators of Local Authority Social Services 1989/90,* Department of Health, London.

Department of Health (1992) *Committed to Quality: Quality Assurance in Social Services Departments,* Department of Health, London.

Department of Health (1993) *Monitoring and Development: Assessment Special Study,* Department of Health, London.

Department of Health (1994a) *A Framework for Local Community Care Charters in England,* Department of Health, London.

Department of Health (1994b) *Review of Key Indicators for Local Authority Social Services,* Department of Health, London.

Department of Health (1994c) *Monitoring and Development: Care Management Special Study,* Department of Health, London.

Department of Health (1994d) *Hospital Discharge Workbook,* Department of Health, London.

Department of Health (1997a) *Better Value for Money in Social Services. A Review of Performance Trends in Social Services in England,* Department of Health, London.

Department of Health (1997b*) Responsibilities of Council Social Services Departments: Implications of Recent Judgements,* LASSL (97) 13, Department of Health, London.

Department of Health (1997c) *Better Services for Vulnerable People,* EL (97)62 CI (97)24, Department of Health, London.

Department of Health (1998a) *The New NHS Charter – a Different Approach*, Department of Health, Leeds.

Department of Health (1998b) *Modernising Health and Social Services: National Priorities 1999/00 – 2001/02*, Department of Health, London.

Department of Health (1998c) *The New NHS Modern and Dependable: A National Framework for Assessing Performance*, Department of Health, Leeds.

Department of Health (1998d) *Key Statistics of local authority personal social services: Activity and Expenditure 1997–98; Budgets 1998 99*, Department of Health, London.

Department of Health (1998e) *Information for Health*, Department of Health, London.

Department of Health (1999a) *A New Approach to Social Services Performance. Consultation Document*, Department of Health, London.

Department of Health (1999b) *Social Services Performance in 1998–99. The Personal Social Services Performance Assessment Framework*, Department of Health, London.

Department of Health (1999c) *The RAP Project: Referrals Assessments and Packages of Care in Adult Personal Social Services. Report of the First Dress Rehearsal*, Department of Health, London.

Department of Health (2000) *A Quality Strategy for Social Care*, Department of Health, London.

Department of Health (2001a) *National Service Framework for Older People*, Department of Health, London.

Department of Health (2001b) *Information on Referrals, Assessments and Packages of Care (RAP) in Adult Social Services – Data Collection Documents*, Department of Health, London.

Department of Health (2002a) *Fair Access to Care Services: Guidance on Eligibility Criteria for Adult Social Care*, LAC (2002) 13, Department of Health, London.

Department of Health (2002b) *Key Indicators Graphical System 2002: Personal Social Services Statistics*, Department of Health, London.

Department of Health (2002c) *Guidance on the Single Assessment Process for Older People*, HSC 2002/001, LAC(2002)1, Department of Health, London.

Department of Health (2002d) *Social Services Performance Assessment Framework Indicators 2001–2002 and mid 2002–03*, Department of Health, London.

Department of Health (2003) *Key Indicators Graphical System 2003: Personal Social Services Statistics*, Department of Health, London.

Department of Health (2004) *National Standards, Local Action: Health and Social Care Standards and Planning Framework 2005/06–2007/08*, Department of Health, London.

Department of Health (2005) *Performance Indicators Comparison System (PICS)*, www.pics.nhs.uk/Ardentia/portal/jsp/index.jsp, Department of Health, London.

Department of Health and Social Security (DHSS) (1972a) *Minutes of Evidence (presented to the Employment and Social Services Sub Committee of the Expenditure Committee)*, HC 281-i, session 1971–2, HMSO, London.

Department of Health and Social Security (DHSS) (1972b) *Local Authority Social Services Ten Year Plans 1973–1983*, Circular 35/72, DHSS, London.

Department of Health and Social Security (DHSS) (1972c) *Management Arrangements for the Reorganised National Health Service*, HMSO, London.

Department of Health and Social Security (DHSS) (1976) *Priorities for the Health and Social Services in England*, HMSO, London.

Department of Health and Social Security (DHSS) (1977) *Forward Planning of Local Authority Social Services*, Circular LASSL (77) 13, DHSS, London.

Department of Health and Social Security (DHSS) (1982a) *Steering Group on Health Services Information 1st Report to the Secretary of State for Social Services* (the Korner Report), HMSO, London.

Department of Health and Social Security (DHSS) (1982b) *Performance Indicators in the NHS: Progress Report on Joint Exercise between DHSS and Northern Region*, RA (82) 34, HMSO, London.

Department of Health and Social Security (DHSS) (1983a) *Performance Indicators: National Summary for 1981*, HMSO, London.

Department of Health and Social Security (DHSS) (1983b) *Health Care and its Costs. The Development of the National Health Service in England*, HMSO, London.

Department of Social and Health Services (1986) *Final Information and Assistance/Case Management Standards*, Department of Social and Health Services, Washington D.C.

Deyo, R.A., Inui, T., Leininger, J.D. and Overmann, S.S. (1983) Measuring functional outcomes in chronic disease: a comparison of traditional scales and a self administered health status questionnaire in patients with rheumatoid arthritis, *Medical Care*, 21, 180–192.

Donabedian, A. (1980) *Explorations in Quality Assessment and Monitoring – Volume 1: The Definition of Quality and Approaches to its Assessment*, Health Administration Press, Ann Arbor, Michigan.

Donabedian, A. (1982) *The Criteria and Standards of Quality*, Health Administration Press, Ann Arbor, Michigan.

Downey, G. (1983) How efficient is the NHS? *Hospital and Health Service Review*, 79, 3, 117–121.

Duncan, I.B., Race, D.G., Macfarlane, S.B.J. and Tate, M.J. (1974) *The Care of the Elderly*, Operational Research (Health Services) Unit Report, Department of Applied Statistics, University of Reading.

Duncan, R. St A. and Warburton, R.W. (1987) *Validity and Reliability of Indicators of Social Services*, Social Services Inspectorate, Department of Health, London.

Dunnachie, H. (1992) Approaches to quality systems, in Kelly, D. and Warr, B. (eds) *Quality Counts. Achieving Quality in Social Care Services*, Whiting and Birch, London.

Eccles, R.G. (1991) The performance measurement manifesto, *Harvard Business Review*, Jan–Feb, 131–137.

Ehreth, J.L. (1994) The development and evaluation of hospital performance measures for policy analysis, *Medical Care*, 32, 6, 568–587.

Elcock, H. (1983) Disabling professions: the real threat to local democracy, *Public Money*, 3, 23–27.

Emmanuel, C., Otley, D. and Merchant, K. (1990) *Accounting for Management Control*, Chapman and Hall, London.

Etzioni, A. (1960) Two approaches to organisational analysis: A critique and a suggestion, *Administrative Science Quarterly*, 5, 257–278.

Euroqol Group (1990) Euroqol: A new facility for the measurement of health related quality of life, *Health Policy*, 16, 199–208.

Evans, B., Hughes, B. and Wilkin, D. with Jolley, P. (1981) *The Management of Mental and Physical Impairment in Non-Specialist Residential Homes for the Elderly*, Department of Psychiatry and Community Medicine, University of Manchester.

Falk, N. and Lee, J. (1978) *Planning the Social Services*, Saxon House, Farnborough.

Farrell, M.J. (1957) The measurement of productive efficiency, *Journal of the Royal Statistical Society, Series A General*, 120, 253–290.

Ferguson, B. and McGuire, A. (1984) *A Short History and Review of the Performance Indicators Issued by the DHSS*, Discussion Paper No. 09/84, Health Economics Research Unit, University of Aberdeen.

Ferlie, E., Challis, D. and Davies, B. (1989) *Efficiency-Improving Innovations in Social Care of the Elderly*, Avebury, Gower.

Fisher, B. and Kenny, R. (2000) Introducing a business information system into an engineering company, *Information Knowledge Systems Management*, 2, 207–221.

Flapper, S.D.P., Fortuin, L. and Stoop, P.P.M. (1996) Towards consistent performance management systems, *International Journal of Operations and Production Management*, 16, 7, 27–37.

Fletcher, K. (1990) Ways to appraise, *Social Services Insight*, 5, 11, 25 29.

Flynn, N. (1986) Performance measurement in public sector services, *Policy and Politics*, 14, 3, 389–404.

Flynn, N. (1993) *Public Sector Management*, Harvester Wheatsheaf, London.

Folstein, M., Folstein, S. and McHugh, P.R. (1975) Mini-Mental State: a practical method for grading the cognitive state of patients for the clinician, *Journal of Psychiatric Research*, 12, 189–198.

Fortin, Y. (1996) Autonomy, responsibility and control – the case of central government agencies in Sweden, in OECD, *Performance Management in*

Government. Contemporary Illustrations, Public Management Occasional Paper No.9, OECD, Paris.

Fortuin, L. (1988) Performance indicators – why, where and how? *European Journal of Operational Research*, 34, 1–9.

Fry, T.D. and Cox, J.F. (1989) Manufacturing performance: local versus global measures, *Production and Inventory Management Journal*, 30, 2, 52–56.

Garvin, D.A. (1993) Building a learning organisation, *Harvard Business Review*, 71, 78–91.

Geron, S.M. (1998) Assessing the satisfaction of older adults with long-term care services: measurement and design challenges for social work, *Research on Social Work Practice*, 8, 1, 103–119.

Geron, S. and Chassler, D. (1994) *Guidelines for Case Management Practice Across the Long-term Care Continuum*, Connecticut Community Care Inc, Boston University School of Social Work.

Gibbs, I. and Smith, P. (1989) Private nursing homes: providing good value? *Public Money and Management*, 9, 55–59.

Gibbs, I. and Sinclair, I. (1992a) Checklists; their possible contribution to inspection and quality assurance in elderly people's homes, in Kelly, D. and Warr, B. (eds) *Quality Counts. Achieving Quality in Social Care Services*, Whiting and Birch, London.

Gibbs, I. and Sinclair, I. (1992b) Residential care for elderly people: The correlates of quality, *Ageing and Society*, 12, 4, 463–482.

Giller, H. and Morris, A. (1981) *Care and Discretion: Social Workers' Decisions with Delinquents*, Burnett Books, London.

Glastonbury, B., Spackman, A. and Gilbert, D. (2000) *Evaluation of the Referrals, Assessments and Packages of Care (RAP) Dataset for Adults*, Department of Health, London.

Glendinning, C. (1998) The continuing care guidelines and primary and community health services, *Health and Social Care in the Community*, 6, 3, 181–188.

Glover, G., Knight, S., Melzer, D. and Pearce, L. (1997) The development of a new minimum data set for specialist mental health care, *Health Trends*, 29, 2, 48–51.

Goldacre, M. and Griffen, K. (1983) *Performance Indicators: A Commentary on the Literature*, Unit of Clinical Epidemiology, University of Oxford.

Goldberg, E.M. (1970) *Helping the Aged*, Allen and Unwin, London.

Goldberg, E.M. (1980) Directions for research in social work and the social services, *British Journal of Social Work*, 10, 207–217.

Goldberg, E.M. (1981) Monitoring in the social services, in Goldberg, E.M. and Connelly, N. (eds) *Evaluative Research in Social Care*, Heinemann Educational, London.

Goldberg, E.M. and Warburton, R.W. (1979) *Ends and Means in Social Work*, George Allen and Unwin, London.

Goldstein, H. and Spiegelhalter, D.J. (1996) League tables and their limitations: statistical issues in comparisons of institutional performance, *Journal of the Royal Statistical Society A*, 159, 385–443.

Gorbach, P. and Sinclair, I. (1989) Monitoring the home help service: clues to improving performance from analysing data in a computerised client information system, *Research, Policy and Planning*, 7, 1, 24–30.

Gostick, C. (1989) A good start is not enough, *Insight*, 4, 8, 15–16.

Gray, A. and Jenkins, B. (1983) *Policy Analysis and Evaluation in British Government*, Royal Institute of Public Administration, London.

Greer, P. and Carter, N. (1995) Next steps and performance measurement, in O'Toole, B.J. and Jorden, G. (eds) *Next Steps: Improving Management in Government*, Dartmouth, Aldershot.

Griffiths, E.R. (1983) *NHS Management Inquiry*, Department of Health and Social Security, London.

Griffiths, R. (1988) *Community Care: Agenda for Action*, HMSO, London.

Grimley Evans, J. (1993) Healthy active life expectancy (HALE) as an index of effectiveness of health and social services for elderly people, *Age and Ageing*, 22, 297–301.

Gunther, J. and Hawkins, F. (1996) *Total Quality Management in Human Service Organizations*, Springer, New York.

Hall, D. (1993) *Measuring the Measurers: Does Performance Measurement Work?* Unpublished M.Soc.Sc. Research Dissertation, University of Birmingham.

Harding, T. (1999) Enabling older people to live in their own homes, in Henwood, M. and Wistow, G. (eds) *With Respect to Old Age: Long Term Care – Rights and Responsibilities, Research Volume 3 Evaluating the Impact of Caring for People*, The Stationery Office, London.

Hardingham, S. (1986) Angels and options, *Insight*, 1, 31, 12–13.

Harper, E. (1986) Measuring performance – a new approach, *Hospital and Health Services Review*, Jan, 26–28.

Hartle, F. (1995) *Transforming the Performance Management Process*, Kogan Page, London.

Hay, D.A. and Morris, D.J. (1979) *Industrial Economics: Theory and Evidence*, Oxford University Press, Oxford.

Heald, D. (1983) *Public Expenditure: Its Defence and Reform*, Robertson, Oxford.

Heaton, J., Arksey, H. and Sloper, P. (1999) Carers' experiences of hospital discharge and continuing care in the community, *Health and Social Care in the Community*, 7, 2, 91–99.

Helfert, E.A. (1965) *Techniques of Financial Analysis*, McGraw-Hill, New York.

Henderson, A.S., Duncan-Jones, P., Byrne, D.G. and Scott, R. (1980) Measuring social relationships: the Interview Schedule for Social Interaction, *Psychological Medicine*, 10, 723–734.

Henderson-Stewart, D. (1990) Performance measurement and review in local government, in Cave, M., Kogan, M. and Smith, R. (eds) *Output and*

Performance Measurement in Government: The State of the Art, Jessica Kingsley, London.

Henkel, M. (1991) *Government, Evaluation and Change*, Jessica Kingsley, London.

Holloway, J., Lewis, J. and Mallory, G. (eds) (1995) *Performance Measurement and Evaluation*, Open University/Sage, London.

Holmes, C., Cooper, B. and Levy, R. (1995) Dementia known to mental health services: first findings of a case register for a defined elderly population, *International Journal of Geriatric Psychiatry*, 10, 875–881.

House of Commons (1972) *Eighth Report from the Expenditure Committee. Relationship of Expenditure to Needs*, HC 515, HMSO, London.

House of Commons (1995) Carers *(Recognition and Services) Act 1995 (c.12)*, HMSO, London.

House of Commons (2003) *Community Care (Delayed Discharges etc.) Act 2003* (c.5), The Stationery Office, London.

House of Commons Social Services Committee (1980) *The Government's White Papers on Public Expenditure: The Social Services. Third Report, session 1979–80*, HC 702, HMSO, London.

House of Commons Social Services Committee (1982a) *1982 White Paper: Public Expenditure on the Social Services. Vol I Report*, HC 306, para. 77, HMSO, London.

House of Commons Social Services Committee (1982b) *1982 White Paper: Public Expenditure on the Social Services. Minutes of Evidence*, HC 306, i–iv, para. 95, HMSO, London.

Hoyes, L., Means, R. and LeGrand, J. (1992) *Made to Measure? Performance Measurement and Community Care*, Occasional Paper 39, School for Advanced Urban Studies, University of Bristol.

Huber, N. (1999) 'At risk' local authorities could lose their social services, warns Hutton, *Community Care*, 25 Nov – 1 Dec, 2–3.

Hudson, B. (1999) Signs of a controlling interest, *Health Service Journal*, 109, 5644, 16–17.

Hunt, S.M., McEwan, J. and McKenna, S.P. (1986) *Measuring Health Status*, Croom Helm, Beckenham.

Hunter, T. (1989) Fine tuning for maximum feedback, *Social Services Insight*, 4, 28, 16–18.

Huxley, P. (1993) Case management and care management in community care, *British Journal of Social Work*, 23, 4, 365–381.

Ikegami, N., Yamauchi, K. and Yamada, Y. (2003) The long term care insurance law in Japan: impact on institutional care facilities, *International Journal of Geriatric Psychiatry*, 18, 217–221.

Imber, V. (1977) *A Classification of the English Personal Social Services Authorities*, Statistical and Research Report Series 16, HMSO, London.

Institute of Health and Economic Programmes (IHEP) (2002) *Study on Evaluation Methods of the Effectiveness of Long Term Care Insurance*, IHEP, Tokyo.

Institute of Municipal Treasurers and Accountants (IMTA) (1972) *Output Measurement Personal Social Services*, IMTA, London.

Irwin, T. (1996) An analysis of New Zealand's new system of public sector management, in OECD, *Performance Management in Government. Contemporary Illustrations*, Public Management Occasional Paper No.9, OECD, Paris.

Isaacs, B. (1981) Is geriatrics a speciality? in Arie, T. (ed.) *Health Care of the Elderly*, Croom Helm, London.

Isaacs, B. and Neville, Y. (1976) The Measurement of need in old people, *Scottish Health Services Studies*, 34, Scottish Home and Health Department, Edinburgh.

Jackson, P.M. (1988) The management of performance in the public sector, *Public Money and Management*, 8, 4, 11–16.

Jackson, P. (1990) *Measuring Performance in the Public Sector*, University of Leicester, Leicester.

Jackson, P.M. (1993) Public service performance evaluation: a strategic perspective, *Public Money and Management*, 13, 4, 9–14.

Jackson, P. and Palmer, B. (1989) *First Steps in Measuring Performance in the Public Sector: A Management Guide*, Public Finance Foundation/Price Waterhouse, London.

James, A. (1987) Performance and the planning process, *Social Services Insight*, 2, 10, 12–14.

James, A. (1992) Quality and its social construction by managers in care service organisations, in *Quality Counts: Achieving Quality in Social Care Services*, Whiting & Birch/Social Care Association, London.

Jones, J., Lewis, S. and Jordan, P. (1988) *Output and Performance Measurement in Central Government: Technical Guide*, HM Treasury, London.

Jowett, P. and Rothwell, M. (1988) *Performance Indicators in the Public Sector*, Macmillan, Basingstoke.

Justice, D. (1993) *Case Management Standards in State Community Based Long-term Care Programs*, Congressional Research Service, Washington, D.C.

Kane, R.L. (1990) *What is Case Management Anyway?* Long-term Care Decisions Resource Centre, University of Minnesota, Minneapolis.

Kane, R.A. and Kane, R.L. (1981) *Assessing the Elderly: a Practical Guide to Measurement*, Lexington Books, Toronto.

Kane, R.L. and Kane, R.A. (2000) *Assessing Older Persons: Measures, Meaning and Practical Applications*, Oxford University Press Inc., New York.

Kaplan, R.S. and Norton, D.P. (1992) The balanced scorecard - measures that drive performance, *Harvard Business Review*, Jan–Feb, 71–79.

Kaplan, R.S. and Norton, D.P. (1993) Putting the balanced scorecard to work, *Harvard Business Review,* Sept–Oct, 134–142.

Kaplan, R.S. and Norton, D.P. (1996) Using the balanced scorecard as a strategic management system, *Harvard Business Review,* Jan–Feb, 75–85.

Katz, S., Ford, A.B., Moskowitz, R.W., Jackson, B.A. and Jaffee, M.W. (1963) Studies of illness in the aged. The index of ADL: a standardised measure of biological and psychosocial function, *Journal of the American Medical Association,* 185, 12, 914–919.

Kaydos, W. (1991) Key performance factors, in *Measuring, Managing, and Maximizing Performance,* Productivity Press, Cambridge, MA.

Kelly, D. and Warr, B. (1992) *Quality Counts. Achieving Quality in Social Care Services,* Whiting and Birch, London.

Kendall, J. and Knapp, M. (1998) Measuring the performance of voluntary organisations, *Public Management,* 2, 1, 105–132.

Kettner, P.M. and Martin, L.L. (1993) Performance, accountability and purchase of service contracting, *Administration in Social Work,* 17, 61–79.

Kettner, P.M., Moroney, R.M. and Martin, L.L. (1999) *Designing and Managing Programs: An Effectiveness-Based Approach,* Sage, Thousand Oaks, California.

King County Division on Aging (1986) *Case Management Program Policies and Procedures Manual,* King County Division on Aging, Seattle.

Klein, R. (1972) The Politics of PPB, *Political Quarterly,* 43, 3, 270–281.

Klein, R. (1982a) Performance, evaluation and the NHS: a case study in conceptual perplexity and organisational complexity, *Public Administration,* 60, 385–407.

Klein, R. (1982b) Auditing the NHS, *British Medical Journal,* 285, 672–673.

Klein, R. (1995) *The New Politics of the NHS,* Longman, London.

Klein, R. and Carter, N. (1988) Performance measurement: a review of concepts and issues, in Beeton, D. (ed.) *Performance Measurement: Getting the Concepts Right,* Public Finance Foundation, Paper 18, Public Finance Foundation, London.

Kline, C.A. and Hessler, H.C. (1960) The duPont chart system for appraising operating performance, in Thomas, W. E. (ed.) *Readings in Cost Accounting, Budgeting and Control,* Southwestern Publishing Co., Cincinnati.

Knapp, M. (1983) The outputs of old people's homes in the post-war period, *International Journal of Sociology and Social Policy,* 3, 3, 55–85.

Knapp, M. (1984) *The Economics of Social Care,* Macmillan, London.

Knapp, M. (1987a) Wrong numbers, *Insight,* 2, 29, 20–23.

Knapp, M. (1987b) Searching for efficiency in long-term care: de-institutionalisation and privatisation, *British Journal of Social Work,* 18, 149–171.

Knapp, M. (1998) Making music out of noise: the cost function approach to evaluation, *British Journal of Psychiatry Supplementum,* 36, 7–11.

Knapp, M., Hardy, B. and Forder, J. (2001) Commissioning for quality: ten years of social care markets in England, *Journal of Social Policy*, 30, 2, 283–306.

Knox, E.G. (ed.) (1987) *Health-Care Information. Report of a Joint Working Group of The Korner Committee on Health Services Information and the Faculty of Community Medicine*, Occasional Papers 8. Nuffield Provincial Hospitals Trust, London.

Lawton, M.P. (1975) The Philadelphia Geriatric Center Morale Scale: a revision, *Journal of Gerontology*, 30, 85–89.

Lawton, M.P. and Cohen, J. (1974) The generality of housing impact on the well-being of older people, *Journal of Gerontology*, 29, 194–204.

Leigh, A. (1988) *Effective Change: Twenty Ways to Make it Happen*, Institute of Personnel Management, London.

Leininger, S.M. and Cohen, P.Z. (1998) The quality circle of hip fracture care, *Nursing Case Management*, 3, 5, 220–226.

Levitt, M.S. and Joyce, M.A.S. (1987) *The Growth and Efficiency of Public Spending*, Cambridge University Press, Cambridge.

Lewis, S. (1986) *Output and Performance Measurement in Central Government: Progress in Departments*, Working Paper No. 28. HM Treasury, London.

Linn, M.W., Gurel, L. and Linn, B.S. (1977) Patient outcome as a measure of quality of nursing home care, *American Journal of Public Health*, 67, 337–344.

Llewellyn, S. (1994) Applying efficiency concepts to management in the social services, *Public Money and Management*, 14, 2, 135–141

Logan, R.F.L., Ashley, J.S.A., Klein, R.E. and Robson, D.M. (1972) *Dynamics of Medical Care: The Liverpool Study Into Use of Hospital Resources*. London School of Hygiene and Tropical Medicine, London.

Lupton, C. (1989) Measuring performance in local authority social services departments, *Assignation*, 7, 1, 20–23.

Macdonald, G. (1999) Evidence-based social care: wheels off the runway? *Public Money and Management*, Jan–March, 25–32.

Macdonald, A. (2002) The usefulness of aggregate routine clinical outcomes data: the example of HoNOS 65+, *Journal of Mental Health*, 11, 645–656.

Mahoney, F.I. and Barthel, D.W. (1965) Functional evaluation: the Barthel Index, *The Maryland State Medical Journal*, 14, 61–65.

Martin, L. (1993) *Total Quality Management in Human Service Organisations*, Sage, Newbury Park CA.

Martin, L.L. and Kettner, P.M. (1996) *Measuring the Performance of Human Service Programs*, Sage, Thousand Oaks, California.

Mason, A. and Morrison, V. (eds) (1985) *Walk, Don't Run. A Collection of Essays on Information Issues Published To Honour Mrs Edith Korner*, King Edward's Hospital Fund for London, London.

Maxwell, R.J. (1992) Dimensions of quality revisited: from thought to action, *Quality in Health Care*, 1, 3, 171–177.

McCarthy, M. (1983) Are efficiency measures effective? *Health and Social Services Journal*, 60, 403.

McDonald, A. (1999) *Understanding Community Care: A Guide for Social Workers*, Macmillan, London.

McDowell, I. and Newell, I. (1987) *Measuring Health: A Guide to Rating Scales and Questionnaires*, Oxford University Press, New York.

Metcalfe, L. and Richards, S. (1987) The efficiency strategy in central government: an impoverished concept of management, *Public Money*, 7, 1, 29–32.

McKee, M. (1997) Indicators of clinical performance, *British Medical Journal*, 315, 142.

McNair, CJ., Lynch, RL. and Cross, K.F. (1990) Do financial and non-financial performance measures have to agree? *Management Accounting*, November, 28–36.

Midwinter, A. (1994) Developing performance indicators for local government: the Scottish experience, *Public Money and Management*, April–June, 37–43.

Miller, N. (1986) Management information and performance measurement in personal social services, *Social Services Research*, 4/5, 7–55.

Mitchell, S. and Tolan, F. (1994) Performance review through inspection and monitoring by central government, in Connor, A. and Black, S. (eds) *Performance Review and Quality in Social Care*, Research Highlights in Social Work 20, Jessica Kingsley Publishers, London.

Mor, V., Angelelli, J., Gifford, D., Morris, J. and Moore, T. (2003) Benchmarking and quality in residential and nursing homes: lessons from the US, *International Journal of Geriatric Psychiatry*, 18, 258–266.

Morris, J.N., Hawes, C., Fries, B.E., Phillips, C.D., Mor, V., Katz, S., Murphy, K., Drugovich, M.L. and Friedlob, A.S. (1990) Designing the National Resident Assessment Instrument for nursing homes, *The Gerontologist*, 30, 3, 293–307.

Mozley, C., Sutcliffe, C., Bagley, H., Cordingley, L., Challis, D., Huxley, P. and Burns, A. (2004) *Towards Quality Care: Outcomes for Older People in Care Homes*, Ashgate, Aldershot.

Mulligan, J., Appleby, J. and Harrison, A. (2000) Measuring the performance of health systems, *British Medical Journal*, 321, 191–192.

Murphy, P. and Stroud, J. (1996) *Interim Proposal for Measurement and Monitoring of Community Care: Responses to the Interim Proposals*, Department of Health/ FPA Performance Analysis, Leeds.

Myers, A.H., Palmer, M.H., Engel, B.T., Warrenfeltz, D.J. and Parker, J.A. (1996) Mobility in older patients with hip fractures: examining prefracture status, complications and outcomes at discharge from the acute care hospital, *Journal of Orthopaedic Trauma*, 10, 2, 99–107.

National Consumer Council (1983) *Measuring the Performance of Local Authorities in England and Wales – Some Consumer Principles*, National Consumer Council, London.

National Consumer Council (1986) *Measuring Up – Consumer Assessment of Local Authorities: A Guidline Study*, National Consumer Council, London.

Netten, A. (1997) Editorial. Gaps in knowledge about unit costs: old problems and new threats, in Netten, A. and Dennett, J. (eds) *Unit Costs of Health and Social Care 1997*, Personal Social Services Research Unit, University of Kent, Canterbury.

Netten, A., Ryan, M., Smith, P., Skatun, D., Healey, A., Knapp, M. and Wykes, T. (2002) *The Development of a Measure of Social Care Outcome for Older People*, PSSRU Discussion Paper 1690/2, Personal Social Services Research Unit, University of Kent, Canterbury.

Neugarten, B.L., Havighurst, R. and Tobin, S.S. (1961) The measurement of life satisfaction, *Journal of Gerontology*, 16, 134–143.

Nocon, A., Qureshi, H. and Thornton, P. (1997) *The Perspectives of Users' and Carers' Organizations*, Outcomes in Community Care Practice Series, No. 4, Social Policy Research Unit, University of York.

Osborne, S.P. (1992) The quality dimension: evaluating quality of service and quality of life in human services, *British Journal of Social Work*, 22, 437–453.

Owen, J.M. and Rodgers, P.J. (1999) *Program Evaluation: Forms and Approaches*, Sage, Thousand Oaks, CA.

Ozcan, Y.A., Luke, R.D. and Haksever, C. (1992) Ownership and organisational performance: a comparison of technical efficiency across hospital types, *Medical Care*, 30, 9, 781–794.

Parker, R. (1990) Elderly people and community care: the policy background, in Sinclair, I., Parker, R., Leat, D. and Williams, J. (eds) *The Kaleidoscope of Care*, HMSO, London.

Parsloe, P. and Stevenson, O. (1978) *Social Service Teams: The Practitioners' View*. HMSO, London.

Payne, M. (1995) *Social Work and Community Care*, Macmillan, Basingstoke.

Pedler, M., Burgoyne, J. and Boydell, T. (1991) *The Learning Company*, McGraw-Hill, London.

Peterborough UK (2004) *Health and Welfare, Residential and Nursing Homes*, www.Peterborough.net/ulrectory.

Philp, I. (ed.) (1993) *Assessing Elderly Patients*, Farrand Press, London.

Pollitt, C. (1984) Blunt tools: performance measurement in policies for health care, *OMEGA International Journal of Management Science*, 12, 2, 131–140.

Pollitt, C. (1985) Measuring performance: a new system for the National Health Service, *Policy and Politics*, 13, 1, 1–15.

Pollitt, C. (1986) Beyond the managerial model: the case for broadening performance assessment in government and the public services, *Financial Accountability and Management*, 2, Autumn, 155–170.

Pollitt, C. (1988) Bringing consumers into performance measurement: concepts, consequences and constraints, *Policy and Politics*, 16, 2, 77–87.

Pollitt, C. (1990) Performance indicators, root and branch, in Cave, M., Kogan, M. and Smith, R. (eds) *Output and Performance Measurement in Government: The State of the Art*, Jessica Kingsley, London.

Pollitt, C. (1994) The Citizen's Charter: a preliminary analysis, *Public Money and Mangagement*, 14, 2, 9–14.

Pugh, D.S. and Hickson, D.J. (1968) The comparative study of organisations, in Pym, D. (ed.) *Industrial Society*, Penguin, Harmondsworth.

Qureshi, H. (1999) Outcomes of social care for adults: attitudes towards collecting outcome information in practice, *Health and Social Care in the Community*, 7, 257–265.

Qureshi, H. and Nicholas, E. (2001) A new conception of social care outcomes and its practical use in assessment with older people, *Research Policy and Planning*, 19, 11–25.

Radical Statistics Health Group (1995) NHS "indicators of success": what do they tell us? *British Medical Journal*, 310, 1045–1050.

Ramsay, J.D., Sainfort, F. and Zimmerman, D. (1995) An empirical test of the structure, process and outcome quality paradigm using resident-based nursing facility assessment data, *American Journal of Medical Quality*, 10, 2, 63–75.

Ranson, S. and Stewart, J. (1994) *Management for the Public Domain: Enabling the Learning Society*, Macmillan, London.

Rawls, J. (1972) *A Theory of Justice*, Clarendon Press, Oxford.

Ridley, C. and Simon, H.A. (1938) *Measuring Municipal Activities: A Survey of Suggested Criteria for Appraising Administration*, International City/County Management Association, Washington, D.C.

Ritchie, P. (1992) Establishing standards in social care, in Kelly, D. and Warr, B. (eds) *Quality Counts. Achieving Quality in Social Care Services*. Whiting and Birch, London.

Rosser, R.M. and Watts, V.C. (1972) The measurement of hospital output, *International Journal of Epidemiology*, 1, 4, 361–368.

Roberts, H. (1990) Performance and outcome measures in the health service, in Cave, M., Kogan, M. and Smith, R. (eds) *Output and Performance Measurement in Government. The State of the Art*, Jessica Kingsley, London.

Roberts, J.A. (1993) Managing markets, *Journal of Public Health Medicine*, 15, 305–310.

Rouse, J. (1997) Resource and performance management in public service organizations, in Isaac-Henry, K., Painter, C. and Barnes, C. (eds) *Management in the Public Sector: Challenge and Change*, International Thomson Business Press, London.

Royal College of Physicians and British Geriatrics Society (1992) *Standardised Assessment Scales for Elderly People*, RCP/BGS, London.

Rubenstein, L., Wieland, D. and Bernabei, R. (1995) *Geriatric Assessment Technology: The State of the Art*, Ediris Curtis, Milan.

Rutherford, B.A. (1983) *Financial Reporting in the Public Sector*, Butterworths, London.

Schneider, J., Kavanagh, S., Knapp, M., Beecham, J. and Netten, A. (1993) Elderly people with advanced cognitive impairment in England: resource use and costs, *Ageing and Society*, 13, 27–50.

Scrivens, E. and Charlton, J. (1983) Warning lights? *Health and Social Services Journal*, 1501 1502.

Senge, P.M. (1990) *The Fifth Discipline. The Art and Practice of the Learning Organization*, Doubleday, New York.

Shapiro, E. and Tate, R.B. (1995) Monitoring the outcomes of quality of care in nursing homes using administrative data, *Canadian Journal on Aging*, 14, 4, 755–768.

Sheldon, B. (1978) Theory and practice in social work: a re-examination of a tenuous relationship, *British Journal of Social Work*, 8, 1–22.

Sheldon, R. (1986) *The Rayner Scrutiny Programmes 1979 to 1983: Thirty Ninth Report from the Committee of Public Accounts, Session 1985/86*, HMSO, London.

Simmons, P. and Orrell, M. (2001) State funded continuing care for the elderly mentally ill: a legal and ethical solution? *International Journal of Geriatric Psychiatry*, 16, 10, 931–934.

Smith, P. (1993) Outcome-related performance indicators and organizational control in the public sector, *British Journal of Management*, 4, 135–151.

Social Information Systems (1988) *Management Information for the Performance Review of Services for Elderly People: The Way Forward*, Social Information Systems, Knutsford.

Social Services Inspectorate (1987) *From Home Help to Home Care: An Analysis of Policy Resourcing and Service Management*, HMSO, London.

Social Services Inspectorate (1989) *Homes Are For Living In*, HMSO, London.

Social Services Inspectorate (1990) *Inspecting Home Care Services: A Guide to the SSI Method*. Department of Health, London.

Social Services Inspectorate (1992) *Caring for Quality in Day Services*, Department of Health, London.

Social Services Inspectorate (2002), *A Guide to Social Services Performance "Star" Ratings*, Department of Health, London.

Social Services Inspectorate/Audit Commission (1998a) *Reviewing Social Services – Guiding You Through*, Department of Health/Audit Commission, London.

Social Services Inspectorate/Audit Commission (1998b) *Getting the Best from Social Services: Learning the lessons from Joint Reviews*, Department of Health/Audit Commission, London.

Social Services Inspectorate/Audit Commission (1998c) Messages for Managers: *Learning the Lessons from Joint Reviews of Social Services*, Department of Health/Audit Commission, London.

Social Services Inspectorate and Social Work Services Group (1991) *Care Management and Assessment: Manager's Guide*, Social Services Inspectorate and Social Work Services Group, HMSO, London.

Sorber, A. (1996) Developing and using performance measurement: the Netherlands experience, in OECD, *Performance Management in Government. Contemporary Illustrations*, Public Management Occasional Paper No.9. OECD, Paris.

Spano, R.M., Kiresuk, T.J. and Lund, S.H. (1977) An operational model to achieve accountability in social work, *Social Work in Health Care*, 3, 2, 123–144.

Spano, R.M. and Lund, S.H. (1986) Productivity and performance: keys to survival for a hospital-based social work department. *Social Work in Health Care*, 11, 3, 25–39.

Stamp, J. (1929) *Some Economic Factors in Modern Life*, King and Son, London.

Stevenson, O. and Parsloe, P. (1993) *Community Care and Empowerment*, Joseph Rowntree Foundation, York.

Stewart, J. and Walsh, K. (1994) Performance measurement: when performance can never be finally defined, *Public Money and Management*, 14, 2, 51–56.

Stewart, K., Challis, D., Carpenter, I. and Dickinson, E. (1999) Assessment approaches for older people receiving social care: content and coverage, *International Journal of Geriatric Psychiatry*, 14, 147–156.

Stewart, K., Hughes, J., Challis, D., Weiner, K. and Darton, R. (2003) Care management for older people: access, targeting and the balance between assessment, monitoring and review, *Research Policy and Planning*, 21, 3, 13–22.

St Leger, A.S., Schnieden, H. and Walsworth-Bell, J.P. (1992) *Evaluating Health Services' Effectiveness*, Open University Press, Milton Keynes.

Styrborn, K., Larsson, A. and Drettner, G. (1994) Outcomes of geriatric discharge planning: a quality assurance study from a geriatric rehabilitation ward, *Scandinavian Journal of Rehabilitation Medicine*, 26, 167–76.

Sumpton, R. (1995) Measuring performance, *Care Plan*, June, 20–23.

Syrett, M. (1993) The best of everything, *Human Resources*, Winter, 83–86.

Tanaka, H. and Ono, T. (2002) *Performance Measurement Utilization in Japan: A Critical View*, Paper Prepared for Presentation at the Annual Conference of the American Society for Public Administration, Phoenix, AZ.

Thanassoulis, E. (2001) *Introduction to the Theory and Application of Data Envelopment Analysis*, Kluwer Academic Publishers, Dordrecht.

Treasury and Civil Service Committee (1990) *Progress in the Next Steps Initiative, 8th Report, Session 1989–90*, HMSO, London

Tyrrell, M. (1975) *Using Numbers for Effective Health Services Management*, Heinemann, London.

United Nations (2002) *Report of the Second World Assembly on Ageing, Madrid 8–12 April 2002*, United Nations, New York.

United States Congress (1993) *Government Performance Results Act*, Public Law 103–62, 103rd Congress, 1st Session, S. 20, Office of Management and Budget, United States Congress, Washington.

Vinten, G. (1993) Health and personal services since 1979: the new managerialism, *Journal of the Royal Society of Health*, 113, 4, 195–200.

Wagner, G. (chair) (1988) *Residential Care: A Positive Choice: Report of the Independent Review of Residential Care*, HMSO, London.

Walsh, K. (1991) Quality and public services, *Public Administration*, 69, 503–514.

Walsham, G. (1993) *Interpreting Information Systems in Organisations*, Wiley, Chichester.

Warburton, R.W. (1988) *Key Indicators of Local Authority Social Services: A Demonstration Package*, Social Services Inspectorate, Department of Health, London.

Warburton, R.W. (1989) Indicate precisely what you mean to say, *Social Services Insight*, 4, 8, 12–14.

Warburton, W. (1993) Performance indicators: what is all the fuss about? *Community Care Management and Planning*, 1, 4, 99–107.

Warburton, R. (1999) *Meeting the Challenge – Improving Management Information for the Effective Commissioning of Social Care Services for Older People*, Department of Health, London.

Webb, A. and Wistow, G. (1986) *Planning, Need and Scarcity. Essays on the Personal Social Services*, Allen and Unwin, London.

Weinberg, A., Williamson, J., Challis, D. and Hughes, J. (2003) What do care managers do? A study of working practice in older people's services, *British Journal of Social Work*, 33, 901–919.

Weiner, K., Stewart, K., Hughes, J., Challis, D. and Darton, R. (2002) Care management arrangements for older people in England: key areas of variation in a national study, *Ageing and Society*, 22, 419–439.

Whitney, J.O. (1993) *The Economics of Trust: Liberating Profits and Restoring Corporate Vitality*, McGraw-Hill, New York.

Which? (1999) Off the rails, *Which?*, Jan, 8–11.

Whitfield, L. (1998) Demand for re-think on 'flawed' charter, *Health Service Journal*, 108, 5633, 10.

Wholey, J. and Hatry, H. (1992) The case for performance monitoring, *Public Administration Review*, 52, 6, 604–610.

Williams, A. and Anderson, R. (1975) *Efficiency in the Social Services*, Basil Blackwell, Oxford.

Williams, A. and Kind, P. (1992) The present state of play about QALYs, in Hopkins, A. (ed.) *Measures of the Quality of Life and the Uses to which They May Be Put*, Royal College of Physicians, London.

Wisconsin Department of Health and Social Services (WDHSS) (1991) *Community Options Program Guidelines and Procedures*, Division of Community Services, Madison, Wisconsin.

Wistow, G. (1995) Paying for long-term care: the shifting boundary between health and social care, *Community Care Management and Planning*, 3, 3, 81–89.

Wistow, G., Knapp, M., Hardy, B. and Allen, C. (1994) *Social Care in a Mixed Economy*, Open University Press, Buckingham.

Wittels, I. and Botwinick, J. (1974) Survival in relocation, *Journal of Gerontology*, 29, 440–443.

Woodham, J.B. (1980) Local government – central control and local stewardship, *Local Government Studies*, 6, 3–16.

World Health Organisation (WHO) (2000) *World Health Report 2000 – Health systems: improving performance*, World Health Organisation, Geneva.

Yates, J.M. (1981) Staff patient ratios and hospital enquiries, *Nursing Times*, December 9, 2143–2145.

Yates, J. (1983) When will the players get involved? *Health and Social Service Journal*, 15 September, 1111–1112.

Yates, J. (1988) *Health Service Performance Indicators*, Inter-Authority Comparisons and Consultancy Group, London.

Yates, J.M. and Vickerstaff, L. (1982) Inter hospital comparisons in mental handicap, *Mental Handicap*, 10, 45–47.

Yates, J.M. and Davidge, M.G. (1984) Can you measure performance? *British Medical Journal*, 288, 1935–1936.

Yesavage, J.A., Brink, T.L., Rose, T.L., Lum, O., Huang, V., Day, M. and Leirer, V.O. (1983) Development and validation of a Geriatric Depression Screening Scale, *Journal of Psychiatric Research*, 17, 37–49.

Yeung, Y.C. (1989) *Performance Measurement in English Local Authorities*, Unpublished MA (Econ) Thesis, University of Manchester.

Zeithaml, V., Parasuraman, A. and Berry, L. (1990) *Delivering Quality Services*, Free Press, New York.

Zimmerman, D., Karon, S., Arling, G., Clarke, B.R., Collins, E., Ross, R. and Sainfort, F. (1995) The development and testing of Nursing Home Quality Indicators, *Health Care Financing Review*, 16, 107–127.

Zimmerman, D.R. (2003) Improving nursing home quality of care through outcomes data: the MDS quality indicators, *International Journal of Geriatric Psychiatry*, 18, 250–257.

Index of Citations

Subject Index